Strategic Environmental Assessment in Action

Strategic Environmental Assessment in Action

Second Edition

Riki Therivel

publishing for a sustainable future

London • Washington, DC

Earthscan Ltd, Dunstan House, 14a St Cross Street, London EC1N 8XA, UK
Earthscan LLC, 1616 P Street, NW, Washington, DC 20036, USA

Earthscan publishes in association with the International Institute for Environment and Development

For more information on Earthscan publications, see www.earthscan.co.uk or write to earthinfo@earthscan.co.uk

ISBN: 978-1-84971-064-0 hardback
        978-1-84971-065-7 paperback

Typeset by MapSet Ltd, Gateshead, UK
Cover design by Clifford Hayes

A catalogue record for this book is available from the British Library

Library of Congress Cataloging-in-Publication Data has been applied for

At Earthscan we strive to minimize our environmental impacts and carbon footprint through reducing waste, recycling and offsetting our CO_2 emissions, including those created through publication of this book. For more details of our environmental policy, see www.earthscan.co.uk.

Printed and bound in the UK by TJ International, an ISO 14001 accredited company. The paper used is FSC certified and the inks are vegetable based.

This edition is dedicated to the next generation:
Sheila, Stephanie, Ian, Alessandra and Gabriella

Contents

Part I
Introducing Strategic Environmental Assessment

Part II The SEA Process

Part III Ensuring SEA Effectiveness

List of Figures, Tables and Boxes

Figures

Tables

Boxes

List of Acronyms and Abbreviations

AQMA	Air Quality Management Area
APHIS	Animal and Plant Health Inspection Service
BPA	Bonneville Power Administration
CAEP	competent authority of environmental protection
CBA	cost–benefit analysis
CEC	Commission of the European Communities
CEQ	Council on Environmental Quality
CLG	Communities and Local Government
CPRE	Campaign to Protect Rural England (formerly Council for the Protection of Rural England)
DBERR	Department for Business, Enterprise and Regulatory Reform
DCENR	Department for Communications, Energy and Natural Resources
DECC	Department of Energy and Climate Change
DTP	district transport plan
EA	environmental assessment
EIA	environmental impact assessment
EIR	environmental impact report
EIS	environmental impact statement
EPA	Environmental Protection Agency
EPDGHKSAR	Environmental Potection Department of the Government of the Hong Kong Special Administrative Region
EqIA	equality impact assessment
FONSI	finding of no significant impact
GIS	geographical information system
HDA	Habitats Directive assessment
HRA	Habitat Regulations assessment
HS2	High Speed 2
IAIA	International Association for Impact Assessment
IDeA	Improvement and Development Agency
IROPI	imperative reasons of overriding public interest
IUCN	International Union for the Conservation of Nature

IWAPHD	International Workshop on Assessment of Plans under the Habitats Directive
LCA	life cycle analysis
LUC	Land Use Consultants
MCA	multi-criteria analysis
NASA	National Aeronautics and Space Administration
NCEA	Netherlands Commission for Environmental Assessment
NDPC	National Development Planning Commission
NEPA	National Environmental Policy Act
NPFA	National Playing Fields Association
ODPM	Office of the Deputy Prime Minister
PAS	Planning Advisory Service
PDGHKSAR	Planning Department of the Government of the Hong Kong Special Administrative Region
PDR	People's Democratic Republic
PEAA	planning examination approval authority
PEIA	plan environmental impact assessment
PEIS	programmatic environmental impact statement
QoLA	quality of life assessment
RDC	République Démocratique du Congo
RECCEE	Regional Environmental Centre for Central and Eastern Europe
RTPI	Royal Town Planning Institute
SA	sustainability appraisal
SANGS	Suitable Accessible Natural Green Space
SDC	Sustainable Development Commission
SEA	strategic environmental assessment
SEPA	State Environmental Protection Agency
SPA	Special Protection Area
TMfS	Transport Model for Scotland
UNDP	United Nations Development Programme
UNECE	United Nations Economic Commission for Europe
USAID	United States Agency for International Development
USDoE	United States Department of Energy
USDoI	United States Department of the Interior
WCED	World Commission on Environment and Development

Acknowledgements

I am very grateful to many people who have, directly, indirectly and cumulatively helped me with the first and second editions of this book.

Roger Levett, my business partner, has been wonderfully inspiring over the years: he wrote the sections of the book that discuss how sustainability and the environment inter-relate, commented on the section on environmental limits, and suggested rules for how not to carry out strageic environmental assessment (SEA). The 'SEA and HRA covens', particularly Steve Smith, Orlando Venn, Jo Hughes, Jeremy Owen, Ric Eales and Rob Gardner have been a consistent source of new ideas for how to improve SEA practice, and have been enthusiastic and pleasant collaborators on many SEA consultancy projects. My colleagues at Oxford Brookes University, notably Elizabeth Wilson, John Glasson, Graham Wood and Stewart Thompson, have been unfailingly helpful and are a pleasure to work with.

Students on my SEA unit at Oxford Brookes University, and participants on various SEA training courses that I have run, have contributed ideas, examples and enthusiasm. Thank you to my SEA clients, many of whom work very hard to promote good practice SEA, and without whom I would not have so much practical SEA experience. I am also grateful to many other fellow SEA practitioners and researchers who have contributed in major ways to the evolution of SEA, and forward-thinking government officials responsible for administering and implementing SEA.

For this edition, Ron Bass kindly reviewed, and made many helpful changes to the section in Chapter 4 on the US system of SEA. Elvis Au provided much useful information on the Chinese SEA system, Olivia Bina helped to find a translator, and Kai-Yi Zhou did a lovely job of translating the Chinese regulations on plan environmental impact assessment at short notice. Jimena Puyana provided the Colombian SEAs and helped me to translate relevant sections. Orlando Venn and Jan Bakker commented on a draft of Appendix D, and Roger Smithson made some very helpful comments on a near-final draft of the book.

I am also grateful to:

- Chris Wood for permission to use Figure 2.3;
- Leicester City Council for permission to use Figure 6.2;
- Transport Scotland for permission to use the figure in Box 6.4;
- Michael Noble for permission to use the figure in Box 6.5;
- Saskatchewan Environment for permission to use the figures in Box 6.7;
- The Environment Agency for permission to use the figures in Boxes 7.3 and 9.2;
- Oxfordshire County Council for permission to use Figure 7.3;
- Wigan Council for permission to use Figure 8.2;
- Leeds City Council for permission to use Figure 8.4;
- The Royal Society, Mark Desholm and Johnny Kahlert for permission to use Figure 8.6;
- Planungsgemeinschaft Halle for permission to use the figure in Table 8.6;
- HS2 Ltd., Booz & Company, Temple Group and particularly Nick Giesler and Vicky Ward for permission to use the photos in Box 8.5;
- the (then) Council for the Protection of Rural England for permission to use Figure C.2;
- John Lee, Stewart Thompson and others for permission to use Figure C.3;
- the European Environment Agency for permission to use Figure C.4;
- Dublin City Council and RPS Ireland for permission to use Figure C.5;
- Gedling Borough Council for permission to use Figure C.6.

Other people who helped with the first edition of this book include (in alphabetical order) Charles Aston, Joan Bennett, Nick Bonvoisin, Jean-Denis Bourquin, Clare Brooke, Lex Brown, Helen Byron, Cheryl Cowlin, Jenny Dixon, Chris Fry, Halldóra Hreggviðóttir, Simon Hooton, Emma James, Norman Lee, Phill Minas, Peter Nelson, Stephen Pickles, David Saul, Deb Seamark, Nick Simon, Chris Smith, Asdis Hlökk Theodorsðóttir, Paul Tomlinson, Ben Underwood and Chris Wood.

Thank you to the Earthscan team, particularly editors Jonathan Sinclair Wilson, Rob West and Nicki Dennis, for their help over the years.

Finally, Tim O'Hara triggered the idea for this second edition, got my laptop fixed when it broke down in the middle of the rewriting process, and patiently listened to 'fascinating' book-related stuff more than anyone should ever have to. As always, I owe much of my sanity and happiness to him.

Part I

Introducing Strategic Environmental Assessment

Chapter 1

Introduction

Strategic environmental assessment (SEA) is a process that aims to integrate environmental and sustainability considerations into strategic decision-making. It has the potential to make the world a greener and more liveable place. It also has the potential to be a dreary and resource-intensive formality, applied in a grudging minimalist fashion by people who just *hate* having to do it, adding still further to some great useless administrative burden paid for by hapless taxpayers. This book is intended to help people to set up good SEA processes and carry out effective, efficient SEAs: it is a manual for SEA. It presents straightforward SEA approaches and techniques that achieve the objectives of SEA – green, equitable – but with a minimal burden.

Book structure

Part I of this book introduces SEA generally and three SEA systems in particular:

- Chapter 2 explains what strategic actions and SEA are, and the benefits and constraints of SEA.
- Chapter 3 presents an example of SEA to explain how the whole process hangs together. It considers what aspects of SEA are crucial and less crucial. It also presents a quality assurance checklist for SEA.
- Chapter 4 discusses the development, requirements and issues raised by the US National Environmental Policy Act of 1969, European SEA Directive of 2004, and Chinese regulations on plan environmental impact assessment (PGIA) of 2009. Appendices A and B present the European and Chinese legislation in full.

Part II discusses techniques, approaches and issues related to different stages of SEA:

- Chapter 5 discusses the context in which SEA is carried out: what strategic actions require SEA, how SEA links with decision-making and other assessment requirements, and who should be involved in SEA.
- Chapter 6 explains how to describe links between the strategic action and other strategic actions, the baseline environment, and relevant environmental and sustainability problems.
- Chapter 7 considers different types of alternatives to a strategic action, how they can be identified, and which can be eliminated from further consideration.
- Chapter 8 explains how the impacts of strategic actions and alternatives can be predicted. It is closely linked to Chapter 9, which discusses how impact significance can be evaluated, negative impacts can be minimized and positive ones can be enhanced, and trade-offs can be made explicit. Appendix C presents a range of impact prediction and evaluation techniques, and the circumstances in which they might be used.
- Chapter 10 looks at how the SEA process can be documented, and approaches to monitoring the environmental impacts of strategic actions. Appendix D discusses Habitats Directive assessment (HDA), a narrow and precautionary form of SEA used in Europe to assess strategic actions' impacts on sites of international importance for nature conservation.

Part III contains a final chapter that revisits the concept of SEA quality and how to assure it. Chapter 11 also discusses how long SEA takes and what resources it requires. It concludes with ideas for SEA capacity building. Appendix E presents a series of exercises to give further understanding of SEA in action.

Some chapters and appendices of this book will be more applicable to some readers than others. Table 1.1 summarizes which might be of most use to different reader groups.

Other resources

This book takes a practical, 'how to do it' approach. For this, it assumes that the reader has some understanding of SEA theory, the process by which strategic actions are developed and adopted, and project level environmental impact assessment. Additional reading that may help to provide background information, flesh out certain aspects of this book or provide more detailed information about SEA practice in specific countries, include:

- Aschemann et al (forthcoming, 2011) *Handbook of Strategic Environmental Assessment*, Earthscan

Table 1.1 *Parts of the book likely to be of particular relevance for specific readers*

For	Particularly relevant parts of the book
People who write SEA regulations and guidance	Chapters 3, 4, 5 and 11 Appendices A, B and D
People who carry out SEAs and students of environmental management	Chapters 2–11 Appendix E
People who carry out HDA and students of ecological impact assessment	Appendix D
People who want to influence strategic actions, or are responsible for SEA quality assurance	Chapters 2, 3, 5 and 11 Chapter 3 checklist Appendix E
Environmental lawyers and law students	Chapters 2 and 4 Appendices A, B, D and E

- Dalal-Clayton and Sadler (2005) *Strategic Environmental Assessment: A Sourcebook and Reference Guide to International Experience*, Earthscan
- Dalal-Clayton and Sadler (forthcoming, 2010) *Sustainability Appraisal*, Earthscan
- Fischer (2007) *Theory and Practice of Strategic Environmental Assessment*, Earthscan
- Glasson et al (2005) *Introduction to Environmental Impact Assessment*, Routledge
- Jones et al (2005) *Strategic Environmental Assessment and Land Use Planning: An International Evaluation*, Earthscan
- Marsden (2008) *Strategic Environmental Assessment in International and European Law*, Earthscan
- Morris and Therivel (eds) (2009) *Methods of Environmental Impact Assessment*, Routledge
- Schmidt et al (2005) *Implementing Strategic Environmental Assessment*, Springer
- Therivel and Partidário (eds) (1996) *The Practice of Strategic Environmental Assessment*, Earthscan

Other useful reports and websites on SEA have been published by organizations such as the OECD (2006), United Nations University (2005) and World Bank (date unknown). The journals *Environmental Impact Assessment Review* and *Impact Assessment and Project Appraisal* frequently publish articles about SEA, as do other journals, though more sporadically. The annual conference of the International Association for Impact Assessment (IAIA) (www.iaia.org) is a good source of inspiration, as well as information on emerging SEA practice worldwide.

Many SEA reports are published online. Words to search for include 'strategic environmental assessment', 'sustainability appraisal', 'programmatic environmental impact statement' (for the US), 'évaluation environnementale stratégique' (for French-speaking countries) and 'evaluación ambiental estratégica' (for Spanish-speaking countries). An annual list of recommended good practice SEA reports is published at www.levett-therivel.co.uk.

SEA changes since 2003

This second edition has been a particular pleasure to write. It has allowed me to review the many changes to the theory and practice of SEA that have taken place over the last six years, and to get a sense of likely future directions in which SEA might go. The European SEA Directive has been implemented in most of its 27 member states; China's EIA Law of 2003 has been superseded by new SEA legislation; and many other countries have seen a rapid evolution in SEA practice, sometimes triggered by requirements of donor organizations. Many new books and articles on SEA have been published, and most of the references for this edition are from post-2003.

These changes have led to an explosion in the number of SEAs carried out worldwide, an improvement in their general quality, and a rapid evolution in SEA approaches and techniques. As a result, I have had a wide range of SEA reports from all parts of the world to use as case studies and examples in this book. Table 1.2 shows some of these. Whereas the first edition of this book used mostly theoretical examples, all of the examples in this edition are from real life (though I have anonymized some them for reasons that will become clear).

What has also become clear is that SEA practice alone is not leading to more environmentally sound decisions. Much of the recent SEA literature concerns the limitations of carrying out rationalist SEAs whose findings must only be 'taken into account' in a non-rationalist, politically driven world. My experience as a consultant bears this out. As such, this edition contains more information about decision-making processes and possible forms of bias inherent in these.

An interesting counter-example to this is HDA: because of the precautionary nature of the legislation that requires HDA and the fact that plans may not be adopted (except under very restricted circumstances) if they will affect the integrity of sites of European nature conservation importance, HDA is proving to be much more effective than SEA in leading to changes in strategic actions. This is discussed further at Appendix D.

Table 1.2 *Examples of strategic actions that have been subject to SEA*

Africa	• Logging contracts and forest management, République Démocratique du Congo (RDC, 2009) • Mining sector reform, Sierra Leone (World Bank, 2008) • Ghana Poverty Reduction Strategy (EPA and NDPC, 2003) • Eskom master plan – Central region, South Africa (Eskom distribution, 2007)
Asia	• Lao People's Democratic Republic hydropower development (Lao PDR and World Bank, 2004) • Tourism strategy for Guizhou, China (World Bank, 2007) • Hydropower masterplan for Viet Nam (Asian Development Bank, 2009) • Hong Kong 2030 – Planning vision and strategy (PDGHKSAR, 2007)
Australia and Pacific Islands	• Defence activities in the Great Barrier Reef Heritage Conservation Area, Australia (Department of Defence, 2006) • Development of a liquefied natural gas precinct (Government of Western Australia, 2009) • Tourism strategy for Fiji (Levett and McNally, 2003)
Europe and Eurasia	• Scottish strategic transport projects review (Transport Scotland, 2008) • River Basin Management Plan for the Loire-Bretagne basin, France (Comité de Bassin Loire-Bretagne, 2007) • Water provision for Dublin, Ireland (Dublin City Council, 2008) • Flood risk management on the tidal River Thames, England (Environment Agency, 2009) • Yerevan City masterplan, Armenia (UNDP and RECCEE, 2005) • Development principles for the cross-border area between Slovenia and Croatia (Republic of Slovenia, 2007) • National policy statement on nuclear power, UK (DBERR, 2008a) • Regional plan for Halle, Germany (Planungsgemeinschaft Halle, 2009)
North America	• Economic diversification in areas infested by mountain pine beetles, Canada (Natural Resources Canada, 2007) • Revision of US regulations on genetically engineered organisms (US Department of Agriculture, 2007) • Designation of energy corridors on federal land, US (USDoE and USDoI, 2008) • Planning for development in the Great Sand Hills areas, Canada (Great Sand Hills Advisory Committee, 2007) • Californian light brown apple moth eradication (California Department of Food and Agriculture, 2009) • Fish and wildlife management plan for the Bonneville Power Administration (BPA, 2003) • Constellation program of space exploration (NASA, 2008)
South America and the Caribbean Islands	• Colombian biofuel production (Lozano et al, 2008) • National sugar adaptation strategy, Trinidad & Tobago (European Commission, 2009a) • Policy for reducing atmospheric contamination in urban centres in Colombia (Burgos et al, 2008)

Chapter 2

Strategic Environmental Assessment: An Overview

This chapter provides a background for the rest of this book. It explains:

- the aims and principles of SEA;
- what strategic actions are and what they look like; and
- the benefits and problems of SEA.

It talks about SEA generically, not the specific form of SEA required in any particular country. Readers who are familiar with SEA may wish to skip this chapter and go directly to Chapter 3.

Aims and principles of SEA

The ultimate *aim of SEA* is to help to protect the environment and promote sustainability. Of course, there are many ways of doing this, but SEA contributes to this by helping to integrate environmental (or sustainability) issues in decision-making:

> *SEA is a systematic process for evaluating the environmental consequences of proposed policy, plan or programme initiatives in order to ensure they are fully included and appropriately addressed at the earliest appropriate stage of decision making on par with economic and social considerations.* (Sadler and Verheem, 1996)

There are many other definitions of SEA (e.g. Therivel et al, 1992; Partidário and Clark, 2000), but they are all essentially variants on this theme.

Just how environmental concerns should be integrated in strategic decision-making is the subject of many guidance documents and

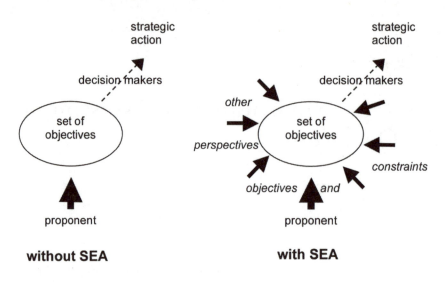

Note: The proponent is typically also the decision-maker
Source: Adapted from Therivel and Brown (1999)

Figure 2.1 *SEA as a decision-making process that takes on board a broader range of perspectives, objectives and constraints*

regulations worldwide, and of Part II of this book. However, there is general agreement on some basic *principles of SEA*, which in turn start to suggest SEA stages and techniques.

First, SEA is a tool for *improving the strategic action*, not a post-hoc snapshot. The strategic action may well be changed as a result of the SEA, with different objectives, different means of achieving these objectives, and different forms of implementation. This suggests that the SEA should be started early, be integrated in the decision-making process, and focus on identifying possible alternatives and modifications to the strategic action. The decision-maker should be involved in the SEA process in an active capacity, to ensure that the SEA findings are fully taken into account in decision-making.

Second, SEA should *promote participation of other stakeholders* in the decision-making process. Essentially, SEA aims to expand the decision-maker's focus to include issues that go beyond their main area of concern – sustainability and environmental issues. This is illustrated in Figure 2.1. As such, SEA should involve a range of stakeholders, normally including the public. It should also document what has been done, why decisions have been made, and assumptions and uncertainties.

Third, to fit into the timescale and resources of the decision-making process, SEA should *focus on key environmental/sustainability constraints*, thresholds and limits at the appropriate plan-making level. It should not aim to be as detailed as project environmental impact assessment (EIA), nor be a giant collection of baseline data which does not focus on key issues. A scoping stage is always important to sort out what the key issues are.

Fourth, SEA should help to *identify the best option* for the strategic action. It should thus assist in identifying and assessing different plan options; for instance, options that meet demands but minimize damage, and options for demand management – modifying forecast demand rather than accommodating it.

Fifth, SEA should aim to *minimize negative impacts, optimize positive ones, and compensate for the loss of valuable features and benefits*. SEA should apply the precautionary principle: if the value of development and its impacts are uncertain there should be a presumption in favour of protecting what exists. Impact mitigation in SEA often takes other forms than end-of-pipe technology: it could include changing aspects of the strategic action to avoid the negative impact, influencing other organizations to act in certain ways, or setting constraints on subsequent project implementation.

Finally, SEA should *ensure that strategic actions do not exceed limits beyond which irreversible damage from impacts may occur*. This requires identification of such limits. It calls for the prediction of the effects of the strategic action; comparing the likely future situation without the strategic action – the baseline – against the situation with the strategic action. It also requires a judgement about whether the effect is significant and whether it will cause environmental limits to be exceeded.

Strategic actions

So far, the discussion has been about strategic actions generally. However, this term covers a huge range of activities. Strategic actions include:

- Policy: legislation, Green and White Papers, policy statements, budgets, economic policies, trade agreements. Examples include (from Table 1.2) national policy on nuclear power, reform of the mining sector, regulations on genetically modified organisms and principles for developing cross-border areas.
- Spatial plans and programmes: national, regional/territorial, local/town, multi-project programmes, conservation areas (World Heritage, national parks).
- Sectoral plans and programmes, e.g. for agriculture, transport, waste. Examples include hydropower master plans, tourism strategies, forest management plans and national transport programmes.

- Policies, plans or programmes to achieve environmental or social ends, e.g. employment development, international aid, ecosystem management. Examples include poverty reduction strategies, policies for improving air quality, flood risk management plans and economic diversification strategies.

Strategic actions are normally developed by public agencies such as land-use planning departments or energy planning agencies. However, they can also be developed by private or semi-private companies. For instance, telecommunications or water companies will have programmes for where to site their infrastructure.

All strategic actions are composed of one or more *objectives* plus more detailed *statements* about how the objective(s) will be implemented. The objective can also be called an aim, vision, strategic policy, and so on; and the statements can also be called actions, measures, implementation plans, policies, and so on. But an objective will look roughly like this:

> *This plan aims to secure within an available level of expenditure that motorists, those without cars, pedestrians and commercial vehicles are given the maximum freedom of movement and parking compatible with the achievement of convenient and prosperous conditions for all and an acceptable quality of environment.*

(This is not a good objective, as we will see in Chapter 3, but it is typical.) The statements – and there could be hundreds of these in a single strategic action – will look roughly like this:

> *New housing developments will provide at least as many car parking spaces as there are bedrooms in the house.*

As vague as the objective looks, it is very important because it sets the tone for the rest of the strategic action. Consider, for instance, the two objectives of Box 2.1, both based on real-life examples (Sustainable Development Commission, 2001). Both objectives read like motherhood and apple pie, but what very different activities they would lead to on the ground. Objective A would lead to statements promoting large-scale agribusiness, large food distribution and retailing centres, use of herbicides and fertilizers to ensure optimal productivity, trade liberalization, and responsiveness to consumer demands. Objective B would lead to statements promoting small-scale farms and abattoirs, support for local foods via farmers' markets and farm shops, reduced use of herbicides and fertilizers, and education of consumers on sustainable consumption. These different activities and projects would in turn have very different environmental, social and economic impacts. The role of SEA is to identify these impacts early

---

Box 2.1 Two examples of objectives for a national policy on farming and food

Objective A
The UK farming and food sector should be profitable, able to compete internationally, and responsive to consumer demands. It should provide:

- choice of a range of fresh produce all year round;
- high-quality convenience foods at stores that provide a wide range of foods under one roof; and
- value for money and low prices, in keeping with the trends of the last ten years.

Objective B
The farming and food sector should provide sustainability, health and livelihoods for UK citizens. In doing so it should, at worst, not undermine the provisions of the same for other countries, and at best, contribute to achieving these goals for other countries. Elements of such a system include:

- natural genetic diversity in farmed plants and animals, to reduce vulnerability to diseases, preserve the heritage and enrich diets;
- careful husbandry of non-renewable natural resources and reduced reliance on fossil fuels;
- a food supply that is nutrient-dense and fibre-rich;
- access to the best quality food for the most vulnerable in society;
- jobs in the food and farming sector that provide a living wage; and
- direct links between primary food producers and purchasers.

Source: Adapted from Sustainable Development Commission (2001)

---

on, and suggest ways to minimize negative and maximize positive impacts.

Strategic actions arise for various reasons. In some cases, organizations are legally required to produce them. In other cases, they evolve out of a perceived need, or a political manifesto, or simply because there is a tradition of devising such strategic actions. Sometimes a decision is made to stop producing them, for instance, where there is no longer a need for them.

Figure 2.2 shows the broad stages of strategic decision-making. Once the strategic action's objective is decided on, alternative ways of achieving the objective are considered. These can be either/or alternatives, such as different approaches to the international food trade (liberalize completely v. liberalize with some environmental and animal welfare safeguards; focus on 'fair trade' v. regional self-sufficiency etc.); or mix-and-match statements (promote farmers' markets, promote 'fair trade' foods, give subsidies to farmers to help

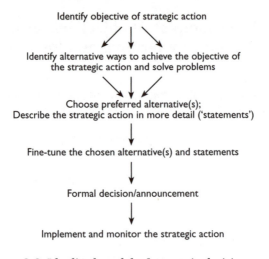

Identify objective of strategic action

Identify alternative ways to achieve the objective of
the strategic action and solve problems

Choose preferred alternative(s);
Describe the strategic action in more detail ('statements')

Fine-tune the chosen alternative(s) and statements

Formal decision/announcement

Implement and monitor the strategic action

Figure 2.2 *Idealized model of strategic decision-making*

them to compete internationally); or broad alternatives leading to a choice of preferred alternatives, in turn leading to more detailed statements of how the preferred alternative will be implemented. Once a preferred alternative and/or more detailed statements have been drafted, they are fine-tuned until a final strategic action is agreed, announced, implemented and monitored.

Of course, in reality this assumption of sequential, rational strategic decision-making rarely holds true, and a key theme in the recent SEA literature is that SEA practitioners need to be more cognisant of the realities of strategic decision-making. Any SEA system needs to be able to operate under these conditions as well as under the more idealized ones. This will be discussed further in Chapter 3.

Policies, plans, programmes and tiering

The SEA literature often refers to strategic actions as 'policies, plans or programmes'. Wood and Djeddour's definition of these terms is still the best one around:

> *a policy may ... be considered as the inspiration and guidance for action, a plan as a set of co-ordinated and timed objectives for the implementation of the policy, and a programme as a set of projects in a particular area.* (Wood and Djeddour, 1991)

Policies, plans and programmes are jointly called 'strategic actions' in this book for the sake of efficiency, and also to reduce confusion over whether something is a policy, a plan or a programme.

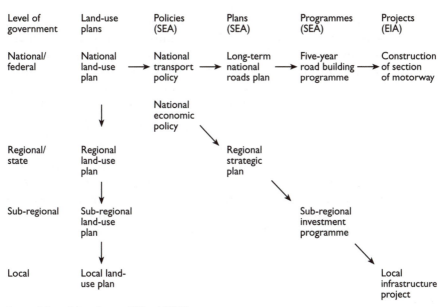

Level of government	Land-use plans	Policies (SEA)	Plans (SEA)	Programmes (SEA)	Projects (EIA)
National/ federal	National land-use plan	National transport policy	Long-term national roads plan	Five-year road building programme	Construction of section of motorway
		National economic policy			
Regional/ state	Regional land-use plan		Regional strategic plan		
Sub-regional	Sub-regional land-use plan			Sub-regional investment programme	
Local	Local land-use plan				Local infrastructure project

Source: Adapted from Lee and Wood (1987)

Figure 2.3 *Tiering of policies, plans and programmes*

For instance, a policy on food and farming with Objective A (Box 2.1) might focus on improving the efficiency and competitiveness of the agricultural sector; related plans might focus on developing networks of efficient large-scale food storage, processing and distribution centres built to the highest international specifications, and effective ways of marketing UK products abroad over the next decade; and related programmes might be for the construction of large abattoirs in region X (note that the same players are not responsible for writing and implementing all of these policies, plans and programmes). A policy with Objective B might emphasize diversity, local provenance and nutrition; related plans could promote the establishment of producer–consumer networks and labelling schemes; and related programmes in area Y could be for the establishment of weekly farmers' markets, the conversion of farmland to organic status, and schools procuring all their food from within 20 kilometres of the school.

The definitions above suggests that there can be a *tiering* of strategic actions, from policy, to plan, to programme and, finally, to project. There can also be a tiering of assessments, from policy SEA down to programme SEA and project EIA; this is shown at Figure 2.3. In theory, aspects of decision-making and SEA carried out at one level do not need to subsequently be revisited at 'lower' levels, which means that tiering of decision-making and SEA can save time and resources.

Of course, the reality, again, is not so clear-cut. Higher-level policies may not be reflected in lower-level plans and projects. Lower-level plans may be adopted before the higher-level 'parent' policies. Strategic decision-making often skips stages: for instance there are no steps between the European Commission's Common Agricultural Policy, which determines levels and rules for agricultural subsidies, and the activities of farmers at individual sites. Many strategic actions are not called what they are (for instance, UK local 'plans' include sub-component 'policies'), or combine aspects of policy, plan and programme all in one strategic action. Sectors overlap, for instance transport and energy, or minerals and waste, so that strategic actions for one cannot be neatly disentangled from strategic actions for the other. However, the concept of 'tiering' is an important one, particularly in terms of the type of information that is presented in SEAs; this is discussed in Chapter 9.

Stages of SEA

The SEA principles discussed earlier, and particularly the need for SEA to inform the decision-making process from the start, suggest particular stages and approaches to SEA. Figure 2.4 shows the basic

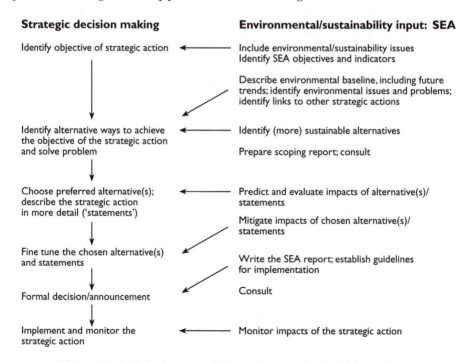

Figure 2.4 *Links between SEA and strategic decision-making*

Table 2.1 *SEA outputs*

SEA stage	What to decide	What to record
1. Identify environmental/ sustainability issues; identify SEA objectives and indicators	What environmental/ sustainability issues to consider, and possibly what objectives, targets and/or indicators to test the plan options and statements against	Issues that are scoped in and scoped out; possibly an SEA framework of objectives, indicators and targets
2. Describe environmental baseline, including future trends; identify environmental issues and problems	What constraints to consider during decision-making	Data on the baseline environment; list of relevant environmental/sustainability issues and constraints
3. Identify links to other relevant strategic actions	What other strategic actions influence the strategic action in question and how	List of relevant strategic actions, their requirements, and any constraints or conflicts with the strategic action in question
4. Identify (more sustainable) alternatives for dealing with the problems and implementing the strategic action objective	What alternatives or options to consider	List of alternatives or options; any alternatives considered and eliminated early in decision-making
5. Prepare scoping report; consult	What to include in the scoping report, whom to consult about scoping	Results of stages 1–4; agreed written statement of how to proceed with subsequent SEA stages
6. Predict and evaluate impact of alternatives/ statements; compare alternatives; mitigate impacts of chosen alternative(s)/statements	What are the environmental and sustainability effects of the alternatives/options and statements; what are the preferred alternatives; what mitigation measures to include	Summary of effects of alternatives/options and statements; list of preferred alternatives; explanation of why these are preferred; mitigation measures proposed
7. Write the SEA report; establish guidelines for implementation	How to present the data from stages 1–6	Prepare the SEA report
8. Consult	Whom to consult; how to respond to consultation results	How consultation results were addressed
9. Monitor the environmental/ sustainability impacts of the strategic action	How to deal with any negative impacts of the strategic action	How the strategic action's impacts will be monitored and significant effects dealt with

steps of SEA and how they feed into various stages of decision-making. Note all of the arrows from right to left: the aim throughout is to ensure that environmental/sustainability considerations (Chapter 5 discusses which of these should be the focus of SEA) are taken on board at each stage of decision-making. Table 2.1 gives an indication of possible SEA outputs. The example SEA in Chapter 3 gives more detail on these SEA stages.

Advantages of SEA

Why is SEA needed? What is its 'value added' over project EIA or other systems of environmental management, footprinting or standards?

First, SEA begins earlier. Strategic actions lead to and shape projects, so appraising them offers the chance to influence the *kinds* of projects that are going to happen, not just the details once projects are being considered.

Second, SEA deals with impacts that are difficult to consider at the project level. It considers the cumulative and synergistic impacts of multiple projects, for instance the transport implications of the redevelopment of an entire area. These are very difficult to address at a project-by-project level. Box 2.2 gives an example of cumulative impacts addressed in SEA. Similarly, SEA can deal with larger-scale environmental impacts, such as those on biodiversity or global warming, more effectively than can individual EIAs.

SEA promotes a better consideration of alternatives. By the time most projects are proposed, many alternatives have already been thrown out because of higher-level decisions. For instance, renewable

---

Box 2.2 Example of cumulative impacts identified as part of SEA

An SEA ('IOSEA3') was carried out for a plan to issue oil and gas exploration licences for the Rockall Basin, north-west of Ireland. Previous SEAs had been prepared for two neighbouring basins. Oil and gas exploration involves seismic surveys in which ships move in a grid pattern towing air guns that produce very loud, low frequency sounds that penetrate and reflect off the sea bed and underlying rock strata. When exposed to loud noise, many marine mammals move away, surface less frequently and for shorter periods of time, and/or change their vocalizations. IOSEA3 considered a scenario where several survey ships in the Rockall Basin or adjacent basins operate simultaneously near each other: in such a scenario, the marine mammals could have nowhere to go. As mitigation, it proposed coordination of survey activities to ensure that marine mammals have a chance to avoid areas of high noise (DCENR, 2008).

Box 2.3 Example of strategic alternatives identified as part of an SEA

The UK government is developing a National Policy Statement (NPS) on ports. The NPS aims to encourage sustainable port development to cater for long-term forecast growth in volumes of imports and exports by sea, promote a competitive and efficient port industry, allow judgements to be made about new port developments, and ensure that such developments satisfy relevant legal, environmental and social constraints and objectives. The 'appraisal of sustainability' (a form of SEA) for the NPS considered seven sets of strategic alternatives for how to meet these objectives:

1. Market-led versus central planning approach to port development
2. Locational NPS versus non-locational NPS
3. Support for development versus no support for development
4. Subsidising versus not subsidising port investment
5. Letting the promoter decide on the need for new development versus consideration by the decision maker
6. Mitigation of impacts versus mitigation of impacts to minimum requirements
7. Developer funding versus state funding of road/rail/inland connections

(Department for Transport, 2009b)

---

energy developments are unlikely to get built in a region with an energy strategy that promotes gas-fired power stations. SEA affects the decision-making process at a stage where more alternatives are available for consideration, including reducing demand (cutting down on the need to travel, promoting accessibility rather than mobility, and the 'business-as-usual' alternative). Box 2.3 gives an example of strategic-level alternatives.

SEA informs decision-makers about the environmental and sustainability consequences of their proposed strategic actions. These can then be considered alongside financial, technical, political and other concerns. SEA thus adds an additional dimension to the decision-making process.

SEA facilitates – in theory, even if not always in practice – public participation in strategic decision-making. Traditionally, strategic actions have been developed with limited public input. At minimum, SEA should provide one opportunity for the public to comment on a strategic action before it is formally agreed. At best, it allows the public to be actively involved throughout the strategic decision-making process.

All of these factors make the decision-making process more transparent and robust. SEA helps to ensure that the strategic action will be implemented effectively and that no unintended impacts will result from the strategic action. It may also help the strategic action to be approved more quickly by any inspectors or auditors. As a side-effect, SEA helps decision-makers to better understand their plans, feel more confident about them and learn about sustainability.

Finally, because of tiering, SEA has the potential to promote more streamlined decision-making, where decisions taken at one planning stage (using SEA) may not need to be revisited at subsequent tiers of decision-making (and their SEA or EIA). It could obviate, for instance, the need for lengthy project-level inquiries that consider strategic-level issues, though in practice it is rarely possible to fully separate the strategic and project levels.

To conclude, SEA can help achieve clearer and more environment-friendly and publicly acceptable strategic actions that are approved more quickly.

Problems with SEA

On the other hand, SEA has some limitations.

First, it takes time and resources. Just how much time and resources depends on the type of strategic action and how efficiently the SEA is carried out. Arguably much or all of this could be recouped with easier, faster approval and implementation of the strategic action. Nevertheless, it is an up-front cost, which is normally incurred just when planners are particularly busy and there are already other costs (e.g. feasibility or capacity studies). And, if SEA is done badly – late, as an artificial add-on, with no real intention of using its results to inform the decision-making process – then all of its costs can be incurred with no benefits in terms of an improved strategic action. This is discussed further at Chapter 11.

Second, SEA is still a relatively new process. Appropriate baseline data may not be available. Mechanisms for public consultation may not be set up. Planners may need to go through the learning curve associated with any new decision-making tool. In most countries, special SEA resourcing and capacity-building will be needed.

SEA needs to cope with a huge range of decision-making situations, from the broadest international policy down to almost project-level local detail. Strategic actions cover large areas with many potential projects. They can last for many years with associated uncertainties about what will happen during that time, for example, the possibility of drought, changes in petrol prices, or technical developments (In the UK alone, 2007–2009 brought a severe economic recession, a sharp slump in housing construction, the first decrease in vehicle miles travelled since 1979, severe floods and fear of a swine flu pandemic.) In many cases, the decision-making process will not be neatly charted out, and some decisions may need to be made very quickly. SEA thus needs to be responsive, adaptable and quick. This often means that SEA cannot be as robust, detailed and 'scientific' as one might like.

Finally, after all the hard work and agony put into SEAs, they still end up being only one part of the decision-making process. Often the decision will be made for reasons that the decision takers find compelling but that are unconnected with, or opposed to, environmental/sustainability principles. At that point, the SEA practitioners have to pick themselves up, dust themselves off, and move on to the next strategic action.

But there are also times when, in the middle of filling in an SEA assessment matrix or thinking about alternatives to the strategic action, the decision-maker comes up with a new, elegant approach to a problem. Or where a doubtful politician is convinced to take a more sustainable option because of the findings of an SEA. Or where the decision-maker starts approaching their strategic action in a different way because the SEA made them explicitly aware of an environmental problem that they had only vaguely appreciated before. Those moments, in my mind, make it all worthwhile.

Conclusions

If there is only one thing that I would like the reader to learn from this book it would be this: SEA is meant to improve – change – the strategic action. This concept carries with it all of the other principles about timing, whom to involve, techniques to use, and so on. Chapter 3 now gives an example of SEA in action.

Chapter 3

SEA in Plan-Making

This chapter aims to give an understanding of how the SEA process as a whole interacts with the plan-making process: how it affects the strategic action, what are the SEA outcomes, and what to look out for. It considers the application of SEA to a hypothetical district transport plan (DTP), then considers what makes SEA effective. It concludes with a quality assurance checklist for SEA. Chapters 5–10 in Part II explain the reasoning behind some of the approaches used, variants on these approaches, and pitfalls to avoid.

Hypothetical example of SEA

Tooton Rush district is an imaginary but typical English local authority with one main town, Standstill, and two smaller towns, Rushmore and Walkerton. A very brief DTP has been in place for many years; see Box 3.1. It consists of a broad objective and three more detailed statements on how the objective will be implemented (in reality there would probably be dozens of detailed statements).

The new, bright chief transport planning officer, Wanda Duright, wants to get her team to rewrite the DTP, integrating SEA into the plan-making process. She has already noted that the old DTP objective gives little weight to the environment, is unwieldy, and is not in keeping with current government advice on reducing the need to travel. She has also noted that two of the detailed statements are potentially contradictory (improve roads but give priority to pedestrians), and one is vague (which of the district's roads are in the proposed primary network?). The SEA will hopefully help to solve these problems and ensure that the new DTP is as sustainable as possible, but where should she start?

The following sections give a brief explanation of how SEA could be carried out for Tooton Rush's DTP (although other approaches would be possible too). It is structured according to the main SEA

Box 3.1 The bad old District Transport Plan for Tooton Rush District

Objective: This DTP aims to secure, within an available level of expenditure, that motorists, those without cars, pedestrians and commercial vehicles are given the maximum freedom of movement and parking compatible with the achievement of convenient and prosperous conditions for everyone in Tooton Rush and an acceptable quality of environment.

T1. Improvements will be made to a primary network of high-quality roads, which will serve as the major routes for through and lorry traffic.

T2. New housing developments will provide at least as many car parking spaces as there are bedrooms in the house. New industrial, shopping and employment developments will provide enough parking for current and likely future demand.

T3. In Standstill, priority will be given to pedestrians and public transport. Appropriate comprehensive local policies for service areas will be sought.

---

stages that are covered in more detail in the next five chapters:

1   Set the institutional structure: get the timing right, determine who should be involved in the SEA and how it fits with other assessment requirements.
2   Describe the context: identify constraints and objectives set out by other strategic actions, describe the current and likely future baseline environment, identify environmental problems.
3   Clarify the strategic action's objectives, and identify sustainable options for achieving this objective.
4   Identify, assess and evaluate the likely environmental impacts of the options, choose the preferred option(s), mitigate significant negative impacts.
5   Document the process and monitor the impacts.

Set the institutional structure

Wanda has a small and relatively inexperienced team of planners. She decides to involve all of them in the SEA to help them understand the links between transport and sustainable development. There is already an established form of public consultation on DTPs, which she plans to expand to include consultation on the SEA.

Tip: SEA can be an educational process, not just an administrative procedure.

She decides to begin the SEA process at the same time as the plan-making process, so that information gathered for one can inform the other, and so that the SEA does not become a late and expensive add-on. The DTP is also subject to a health impact assessment; she decides to integrate the two forms of assessment so as to minimize duplication of work and identify win–win solutions where possible.

Tip: The SEA process is, in many ways, a model for good plan-making. The more the plan-making and assessment process(es) is integrated, the more effective the assessment is likely to be.

Describe the context

Wanda's team review existing higher-level (national and regional) strategic actions relating to their plan. This helps to identify what the DTP must do, may not do and should ideally do. They note that the government is now focusing on promoting transport choice and reducing the need to travel, rather than on improving people's ability to move around easily. They also refer to a recent local residents' visioning process, which shows that residents' priorities in terms of travel are speed, comfort and safety.

The team describe the baseline environment so as to get a feel for what the area's environmental problems are, and to provide a basis for future impact predictions and monitoring. They do this through a combination of overlay/constraints maps and a table that shows, for various aspects of the environment, current baseline levels, comparators, targets and trends.

A first question, though, is to decide what aspects of the environment should be analysed. Wanda opts to use the list of environmental topics from the European SEA Directive (see Box 4.2), plus relevant social and economic topics, adapted to the transport planning context. This provides the first column of Tooton Rush's baseline environment in Table 3.1. Wanda gets one of her planners to spend a week collecting data from various websites and documents, and organizing it in the table and maps.

About half of the data needed for the table – which is based on a real case study – is not available. In particular, many trends cannot be determined because there is no time-series data. With no time in this planning cycle to collect more baseline information, Wanda's team decide to collect the outstanding data by carrying out a survey of local residents and an analysis of Tooton Rush's planning files before the next plan-making cycle.

Tip: Not all the baseline data must be available for an SEA to proceed. The first SEA can be seen as a way of identifying what data need to be collected and monitored in the future.

Table 3.1 *Baseline data for Tooton Rush (hypothetical)*

Topics/ indicators	Quantified data	Comparators, trends, targets	Comments
Water			
River quality	10% fair, 60% good, 30% very good (2010 data)	Tooton Rush 2000: 35% fair, 50% good, 15% very good England: 15% fair, 65% good, 20% very good Water Framework Directive target: 100% good or better by 2015	Improving sharply over time, and better than the England average; may meet demanding target on time
Air and climatic factors			
Distance travelled per person per year by mode of transport (miles)	walking 165, cycling 51, car 6156, public transport 648	England: walking 189, cycling 39, car 5713, public transport 874 Target: double cycling levels by 2012	Tooton Rush has higher car use than the national average. Car use is increasing, walking and cycling decreasing
Number of days of air pollution over national standard	Standstill: 18 (2010)	England & Wales: average 26 (2010) Standard: $40\mu g\ NO_x/m^3$ Target: no exceedances	Better than E&W average but will require significant reductions in vehicle emissions to achieve targets
CO_2 emissions per person per year	10.5 tonnes (2010)	UK: 9.4 tonnes average (2010) UK target: reduce by 34% of 1990 levels by 2020 and 80% by 2050	
Biodiversity, flora, fauna			
Achievement of Biodiversity Action Plan objectives	No district level data available	No national level data available	
Condition of Sites of Special Scientific Interest	25% favourable, 75% unfavourable no change (2010)	England: 44% favourable, 45% unfavourable recovering, 8% unfavourable no change, 4% unfavourable declining Target: 95% in favourable or recovering condition by 2010	Target not being achieved
Human health			
Transport accidents/ billion passenger kilometres	No district level data available	UK: bus 0.3; car 2.8; rail 0.4; pedestrian 47 (2010)	

Topics/ indicators	Quantified data	Comparators, trends, targets	Comments
% households with one or more persons with a limiting long-term illness	33%	32%	
Public concern over noise	21% 'very worried' about noise (2010)	30% of UK respondents affected by traffic noise (2009)	Getting worse (planners' perceptions)
Social inclusiveness and accessibility			
Index of multiple deprivation: access to services	3 out of Tooton Rush's 10 sub-areas (all rural) are in the lowest 20% of accessibility in the UK (2007)	3 out of 10 in lowest 20% of accessibility (2004)	No change
Access to key services	% rural households < 4 kilometres from service: supermarket 81%; primary school 93%; secondary school 74%; bank 70%; doctor 87%	England: supermarket 79%; primary school 92%; secondary school 76%; bank 76%; doctor 87%	Very similar to national average
Access to services for disabled people	No district level data available	GB: difficulty in: shopping 29%; using bank 6%; going to pub/restaurant 15%	Getting better (planners' perceptions)
Landscape			
% land designed for particular quality or amenity value	Area of Outstanding Natural Beauty 3.3%; Green Belt 5%	England: Area of Outstanding Natural Beauty 16%; Green Belt 13%	
Economic and access			
Employment	65% (2010)	GB 63% (2010) Tooton Rush 66% (2008)	No significant issues

Note: This table is not comprehensive, it is for example purposes only.
GB = England, Wales and Scotland; UK = GB plus Northern Ireland

The team then identify environmental problems. They look, in Table 3.1, at where Tooton Rush is worse than its targets or other comparators and likely to get worse: a high percentage of journeys in Tooton Rush are made by car, air quality standards are not being achieved and services in rural areas are not particularly accessible. Wanda presents the team's findings at a meeting of the local elected representatives who identify two further problems: future issues likely to result from developments on the edge of Standstill that have been given planning permission but have not yet been built, and that many people without cars have problems getting to essential services, such as shopping and the doctor.

Tip: The views of planners and others who are familiar with the area are invaluable in SEA. Use 'expert judgement' liberally. The SEA process can also be used as a way of involving politicians in the plan-making process.

By now, Tooton Rush's planners have three sets of information to help them to rewrite their DTP objective: the government's emphasis on transport choice and reducing the need to travel; the results of the local resident visioning process that emphasizes speed, comfort and safety; and the environmental baseline that suggests that residents' health and accessibility are being negatively affected by the over-emphasis on car use, and that this in turn is affected by land-use planning decisions, which makes it difficult for many people to get around without a car. They reassess the DTP objective (parentheses denote their thought processes) as follows.

> *This DTP aims to secure within an available level of expenditure* (This objective puts economics symbolically first: we must change that to emphasize our sustainable development agenda)...

> *that motorists, those without cars, pedestrians and commercial vehicles* (Hm. The focus on different user groups is good, but what strange overlaps! Commercial vehicle drivers are motorists, and pedestrians are people without cars. And what about cyclists or public transport users, whom we should be trying to encourage?)...

> *are given the maximum freedom of movement and parking* (We should instead emphasize accessibility, reducing the need to travel, and speed, comfort and safety: focus on the ends rather than the means)...

> *compatible with the achievement of convenient and prosperous conditions for all in Tooton Rush and an acceptable quality of environment* (Just a last grudging mention of the environment. This has to be made stronger and be linked to sustainable development).

Wanda's team develop a new objective to deal with these problems:

> *This DTP aims to optimize accessibility to jobs and services for all in an efficient, comfortable and safe manner while maintaining or enhancing environmental conditions in the district.*

Whereas the original objective inherently implied the construction of roads and parking lots, the new one describes the outcomes desired unencumbered by assumptions about how best to achieve them. This has three benefits: it facilitates public consultation about what policy should try to achieve; it enables implementation options to be compared empirically and objectively, increasing the chances that what the Council eventually does will help to achieve its aims; and it provides room to manoeuvre to allow these transport-related objectives to be reconciled with other objectives.

Identify sustainable options for meeting the (new) plan objective

Traditionally, at this stage, Tooton Rush's transport planners would have identified locations where accidents were particularly bad or where other improvements were necessary; and then they would have written plan statements that tried to improve transport conditions in those areas. Instead, Wanda encourages her team to brainstorm possible alternative ways of meeting the plan objective: to be proactive rather than reactive. Following good SEA practice, they try to focus particularly on the more strategic issues – reducing the need to travel and broad approaches for dealing with the remaining travel demand. Box 3.2 shows the results.

The team then determines which of these are clearly not feasible (m) and not within its control (a, c, d, g, j, l). Some of these are within the remit of other local authority departments: for instance, school buses are the remit of the education department and the promotion of farm shops that of the economic development department: the transport planners decide to discuss these issues with the responsible departments. Others options, such as petrol charging, are clearly outside the local authority's control and they decide not to take them further (though this should inform the council's response to national policy consultation). The team takes the rest of the options forward for further analysis.

Tip: Where good options are not within the competent authority's remit, it may be worthwhile negotiating with the responsible authority to try to get them implemented.

Box 3.2 Brainstormed options for achieving Tooton Rush DTP's new objective

Reduce the need to travel

a   Provide schools, shops, etc. close to where people live; and build new houses close to existing schools, shops, etc.
b   Congestion charging in Standstill.
c   Provide school buses to obviate the need for parents to drive their children to school.
d   Double the cost of petrol.
e   Reduce the number of parking spaces in towns.
f   Require businesses to prepare travel plans which aim to reduce commuting.
g   Encourage farm shops and locally produced foods.

Alternative modes of travel

h   Pedestrianization of Standstill, Rushmore and Walkerton town centres.
i   Park and Ride system for Standstill.
j   Improved bus fleet with wheelchair access.
k   Separate cycle-only lanes running parallel to each road.
l   Increase safety on footpaths perceived to be unsafe.
m   Tunnel under Standstill, Rushmore and Walkerton to carry through-traffic.

Note: The options given are for example purposes only. The list is not comprehensive.

The team also revisits the original plan statements, and decides to remove T1 and T2 from further consideration because they are clearly not in keeping with the new plan objective. They decide to consider the first sentence of T3 – 'In Standstill priority will be given to pedestrians and public transport' – as a variant to alternative h on full pedestrianization. They decide that the second half of T3 – 'Appropriate comprehensive local policies for service areas will be sought' – should not be a plan statement, as it essentially says 'we know that we should look at this in more detail but can't do it as part of this plan'.

Predict, evaluate and mitigate impacts

Wanda's team then appraises the remaining options using the topics from Table 3.1. They ask themselves:

• What will this option look like on the ground?
• What impact will this option have on each SEA topic?

Table 3.2 Impact appraisal of some of the options for Tooton Rush's District Transport Plan

Option	Impact of option on…							Comments/possible mitigation
	water	air & climate*	biodiversity, flora, fauna	human health*	social inclusiveness & access*	cultural heritage, landscape*	economic development	
b. Congestion charging in Standstill		++		+	+/–		–	Impact depends on whether you are rich or poor and have a car or not. Will have a direct cost to businesses in Standstill that depend on motorized vehicles.
e. Reduce the number of parking spaces in towns		+		+	–		–	Could negatively affect people with mobility problems, also businesses, particularly retail businesses depending on short-term parking.
f. Require businesses to develop travel plans		+		+	–		–	Many impacts depend on implementation, e.g. how travel plans are used, and whether they apply to all businesses (or only large companies, or new businesses).
h. Pedestrianization of town centres		++		+	+	–	–/+	Previous experience with pedestrianization suggests that retailers' earnings go down for the first 6–18 months, then rise to levels above those pre-pedestrianization. Possible impact on people with disabilities and delivery vehicles. Through traffic would need different route around town centre.
h1/T3. Pedestrian priority in town centres		+		+				Could slow down traffic. Extend priority to cyclists and emergency vehicles?
i. Park and Ride system for Standstill	–	+/–	–	+	–	–		P+Rs improve air quality etc. in urban areas but have negative impacts on edge of towns – on land take and wildlife during construction, and on air quality and quality of life for local residents during operation. They could also increase commuting.
k. Cycle lanes parallel to roads		+	–	++	+			Improves conditions for cyclists and could encourage drivers to cycle. Impact on biodiversity depends on whether lane goes on previously developed land or not.

Key: + positive impact; – negative impact; I depends on implementation; * identified as particularly important criterion in previous SEA stage

Table 3.3 *Compatibility appraisal of some of the options for Tooton Rush's District Transport Plan*

	b. Congestion charging	e. Reduce parking spaces	f. Travel plans	h. Pedestri -anization	h1. Pedestrian priority	i. Park and Ride
e. Reduce parking spaces	✔					
f. Travel plans	✔	✔				
h. Pedestrianization	✔	✔	✔			
h1. Pedestrian priority	✔	✔	✔	choose either h or h1		
i. Park and Ride	potential to integrate	where does parking go?	✔	✔	✔	
k. Cycle lanes	✔	✔	✔	who has priority?	who has priority?	potential to integrate

- If the impact is negative, can this be avoided, reduced or offset?
- If the impact is positive, can it be enhanced?
- If the impact depends on how the option is implemented, how can we ensure that it is implemented well?

The resulting analysis is shown in Table 3.2. The team also checks whether the different options are compatible with each other: this is shown in Table 3.3.

Tip: An important side-benefit of SEA is that it can help to identify where the strategic action is not worded clearly, which in turn could lead to future problems in implementation.

Tip: Several rounds of appraisal may be necessary, either to test broad approaches and then more specific ones (e.g. reduce parking or not, then details about location of parking sites) or to get more specific information where an initial appraisal leads to an uncertain appraisal result (e.g. computer modelling of likely traffic flows with and without pedestrianization before deciding whether the impact of pedestrianization would be positive or negative).

They further explore where the Park and Ride sites could be located by preparing constraints overlay maps for possible sites. These show, on one map, the nature conservation, historical, landscape and other constraints and opportunities that could affect the site. From this information they choose two preferred sites.

Table 3.4 *Mitigation measures for impacts identified in Tables 3.2 and 3.3*

Identified impacts	Possible mitigation measure(s)
– Costs to businesses from congestion charging – Impact on those who rely heavily on motorized vehicles	• reduce tax rates for shopkeepers temporarily • provide discount for local residents • provide electric buggies for people who are less mobile • allow cars and deliveries at certain times of day • reduce congestion and parking charges for Standstill residents • hypothecate income from congestion charging and parking for improvements to public transport[*]
+ Improvement in pedestrian environment, visual amenity	• provide spaces for outdoor cafes, benches, sculptures[*]
– Land take and wildlife implications of P+R and new cycle lanes	• ensure that P+R sites and cycle lanes are built on previously developed land where possible • add wildlife-friendly plantings and try to link with wildlife corridors
+ Decreased air pollution, improved health	• put up monitoring station with read-out to 'advertise' improvements and educate on air quality • ensure that P+R buses are low-emission vehicles or use clean fuels[*] • add cycle storage at P+R sites for Park-and-Cycle

Note: * These are outside the remit of the transport planning department and would need discussion with other departments

Based on these analyses, and in discussion with local elected representatives, the planners decide that congestion charging, a Park and Ride system for Standstill, priority for pedestrians in town centres and cycle lanes merit further consideration. They brainstorm possible mitigation measures for the impacts caused by these measures (Table 3.4).

Tip: Positive impacts can be enhanced as well as negative impacts reduced. Mitigation measures can include details of design and construction.

The team then write their final plan statements to include mitigation measures, minimize conflicts and avoid problems with implementation. The final, chosen, mitigated plan statements are:

TA1. Two Park and Ride sites will be built at sites X and Y adjacent to major routes into Standstill. Recycled aggregates and permeable paving will be used in their construction. The sites will be landscaped with indigenous plantings and include bicycle storage and links to the network of cycle lanes. The sites will be operational by June 2017.

TA2. In Standstill, Rushmore and Walkerton, priority will be given, in decreasing order, to wheelchair users, pedestrians and emergency vehicles; cyclists; and public transport; and private vehicles.

TA3. A pilot congestion charging scheme will be operational in Standstill city centre (as defined in Map S) during January–December 2013. The revenues generated from the scheme will be used to improve public transport services. Residents and businesses based in the congestion charging zone will receive an 80 per cent discount. At the end of the pilot period a public referendum will be held to determine whether the scheme should be continued.

TA4. Off-road cycle lanes will be built parallel to roads marked in red on Map T. They will be built on previously developed land where possible. Indigenous plantings will be used to separate the cycle lanes from the roads unless this conflicts with safety considerations.

Document the process

Finally, the team documents the SEA process, which results in an SEA report that looks much like this section of the book. The SEA report is made available for public comment at the same time as the new DTP. There are few public objections to most of the DTP, but a group of local residents protests strongly against one of the Park and Ride sites, citing noise and landscape concerns. The planning team visits the sites with the residents, and they jointly develop a site plan to minimize vehicle movements near residents' homes. The team includes this plan into their schedule for implementing the DTP.

Summing up, the SEA helped to revise the objective of Tooton Rush's DTP, identify options, choose preferred options, refine these options and make the plan-making process more transparent and publicly accountable. The new Tooton Rush DTP bears no resemblance to the old one. The objective has been changed, and only fragments of the original statements remain. The new DTP is more sustainable, more responsive to public concerns, and more in line with higher-level policy. Of course, not all of this is attributable to the SEA: in fact, it is difficult to work out which changes are due to the SEA and which resulted from the plan-making process. Wanda Duright has inextricably integrated the two by starting the SEA early and fully involving her team .

SEA and decision-making

The Tooton Rush example is an idealized one because Wanda Duright (I hope that you have figured out by now that she 'wants to do right') and her team are very open to the idea of integrating SEA and the plan-making process, and follow a form of idealized, rational plan-making process that is rarely found in real life.

One of the main developments in SEA over the last 5–10 years, supported by increasing SEA practice, has been a more subtle understanding of how SEA and plan-making interrelate. This has shown that, if the objective of SEA is to reduce the environmental impacts of plans, then the rationalist concept of SEA as a clearly structured process that provides specified, 'impartial' environmental information to be considered at specified plan-making 'decision windows' and that miraculously leads to an environmentally sensitive plan, is far too simplistic.

All of us, including planners, make decisions based on our previous knowledge and beliefs. We tend to give disproportionate weight to the first information that we receive (much of it very early in our lives), and this acts as an 'anchor' to subsequent thoughts and judgements. We are inclined to be biased towards what is familiar, what has previously been successful and what supports an existing point of view, and tend to discount unfamiliar information. Consciously or unconsciously, we don't like to admit past mistakes, so we often validate past choices (Scott Wilson, 2008a; Stoeglehner et al, 2009).

As such, we mostly operate through 'single loop learning', where our existing approach (our 'action strategy') may be modified, but is unlikely to be radically altered, by its consequences (Figure 3.1). This perpetuates the status quo. Only rarely do we step back and reappraise our action strategy altogether, perhaps when we start a new job, visit a new country or are challenged with radical new information: when our underlying values change and we experience 'double loop learning'. In such cases, we may experience a more fundamental readjustment of our knowledge and beliefs, and our action strategy may change significantly (Argyris and Schön, 1978; Jha-Thakur et al, 2009; Fischer, 2010).

These concepts also apply to the plan-making process, which involves multiple decisions by multiple planners (and often also politicians), and where the inputs are not only the SEA information and public comments on the SEA, but a wide range of additional 'evidence': economic data, national government policies, the latest newspaper headlines and so on. Cherp et al (2007) refer to Mintzberg's (1987) five strategy-making theories, only the first of which follows the rational model of strategy making:

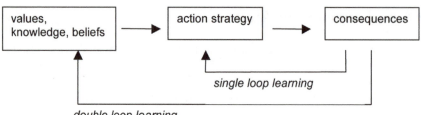

Source: Adapted from Argyris and Schön (1978)

Figure 3.1 *Single- and double-loop learning*

- *Strategy is a Plan – a consciously intended course of action, a set of rules to deal with the situation.*
- *Strategy is a Ploy – a scheme intended to outmaneuver opponents and strengthen useful alliances.*
- *Strategy is a Pattern – in a stream of actions, consistency in behaviour (whether or not intended); here strategies result from actions, not designs.*
- *Strategy is a Position – locating an organisation in its [context…], literally a position on a battlefield.*
- *Strategy is a Perspective – an ingrained way of perceiving the world; 'strategy in this respect is to the organization what personality is to the individual'.* (Cherp et al, 2007)

The development of strategic actions is often an informal and emergent process. Strategic actions evolve over time from vague glimmer to final strategy through brainstorming, discussions and 'negotiations' (aka arm-twisting, horse-trading). They typically proceed in fits and starts, with the timetable for the development of the strategic action often differing wildly from that initially anticipated by decision-makers. Strategic actions may be rushed along if a politician wants to respond to public outcry, held up during elections or made way for an even more urgent policy initiative, or dropped altogether after a change of administration. 'Decision windows' (ANSEA Team, 2002) may be in the form of formal meetings informed by scientific reports, but they may just as easily come through discussion in the ladies room or café.

Decision-makers often start with a fixed idea of their preferred alternative and then write the strategic action's objective around this. Other alternatives may only be considered where there is public outcry, or a legal challenge, or someone makes a truly compelling case for them. In many countries, privatization and decentralization has led to a situation where strategic actions are implemented through private companies more than in the past, so the private sector may be more actively involved in developing the strategic actions (Nilsson et al, 2009).

Strategic actions may also change significantly between initial glimmer and final adopted report. For instance, the UK government's initial idea for new 'eco towns' to help deal with a severe housing shortage in an environmentally friendly manner has evolved significantly over two years, from an initial prospectus of general concepts (CLG, 2007a) to a recent draft planning policy statement (CLG, 2009a). Changes over that time have included reduced emphasis on free-standing development, some dilution of environmental requirements, and a highly contentious site selection process from over 50 bids to four final confirmed locations.

None of these characteristics of strategic actions – informal and fluid development, high level of political and private sector influence, uncertain timing – are particularly compatible with the formal process of SEA. Most commentators (e.g. Owens et al, 2004; Cherp et al, 2007; Nilsson et al, 2009) argue that SEA must adapt to the realities of strategic decision-making: that it should be treated less as a technocratic and rationalist process, and more as a political, collaborative approach aimed at consensus-building.

Unless environmental concerns are already part of an established single loop learning process (for instance, if the whole organization or the boss is already very environmentally aware), or unless the environment miraculously becomes a governing variable (for instance, as a result of a change in political administration, a successful legal challenge or public outcry over an environmental problem), even an impartial and robust SEA will be seen as an external, 'advocacy' tool that represents special interests.

In such a situation, change is slow 'because values and norms differ between actors and the institutions encourage consensuses seeking and gradual, controlled, firmly anchored change' (Nykvist and Nilsson, 2009). SEA may lead to the tweaking of individual statements within a plan, to the addition of mitigation measures, but not to a fundamentally new approach to the plan (Nykvist and Nilsson, 2009; Stoeglehner et al, 2009). This is exemplified by a UK SEA consultant's comments:

> *We've been quite successful in openly telling the planners what we think the implications of the [plan] are. They haven't tried to suppress our messages... We get invited to all the meetings, and [planners] ... talk candidly and I make my comments and they nod their heads... But they'll be tweaking the [plan] around the edges rather than using, for example, climate change as one of the key drivers. The [plan-making] process is driven by government household projections... Degree of influence of the [SEA]: 2 out of 10.* (Therivel et al, 2009)

This also helps to account for the fact that there is no consistent correlation between the quality of SEA information and its effectiveness in influencing plan-making (Retief et al. 2008).

Bina (2007) suggests that 'SEA's greatest potential [is] more in persuading planners – early on – to design more environmentally sustainable initiatives ... and less in confronting proponents with information on negative consequences.' Partidário (2007) notes that, in SEA, 'it is not the data per se that matters, but what you need the data for ... what may be important is to use SEA to help thinking in formulating the right questions'.

On the other hand, Cowell and Owens (2006) argue that SEA exercises may present 'crucial institutional spaces for challenges to the status quo', potentially leading to more sustainable and environmentally conscious patterns of development. This may be particularly the case where there is significant public input in the plan-making and SEA processes. Others suggest that SEA can provide needed rigour and accountability where strategic actions are developed within a highly politicized context (Fischer and Gazzola, 2006). Certainly a one-size-fits-all approach to SEA is inappropriate, and SEA needs to be able to operate under non-ideal as well as ideal conditions.

Even in a single loop context where a given SEA may have only limited direct influence in terms of making the plan in question 'greener', the overall SEA process may still indirectly affect planners' values in a subtle, drip-feed manner, lead to gradual changes in institutional structures and departmental traditions, and improve environmental awareness among stakeholders (Thissen, 2000; Cashmore et al, 2004; Fischer et al, 2009). Figure 3.2 shows the results of a 2006 questionnaire of UK local authority planners, which asked about the indirect effects of SEA: clearly, SEA's benefits go beyond changing individual strategic actions.

Indeed, indirect benefits dominate a recent summary of the strengths of applying the European SEA Directive:

Many Member States report that applying the SEA procedure to individual planning processes has provided a clearer structure and regulatory framework for the plan drafting process, the consultation process with other authorities [and] the public... Furthermore, some Member States have emphasized the fact that planning processes have become more transparent, and even some Member States report that the early consideration of environmental needs have led to a decrease of expensive mitigation measures, because the environment was considered early in the process. (European Commission, 2009b)

In turn, this change in values can be reflected in a gradual increase in the direct effectiveness of SEA. For instance, consecutive surveys of UK local authority planners showed that, over time, SEAs had led to an increasing number of changes to plans: in 1995, 50 per cent of plans subject to 'sustainability appraisal' (SA) had been changed as a result of the appraisal, rising to 78 per cent in 2008 (Therivel, 1995; Therivel

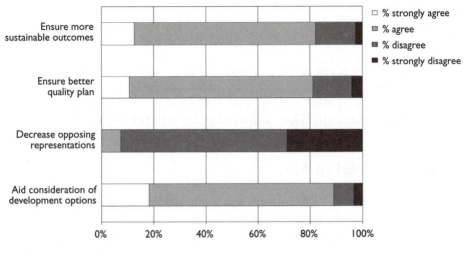

Source: Based on CLG (2007b)

Figure 3.2 *Indirect effects of SEA:*
'Producing sustainability appraisals will...'

and Minas, 2002; Therivel and Walsh, 2006; Sherston, 2008). Similarly, a survey of SEA practitioners showed that 35 per cent of respondents from the UK (where SEA has been carried out for nearly 20 years) thought that lack of real influence of SEA on plan-making was a major problem, compared to 75 per cent of respondents from China (where SEA practice is more recent): 'This again appears to be an indication that the performance of SEA systems may be improving over time' (Fischer and He, 2007).

Ensuring that SEA is effective

All of these points suggest that the concept of 'effective SEA' is multi-faceted. As an *input* to decisions about strategic actions, effective SEA must:

* provide decision-makers with robust, clearly presented information about the environmental impacts of their plan at the right times;
* help to change the values, attitudes and perceptions of stakeholders, including decision-makers;
* increase participation, collaboration, inclusiveness and consensus in the plan-making process, thus helping to provide support and legitimacy; and
* help to change established institutional processes.

This, in turn, should help to reach the direct *outcome* of greener plans, as well as the indirect outcomes discussed above (Cashmore et al, 2004; Fischer, 2009; Jha-Thakur et al, 2009; van Buuren and Nooteboom, 2009).

It is difficult to encompass points 2–4 in an SEA effectiveness review checklist. Box 3.3 presents a checklist which attempts to cover the SEA process as well as its outputs (various reports) and outcomes, but I suspect that better checklists will be developed over the next five years.

What is crucial in SEA?

What is essential to SEA and what is icing, and at what point is SEA so minimal that it is no longer really SEA? There is no one answer to this. In part, legal requirements will determine what has to be done. I would argue that any SEA must be good enough to fulfil the aim of SEA, namely to protect the environment and promote sustainability. This means, at minimum, that one needs to understand the environment well enough to be able to determine whether a strategic action could harm it; assess the impacts of a strategic action enough to identify whether it *would* harm the environment; and mitigate any negative environmental impacts. Colleagues have argued that documentation of the SEA process and consultation of the public are also essential to SEA.

Table 3.5 gives an indicative hierarchy of SEA approaches, including the value added of each approach and who could carry it out.

Conclusions

The SEA process works best when it is fully integrated in the decision-making process. It can act as an educational tool and help to ensure that the plan is as robust and environment-friendly as possible and make its implementation faster and smoother. SEA does not have to be a horrible, daunting process: some aspects are more crucial than others and must be done, while others are refinements on the basic approach. The checklist of Box 3.3 can help to ensure that the SEA is of a good quality. Chapter 4 now discusses three countries' SEA systems.

Box 3.3 SEA effectiveness review checklist

SEA context

The SEA is:

- context specific (integrated with the plan-making process; 'owned' by decision-makers; responsive to cultural context and institutional structures; takes into account learning styles);
- sustainability led (addresses the interrelationship of biophysical, social and economic aspects; explicitly promotes sustainability);
- tiered, efficient and proportional (deals with key issues relevant to the scale and remit of the strategic action; is tiered and linked with lower-tier initiatives and project EIA; is cost- and time-effective; its level of detail is proportional to the level of detail of the strategic action);
- participative (informs and involves all key environmental authorities, the public and other stakeholders in a meaningful way throughout the decision-making process; explicitly responds to stakeholders' inputs and concerns; stakeholders are satisfied with the process);
- proactive (provides assessment results early enough to influence decision-making; helps to ensure that its results are considered in future decision-making);
- professional (carried out with professionalism, rigour, impartiality and balance; review mechanisms are in place; the public has the opportunity to appeal against the process and decision output);
- iterative (there is opportunity for learning and system improvement through regular system review).

SEA process

The SEA process includes:

More detailed checklists are provided at the end of the chapter...

- strategic action description (a clear description of the strategic action objectives and structure is provided; it explains what the plan can and cannot do);   6
- context analysis (the SEA describes the policy context and how this relates to the strategic action; biophysical and possibly social and economic aspects of the area at an appropriate scale and level of detail; existing standards, thresholds and/or environmental limits; likely evolution of these aspects without the strategic action; and environmental opportunities and constraints using a justified methodology);   6

- scoping (more or less detailed assessment is carried out depending on the context and issues; the SEA addresses key issues; environmental authorities, the public and stakeholders are involved in the scoping process); 6
- alternatives (reasonable alternatives are identified, their impacts are assessed, and preferred alternative(s) are chosen and justified); 7
- impact prediction and evaluation (all significant impacts of the strategic action are identified and assessed; assumptions and uncertainties are clearly stated; impact significance is evaluated in relation to a clear and reasonable basis; indirect and cumulative effects are considered; assessment and evaluation techniques are appropriate in terms of context, resources and available data); 8, 9
- mitigation (measures to avoid, mitigate and compensate for impacts (in that sequence) are proposed for all significant adverse effects of the strategic action; the measures are likely to be implemented and effective; any trade-offs have been justified and are reasonable); 9
- monitoring and follow-up (a monitoring framework is proposed that covers all significant impacts; procedures are in place for follow-up and corrective action); and 10
- communication of results (the SEA report presents the results of the SEA process in a clear manner; explains how the strategic action was changed as a result of the SEA; includes a non-technical summary). 10

SEA outcomes

The SEA achieves:

- improved strategic action (the SEA has resulted in amendments / modification to strategic action; identification of preferred alternative(s); an authoritative planning decision);
- effective implementation of the strategic action (the strategic action is implemented as intended; SEA and EIA inform subsequent lower-tier decision-making; monitoring and follow-up is carried out as intended);
- environmental protection and sustainability (environmental and sustainability changes are observed post-SEA that could be attributed to the influence of the SEA); and
- improvements to future plan-making (the SEA accurately identified key environmental issues or, if not, lessons to be learned; planners feel that they have a better understanding of environmental and sustainability issues).

Source: Based on IAIA (2002), ODPM et al (2005), Retief (2007), Environmental Protection Agency (2008a) and Noble (2009)

Table 3.5 *Possible hierarchy of importance of SEA approaches*

SEA approach	Is it needed?	Value added of approach
Develop a vision for a sustainable future: 'visioning'	✔	Helps decision-makers to look at the long term and sustainability, not just short term and fire-fighting
Establish an appraisal framework of environmental/ sustainability indicators, standards and/or thresholds	+✔	Focuses on key environmental/sustainability issues; streamlines the subsequent baseline description and monitoring stages
Describe the environmental baseline	*✔	Provides a base for impact prediction and monitoring; helps to identify environmental problems
Identify problem areas	+*✔	Focuses SEA on key issues
Analyse links with other strategic actions	*✔	Makes transparent how the strategic action is affected by outside factors; suggests ideas for how any inappropriate constraints can be overcome
'Scope' the SEA: agree on assessment methods, environmental criteria, alternatives to consider, level of detail, etc. of the SEA	*✔	Ensures that the SEA covers key issues, helps to streamline the SEA, helps to avoid subsequent critique of the SEA
Identify statements that most/don't need assessment	✔	Focuses the SEA on key aspects of the strategic action
Identify (more) sustainable alternatives and compare alternatives	+*✔	Helps to ensure that the strategic action is as good as possible, including as sustainable as possible
Assess the impacts of the strategic action objectives, alternatives, statements	+*✔	The core of SEA
Avoid or mitigate any significant adverse impacts	+*✔	Also the core
Involve the public and environmental experts in the SEA	+*✔	Ensures comprehensive understanding of the environmental/sustainability baseline, identification of problems, identification of alternatives, and consideration of mitigation measures

Table 3.5 *continued*

SEA approach	Is it needed?	Value added of approach
Ensure that the strategic action objectives and statements are compatible with each other	✔	Ensures that the strategic action is internally coherent and that different elements of the strategic action do not pull against each other
Document the SEA findings	+*✔	
Document the decision making process	*✔	Helps to ensure transparency, and that SEA findings are fully taken into account
Monitor the impacts of the strategic action	*✔	Checks whether the strategic action's actual impacts are the same as those predicted in the SEA; allows future SEAs to be based on more robust data
Take action if strategic action has unintended significant adverse impacts	✔	Deals with a strategic action's unintended consequences

Note: Organized roughly chronologically in terms of when they would be used in the SEA process

Key:
+ fundamental: don't miss this
* legally required for European member states
✔ best practice

Chapter 4

Three SEA Systems:
United States, Europe, China

By late 2009, several dozen countries worldwide had established legal requirements for SEA, and others had developed SEA guidelines. This chapter discusses three quite different SEA systems, to demonstrate the range of institutional structures and legal systems within which SEA can be applied, and SEA approaches used.

The US National Environmental Policy Act of 1969 was the first SEA system, and has by now been in action for 40 years. It continues to evolve, for instance, to allow some projects and plans to be fast tracked. The European SEA Directive of 2001 applies to 27 member states, which are at various stages of implementing it. Agreeing a common approach for so many countries – some with previous SEA systems – was a major undertaking, and the Directive is triggering thousands of SEAs each year. The SEA component of China's Environmental Impact Assessment Law of 2003 has recently been superseded by new Plan Environmental Impact Assessment Regulations, and SEA practice in China can be expected to evolve rapidly in coming years.

More information on the SEA systems of these and other countries is available from, for example, Dalal-Clayton and Sadler (2005), Schmidt et al (2005) and Fischer (2007). Early SEA systems and their evolution were discussed in Sadler and Verheem (1996) and Therivel and Partidário (1996). Readers with no interest in individual SEA systems may wish to go directly to Chapter 5.

The US National Environmental Policy Act of 1969

In the US, the National Environmental Policy Act (NEPA) of 1969 established the world's first SEA legislation as part of a set of wider environmental assessment requirements. NEPA sets out a national environmental policy and, as a means of achieving this policy, requires

---

Box 4.1 NEPA's requirements for environmental assessment (42 USC 4332)

'(2) All agencies of the Federal Government shall— ...

(C) include in every recommendation or report on proposals for legislation and other major Federal actions significantly affecting the quality of the human environment, a detailed statement by the responsible official on—

i) the environmental impact of the proposed action,

ii) any adverse environmental effects which cannot be avoided should the proposal be implemented,

iii) alternatives to the proposed action,

iv) the relationship between local short-term uses of man's environment and the maintenance and enhancement of long-term productivity, and

v) any irreversible and irretrievable commitments of resources which would be involved in the proposed action should it be implemented.

Prior to making any detailed statement, the responsible Federal official shall consult with and obtain the comments of any Federal agency which has jurisdiction by law or special expertise with respect to any environmental impact involved. Copies of such statement and the comments and views of the appropriate Federal, State, and local agencies, which are authorized to develop and enforce environmental standards, shall be made available to the President, the Council on Environmental Quality and to the public as provided by section 552 of title 5, and shall accompany the proposal through the existing agency review processes.'

---

that federal agencies assess the environmental impacts of their actions. It also created the Council on Environmental Quality (CEQ), which is responsible for ensuring compliance with NEPA.

Box 4.1 shows NEPA's requirements for environmental assessment in full. They ask federal government agencies to describe and assess the environmental impacts of their actions and alternatives, consult with other relevant government agencies, and make publicly available a report that documents this process. The CEQ has issued regulations that provide greater detail about how federal agencies must implement NEPA (40 CFR 1500–1517). However, as will become clear, much of NEPA's strength also came from early court rulings.

Actions that require SEA and the assessment process

NEPA does not list the types of strategic actions that require environmental assessment (the 'detailed statement'); rather it requires assessment of all 'proposals for legislation and other major Federal actions significantly affecting the quality of the human environment'. The CEQ regulations interpret the term 'federal action' as meaning 'new and continuing activities, including projects and programs

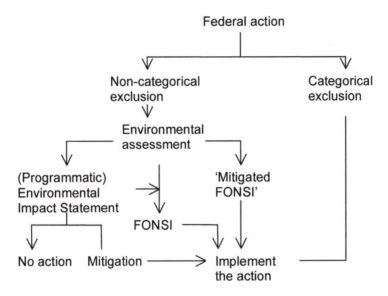

Figure 4.1 *NEPA decision-making process*

entirely or partly financed, assisted, conducted, regulated, or approved by federal agencies; new or revised agency rules, regulations, plans, policies, or procedures; and legislative proposals' (40 CFR 1508.18), and hence assessment is required for strategic actions as well as projects. Under NEPA, agencies must evaluate actions 'significantly affecting the quality of the human environment'. This is a very broad phrase that includes direct and reasonably foreseeable indirect effects to land, water, air, ecosystems and other natural and physical resources (40 CFR 1508.8, 1508.14 and 1508.27), as well as cumulative impacts to the above resources (40 CFR 1508.7). NEPA does not cover non-federal initiatives. However, if non-federal activities require federal approval or obtain federal funding, then NEPA would be triggered.

Unlike in some other countries, NEPA does not distinguish between EIA and SEA. However, the CEQ regulations do identify certain broad federal actions (e.g. plans, programmes and policies) that may be evaluated at a programmatic level (40 CFR 1502.4(c)). Thus, in practice, 'programmatic environmental impact statement' (PEIS) is the generally used term for SEA in the US.

The NEPA environmental assessment process requires federal agencies to carry out up to three stages of progressively more detailed and time-consuming assessment, until they can show that the next stage is not needed: 1. initial analysis including a test of categorical exclusion; 2. environmental assessment; and 3. environmental impact statement (EIS) for a project or PEIS for a strategic action. Figure 4.1 illustrates this process.

For the initial analysis, if a major action is already covered in a previous NEPA document, then the agency must update that document if necessary, and review the action to determine whether it includes any substantial changes that require further analysis, or whether new information has become available, before the action is implemented. The agency also determines if a categorical exclusion – a previous determination that the action will not result in significant impacts – applies.

If the major action is not covered in a previous NEPA document and no categorical exclusion applies, then the agency must determine whether it could have significant environmental impacts. If the agency is certain that the action will have such impacts, then it must prepare a full EIS or PEIS. Where it is uncertain, it prepares a shorter environmental assessment (EA), which 'serves to briefly provide sufficient evidence and analysis for determining whether to prepare an EIS or a finding of no significant impact' (40 CFR 4332(2)(C)). If the EA determines that the action could have a significant impact, then a full EIS or PEIS is required; otherwise it can conclude with a finding of no significant impact (FONSI) or a 'mitigated FONSI'.

An EIS or PEIS is a more in-depth version of an EA. If the lead agency concludes that an action will have significant impacts, then the agency may propose mitigation for these impacts or decide not to proceed with the action. Instead, if a FONSI is made, then the action can proceed without mitigation. The reliance on mitigation to avoid preparation of an EIS is sometime known as a 'mitigated FONSI'. In these situations, the agency must demonstrate that it has taken a 'hard look' at the problem, show that the mitigation measures will reduce the impacts to less-than-significant levels, and confirm that the mitigation measures will actually be implemented and effective.

This already-complex process is often interspersed with legal challenges. These have included challenges to agencies' decisions that a categorical exclusion applies, to not prepare a PEIS, and to conclude with a determination of FONSI or mitigated FONSI, as well as to the adequacy of PEISs and to agencies' decisions of whether to allow an action to go ahead in light of the findings of the EIS (Orloff and Brooks, 1980). El-Jourbagy and Harty (2005) give examples of some of these types of legal challenges. That said, the legacy of legal challenges has made agencies more responsive to public concerns and the process more transparent in the long run (Bass et al, 2001).

Contents of an environmental assessment or programmatic EIS

EAs and EISs/PEISs follow a standard format unless there are good reasons to do otherwise:

(a) Cover sheet, summary, table of contents
(b) Purpose of and need for action
(c) Alternatives, including proposed action
(d) Affected environment
(e) Environmental consequences
(f) List of preparers, list of consultees
(g) Index, appendices (40 CFR 1502.10).

The CEQ NEPA regulations encourage 'tiering' of assessments, to avoid repetitive discussions of the same issues and help ensure that relevant issues are considered at each decision-making stage. Where a PEIS has been prepared for a higher-level policy or plan, lower-level assessments only need to summarize the issues discussed in the PEIS, and then concentrate on the issues specific to the subsequent action (40 CFR 1508.28). A report by the NEPA Task Force (2003), which recommended ways of modernizing NEPA implementation, suggested, with respect to tiering, that:

- first-tier PEISs should include a section that explains the relationship between the PEIS and future tiers of analyses, and describes how stakeholders will be involved;
- PEISs should explain where and when any issues not addressed in the PEIS (deferred issues) will be addressed, and describe the proposed temporal and spatial scales that will be used when analyzing those issues; and
- criteria should be developed to evaluate whether a programmatic document has become outdated.

Little specific guidance is provided on two other issues that particularly affect PEISs: cumulative impacts and strategic level alternatives. The CEQ's (1997) handbook *Considering Cumulative Effects Under the National Environmental Policy Act* describes principles and procedures for assessing cumulative impacts, but is heavily oriented to project EISs. Although a NEPA Task Force (2003) report identified the consideration of alternatives in EISs as requiring modernization, it made no specific recommendations generally, and did not consider alternatives in PEISs specifically.

Good and bad aspects of NEPA

NEPA has gone through distinct phases during its 40-year history. The first 10–15 years were a time of foment: agencies were experimenting with different ways of meeting (and not meeting) NEPA's requirements, guidance was being developed and, as a result of many legal challenges, the courts began to shape the interpretation of NEPA. The next 15–20 years saw a bedding-in of the requirements, where they became a routine – perhaps to an excessive degree – part of agency activity. During this period, many agencies began preparing very long and complex documents to try to ward off legal challenges. For the past ten years, EA practice in the US has been progressively sidelined, with a weakening of the powers and resources of the CEQ, a generally greater emphasis on promoting development rather than on managing its impacts, and an emphasis on streamlining the NEPA process. Initial indications are that the new administration will reverse some of this, although it is also clearly keen to continue to streamline NEPA processes. For instance, the recently adopted American Recovery and Reinvestment Act of 2009 encourages federal agencies to 'ensure the expeditious completion of National Environmental Policy Act reviews under applicable law' (Bass et al, 2009).

NEPA has both very good and very bad aspects. It remains remarkably relevant and unchanged after 40 years, attesting to its forward-looking nature – much like the US Constitution. It showed remarkable foresight in applying to strategic actions as well as projects. Its requirements to consider 'the relationship between local short-term uses of man's environment and the maintenance and enhancement of long-term productivity, and any irreversible and irretrievable commitments of resources' (USC 4332) remain as appropriate and challenging today as they did when NEPA was first written. Its requirements have proven to be flexible enough to accommodate changes, for instance, the requirement for land use PEISs to consider whether the plan would result in disproportionate impacts to low-income or minority populations (White House, 1994). As the world's first EA system, NEPA has also kick-started dozens of similar systems worldwide.

The use of PEISs in particular seems to be increasing, with federal agencies generally finding them helpful (NEPA Task Force, 2003). For instance, the American Recovery and Reinvestment Act of 2009 provides a large fiscal stimulus for renewable energy, water quality and public transit projects, but does not exempt these projects from NEPA requirements. The Bureau of Land Management is currently (late 2009) preparing PEISs for wind and geothermal energy production, which have the potential to streamline the environmental review for some wind and geothermal projects (Latham and Watkins, 2009).

On the other hand, NEPA applies only to actions by federal agencies, which manage about one-third of the geographical area of the US; and only 18 states have adopted parallel 'little NEPA' legislation (Bass, 2005). Most strategic actions in the US are thus not covered by its requirements. NEPA's implementation has always been accompanied by legal challenges, increasing costs and delays to all parties. NEPA documents and processes tend to be very long, technical and complex, with claims of 'analysis paralysis'. In part to avoid legal challenges, PEISs tend to use project-level assessment techniques, and so end up being very detailed and possibly not focused on strategic-level issues and problems. Some commentators are concerned that mitigated FONSIs are increasingly being used to bypass the rigorous EIS/PEIS requirements, while others feel that they are simply reflections of good planning. Improved monitoring and adaptive management is needed, to reflect situations where environmental conditions change in unanticipated ways, inaccurate predictions are made, or subsequent information might affect the originally agreed methods for environmental protection (NEPA Task Force, 2003; Dalal-Clayton and Sadler, 2005; Glasson et al, 2005).

We now move to an SEA system that was inspired by NEPA but that has evolved into a very different beast.

The European SEA Directive of 2004

Discussions about a Europe-wide SEA Directive started at the same time as discussions about an EIA Directive, in about 1975. It was initially intended that one Directive would cover both projects and strategic actions, but by the time that the EIA Directive was approved in 1985 (CEC, 1985), its application was restricted to projects only (Wood, 1988).

In the absence of a Europe-wide SEA requirement, several European member states had already established SEA systems, starting in the late 1980s. For instance, the Netherlands required SEA for certain plans and programmes, and an abbreviated 'e-test' for Cabinet decisions. Denmark required SEA of government proposals under an administrative order. In the UK, an abbreviated form of SEA, 'environmental appraisal', was being carried out for local and regional development plans.

This country-by-country approach meant that SEA systems could be responsive to the specific context of each country. However, it did not encourage the 'level playing field' – establishment of reasonably similar economic conditions throughout Europe – that is a hallmark of European economic policy, nor did it provide the robust environmental protection advocated under successive European Commission Action Programmes on the Environment. The SEA Directive aimed to rectify both of these limitations. The evolution of the SEA Directive from an initial proposal of 1990 to its final adopted form of 2001 is discussed in more detail by Feldmann et al (2001) and Kläne and Albrecht (2005).

The Directive does not have direct effect in the different European member states. Instead, member states were expected to make the Directive operational through implementing its regulations by July 2004. The European Commission (2003) published guidance on how to interpret the Directive's requirements in September 2003. In the end, only nine of the then 25 (now 27) member states had implemented the Directive fully by July 2004 (D. Aspinwall, pers. comm.). Although, by late 2008, most member states had transposed the Directive into law, the European Commission still had 23 active infringement cases related to transposition and non-conformity with the Directive (European Commission, 2009b).

The SEA process

Appendix A provides a full copy of the SEA Directive (CEC, 2001). The Directive's title – 'on the assessment of the effects of certain plans and programmes on the environment' – already gives a clue about many aspects of its requirements:

- It requires not an appraisal but an 'assessment': it is meant to be evidence-based and rigorous.
- It applies to 'certain' plans and programmes, and so does not apply to certain others. It has exclusions.
- It does not apply to policies.
- It considers effects on the 'environment', not sustainability (though its objective refers to sustainable development and its definition of environment is quite wide).

Article 1 of the Directive states its objectives:

> *to provide for a high level of protection of the environment and to contribute to the integration of environmental considerations into the preparation and adoption of plans and programmes with a view to promoting sustainable development, by ensuring that … an environmental assessment is carried out of certain plans and programmes which are likely to have significant effects on the environment.*

The rest of the Directive is quite concise and well-structured, with four main clusters of requirements:

- Articles 2–4 and Annex II, which explain what strategic actions the Directive applies to, when SEA should be carried out, and some basic definitions;
- Articles 5–7 and Annex I, which explain the key SEA inputs to the decision-making process: the environmental report, consultation with the public and 'authorities', and consultation with other member states where appropriate;
- Articles 8 and 9 which require the information arising from Articles 5–7 to be taken into account in decision-making and explain how this needs to be documented; and

- Articles 10–15, which deal with miscellaneous other requirements, including monitoring.

The first three of these are now considered one by one.

Plans and programmes that require SEA

Articles 2 and 3 of the Directive establish a complicated set of tests for determining whether a given strategic action requires SEA or not. Strategic actions that require SEA are plans and programmes that:

1   are subject to preparation and/or adoption by an authority (Art. 2(a)); *and*
2   are required by legislative, regulatory or administrative provisions (Art. 2(a)); *and*
3   are likely to have significant environmental effects (Art. 3.1) as determined by using the criteria set out in Annex II of the Directive; *and*
4a are prepared for agriculture, forestry, fisheries, energy, industry, transport, waste management, water management, telecommunications, tourism, town and country planning or land use *and* set the framework for development consent of projects listed in the EIA Directive (Art. 3.2(a)); *or*
4b in view of the likely effect on sites, require an appropriate assessment under the Habitats Directive (Art 3.2(b)); *or*
4c are other plans and programmes determined by member states to set the framework for future development consent of projects (Art. 3.4).

This is summarized in Figure 4.2.

Member states can also require SEA for other plans and programmes that set the framework for development consent of projects *and* are likely to have significant environmental effects (Art. 3.4). For instance, Scotland requires SEA for all plans and programmes that are likely to have significant environmental effects, except for those listed at 5–7 below. Belgium, Finland, France and Hungary require SEA for all land-use plans, regardless of whether they fulfil the additional requirements of the Directive (European Commission, 2009b).

Strategic actions that do not require SEA under the Directive are plans and programmes that:

5   determine the use of small areas at local level or are minor modifications to plans and programmes that would otherwise require SEA *and* that are unlikely to have significant environmental effects (Art. 3.3); *or*

6   are financial or budget plans or programmes (Art. 3.8); *or*
7   have the sole purpose is serve national defence or civil emergency (Art. 3.8).

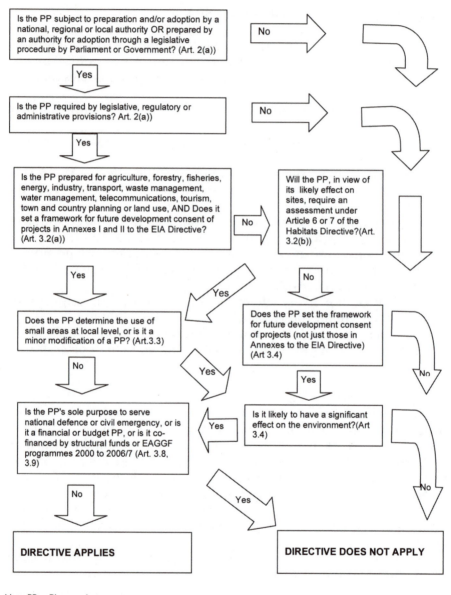

Figure 4.2 *Screening under the SEA Directive*

Some examples of these rules in action might be helpful. Land-use management plans prepared by voluntary bodies (for instance, for land held by an environmental charity) would not require SEA because such an organization is not an 'authority' (1 above). Many plans and programmes prepared by private companies will not require SEA because the companies are not 'authorities', although plans and programmes prepared by some privatized companies that perform public services as part of their statutory duties (e.g. water or electricity provision) may require SEA. A local authority's voluntary tourism strategy would not need SEA because the strategy is not 'required' (2 above), whereas its mandatory land-use plan would require SEA. Many national-level plans and programmes are also likely to be exempt from SEA because they are not 'required'. Appropriate assessment (see Appendix D) triggers SEA, but the opposite does not necessarily hold true (4b above). Plans that are very strategic – for instance, a regional strategy on how to deal with genetically modified organisms – do not require SEA because they do not set the framework for development consent of projects (4a). Neither do plans for war (7), despite the devastating environmental impact that armed conflict can have. However, plans for the management of military training grounds may need SEA where such land is used for recreational as well as military purposes.

The Directive does not apply to policies, which set the framework for plans and programmes: as such, SEAs are required for strategic actions whose predecessors do not require SEA, with all the possible inconsistencies and conflicts this raises. There are no signs of this changing soon.

Contents of the environmental report and consultation

Box 4.2 summarizes, for a given plan or programme, what the SEA Directive requires. It asks for three major SEA inputs to be taken into account in decision-making: the environmental report, the consultation responses of the public and 'authorities', and the consultation responses of other member states where appropriate.

Several aspects of the requirements concerning the *environmental report* are noteworthy. First, a) to e) provide a clear context for the development of the plan or programme by requiring an analysis of the policy context, a description of the baseline environment with a greater focus on areas likely to suffer significant impacts, and an identification of environmental problems. Arguably b) to e) can be done relatively independently of the plan or programme, and the results can be used for several plans in one area. Second, there is a clear emphasis on alternatives: they are mentioned several times, and the Directive does not distinguish between the level of analysis needed for the plan or

Box 4.2 Summary of SEA Directive requirements for a given plan or programme

Preparation of an environmental report in which the likely significant effects on the environment of implementing the plan or programme (the term 'plan' is used hereafter to denote both), and reasonable alternatives are identified, described and evaluated. The information to be given is (Art. 5 and Annex I):

a) the contents and main objectives of the plan, and its relationship with other relevant plans and programmes;
b) the relevant aspects of the current state of the environment and the likely evolution thereof without implementation of the plan;
c) the environmental characteristics of areas likely to be significantly affected;
d) any existing environmental problems that are relevant to the plan;
e) environmental protection objectives that are relevant to the plan, and the way those objectives and any environmental considerations have been taken into account during its preparation;
f) the likely significant effects of the plan on the environment;
g) proposed ways of mitigating any significant adverse environmental effects;
h) the reasons for selecting the alternatives dealt with, and a description of how the assessment was undertaken;
i) proposed monitoring measures; and
j) a non-technical summary of the above.

The report must include the information that may reasonably be required, taking into account current knowledge and methods of assessment, the contents and level of detail in the plan, its stage in the decision-making process and the extent to which certain matters are more appropriately assessed at different levels in that process in order to avoid duplication of the assessment (Art. 5.2).

The environmental reports should be of a sufficient standard to meet the requirements of the SEA Directive (Art. 12.2).

Consultation

• of environmental authorities when deciding on the scope and level of detail of the information that must be included in the environmental report (Art. 5.4);
• of environmental authorities and the public, who must be given an early and effective opportunity within appropriate timeframes to express their opinion on the draft plan and the accompanying environmental report before the plan's adoption (Art. 6.1, 6.2); and
• of other EU member states where the plan's implementation is considered likely to have significant effects on the environment of those states (Art. 7).

The environmental report and the results of the consultations must be taken into account in decision-making (Art. 8).

Provision of information on the decision

When the plan is adopted, the public, the environmental authorities and any EU member state consulted under Art. 7 must be informed and the following items made available to them:

- the plan as adopted;
- a statement summarizing how environmental considerations have been integrated into the plan and how the environmental report of Art. 5, the opinions expressed pursuant to Art. 6 and the results of consultations entered into pursuant to Art. 7 have been taken into account in accordance with Art. 8, and the reasons for choosing the plan as adopted, in the light of the other reasonable alternatives dealt with; and
- the measures decided concerning monitoring (Art. 9).

Monitoring of the significant environmental effects of the plan's implementation (Art. 10).

---

programme and its alternatives (European Commission, 2003). This is a clear improvement on the EIA Directive, which requires only 'an outline of the main alternatives studied by the developer' (CEC, 1985), and no identification and evaluation of the alternatives' environmental impacts. Third, the SEA Directive includes a requirement for monitoring of effects, which is also absent in the EIA Directive.

The Directive's requirements raise questions about the link between the environment and sustainable development. Just how does protecting the environment promote sustainable development, as implied in Article 1? Why does the Directive's definition of the 'environment' include population, human health and material assets? Some countries, notably England and Wales, have broadened SEA out to cover the full range of sustainability issues. This is discussed further in Chapter 5.

Clearly, the Directive's requirements have the potential to be extremely onerous and to lead to encyclopaedic environmental reports. Article 5.2 sets bounds on the level of detail needed:

> *The environmental report ... shall include the information that may reasonably be required taking into account current knowledge and methods of assessment, the contents and level of detail in the plan or programme, its stage in the decision-making process and the extent to which certain matters are more appropriately assessed at different levels in that process in order to avoid duplication of the assessment.*

This and Article 4.3 suggest that, where data have been provided and analyses carried out in other SEAs, they do not need to be repeated in the SEA in question: SEAs can be tiered.

The 'authorities' need to be consulted when the environmental report's scope and level of detail is decided (Art. 5.4). Member states can determine which authorities must be consulted. They are those authorities which, 'by reason of their specific environmental responsibilities, are likely to be concerned by the environmental effects of implementing plans and programmes' (Art. 6.3). A legal ruling in Northern Ireland (High Court of Justice in Northern Ireland, 2007) clarified that an 'authority' must be independent from the plan-making body.

Once the environmental report has been prepared, it and the draft plan or programme must be made available for *consultation*. The documents 'shall be made available to the authorities [of Art. 6.3] and the public' who must 'be given an early and effective opportunity within appropriate time frames to express their opinion on the draft plan or programme and the accompanying environmental report before the adoption of the plan or programme' (Art. 6.2). Again, member states can determine which members of the public should be consulted. Other member states that are likely to be significantly affected by the plan or programme must also be consulted. Table 4.1 summarizes the consultation requirements of the Directive.

The environmental report and the consultation comments from the authorities, public and other member states, where appropriate, must be 'taken into account during the preparation of the plan or programme and before its adoption' (Art. 8). After the plan is adopted, the results of the decision-making process must be made available to the authorities, public and other member states in an 'SEA statement' that details:

(a) the plan or programme as adopted;

(b) a statement summarising how environmental considerations have been integrated into the plan or programme and how the environmental report [and consultation opinions] have been taken into account ... and the reasons for choosing the plan or programme as adopted, in the light of other reasonable alternatives dealt with; and

(c) the measures decided concerning monitoring. (Art. 9.1)

This aims to help improve the transparency of decision-making and ensure that the SEA findings are properly taken into account. Significant environmental effects of the implementation of the plan or programme must be monitored 'in order, inter alia, to identify at an early stage unforeseen adverse effects, and to be able to undertake appropriate remedial action' (Art. 10).

Table 4.1 *Summary of the SEA Directive's consultation requirements*

Stage of SEA	Mandatory requirements	Additional requirements where the plan/programme is likely to have significant transboundary effects
Determination if a plan or programme requires SEA	Consultation of authorities (Art. 3.6) Information made available to the public (Art. 3.7)	
Decision on the scope and level of detail of the SEA	Consultation of authorities (Art. 5.4)	
Environmental report and draft plan or programme	Information made available to authorities and the public (Art. 6.1) Consultation of authorities and public in any member state likely to be affected (Art. 7.2)	Consultation of authorities and the public (Art. 6.2)
Adopted plan or programme; statement on how the SEA information has been taken into account in decision-making (Art. 9.1b); monitoring measures	Information made available to authorities and public (Art. 9.1)	Information made available to the consulted member state (Art. 9.1)

Source: Adapted from European Commission (2003)

Good and bad aspects of the SEA Directive

The SEA Directive sets a minimum baseline, which all European member states need to reach; is triggering thousands of SEAs each year, with consequent improvements in SEA experience and development of SEA techniques; and has significantly influenced the UN Economic Commission for Europe (UNECE) (2003) SEA Protocol. A recent European Commission (2009b) study on the Directive's effectiveness suggests that the Directive has made planning processes more structured and transparent, and has strengthened relationships between environmental and planning authorities. SEA has helped to integrate environmental considerations in decision-making, sometimes significantly. For instance, two terminals were removed from the Bulgarian national programme for ports development because of nature conservation concerns; the best alternative from an environmental perspective was chosen for a Romanian regional waste management plan as a result of SEA; and the SEA for a Hungarian water management programme helped to prevent a very expensive project (European Commission, 2009b).

The study also identified problems with the Directive. Several member states noted that its requirements can result in more time-consuming and expensive plan-making. Public involvement was seen as a particular burden. Many member states reported that SEA has led to no or minimal changes in plans and programmes. Remaining difficulties in implementation include confusion about what are 'administrative provisions' and 'reasonable alternatives', lack of relevant baseline data, and limited monitoring of impacts. However, overall the study concluded that these problems were small compared with the profound nature of the Directive (European Commission, 2009b).

The Chinese Plan Environmental Impact Assessment Regulations of 2009

China's SEA system[1], even more than those of the US and Europe, evolved from its system of project EIA, which has been in place since the Environmental Protection Act of 1979. In 1993, the State Environmental Protection Agency (SEPA) required 'regional EIA' of development zones through its 'Circular on Strengthening EIA Management of Construction Projects' (SEPA, 1993), but in practice this was done only sporadically and in a limited fashion. Starting in the mid-1990s, a range of academic reports promoted the expansion of EIA to strategic actions, in part to deal with limitations of project EIA. Some proto-SEAs were also carried out, for instance, for the five-year plans of three large iron and steel companies, some very large projects (e.g. west-to-east electricity transmission project, south-to-north water transfer project), and some land-use plans (Zhu and Ru, 2008). These were based heavily on project EIA methodologies.

SEA practice in China leapt forward when the Environmental Impact Assessment Law of the People's Republic of China – the 'EIA Law' – was approved in 2002 and became operational in September 2003. The EIA Law applied to both plans and projects, and aimed to 'implement the strategy of sustainable development, prevent adverse environmental impacts of plans and construction projects, and promote coordinated development of the economy, society and environment' (adapted from Bina, 2008, and GTZ, 2009). The last of these points is particularly important in a country where there is limited collaboration between ministries, and a clear distinction between 'environmental' and 'non-environmental' ministries (Bina, 2008).

To help implement the EIA Law's SEA requirements, the State Environmental Protection Agency (now Ministry of Environmental Protection) published a technical guide on SEA of provincial level land-use plans in 2003 (SEPA, 2003); a detailed list of the types of strategic actions that require SEA in 2004; lists of about 250 institutes that it recommends as being competent to carry out SEAs; and draft SEA review guidelines in December 2007 (the latter have since been superseded). Since 2005, it has carried out a series of SEA pilots and experimental applications, and organized several conferences on SEA (Li et al, 2006; Dusik and Xie, 2009). Several provinces and cities have also issued SEA regulations and guidance documents (Li et al, 2006).

In August 2009, the Chinese government published new regulations on plan environmental impact assessment (PEIA), which apply specifically to strategic actions. They are based heavily on the EIA Law of 2003. Appendix B provides a translation of the full PEIA regulations, and their requirements are discussed further below.

Actions that require SEA and the SEA process

The main SEA actors in China are:

- planning authorities at the national, provincial or local ('municipal with districts') level that prepare plans and are responsible for their PEIAs.
- authorization authorities. These are at a higher level of government than the plan-making authorities. They review drafts of the plans and their PEIAs, and authorize the plans.
- relevant institutions, experts and the public, who are consulted on the plans and their PEIAs.

Two types of strategic actions require SEA in China. The shorter, Type A, process relates to 'comprehensive plans': land-use plans, regional development plans, watershed and marine development plans, construction and utilization plans, and high-level conceptual or directive plans. For such plans, the planning authority must prepare an environmental impact chapter or note (Art. 10.1), which is submitted to the authorization authority alongside the draft plan (Art. 15). The planning authority should make the PEIA information publicly available (Art. 4), but more active attempts to involve the public are not required. The authorization authority may not approve a plan that has no environmental impact chapter or note, but the PEIA regulations do not prescribe a particular form of review process. The planning authority must monitor the environmental impacts of implementing the plan, and put in place remedial measures if it has adverse environmental impacts (Arts 24–29).

A more rigorous, Type B SEA process is required for 'special plans' for industry, agriculture, animal husbandry, forestry, energy, water management, transport, urban-development tourism and natural resources. Drafts of these plans must be accompanied by a full environmental impact report (EIR) (Art. 10.2). The planning authority must seek the opinions of relevant institutions, experts and the general public on the draft plan and its EIR, for instance, through public meetings or hearings; arrange follow-up meetings with various parties if they have strongly divergent views; and include details in the final EIR information of whether the opinions were adopted or refused (Art. 13). The relevant environmental protection authority must convene experts and representatives of relevant departments to form a review group that examines the EIR and submits its opinion in written form (Art. 17). The authorization authority must use the conclusions of the EIR and the review group as the main basis for its decision on the plan, and must keep records of where the EIR's conclusions or reviewers' opinions were not implemented (Art. 22). Monitoring and follow-up is required as for the comprehensive plans.

Contents of an environmental impact chapter or SEA report

Both Type A environmental impact chapters and Type B EIRs should include:

- prediction and evaluation of the likely environmental effects of implementing the plan, including an analysis of carrying capacity, adverse environmental impacts, and the environmental compatibility of the plan with other relevant plans;
- proposed measures to avoid or reduce adverse environmental impacts (Art. 11.1).

EIRs should also include conclusions from the PEIA process, including the environmental rationality and feasibility of the draft plan, the rationality and feasibility of the proposed mitigation measures, and suggestions for how to adjust the draft plan (Art.11.2). PEIAs in China generally focus on environmental issues, although social issues, such as minority cultures or resettlement of populations, are also sometimes addressed (Tao et al, 2007; Dusik and Xie, 2009).

Some of the details of the regulations have yet to be clarified, including what is meant by 'rationality' of the plan and mitigation measures; who decides whether a spatial plan will have adverse environmental impacts and affect the interests of the public, and hence whether public participation in its SEA process is required; what spatial plans are 'legally classified' and thus are not subject to some SEA requirements; and who determines whether a plan is likely to have significant environmental impacts and thus requires monitoring and follow-up. In Chinese legislation, lacunas and limited coverage tend to reflect areas of dilemma or controversy, so one could expect further debate and possibly future guidance on these topics.

Good and bad aspects of the EIA Law

A particularly strong aspect of the new Chinese PEIA regulations is their emphasis on ensuring that plan-makers really take account of the findings of PEIAs. For special plans, plan-makers are expected to consult with a range of organizations and individuals, and include in the EIR information about how their comments have been taken into account (Art. 13). A review group checks on the quality of the EIR (Art. 19). The authorization authority is expected to base its decision about the plan primarily on the conclusions of the PEIA process and the review group's findings, and to justify any cases where they do not adopt recommendations made by the review group (Art. 22). That said, none of these requirements apply to comprehensive or high-level conceptual plans.

In addition to these procedural requirements, the regulations also have a strong substantive basis. PEIAs are expected to discuss cumulative impacts (Art. 8) and include an analysis of carrying capacity (Art. 25). For special plans, where it is not possible to assess the scale and extent of the plan's environmental impacts, or where significant environmental impacts would remain after mitigation measures are fully considered, the review team is expected to reject the EIR (Art. 21). In extreme cases, environmental conditions can prevent a plan from being approved:

> *If the total emissions of a key pollutant exceed the national limit or regional limit within the implementation area of a given plan, the examination and approval of EIRs of new plans that increase the concentration of the key pollutant within the area should be suspended.*
> (Art. 30)

The regulations also clearly aim to lead to progressive improvements in the quality of SEA techniques and effectiveness of mitigation measures. The review of EIRs should include consideration of the provenance of the baseline data, robustness of impact prediction methods, effectiveness of proposed mitigation measures, and overall 'scientific rationality' of the conclusions of the PEIA process (Art. 19). The monitoring and follow-up process involves comparing the actual impacts of implementing the plan against those predicted in the PEIA, and assessing the effectiveness of mitigation measures (Art. 25); both of these should provide information that allows future PEIAs to become increasingly robust and well justified.

Some of the new regulatory requirements seem designed to deal with past problems of implementing SEA in China. To date, many special plans have been authorized without EIRs being prepared for them, either because the planning and authorization authorities were not aware of the SEA requirements or because they were avoiding them. SEAs were often carried out late in the plan-making process, sometimes after the plan had been authorized, and often too late to influence its development (Bina, 2007; Dusik and Xie, 2009; YEPB and Sida, 2009; Zhu and Ru, 2008). The new regulations require PEIAs to be prepared 'during the course' of plan-making (Art. 7); and plans submitted without the proper environmental impact chapter or EIR should not be approved (Arts 15 and 16). Four of the 35 articles in the regulations deal with legal liabilities if various parties do not abide by the regulations' requirements (Arts 31–34).

Other limitations of current SEA practice in China have not been so directly addressed by the regulations. Most of the organizations recommended by the SEPA as being competent to carry out PEIAs have expertise in project EIA, and are carrying over this expertise to plan EIAs. As a result, PEIAs often feel very much like EIAs: they emphasize quantifiable impacts, modelling and mitigation of impacts through technical means rather than avoidance of impacts in the first place. This EIA-based approach is reinforced by the regulations' emphasis on PEIA as 'improving the scientific rationality of planning' (Art. 1). The SEA requirements for comprehensive plans are still limited despite these plans' potentially significant environmental impacts, due to methodological, institutional and political difficulties, and because such SEAs tend to be very different from project EIAs.

The links between planning authorities and authorization authorities can be very close, so that the rigour and impartiality of the plan approval process may be more limited in practice than is implied by the regulations. Many provinces and cities also have different ways of designating authorizations for different types of plans, making consistent application of the statutory requirements difficult.

The PEIA regulations are ambiguous about the role of environmental authorities in the review and authorization of plans. Article 18 requires review groups to be chosen randomly from a list of experts, but environmental authorities may not be chosen and could thus not have a presence in these groups. Attempts by the SEPA to develop review guidelines that establish a clearer role for environmental authorities have been criticized by other agencies (Zhu and Ru, 2008; Dusik and Xie, 2009). Chinese SEA practitioners are also facing typical problems of early SEA practice: limited relevant baseline data, inconsistency of data collection between authorities and limited sharing of data, a lack of understood SEA techniques, and a general need for more capacity-building (Li et al, 2006).

At the time of writing (late 2009), SEA practice in China is still in its relatively early days. Many of China's SEAs are still pilots, supported by the Ministry of Environmental Protection and international bodies. Many planning authorities are still working out how to carry out PEIAs, and environmental authorities are trying to ensure that the environmental impacts of plans that will influence China during a period of very rapid growth are fully taken into account. China seems to be at the stage of rapid evolution, experimentation and vigorous debate that characterized SEA practice in the US in the late 1970s and in Europe around the time that the SEA Directive became operational. The PEIA regulations are a powerful step forward, and SEA practice in China is likely to evolve rapidly over the coming decade.

Conclusions

This chapter has reviewed three SEA systems at different stages of development. It shows that all SEA systems go through teething pains, and that they all struggle with common issues:

- Should SEA focus on environmental impacts or also cover social and economic impacts?
- Should SEA apply to policies or just to plans and programmes?
- Should different types of strategic actions require different types of SEA?
- Should SEA use the same techniques as project EIA or are there separate 'SEA techniques'?
- What information should be considered at what 'tiers' of planning and SEA?
- How can the costs of SEA be minimized and its benefits be optimized?

These points are explored further in Part II. Chapters 5–10 provide a range of approaches for carrying out SEA. They cover, in turn, the context for SEA; the baseline environment and links to other strategic actions; alternatives; prediction, evaluation and mitigation of impacts; and SEA documentation and decision-making.

Footnote

1   This section discusses the SEA system of the People's Republic of China, not that of the Hong Kong Special Administrative Region, which has evolved quite separately and has its own environmental assessment ordinance and system. For information about the latter, the reader is referred to the Hong Kong Environmental Protection Department (2009).

Part II

The SEA Process

Chapter 5

Setting the Context for SEA

This chapter considers the early, context-setting stages of the SEA process:

A   Understanding various dimensions of the strategic action and how they affect the SEA.
B   Screening: deciding whether a given strategic action requires SEA.
C   How to link SEA and the strategic action, especially in terms of timing.
D   Who should be involved in SEA, including environmental/ sustainability authorities and the public.
E   How SEA can fit with other existing assessment requirements.
F   Three early, interlinked questions, which influence many aspects of the SEA process: whether SEA should focus on the environment or sustainability; whether it should be objectives-led or baseline-led; and whether the report should be task-based or topic-based.

Understanding the strategic action

The first step in SEA is to understand some basic aspects of the strategic action, since this will influence many aspects of the SEA.

Who is developing the strategic action? The authority that is developing the strategic action will typically also be responsible for its SEA, although the actual SEA work may be carried out by others.

What is the spatial scale of the strategic action and what will be its level of detail? Is the strategic action at an international, national, regional/province, local or sub-local/site level? Will it provide broad-brush guidelines or propose specific types of development in specific locations? How spatially specific will it be? The level of detail of SEA should be broadly proportional to that of the strategic action, so the smaller the scale and greater the level of detail (including spatial) of the strategic action, the more detailed and specific the SEA should be.

Is the strategic action sectoral or spatial? Does it deal with a specific sector such as waste, transport or forestry; or does it cover all activities in a particular area? Spatial strategic actions will typically have many different types of impacts. Sectoral strategic actions' impacts, instead, may be more specific, and some impact types may not need to be covered in their SEAs at all.

What is the strategic action's temporal scale, and is it cyclical or one-off? Over what period is the strategic action meant to apply? When (if at all) will it be reviewed and revised? Is it a revision of an already-existing strategic action? The strategic action's temporal scale will influence how far into the future the SEA's baseline should be projected, and what will be the short-term and long-term impacts of the strategy. A cyclical strategic action – one that is rewritten every (say) five or 20 years – allows for a clearer cycle of impact prediction, monitoring and future improved predictions based on the monitoring information. However, cyclical strategic actions may also be more mired in set institutional structures, which could prevent innovative 'second loop' thinking towards the strategic action and its SEA.

Is the strategic action required or voluntary? If the strategic action is required, under what legislation, and what does that legislation say that the strategic action must do or include? If it is voluntary, SEA may not be legally required but could still be beneficial for the reasons discussed in Chapter 2.

A template can be set up for these questions: Box 5.1 shows such a template prepared by the Scottish Executive (2006). The answers to these questions can be summarized in a short paragraph, which can act as an introduction to the SEA report. Box 5.2 shows two examples of such paragraphs.

Deciding whether the strategic action requires SEA: 'screening'

Once the basic aspects of the strategic action have been understood, it should be possible to determine whether the strategic action requires SEA: this is the screening process. The faster and more definite the screening process is, the less uncertainty and wasted time (and apprehension) will result.

Different countries have different screening requirements. In some countries and organizations, SEA requirements are limited to a

Box 5.1 Template for describing the strategic action

Plan-making authority	
Title of the strategic action	
Purpose of the strategic action	
What prompted the strategic action (e.g. a legislative or administrative provision)	
Subject (e.g. transport)	
Period covered by the strategic action	
Frequency of updates	
Geographic area of the strategic action (attach a map)	
Summary of nature/content of the strategic action	
Proposed objectives of the strategic action, if available	

Source: Based on Scottish Executive (2006)

particular type of strategic action, for instance, regional and sectoral development activities by the World Bank, proposals to Parliament in Denmark, policies and plans that cover resource consents in New Zealand (Dalal-Clayton and Sadler, 2005). The US National Environmental Policy Act requires a 'detailed statement' to be prepared for all 'major federal actions significantly affecting the quality of the human environment'. The flexibility inherent in this definition has led to great uncertainty and a truly impressive number of lawsuits about whether any given activity is major, federal, an action, and with significant effects on the human environment. The European SEA Directive has complex 'and/or' screening requirements (Figure 4.2), which are easy to apply to some strategic actions but provide less clear-cut answers for others.

An interesting aside here is that legislative wording can have a strong influence on whether a given plan or programme requires SEA

Box 5.2 Two examples of descriptions of strategic actions

1 One-off, regional scale, sectoral programme: 'Eskom Master Plan – Central Region', South Africa

   Eskom Distribution, in an effort to proactively plan for the energy needs for the study area, commissioned NETGroup South Africa (Pty) Ltd as consulting electrical engineers to evaluate and recommend a master plan of energy supply in the areas south of Johannesburg. The study area includes ... Eskom Networks within Emfuleni and the Midvaal Local Municipalities and Johannesburg Metropolitan Municipality. The Eskom Master Plan Central Region study specifically deals with the siting, sizing and timing of new high voltage (400kV to 11kV) electric infrastructure, with the main focus on the sub-transmission network (275/132kV to 88kV and associated distribution substations and lines) within the study area. The primary drivers for this new infrastructure are typically growth in the existing electricity demand, expected future demand, infrastructure renewal requirements and network performance improvement requirements.

2 Cyclical, local scale, spatial plan: Killarney Town Plan 2009–2015, Ireland

   The Killarney Town Plan sets out the overall strategy for the sustainable development of the town. The existing Town Development Plan was adopted in 2003 and remains in force until October 2009. Killarney Town Council is currently preparing a new Town Development Plan under The Planning and Development Act (2000) which requires the Planning Authority to prepare a 'Development Plan' every six years for its jurisdiction... The plan, as the main public statement of the town council, provides a vision for the town to evolve, giving statutory context for guiding development in the interests of the proper planning and sustainable development of the town. The key objectives of the Plan are:

   - to promote the sustainable development of the town in fulfilling it is role as part of the Tralee/Killarney Hub;
   - to afford all citizens of and visitors to Killarney the highest quality living environment as possible;
   - to channel development in the town in a manner that promotes compact urban form...

Sources: 1 Eskom Distribution (2007); 2 Killarney Town Council (2008)

---

or not. For instance, the UK Planning Act 2008 establishes a new form of strategic action, national policy statements, which will form the main basis for future planning decisions about major new infrastructure projects (transport, energy, water, etc.). National policy statements are prepared by government departments. They can specify suitable locations for new infrastructure projects, and the amount, type or size of specified types of developments. Clearly, they are prepared by a formal authority, relate to sectors specifically listed in the SEA Directive, could have significant environmental effects, and could set the framework for development consent of projects: in all but one respect, they trigger SEA under the SEA Directive (see Figure 4.2). However, section 5(1) of the UK Planning Act 2008 states that 'The Secretary of State *may* designate a statement as a national policy statement' (my emphasis): thus national policy statements are not 'required' and therefore they do not require SEA.[1]

Even where SEA is not legally required for a given strategic action, authorities should consider carrying out SEA, especially where the strategic action influences lower-levels ones that require SEA or EIA. Otherwise, where SEAs/EIAs for the lower-level strategic actions identify that the higher-level strategic action is not sustainable or environmentally sound, then the higher-level strategic action's validity may be in doubt. Where no SEA is deemed to be required, it may be useful to write a justification for this. Where an SEA has already been carried out on an earlier version of the strategic action, the new SEA should probably aim, on efficiency grounds, to update the original SEA rather than starting afresh.

Links between SEA and decision-making

SEA should be started early in the process of developing the strategic action, and should influence the plan-making process from beginning to end: for instance, the Chinese SEA legislation (Appendix B) notes that SEA should be carried out 'during the course of plan-making', and the SEA Directive (Appendix A) expects SEA to be carried out 'during the preparation of a plan or programme and before its adoption or submission to the legislative procedure'. The early, context-setting stages of SEA should help to identify constraints and opportunities for the strategic action. In the middle stages of the development of the strategic action, the SEA should help to identify and inform the choice of alternatives. As the details of the strategic action become finalized, the SEA process should identify ways of avoiding or minimizing its negative impacts and optimizing its positive ones. After adoption of the strategic action, the SEA monitoring process should help to ensure that the strategic action is implemented well and modified if necessary.

Although it is virtually impossible to accurately foretell what will be actual 'decision windows' – times in which key decisions are made (ANSEA Team, 2002) – in the plan-making process, it will still be worthwhile mapping out any formally required stages of decision-making and deciding how to best integrate it in the SEA. Figure 5.1 shows such a flowchart for the Tooton Rush example of Chapter 3.

In most cases, SEA should fit elegantly with the strategic decision-making process. In fact, there is potential for so completely integrating planning processes and SEA that the only added requirement for formal SEA would be the documentation of this process.

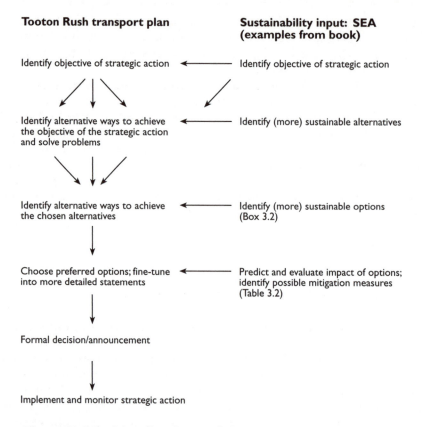

Tooton Rush transport plan

Identify objective of strategic action

Identify alternative ways to achieve the objective of the strategic action and solve problems

Identify alternative ways to achieve the chosen alternatives

Choose preferred options; fine-tune into more detailed statements

Formal decision/announcement

Implement and monitor strategic action

Sustainability input: SEA (examples from book)

Identify objective of strategic action

Identify (more) sustainable alternatives

Identify (more) sustainable options (Box 3.2)

Predict and evaluate impact of options; identify possible mitigation measures (Table 3.2)

Figure 5.1 *Decision flowchart and SEA inputs for Tooton Rush*

Who should be involved in the SEA

Three groups of people and organizations are likely to be involved in an SEA: the decision-maker and possibly their consultants; environmental or sustainability authorities; and the public. Inspectors, auditors and others interested in quality assurance of the SEA process may also participate. Normally, the SEA will be carried out by the decision-maker with involvement from the other groups.

Decision-maker or consultant?

Whereas project EIA is primarily carried out by consultants because of the specialist skills it requires, SEAs are often carried out by the decision-makers themselves. For instance, in the UK, slightly over half of local authority planning departments are carrying out SEAs solely within their authority; about 20 per cent are delegating the work completely to consultants; in about 20 per cent of cases, the SEAs are undertaken jointly by local authority personnel and consultants; and, in a few cases, SEAs are carried out by a wider group of stakeholders, either within the authority or with other authorities (Therivel and Walsh, 2006; Fischer, 2010). On the other hand, most South African SEAs between 1996 and 2003 were carried out by consultants, most early Chinese SEAs were carried out by universities acting in the role of consultants, and in some countries (e.g. Estonia, Czech Republic, Belgium) SEAs must be carried out by licensed environmental experts who are typically also EIA experts (Schmidt et al, 2005; Retief et al, 2008; Zhu and Ru, 2008).

Integration of SEA with the strategic action development process is a key factor in SEA effectiveness, so SEAs carried out quite separately from the strategic action – for instance, by remote consultants or by a single junior planner – are likely to be less effective than those carried out in, say, group workshops involving the plan-makers (ODPM et al, 2005). Retief et al (2008) argue that consultants are unlikely to be fully cognisant of the real-life, value-driven context within which plan-makers operate, and more likely to promote an artificial (and thus ineffective) technical–rational approach to plan-making. EIA experts may well have difficulty in coping with the uncertainty, fluidity and political aspects of strategic-level decision-making. A survey of UK SEA pilot authorities concluded that the plan-making team should carry out SEA 'because of the importance of making it an integral part of decision-making and having full knowledge of all the judgements made within [SEA]' (PAS, 2006). However, the same study adds that there is still value in using consultants as 'critical friends': for training, review of SEA documents and other support to planning staff.

That said, planners face many constraints, and SEA may be one work package that is relatively easy to outsource. Consultants are likely to be more familiar with data sources and legal requirements for SEA, and so may be particularly efficient in the context-setting stage of SEA. Consultants can provide more independent views, less dominated by long-established institutional networks and mindsets. They may be able to 'cross-fertilize' good practice between their client authorities. Studies of UK environmental appraisal practice (e.g. Therivel, 1995; Therivel and Minas, 2002; Therivel and Walsh, 2006; Sherston, 2008) show mixed results in terms of whether SEAs carried out by consultants, planners, one planner or mixed groups of consultants and planners lead to most changes in the strategic action.

The use of consultants may seem particularly attractive at the late stages of plan-making, when planning deadlines are looming and planners' time is short. Fischer (2009) found that less than 30 per cent of scoping reports (early stages of SEA) compared with more than half of later-stage SEA reports, were prepared by consultants. Unfortunately, the assessment stage is probably the one where planners' involvement is most crucial, since it is at this stage that plan impacts are identified, and ideas for changes to the plan raised and adopted.

Table 5.1 summarizes advantages and disadvantages of SEAs carried out in-house or by consultants. However, perhaps more useful than this simple categorization is the concept that the SEA team should have the right competences: independence, the authority to implement the SEA's recommendations, and experience. Independence, objectivity and credibility could be achieved through post-audit review (e.g. a citizens review panel) or through involvement with external agencies, such as consultants or academics. Close integration between the SEA and the decision-making process – which is needed so that SEA recommendations can be taken on board easily and efficiently – is probably most easily done by involving the planners in the SEA. Where external consultants are employed, then a close working partnership with the planners should be stressed, and how the resulting formal recommendations are taken on board by the authority should be documented. Experience is needed in terms of full coverage of relevant social, economic, environmental, health and public participation issues; understanding of the decision-making process; and a knowledge of the local area.

Table 5.1 *Advantages and disadvantages of different approaches to who should carry out the SEA*

	Advantages	Disadvantages
In-house	• Planners are better placed to conduct an iterative process that extends throughout the development of the strategic action • Planners gain a better understanding of the strategic action and sustainability issues	• Planners may not have previous SEA expertise • Resource/time problems • If undertaken by planners who wrote the plan, not independent
Consultants	• Ensures expertise in environmental/ sustainability issues and SEA; can 'cross-fertilize' between authorities by highlighting good practice from other authorities • Provide independent, fresh outlook and ideas • Prevents accusations of bias	• Consultants are unlikely to know local circumstances and context • Does not deal with 'real-life decision-making' and 'value driven' approaches to plan-making (Retief et al, 2008) • Financial cost to the plan-making authority, especially if consultants are involved throughout the decision-making process • Difficult to do as an integral process of the development of the strategic action

Involving environmental/sustainability authorities

Environmental/sustainability authorities – also known as competent authorities, expert bodies or statutory consultees – are government agencies responsible for various aspects of environment or sustainability. They could, for instance, be a country's environment department, nature conservation bureau or pollution inspectorate. In England, they are the Environment Agency (air, water, soil), Natural England (biodiversity, flora, fauna, landscape), English Heritage (archaeological, historical and cultural issues), and increasingly also more socially oriented organizations, such as the Department of Health and the police. They could also include NGOs, such as wildlife trusts and local government environmental departments.

Environmental/sustainability authorities are often key players in SEA. They are able to provide environmental data; help identify environmental problems; help decide the level of detail that the SEA should go into, methods it should use, and alternatives it should consider ('scoping'); identify other strategic actions that influence, or are influenced by, the strategic action in question; suggest sustainable alternatives; help to choose between alternatives; and suggest mitigation measures. The most effective way to obtain this expert input is during the course of the SEA process, for instance, by inviting the organizations to SEA steering group meetings or involving them actively in the analysis of alternatives.

Some SEA systems require that environmental/sustainability authorities are consulted at specific stages of plan-making. For instance, the SEA Directive requires that environmental authorities' views be sought on the 'scope and level of detail' of the SEA and on the draft SEA report, and that these views are 'taken into account' in decision-making. In Flanders (Belgium), a central EIA/SEA unit sets terms of reference for the final SEA report. In the Netherlands, a very similar process that had been in place for many years has recently been scrapped in favour of consultation with a range of environmental bodies; but the Netherlands Commission for Environmental Assessment (NCEA) has the final say on the composition of expert groups who carry out SEAs and carries out a formal quality review of SEA reports before plans are approved. In Scotland, an 'SEA Gateway' coordinates the views of all of the environmental/sustainability authorities, to ensure that these views are not contradictory. In other cases, for instance China, the role of environmental/sustainability authorities is more uncertain (Schmidt et al, 2005; Zhu and Ru, 2008; NCEA, 2009).

More proactively, some environmental/sustainability authorities have set out information explaining what they will and will not comment on (e.g. English Nature et al, 2004); others have prepared SEA guidance on their specialist areas (e.g. Countryside Council for Wales, 2007;

Department of Heath, 2007); and still others have set up formal SEA review criteria (e.g. Environmental Protection Agency, 2009).

Involving the public

Involving the public in decision-making and SEA takes advantage of local skills, knowledge and resources, leads to more socially and politically acceptable decisions, improves 'ownership' of decisions and makes the strategic action more likely to be implemented, can resolve conflict between stakeholder groups, and improves democracy by ensuring that community views are taken into account in decision-making. Public participation is a key principle of sustainable development. It is also in line with the Aarhus Convention, which aims to 'ensure that the public are given early and effective opportunities to participate in the preparation and review of [strategic actions]' (UNECE, 1998).

Public involvement in the SEA process can help to ensure that the strategic action meets people's aspirations for the future and does not just respond to today's problems. The public can contribute to setting the SEA objectives; help to ensure that baseline data is comprehensive and that the full range of environmental/sustainability problems are understood; identify innovative, sustainable and/or politically acceptable alternatives; choose between alternatives; identify mitigation measures; and ensure that the strategic action is implemented effectively.

On the other hand, public participation may not result in the most environmental or sustainable solution, or even come close to it. Participants may only become involved when they feel threatened, so NIMBY (not in my back yard) approaches can dominate. It may be difficult to identify and engage the public, and there may be 'consultation fatigue'. Specialist skills are often needed to achieve effective participation and, if done poorly, the public's expectations can be raised unrealistically and participants can be left feeling frustrated.

I have to be honest here (and I get told off about this regularly, so do feel free to disagree): involving the public in SEA is not easy, and I am not certain that the benefits of such involvement outweigh its costs in all circumstances. Most members of the public don't understand the planning process, much less SEA. SEAs and the strategic actions they relate to are often too strategic, too removed from people's everyday concerns to elicit 'participation' from more than an extremely limited and unrepresentative group of people. Heiland (2005) refers to the 'participation paradox': the public do not participate at the more strategic stages of plan-making where they could have more influence, but participate at more detailed, concrete stages of plan- and project-making where possibilities to influence them are reduced.

Table 5.2 *Public participation techniques and approaches*

Type	Public consultation	Public involvement
Applied through	Individuals, separately	Groups, collaboratively
Kinds of value/style of input most encouraged	Private interest/adversarial	Public interest/consensus seeking
Prevailing tone	Argumentative	Deliberative
Common techniques	Public meetings Printed materials Newspaper articles/ads Information on websites Draft SEA reports for comment Questionnaires Planning inquiries	Small meetings, focus groups Workshops, e.g. SEA assessment exercises Citizens' juries Future Search Planning for Real Visioning

Source: Adapted from CAG (2000)

Public participation techniques range from basic consultation – provision of information and the opportunity to comment – through to extended involvement as members of an SEA steering group or SEA team, with the ability to genuinely influence the SEA and planning processes. Table 5.2 summarizes some of the key techniques for public participation, along with their underlying philosophies. Further information on these techniques can be found in publications by, for example, the Audit Commission (1999), Institute of Environmental Management and Assessment (2002) and World Bank (1996).

Most countries' SEA systems – including the SEA Directive – require only a minimal form of public consultation in the form of an opportunity to comment on an SEA report. This is unfortunate, since merely making reports available on the authority website or sending them out alongside the draft plan is unlikely to generate much public response. For instance, a 2005 survey of UK local authority planners asked them to explain how they had consulted the public on SEA and how helpful the response had been, from 1 very helpful to 4 unhelpful. Typical responses were:

- *'[SEA] went out to public (>1000 people): 2 responses received for one document, 3 on the other. One was useful, the others less so.'*
- *'Copies of the documents posted to consultees – some useful feedback (2); Website consultation – limited feedback (3); Workshops (parish councils, key service providers) – (1) very helpful.'*
- *'Comments from general public were 3/4, as they either miss the point of the exercise/didn't understand or were pushing their own agenda.'*

- *'Overall helpful. Response rate was reasonable but not brilliant (approx 33 replies to scoping report). However, quality of responses was very good.'* (Therivel and Walsh, 2006)

SEA public participation methods that are most likely to lead to tangible outcomes are those that are most targeted and intensive, and that involve a large element of initial capacity-building, for instance workshops, citizen panels and discussions to elected representatives (CLG, 2009b). Box 5.3 provides some ideas for SEA workshops of different lengths, with different types of groups, based on real-life examples.

Getting meaningful input to the SEA process from groups that have traditionally been disenfranchised – for instance, Aboriginal and other indigenous people, young people, the homeless, and gypsies and travellers – is particularly difficult. In some cases, this is because they are physically difficult to reach or because of language barriers. Consultation processes involving newsletters, public meetings and requests for written feedback are biased against participants who are not comfortable attending meetings, speaking in public or writing letters. There may also be a profound social gulf between mainstream planners and some of the people whom they are planning for, including racism, centuries-old tribal enmity, and the reluctance of some groups to participate in government processes that have treated them poorly in the past. In such cases, small group meetings on people's home ground, story-telling, or informal engagement may be the only effective approaches (O'Faircheallaigh, 2009). These techniques are very resource intensive, and probably justified only where these groups are likely to be significantly affected by a strategic action.

An alternative to 'public' participation is to involve representatives of the wider public in the SEA. These could be elected representatives or politicians, or pressure groups that represent various public views (business organizations, environmental organizations, etc.). In some SEA processes, steering groups made up of representatives of the public oversee the entire process or carry out the assessment themselves.

It may be useful, early in the SEA process, to set up a public participation programme that identifies the role of the public, representatives and/or stakeholders; how and when they will be involved; and expected outputs. This will help to ensure that participation occurs early enough to influence the strategic action, that adequate time and resources are set aside, and that appropriate techniques are used.

Box 5.3 Examples of SEA workshops

Half-hour meeting to inform about 20 local politicians (who tend to be very opinionated and vocal) about the basics of the SEA process early in the process, to help ensure their subsequent involvement.

- Five-minute introduction explaining that, as part of the plan-making process, the plan's environmental impacts will need to be assessed, and that part of the assessment involves identifying existing problems that the plan will seek to remediate.
- Hand out draft list of a dozen existing problems already identified by consultants as part of the SEA context-setting stage; ask the politicians 1. whether the list is correct, and 2. to put stars next to those problems that they feel are particularly acute.
- Fifteen-minute discussion by the politicians, which removes some 'problems', adds some others, and puts stars next to several of the problems.
- Ten-minute explanation of how this stage fits into the entire SEA process, and the next (impact assessment of options) step in which politicians can expect to be involved in.

One-and-a-half-hour meeting with about 30 health and social services professionals (with no previous SEA experience) to help identify a 'social baseline' and problems.

- Participants sit down at four square tables, each with a large map of the district, coloured pens and pads of sticky-backed note paper.
- Ten-minute Powerpoint presentation of the plan-making process and the role of SEA in it, with a particular focus on what the future plan will and will not be able to do.
- Participants are asked to mark on the maps: existing health/social problem areas in red pen, existing health/social aspects that work well in green pen, suggestions for how the future plan might be able to improve the situation in blue pen. Extra notes can be made on the sticky-backed notes. Two of the groups are asked to focus on, respectively, the urban and rural parts of the district, and one is asked to focus on sub-groups of the population that might have difficulty in getting to health/social facilities.
- Ten-minute plenary to allow the groups to share their main findings.
- Ten-minute conclusion about how the workshop information will be used, and explanation of next steps.

One-and-a-half-hour to two-hour meeting with about 60 members of the public and local politicians to help inform them about the SEA assessment stage, and ensure that planners have a full understanding of local factors when choosing between three broad spatial options for providing more housing in the district.

- Ten-minute Powerpoint presentation of the plan-making process and the role of SEA in it, with a particular focus on what the future plan will and will not be able to do.

- Participants are split into groups of about eight people, each around a square table with one facilitator and one note-taker (both planners). Each table has maps showing existing constraints (e.g. flood plain, nature conservation designations) and blank assessment matrices. Each group is given four SEA topics (e.g. air quality, transport, employment, landscape), and is asked to discuss the impacts of each option on each topic, informed by the constraints maps, and using the matrix to record its findings. Only being asked to comment on a few SEA topics means that participants cannot try to work the appraisal process so as to achieve a predetermined solution; also planners must be clear about the fact that the workshop findings will feed into the assessment process rather than being the assessment.
- Fifteen-minute plenary in which planners summarize key points arising at their tables, and participants are reminded of forthcoming stages of the SEA process.

Fitting SEA with other assessment requirements

In many countries, SEA will be one of a range of assessments required for strategic actions. Others could include, for instance, assessment of the strategic action's compliance with other regulations and effect on health, equity, vulnerable groups (e.g. the elderly, minorities, farmers), businesses or sustainability. In European Union countries, 'appropriate assessment' under the Habitats Directive is also required for plans (see Appendix D).

Where other assessment systems already exist, a decision will need to be made about whether the SEA and other systems can be integrated, or whether they should run side-by-side. Whether or not to integrate will depend on the degree of overlap of the different assessment systems in terms of what strategic actions they apply to (policy/plan/programme, what sectors); the impacts that they consider (e.g. health); whether they focus on a particular receptor group; and the rigour of their requirements. Many of these other forms of assessment – especially various forms of social impact assessment – are, if anything, less well-developed than SEA is, and the SEA process may act as a useful framework for them.

Generally integration is preferable on grounds of efficiency, for instance, in collecting and presenting baseline data, or reducing the number of separate consultation exercises. However, it could reduce SEA's emphasis on the environment, and the legal requirements for the two sets of assessment may vary. For instance, European planners only need to 'take into account' the findings of SEA, but must protect the integrity of internationally important nature conservation sites under 'appropriate assessment'. Any integrated system will also require collaborative working between agencies that may well not have a tradition of cooperation.

A range of approaches are possible:

- carry out separate SEA and other assessment(s);
- carry out SEA, plus an additional separate analysis of those aspects of the current assessment system(s) not covered by SEA;
- carry out the other assessment(s), plus an additional separate analysis of those aspects of SEA not covered by the current assessment system(s); or
- integrate SEA and the other assessment systems.

Table 5.3 summarizes some of their advantages and disadvantages.

Table 5.3 *Advantages and disadvantages of different approaches to fitting SEA with other assessment systems*

Option	Advantages	Disadvantages
Separate SEA + other assessment	• Easiest to write regulations and guidance for • Copes most easily with different areas of application (policy, plan, programme; different sectors)	• Confusing for implementing bodies • Inefficient
SEA + separate analysis of aspects of other assessment systems not covered by SEA	• Where SEA is legally required and other assessment systems are discretionary, then SEA provides a regulatory basis and should thus be the main basis for guidance	• Somewhat confusing for implementing bodies • Sustainability is often best tackled in an integrated (environment – social – economic) manner rather than by treating them as separate issues
Integrate SEA + other assessment systems	• Efficient; eliminates duplication • Easy to understand for implementing bodies • Can incorporate best practice from the different assessment systems • Sustainability is often best tackled in an integrated (environment – social – economic) manner rather than by treating them as separate issues	• Potentially the most difficult to write guidance for, not least because it requires approval by officials responsible for the other systems of assessment • Could dilute SEA's emphasis on the environment

Environmental assessment or sustainability assessment?

The question of whether SEA should be limited to biophysical/environmental issues or broadened out to include the full range of sustainability issues is a key early question in the SEA process. Unfortunately, it is also a particularly complex one.

Different SEA systems take different approaches to this issue. For instance, Chinese SEA practice focuses relatively clearly on the biophysical environment. The US National Environmental Policy Act focuses on the 'human environment'; PEISs typically cover biophysical issues plus social issues, such as environmental justice, health and safety, land use and cultural resources. The SEA Directive aims to provide for a high level of protection of the environment 'with a view to promoting sustainable development'. In other words, it implies that environmental protection and sustainable development are distinct goals; integrating the environment into strategic actions will promote sustainable development; and environmental assessment (not sustainability assessment) is a good way to do this.

Both approaches have advantages and disadvantages. Those in favour of subsuming SEA within a wider sustainability assessment process, refer back to the fundamental reasons why we value the environment. They go as follows:

Sustainable development is an anthropocentric concept: it puts human interests first. The classic Brundtland definition, 'development which meets the needs of the present without compromising the ability of future generations to meet their own needs' (WCED, 1987), does not even mention the environment. According to this definition, sustainable development has things to say about the environment because, and only because, the way that humans are currently treating it in order to meet some of the 'needs of the present', notably through economic production and consumption, is interfering with other 'needs of the present'. These include healthy and pleasant living conditions (especially for poorer people and countries), and jeopardizing the ability of future generations to meet basic needs, such as water, food and land tolerably free from floods, droughts and other climatic disasters.

Another widely accepted definition of sustainable development is 'improving the quality of life within the carrying capacity of supporting ecosystems' (IUCN, 1991). This makes explicit reference to one aspect of the environment, but it is the instrumental one of avoiding breaches of carrying capacities because they could undermine the future quality of (human) life. It does not exclude concern for other aspects of the environment, although they would have to come under the 'quality of life' part of the definition, not the 'carrying capacities' one.

In contrast, the SEA Directive's phrase, 'protection of the environment', implies a moral aim to protect the external world for its own sake – an ecocentric view. This begs the question of precisely what should be protected, which in turn begs the question of what constitutes 'damage'. Every time a human being eats, breathes or walks across a lawn, they are altering the environment, so how do we decide which alterations the environment should be protected from? The environment has never been in a state of equilibrium: land masses form and reform, mountains are created and erode, species evolve and become extinct. So, from an earth-centred perspective, it is hard to say why recent human impacts on the environment should be wrong when the same kinds of impacts have happened throughout time.

It is also very difficult to distinguish where the environment stops and where society or the economy begins. The economy and people's well-being are inextricably linked to the state of the environment, so the concept of 'environment' can also be considered to encompass the other two concepts.

The environment matters because it affects human well-being. For example, climate change is important not because it is wrong or unnatural, but because the rapid and extreme climate change that human greenhouse gas emissions are causing is likely to lead to vast human suffering (e.g. loss of low land, changes in crop patterns). Likewise, maintenance of biodiversity does not matter because every species has a right to live forever: species are always emerging and disappearing. It matters because humans benefit from the range of useful medicinal products, the resilience, and the delight of exquisite variety and natural beauty that diversity provides. In other words, the apparently ecocentric idea of 'protection of the environment' rapidly bring us back to anthropocentric judgements about what matters for human quality of life. There is no list of environmental imperatives that can be 'read off' purely from science without the intervention of any normative judgements about what matters to humankind.

If this is so (and many environmentalists and philosophers would hotly dispute it) there are interesting consequences for SEA. If the basis of even apparently 'environmental' objectives is human well-being, there is no profound difference in principle between assessing the effects of a strategic action on the environment, and assessing its effects on a wider range of outcomes that matter for human well-being. It follows that environmental assessment (and, using the same argument, economic assessment) should be understood simply as a subset of sustainability assessment. 'Protection of the environment' is not a separate policy goal from sustainable development, as the Directive and Protocol imply, but must be understood as a contributor to or sub-goal of it.

Separating social, economic and environmental issues into artificial assessment ghettoes can also make it harder to integrate environmental issues in decision-making, as they come to be seen as a special interest subject, which constrains other aspirations. Such a separation also makes it harder to have transparent decisions and to identify win–win–win solutions that integrate all three.

Arguments for limiting SEA to biophysical/environmental concerns are as follows. First, many requirements for environmental assessment (including all three SEA systems discussed at Chapter 4) were prompted by concerns that environmental consequences of decisions are being given insufficient weight compared to social ones, and particularly to the economic ones, which arguably dominate policy. If the point of environmental assessment is to redress this balance, then expanding it to include social and economic elements would be both unnecessary and self-defeating.

Second, environmental assessment depends on evidence about the physical world, even if the evidence that should be collected and how it is interpreted are matters of judgement, and even if, in practice, there are gaps and uncertainties in the data that have to be filled and clarified by further judgement. Economic assessment can also use ostensibly 'objective' data, despite debate about how well economic indicators measure quality of life. However, for the non-economic aspects of quality of life, the question of 'evidence' is elusive: measuring issues such as contentment, security and quality of social life is notoriously difficult. So, sustainability assessment would be trying to compare apples and oranges, which might be better analysed separately.

Third, sustainability assessment increases the risk that, beneath the comforting rhetoric of integration and 'joining up', environmental concerns continue to be marginalized because economic interests continue to have the institutional power. Box 5.4 shows an example of this. The Royal Commission on Environmental Pollution (2002) also voiced concern that:

> *sustainability appraisal can in fact marginalise the very environmental and social appraisals that it is supposed to bolster as a counterpoint to dominant financial and economic assessments… [Where] the driver or imperative for a policy, plan or programme is an economic one, as it often is, appraising the effects of the policy, plan or programme in terms of economic criteria and subsequently justifying it on that basis renders the appraisal meaningless.*

By keeping environmental arguments separate, a clear environmental case can be made and environmental constraints clearly stated, so it will at least be clear if they are set aside.

If a wider approach is taken to the SEA, there is still a range of approaches to integrating (or not) environmental, social and economic issues. In its least integrated form, SEA can be expanded to also cover some social and economic issues; the SEA aims to minimize adverse impacts on all issues, and trade-offs between these issues can take place.

Box 5.4 Social, environmental and economic impacts of plans subject to 'sustainability appraisal'

The findings of 45 UK sustainability appraisals incorporating SEA (SA/SEA) of 'core strategies' were analysed, to determine the kinds of impacts that the strategies were expected to have. Core strategies are the main UK local-level spatial planning document, with a broad remit to promote sustainable development, and they are subject to SA/SEA throughout the plan-making process. As such, one would expect them to promote social, economic and environmental sustainability.

Predicted impacts of core strategies: Finding of analysis of 45 SA/SEA reports

Broadly social	Accessibility	1.27
	Crime	0.59
	Equity, inclusion	1.16
	Health	1.04
	Housing	1.23
	Average	**1.06**
Broadly environmental	Air	-0.21
	Biodiversity	0.26
	Climate change, energy	0.09
	Landscape, historical	0.67
	Resources	0.20
	Water	-0.04
	Waste	-0.34
	Average	**0.09**
Broadly economic	Economic growth, investment	1.18
	Employment	1.17
	Skills	0.68
	Average	**1.01**
	Flooding	-0.30
	Land use	1.04

Key: +2 very positive impact, +1 positive impact, 0 neutral or no impact, -1 negative impact, -1 very negative impact

The analysis of the findings of the SA/SEA processes, shown above, suggest that core strategies overall have significant social and economic benefits, but between mildly positive and mildly negative impacts on the environment. If anything, the SA/SEAs seemed to understate some of the core strategies' negative environmental impacts. This suggests that SAs are not helping to ensure that plans are environmentally sustainable.

Local authority planners were also sent a questionnaire, which asked whether they felt that the planning and SA/SEA processes favour the environment, economy or social factors. Of 14 respondents, five felt that the plan-making process favours the economy, four that it favours social and economic dimensions, and four that it is balanced. Eight respondents felt that the SA/SEA process is balanced and six that it favours the environment. The respondents overwhelmingly felt that the SA/SEA process changes plan-making to be more balanced (see Figure 5.2).

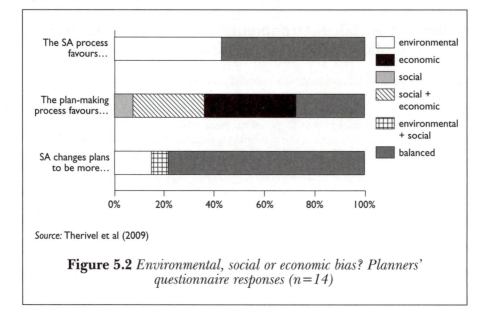

Source: Therivel et al (2009)

Figure 5.2 *Environmental, social or economic bias? Planners'*
questionnaire responses (n=14)

In the middle, SEA can cover a similarly wider remit, but trade-offs between social, economic and environmental parameters cannot be made; win–win–win solutions are expected; and mitigation beyond the normal scope of impact assessment practice (e.g. offsets) may be required. The most integrated forms of assessment consider sustainability as an integrated concept, and planning decisions are made based on clear cross-cutting approaches and rules that do not treat the three parameters as 'warring houses' (Pope et al, 2004; Morrison-Saunders and Therivel, 2006). Table 5.4 summarizes advantages and disadvantages of integrating environmental, social and economic issues in one SEA.

Cross-cutting approaches

Some approaches to development – for instance, increasing accessibility, providing for local needs locally, and redressing social inequalities – are genuinely better environmentally, socially *and* economically. The Local Government Management Board's (1994) sustainability themes, shown in Box 5.5, are an example of where all three are integrated. These themes have been used as a framework for many English SEAs.

A key cross-cutting component of sustainability is *equity*, both intra-generational (between groups of people who are currently alive) and inter-generational (between today's generations and future ones). The concept of equity brings together environmental (future generations enjoying the same environmental benefits as current ones) and

Table 5.4 *Arguments for and against integration in SEA*

Arguments in favour of integration	Arguments against integration
Improves coherence and efficiency; reduces duplication of reports.	Given that time and resources are limited for any assessment, there will necessarily be a loss of depth in consideration of the environment if social and economic objectives and criteria are considered simultaneously.
Separating social, economic and environmental issues into assessment ghettoes can make it harder to integrate environmental issues in decision-making, as they come to be seen as a special interest subject, which constrains other aspirations. Environmental, social and economic 'pillars' become 'warring houses'.	
	Removes questions of an essentially political nature from the realm of democratically accountable decision-making and presents them as reconcilable by technical and rational methodologies or procedures.
Helps to identify win–win–win solutions that integrate all three.	
Allows better identification and documentation of indirect and synergistic effects that result from linkages between environmental, social and economic impacts, which otherwise might be overlooked in separate, more specialized assessments.	Increases the risk that environmental concerns continue to be marginalized under a rhetoric of 'sustainability'; keeping environmental arguments separate allows a clear environmental case to be made and environmental constraints to be clearly stated.
	Carrying out the assessment in aggregate allows trade-offs between individual aspects or components to be hidden. A deterioration in quality of life for some social groups may not become apparent, and potentially unsustainable environmental effects may go undetected.

Source: Based on Morrison-Saunders and Therivel (2006)

economic (improved access and skills, reduced dependence, etc.) as well as social issues. An underlying objective of any strategic action should be to help redress – or at least not exacerbate – any existing imbalances in equity. SEA should thus ask who would win and lose under the strategic action, focusing on those groups who might be particularly disadvantaged.

Another cross-cutting aspect of sustainability is *resilience*, or lack of vulnerability. A strategic action should be able to withstand and counter problems such as changes in climate, petrol prices, subsidies and currency exchange rates; and disease, war and terrorism. Resilience is one way to operationalize long-term thinking and the precautionary principle. For instance, approaches to food and farming that enhance resilience are those that reduce:

Box 5.5 Local Government Management Board sustainability themes

1   Resources are used efficiently and waste is minimized by closing cycles.
2   Pollution is limited to levels that natural systems can cope with and without damage.
3   The diversity of nature is valued and protected.
4   Where possible, local needs are met locally.
5   Everyone has access to good food, water, shelter and fuel at reasonable cost.
6   Everyone has the opportunity to undertake satisfying work in a diverse economy.
7   The value of unpaid work is recognized, while payments for work are fair and fairly distributed.
8   Peoples' good health is protected by creating safe, clean and pleasant environments and health services that emphasize prevention of illness as well as proper care for the sick.
9   Access to facilities, services, goods and other people is not achieved at the expense of the environment or limited to those with cars.
10 People live without fear of personal violence from crime or persecution because of their personal beliefs, race, gender or sexuality.
11 Everyone has access to the skills, knowledge and information needed to enable them to play a full part in society.
12 All sections of the community are empowered to participate in decision-making. Opportunities for culture, leisure and recreation are readily available to all.
13 Places, spaces and objects combine meaning and beauty with utility. Settlements are 'human' in scale and form. Diversity and local distinctiveness are valued and protected.

Source: Local Government Management Board (LGMB) (1994)

- the need to travel – and thus dependence on petrol and the rapid spread of diseases – through more farmers' markets, shorter supply chains, fewer animal movements and more local abattoirs;
- the likelihood of, and vulnerability to, flood and droughts by paying farmers for flood control and carbon banks ('trees'), and the managed retreat of coastlines;
- the likelihood of disease through better food standards, less reliance on animal drugs and supplements (leading, over time, to increased resilience in animal stocks), greater variety of crops, better maintenance of the soil resource, and decreased application of herbicides, pesticides and fertilizers;
- the risk of farmers facing economic failure by promoting a wider variety of income streams for them so that any effects on one commodity are buffered by its relatively small market share, reducing subsidies, use of the same amount of subsidies for a wider

---

Box 5.6 Integrated sustainability decision criteria

1   socio-ecological integrity – recognition of life support functions on which human and ecological well-being depends;
2   livelihood sufficiency and opportunity – ensuring a decent life for all people without compromising the same possibilities for future generations;
3   intra-generational equity – ensuring equity of sufficiency and opportunity for all people;
4   intergenerational equity – favouring options most likely to preserve or enhance opportunities for future generations to live sustainably;
5   resource maintenance and efficiency – reducing extractive damage, avoid waste and reduce overall material and energy use per unit of benefit;
6   socio-ecological and democratic governance – delivering sustainability requirements through open and better informed deliberations, reciprocal awareness, collective responsibility and other decision-making practices;
7   precaution and adaptation – respect for uncertainty, avoidance of poorly understood adverse risks, planning to learn, designing for surprise and managing for adaptation; and
8   immediate and long term integration – applying all principles of sustainability at once, seeking mutually supportive benefits and multiple gains.

Source: Gibson (2005)

---

range of schemes, promoting value added close to source (e.g. processing and packaging of crops), and greater genetic diversity; and

• the likelihood of political instability by promoting fair trade and reducing inequitable subsidy schemes and reliance on (and thus conflict over) non-renewable resources (SDC, 2001).

Gibson (2005) has brought together many of these concepts into a set of sustainability decision criteria, which aims to avoid compartmentalizing sustainability into separate economic, social and environmental parameters, and set a framework for testing progress towards sustainability. It is shown at Box 5.6.

Objectives-led or baseline-led approach?

Approaches to SEA impact prediction – and to the type of context-setting information needed to support the predictions – can be broadly classified into baseline-led and objectives-led. Baseline-led (also called impact-led) approaches seek to predict changes in the current state of the environment/sustainability due to the implementation of a strategic action. They are similar to project EIA techniques in that they build up a story:

- What is the current state of the environment?
- What is likely to be the future state of the environment without the strategic action?
- How might the future state of the environment be affected by the strategic action?
- How can any adverse impacts of the strategic action – the difference between the future state of the environment with and without the strategic action – be minimized?
- What are the residual, post-mitigation impacts?

Objectives-led assessment, instead, identifies a framework of aspirational environmental/sustainability objectives, and tests whether the strategic action will help to achieve these objectives. At the assessment stage, the SEA objectives (those in Box 5.5 are an example) will typically be placed on one axis of a matrix, the components of the strategic action on the other, and the cells are filled in to show, in each case, whether the strategic action component supports or does not support the SEA objective. As such, objectives-led assessment typically takes the form of quite lengthy assessment tables.

Fothergill (2008) has illustrated the different outcomes of the two approaches:

- Objectives-led: 'Option H1 is likely to generate minor negative effects potentially detracting from the achievement of SEA Objective 1 (conserve and enhance biodiversity).'
- Baseline-led: 'Option H1 will lead to new development in the east of town, which is likely to reduce connectivity between six locally important wildlife sites. This has the potential to affect the viability of a population of water voles (a Biodiversity Action Plan species) that are present across these sites.'

Objectives-led assessment has been most commonly applied to English and Welsh spatial plans, for which 'SA' is required. As such, to date, most objectives-led SEAs have also been wider sustainability assessments. However an objectives-led assessment can be limited to environmental issues, and a sustainability assessment can be baseline-led.

Both approaches have strengths and weaknesses. The baseline-led approach assumes that the physical development of an area is directly shaped by the implementation of a strategic action, and so tends to be more spatially specific, detailed and quantitative than the objectives-led approach. It can provide a good vehicle for bringing together other forms of predictions, for instance, transport models or population predictions. It can assess cumulative impacts on the receiving environment. On the other hand, it is likely to be less precise about non-spatial impacts, including most social and economic impacts. It also does not account for the fact that most strategic actions do not have direct, tangible outcomes but rather act as principles and norms for guiding future development, and thus may have only very indirect, long-term impacts, often acting jointly with other strategic actions. It does not account the inherently political nature of decision-making (Jackson and Illsley, 2007).

The objectives-led approach suggests that SEA should not only minimize negative impacts but also promote positive impacts (Pope et al, 2004). It can be used in situations where there are very few baseline data, and for high-level policies that may only have an impact indirectly, through the implemention of plans and programmes. It can also more easily cover social and economic as well as environmental issues. However, it has been criticized for leading to broad-brush, qualitative, non-replicable predictions. It is based on the assessment authors' interpretation of sustainability, which may be 'light green' in the extreme: taken together, the aspirations expressed through a set of SEA objectives may not constitute what most of us think of as 'sustainable development'. Generally, it makes limited or no reference to baseline data. Scoping consultation often focuses on fine-tuning the SEA framework rather than on substantive environmental issues, and SEA reports focus on whether the plan includes the right aspirational statements rather than on its actual environmental/sustainability effects. It tends to result in long, complex matrices from which it is difficult to draw key findings, and which may create a spurious impression of scientific rigour (Jackson and Illsley, 2007; Fothergill, 2008; CLG, 2009b).

Jackson and Illsley (2007) critique both approaches:

> *Under the baseline-led model, the assessor assumes the mantle of a technical expert lacking a toolkit capable of delivering authoritative guidance to decision-makers. Applying the objectives-led model, the assessor serves as the local agent in a system designed to provide an official rationalisation of the meaning of sustainability. This eliminates any need to question whether the value frame chosen for this purpose is appropriate and helps exclude rival processes of knowledge formulation. Greater transparency about the ambiguous, constructed nature of the decision criteria involved in these expert-driven methodologies would do much to enhance the integrity of SEA practice.*

George (2001) suggests that SEA should not ask 'Is the strategic action contributing to sustainability?' but rather 'Is the strategic action sustainable?', a rather more challenging question. This approach would lead to the use of quite different SEA objectives.

The 'baseline-led' approach tries to solve today's problems; the 'objectives-led' approach tries to achieve tomorrow's vision. The two methods can thus be seen as complementary rather than conflicting.

However, 'baseline-led' approaches must acknowledge that the choice of what to measure is not a neutral, technical issue, but one that implies or presupposes judgements about what matters; and 'objectives-led' approaches must be careful to go beyond a mere test of internal compatibility. A careful choice will need to be made early in the SEA process about what emphasis and techniques will be used. I prefer the 'baseline-led' approach because it better identifies a strategic action's impacts, more clearly relates these to the baseline and does not involve filling in huge assessment matrices.

Task-based versus topic-based reports

Two broad approaches can also be taken to documenting the SEA findings. The 'task-based approach' considers and presents each SEA stage separately, covering all environmental/sustainability components at each task. The 'topic-based approach', instead, uses the environmental/sustainability components as a basis, and carries out each task for each component. Box 5.7 shows a typical SEA table of content for each approach.

The 'task-based approach' allows for better integration of sustainability components and consideration of cross-cutting issues. It lends itself better to objectives-led, policy appraisal type SEA approaches. It may also facilitate a progression from the context-setting to the assessment stage, by allowing 'closure' of some report chapters early in the process. Most of the SEA reports that I reviewed when writing this edition seem to take a task-based approach.

The 'topic-based approach' allows baseline data to be more clearly linked to the impact assessment stage, and then to proposals for impact avoidance and mitigation. It seems to lend itself better to quantitative, detailed, baseline-led assessment approaches, and to tests of environmental limits. Environmental authorities tend to prefer it because it allows them to focus only on chapters related to their expertise. On the other hand, it tends to place impacts and issues into silos, and may make integrated, win–win mitigation measures harder to identify and agree.

Clearly, both approaches can include variants, and the precise approach chosen will depend on what information needs to be presented to whom. However, early agreement on which approach will be taken will help to save time and frustration later on in the SEA process.

Box 5.7 Task-based v. topic-based approach: Typical SEA tables of contents

(Grey shading denotes information typically collected at the context-setting/scoping stage.)

Task-based approach: Adapted from the SEA for the national sugar adaptation strategy for Trinidad & Tobago (European Commission, 2009a)

1. Executive summary
2. Scope
3. Background (justification for the strategy, planned alternatives)
4. Environmental and sectoral policy, legislative and planning framework
5. Approach and methodology
6. Environmental baseline (to 1975, since 1975, existing problems)
7. Analysis of planned alternatives, impacts and micro-level mitigation
8. Mitigation or optimizing measures
9. Institutional capacities and recommended indicators
10. Conclusions and mitigation

Ch. 6 and 7 structured as:
- water resources
- soil quality
- air quality
- biodiversity
- human health
- cultural heritage
- landscape
- social inclusiveness
- economic access
- material assets and infrastructure

Topic-based approach: Adapted from the SEA for the designation of energy corridors on federal lands (USDoE and USDoI, 2008)

Summary
1. Why are federal agencies proposing to designate energy corridors in the west?
2. What are the alternatives evaluated in this [SEA]?
3. What are the potential environmental consequences of corridor designation and land-use plan amendment?
     3.1 Introduction
     3.2 Land use
     3.3 Geological resources
     3.4 Paleontological resources
     3.5 Water resources
     3.6 Air quality
     3.7 Noise
     3.8 Ecological resources
     3.9 Visual resources
     3.10 Cultural resources
     3.11 Tribally sensitive resources
     3.12 Socioeconomic conditions
     3.13 Environmental justice
     3.14 Health and safety
4. Cumulative, unavoidable, short-term, long-term, etc. impacts of the plan
5. List of preparers
6. References and glossary

Sections 3.2 – 3.14 structured as:
- What are the current resources in the 11 western states?
- How were the potential impacts of the plan evaluated?
- What are the potential impacts associated with the plan?
- What types of impacts could result with project development, and how could these impacts be minimized, avoided or compensated?

Conclusions

Several decisions need to be made before any SEA can begin:

- What is the strategic action about?
- Does it require an SEA?
- If so, at what stages of the decision-making process should which aspects of SEA be carried out?
- Who should be involved in the SEA, when and in what capacity?
- Do other assessment processes apply to the strategic action? If so, what is the best way to deal with any overlaps between the assessment systems?
- Should the SEA focus on the environment or broaden out to cover the full range of sustainability issues? Should it be baseline-led or objectives-led? Should the reports be topic-based or task-based?

Once these decisions have been made, the real work can start: describing the baseline, identifying problems, and analysing links to other strategic actions. These are discussed in Chapter 6.

Note

1   The Planning Act requires an 'appraisal of sustainability' for national policy statements but does not specify what this should cover. In practice, government departments and their consultants have assumed that an 'appraisal of sustainability' must be SEA Directive compliant.

Describing the Environmental Baseline, Identifying Problems, Links to Other Strategic Actions

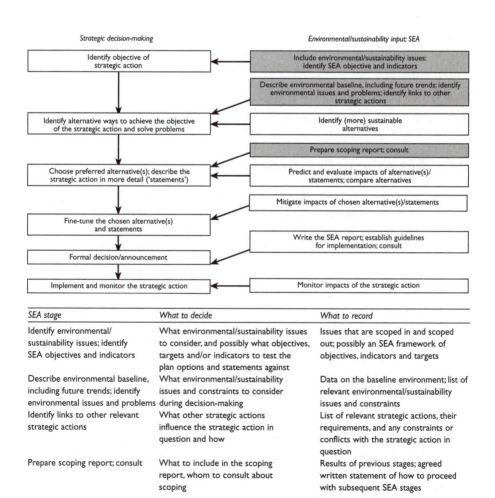

Strategic decision-making / *Environmental/sustainability input: SEA*

SEA stage	What to decide	What to record
Identify environmental/ sustainability issues; identify SEA objectives and indicators	What environmental/sustainability issues to consider, and possibly what objectives, targets and/or indicators to test the plan options and statements against	Issues that are scoped in and scoped out; possibly an SEA framework of objectives, indicators and targets
Describe environmental baseline, including future trends; identify environmental issues and problems	What environmental/sustainability issues and constraints to consider during decision-making	Data on the baseline environment; list of relevant environmental/sustainability issues and constraints
Identify links to other relevant strategic actions	What other strategic actions influence the strategic action in question and how	List of relevant strategic actions, their requirements, and any constraints or conflicts with the strategic action in question
Prepare scoping report; consult	What to include in the scoping report, whom to consult about scoping	Results of previous stages; agreed written statement of how to proceed with subsequent SEA stages

The aims of the context/scoping phase of SEA are to identify and document:

A   the policy context which affects what the strategic action must, should and cannot do;
B   the current environmental/sustainability baseline;
C   the likely future baseline without the strategic action. This sets the basis for the subsequent stages of SEA: impact prediction, evaluation and monitoring;
D   existing environmental/sustainability problems, so that the emerging strategic action does not make the problems worse, and ideally helps to rectify them; and
E   the scope of the SEA: key likely impacts of the strategic action, issues that don't need further analysis (they are 'scoped out'), who needs to be consulted and how, and possibly reasonable alternatives to the strategic action.

The context-setting stage also allows environmental/sustainability authorities and possibly the public to participate in the SEA and plan-making processes at an early stage. This chapter discusses how to carry out these early, context-setting SEA stages. SEA frameworks associated with objectives-led SEAs are discussed near the end of the chapter. Until then, this chapter applies to both baseline-led and objectives-led SEAs.

Describing the policy context

The policy context discusses the strategic action's links with other plans, policies and environmental/sustainability objectives. Chapter 5 already noted that the SEA should mention why the strategic action is being prepared. The policy context description should also discuss:

- other 'higher-tier' policies and plans that influence the strategic action; for instance, requirements for a plan to provide for a certain number of homes, or for a waste management strategy to meet international standards. This could include policies and plans that have not yet been finalized but are in the pipeline.
- 'lower-tier' plans and projects that are influenced by the strategic action, in particular projects that are likely to arise as a result of implementing the strategic action.
- environmental/sustainability objectives that affect the strategic action. From these, the SEA should identify any relevant legal standards (e.g. for air quality or noise), targets (e.g. for reduction in greenhouse gas emissions) and more aspirational objectives (e.g. on improvements in biodiversity). Some of these may overlap with the first bullet point.

Policy context information is important for several reasons. First, environmental/sustainability objectives can set targets or thresholds for the SEA. For instance, national or international air quality standards can act as environmental tests for the strategic action in question.

Second, the other strategic action may limit what the strategic action in question can achieve, and hence its sustainability. For instance, the UK's approach to farming and food production is strongly limited by the Common Agricultural Policy, which (in the past at least) has promoted food production to the detriment of more integrated land management. Similarly, World Trade Organization rules, which do not allow countries to discriminate against imports on the basis of the process and production methods used (e.g. organic, high animal welfare), financially disadvantage and thus discourage those food producers who aim to achieve higher environmental or animal welfare standards. Alternatively, the other strategic action may support the strategic action in question. For instance, policies that require local authorities or the military to procure locally grown food for schoolchildren, nursing home residents or soldiers, would support national government policies on reducing the need to travel and promoting locally produced foods.

Third, the strategic action in question can promote the sustainability of other strategic actions, or conversely close off sustainable options for those strategic actions. A farming policy that focuses on large-scale production and retailing will lead to pressures for the development of large supermarkets on sites outside town centres, and large distribution depots that rely heavily on an efficient system of road distribution. Historically, these developments have made smaller local stores economically unviable, leading to their closure and people having to travel further to buy their food. These cumulative trends put pressures on the road network and support calls for the construction of new (unsustainable) roads. In this example, a strategic action about farming influences retail and transport policy.

The SEA can also help to explain what the strategic action's remit is, and in particular what it cannot do. This information is familiar to plan-makers but is often not apparent to the environmental/ sustainability authorities or the public. For instance, it might be worthwhile explaining (where appropriate) if a plan cannot influence the actions of bus operators, or impose a congestion charge, or force owners of existing homes to install insulation. This could reduce the amount of well-meaning consultation comments that cannot be incorporated into the strategic action because they would go beyond its remit. Box 6.1 provides an example of how different aspects of the policy context can be described.

The findings of the policy context could be presented as a form of story: 'The strategy must... It may not... It should try to achieve...', for instance:

Box 6.1 Example of policy context description: Annotated (in italics) excerpts from the UK Offshore Energy SEA (DECC, 2009)

[The aim of the offshore wind energy component of the strategy is] 'to enable further rounds of offshore wind farm leasing in the UK Renewable Energy Zone and the territorial waters of England and Wales with the objective of achieving some 25GW of additional generation capacity by 2020. The Energy Act 2004 makes provision for the designation of a Renewable Energy Zone outside territorial waters over which the United Kingdom may exercise rights for wind, wave and tidal energy production.' *This is a higher-tier policy which directly affects the strategic action.*

'The Climate Change Act 2008 places a duty on the Secretary of State to ensure that the net UK carbon account for the year 2050 is at least 80% lower than the 1990 baseline.' *Another higher-tier policy with a direct effect – but also an environmental objective.*

'In December 2008 the European Parliament and Council of Ministers reached political agreement on legislation to require that by 2020, 20% of the EU's energy consumption must come from renewable sources. The UK's contribution to this will require the share of renewables in the UK's energy consumption to increase from around 1.5% in 2006 to 15% in 2020. In 2008 the Government consulted on a UK Renewable Energy Strategy, which is due to be published in Spring 2009.' *Discusses forthcoming as well as already-agreed policies.*

'The Crown Estate's permission, in the form of a site option Agreement and Lease, is required for the placement of structures or cables on the seabed. This includes offshore wind farms and their ancillary cables and other marine facilities. Potential offshore wind farm developers also require statutory consents from a number of Government departments before development can take place.' *Explains how projects that will derive from the strategic action will be controlled through other policies.*

Source: DECC (2009)

The plan must:

- *provide for 20,000 new homes over five years under the National Housing Strategy;*
- *provide adequate infrastructure for these homes under the National Housing Strategy; and*
- *protect special areas designated for habitats and birds under international Legislation X and Y.*

The plan should also aim to:

- *improve biodiversity;*
- *reduce the need to travel;*
- *increase housing densities;*
- *site housing on previously developed land where possible.*

Dealing with conflicting strategic actions

What happens if two strategic actions conflict? Examples of such conflict include:

- two conflicting higher-level strategic actions, for instance, one that requires the provision of homes in an area prone to flooding and another that requires flood risk in the area to be reduced;
- a higher-level strategic action constraining the ability of lower-level strategic actions to be sustainable, for instance, national-level strategies on the provision of new housing or airports imposing development on local authorities that make their sustainability targets on land use or air quality impossible to achieve;
- strategic actions at one level being prepared before other plans at the *same* level thus constraining the subsequent strategic actions;
- overlapping strategic actions that partly duplicate each other, for instance, separate plans for flood control, water abstraction and conservation of wetland habitats in the same river catchment, all with slightly different approaches to management of the river; and
- lower-level strategic actions needing, for practical purposes, to be prepared before higher-level ones, thus constraining the higher-level strategic actions, for instance, urgent flood defence works that need to be carried out before an integrated, larger-scale flood management plan can be devised.

The timing of strategic actions – which precedes the other – is often a problem, particularly where neither strategic action has clear precedence. Indeed, an absence of clear hierarchy could lead to an unintended paralysis and inability to change. For instance, assume that a region's economic strategy and its spatial strategy are at the same level. Assume that the economic strategy is written first and includes an unsustainable objective, say increasing GDP by 2 per cent per year. The spatial strategy has to accept this because the economic strategy was written first. The spatial strategy gets adopted complete with the unwanted objective and associated implementation measures. When the time comes to review the economic strategy, even if the economic strategy wanted to abandon the unsustainable objective, it would not be able to do so because it is now in the spatial strategy that has now 'got there first'.

In cases of conflicting strategic actions, the general assumption is that higher-level strategic actions 'win' over lower-level ones, but this is not always the case. For instance, the higher-level strategic action could be due for replacement, clearly unsustainable, or not have been subject to SEA. In such cases, the higher-level (or earlier) strategic actions could be treated not as constraints but as options or scenarios, and queried as being unsustainable. For instance, in the example above, the evolving spatial strategy could treat potentially unsustainable targets set by the economic strategy as one of several possible scenarios.

All of these are not strictly SEA issues, but rather problems already present in decision-making processes that SEA makes more visible and urgent. There are several possible ways forward. Organizations can aim to rationalize their decision-making processes to try to minimize these problems. Governments could clarify, in cases of uncertainty, which plan has precedence. SEA may help ease some of the problems by encouraging the convergence of strategic actions onto common sustainability objectives. Rather less ideally, a lower-level strategic action can simply perpetuate higher-level conflicts. This has been the case, for instance, with UK regional spatial strategies: when interviewed about the sustainability of their strategy, a typical planner's response was:

> *There are conflicting national objectives, and those conflicting objectives and targets are passed down to the regions. Although there is a general understanding that there is sometimes a conflict in objectives, these are not overtly expressed in our [strategy], and the [strategy] does not really try to reconcile them. Officers working on their policy areas – say, housing, transport etc. – seek to ensure that their policies meet the requirements given to them even though these may compromise other objectives such as reduced CO_2 emissions... The [plan-making authority] is not good at making hard decisions and tends not to tell Government (which funds the [plan-making authorities]) that it can only achieve an objective (say CO_2 reductions) if it does not achieve others, such as meeting housing demand or supporting airport expansion.* (CPRE et al, 2007)

In these cases, the best that an SEA can do is to document, not resolve, the conflicts.

Describing the current environmental/sustainability baseline

The environmental/sustainability baseline is the current status of the environment or sustainability, plus its likely future status in the absence of the strategic action. Information about the environmental/sustainability baseline helps to identify existing problems that the strategic action should try to solve; sets a context for the impact prediction and evaluation stage; and provides a basis against which the strategic action's impacts can later be monitored. The next section discusses the future baseline; this section discusses the current baseline.

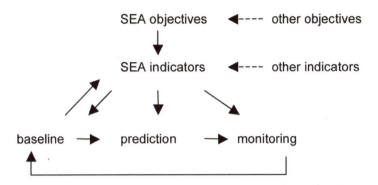

Figure 6.1 *Links between indicators and other aspects of SEA*

SEAs cannot describe the baseline environment in as much detail as project environmental impact assessments (EIAs). Even if it was physically possible to do so, they would include such a welter of detail that the information would become essentially meaningless. Instead, SEAs typically use overarching themes or objectives to represent larger clusters of environmental data, and more detailed indicators to act as representative examples of such data for monitoring purposes. *Themes* are broad categories of impacts, for instance, air pollution or human health. *Objectives* specify a desired direction for change, for instance, 'reduce air pollution' or 'improve human health'. *Indicators* are measures of variables over time, for instance, NO_x levels at specified monitoring stations or traffic accidents in a given region. In SEA, indicators are normally used to describe and monitor the baseline environment (Figure 6.1), and indicators or objectives are used to predict impacts.

The choice of themes/objectives and indicators may be explicit or implicit in an SEA. Table 6.1 shows an example of explicitly listed set of SEA themes, plus indicators at two spatial scales.

Once the SEA themes/objectives and indicators have been agreed, data on the baseline environment is collected using the indicators as a framework. Data sources on the baseline environment include websites and reports from governments at all levels (international to local), universities, non-government organizations, etc.; old maps, which can show trends in land use; surveys of local residents; and information known by experts but not formally recorded. In many cases, data about the baseline environment will be 'hard' quantitative data based on monitoring information. In other cases, it will be 'soft' qualitative and/or perceived data.

The baseline description in SEA can take various forms, including text, maps and matrices/tables. Boxes 6.2 and 6.3 show excerpts from a text-based SEA baseline analyses: a detailed description of a biophysical component (butterfly life cycle) and a more broad-brush description of

Table 6.1 *Example of SEA themes and national and regional/local indicators: SEA for Colombian biofuel production*

Theme	National-level indicator	Regional/local level indicator
Ecology	• All aquatic and terrestrial ecosystems • Arid areas • National and regional-level designated areas • Areas over 3000m altitude (other than those otherwise prioritized) • Ecosystems with moderate levels of intervention (woods and shrublands)	• All aquatic and terrestrial ecosystems • Arid areas • National-, regional- and local-level designated areas • Areas over 3000m altitude (other than those otherwise prioritized) • Analysis of the ecological integrity of ecosystems • Areas needed to restore the ecological connectivity of remnant habitats
Water	• Buffer riparian zones of major water bodies • Areas of infiltration and recharge of groundwater (hydro-geological parameters and use)	• Buffer riparian zones of all components of the water system (rivers, streams, lakes, etc.) • Water supply areas • Areas of infiltration and recharge of groundwater (hydro-geological parameters and use)
Natural hazards	• Key areas for the management of natural hazards (landslides, hydro-climatic conditions for landslides and other forms of geological susceptibility, slopes of more than 45°, floods)	• Key areas for the management of natural hazards (landslides, hydro-climatic conditions for landslides and other forms of geological susceptibility, slopes of more than 45°, floods)
Cultural	• Indigenous reserves • Territories of Afro-Colombian communities and all others identified at national level	• Areas of importance to archaeology, history, education, tourism and landscape at the national, regional and local level
Food security	• Agro-biodiversity hot-spots	• Agro-biodiversity hot-spots and other relevant areas

Source: Lozano et al (2008)

a social component (poverty) including information about causes of existing problems.

Figure 6.2 shows an example of a constraints overlay map. This includes, on one map, a range of different types of constraints: nature conservation, historical, landscape and so on. Such a map allows areas to be identified where there are few constraints and where development may be less of a problem; and conversely areas of greater constraint where development would be more problematic.

Box 6.2 Part of a baseline analysis: SEA for the Californian light brown apple moth eradication programme

This is a good example of baseline data that provides information necessary for a strategic decision. The proposed strategic action involves eradicating an invasive species of moth that has the potential to severely affect California's fruit industry, using a combination of sterile insects, mating disruption pheromone and other techniques. The baseline description not only provides information about the rarity and range of a butterfly species that could be affected by the moth eradication programme, but also about its past population trends, factors that could indirectly affect the butterfly (the kinds of plants on which the larvae feed), and sensitive times in the butterfly's life cycle that could be affected by the eradication techniques.

The bay checkerspot butterfly is federally listed as threatened (Federal Register, 1987). Critical habitat has been designated and revised for this species (Federal Register, 2001, 2008a). The historical range of this butterfly extended from San Francisco and Contro Costa counties south to Santa Clara County. Its distribution may have been more extensive prior to the introduction of non-native grasses and other weeds in the 1700s. The current range of this species is limited to Santa Clara and San Mateo counties (USFWS, 1998). This species is found in areas with shallow, serpentine-derived or similar soils that support both the larval food plants for this species, as well as nectar-producing plants for adults. Habitats for the larval host plants include grassland, coastal sage scrub, foothill woodlands, and chaparral, below 2500 to 3000 feet in elevation.

This butterfly utilizes more than one larval host plant species. Adults emerge from pupae and breed in spring, typically in a 4- to 6-week period from late February to early May. Adults generally live only for about 10 days. Following mid-spring mating, the female butterflies lay their eggs on a native plantain (Plantago erecta). The eggs hatch and the larvae feed on this host until either they have developed to a point at which they may enter dormancy, or the host has begun to dry up from the summer heat... All known populations of the bay checkerspot butterfly occur in the immediate Program Area.

Source: California Department of Food and Agriculture (2009)

Table 6.2 is an example of a baseline data matrix, which shows the current environmental state, comparative data from other authorities, any targets that exist for that topic, and trends in the data. This allows much data to be presented in a very condensed format and clearly identifies data gaps that may need monitoring in the future. It can also be used to identify existing problems: How does the current situation in the relevant local authority compare to other similar authorities? Are things getting better or worse over time? Are environmental or sustainability targets being met?

Box 6.3 Part of a baseline analysis including discussion of causal factors: SEA for a tourism strategy for Guizhou (China)

This baseline describes the socio-economic situation in a Chinese province for which a tourism strategy was being developed. It helpfully describes not only existing problems, but also the reason for some of these problems. This allows the strategic action to focus on causes rather than symptoms.

The 29 million poor people registered in China in 2005 were concentrated in rural areas in western provinces... It is estimated that... 6.9% of the total poor in China live in Guizhou. In general, poverty is higher in the rural and mountainous areas where 74% of the population live. Limited access, lack of social infrastructure, and a poorly developed agricultural-based sector all contribute to poverty in rural areas. The Government is making a sustained effort to reduce poverty...

There are two features that explain the disparity between urban and rural areas in Guizhou. The first one is the unequal pattern of income and employment distribution and the second one is the decline in the traditional agriheritage-based system. In 2003, the annual disposable income of the rural population was only 24% that of urban residents. Government policy aims to promote growth in the secondary and tertiary sectors and provide employment opportunities in urban areas. During the Tenth Five Year Plan, Guizhou's secondary and tertiary sectors grew 11% and 10.6% respectively compared to 3.5% of the primary sector. A direct consequence is insufficient employment growth in rural areas needed to absorb the surplus labour force and to generate income levels to match those of urban residents. The consequence of this is the tendency for young and low middle-age people to migrate to urban areas in search of work.

Source: World Bank (2007)

Issues about SEA indicators and data

Clearly, the themes/objectives and indicators used in SEA will affect what baseline data are collected, what predictions are made, and what monitoring systems are used. Poorly chosen ones will lead to a biased or limited SEA process: for instance (to take an obvious example), an SEA for an energy policy that does not consider CO_2 emissions would lead to very different conclusions about the acceptability of certain forms of power generation than one that does. Below are some pointers about what SEA baseline indicators and data should and should not be used.

SEA indicators and data should *be of an appropriate scale*. In many situations, it makes no sense to use national-level data as an indicator for local-level trends or vice versa. Some issues may be more important at one scale than another: at the national level, for instance, noise is likely to be less important than greenhouse gas emissions. Table 6.1 provides a nice example of this. As such, any generic list of indicators must be checked and adapted to the strategic action in question: local

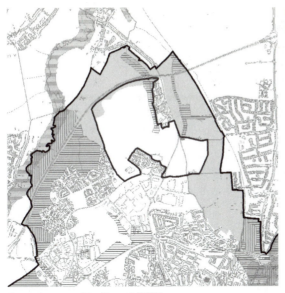

Ashton Green
City Boundary
Green Wedge
Floodplain
Site of Importance for Nature Conservation
Biodiversity Enhancement Site
Listed Building
Building of Local Interest

Source: Leicester City Council (2008)

Figure 6.2 *Example of constraints map: Sustainability appraisal for the Leicester core strategy*

objectives may need to be added to reflect local-level circumstances, objectives that are irrelevant to the area may be deleted; and more detailed objectives may be added.

For specific areas likely to be significantly affected by a strategic action – for instance, proposed sites for housing, new infrastructure or mineral extraction – more detailed and possibly different forms of baseline data may be needed. The SEA Directive, for instance, requires both a general description of 'the relevant aspects of the current state of the environment' and a discussion of 'the environmental characteristics of areas likely to be significantly affected' (Annex I). The SEA should 'zoom down' on these areas, and constraints overlay maps may be particularly appropriate for this.

João (2007) has suggested that the choice of scale of baseline data – both the spatial 'window' of assessment and the amount of detail/resolution provided – can affect not only the data needed for an SEA but also the subsequent SEA findings. Too much detailed data may swamp the assessor and not allow broader patterns to be identified (the wood gets lost for the trees), whereas too little detail could hinder effective assessment and mitigation. João suggests that 'data and/or scale abuse' could potentially take place, where the data or scales are chosen that lead to a preferred answer rather than the solving of the problem. She concludes that:

Table 6.2 *Part of a baseline data matrix: East Cambridgeshire District Council*

Objective	Indicator	Current situation East Cambs	Comparator	Trends East Cambs	Assessment	Source
Minimize the irreversible loss of undeveloped land and productive agricultural holdings	% dwellings completed on previously developed land	29.7% (2006/07)	Cambridgeshire 51% (2006/07)	36% (1999–2007)	Plan target is 30%. Current trend, apart from 2006/07, is favourable	County Council housing monitoring data
	Net density of dwellings completed on major sites	Average density 39.3 dwellings per hectare (2006/07)	Cambridgeshire 44.4 dph (2006/07)	33.7 dph (2001–2007)	Favourable trend, density increasing	County Council housing monitoring data
Reduce the use of non-renewable energy sources	KWh of gas consumed per household per year	18656 (2005)	East of England 18,854 (2005)	19,811 (2001) 20,140 (2003) 19,206 (2004)	Favourable trend, consumption is gradually reducing	Department of Trade and Industry energy statistics
	Generating potential of renewable energy sources	255.2 GWh/y (2005)	323.9 GWh/y (2005)	0 in 1999	Figures show the impact of the straw-burning plant at Sutton	Cambs environmental report 2005
Limit water consumption to levels supportable by natural processes and storage systems	Water use per household	No data available at present	No data available at present	No data available		A method of estimating water consumption at the county level is being investigated

Source: Adapted from East Cambridgeshire District Council (2008)

Issues (defined for example by SEA objectives) should normally come before data collection. This way it can be ensured that issues considered important ... are selected for further assessment (irrespective of the existence or not of data) while at the same time avoiding unnecessary data collection. That said, the selection of issues can be affected by iterative elements, such as data collected... The reality is that not all issues need to be dealt at the same time or with the same level of detail. Therefore, data collection could be incremental and spread through the SEA process. (João, 2007)

Where existing data are not at the right scale, it may be reasonable to make informed assumptions, for instance, about whether national trends may be assumed to hold locally. However, these assumptions should be clearly stated in the SEA, and it may be helpful to subsequently monitor them to make sure that they are accurate.

The amount of data available at different scales may vary considerably. For instance, in the UK, considerable environmental data are available at the national and county levels, less at the regional level (between national and county), and relatively little at the district and ward levels (under county). Different authorities may refer to slightly different boundaries: for instance, local authority boundaries may not be the same as the river catchment boundaries used for water management plans. Again, any inconsistencies should be clearly stated in the SEA report.

Data should be *up to date*. Although individual 'snapshots' of data are better than no data at all, several years' worth of consistently monitored data are much more valuable. Limited data can be particularly problematic where the baseline changes rapidly, for instance, in areas of rapid urban expansion. In such cases, field surveys or discussions with experts may be needed to check whether the data are worth including at all.

SEA objectives and indicators should *say what they mean*, and not be able to be manipulated. For instance, in a laudable attempt to improve the quality of health care in the 1990s, the UK government set targets for reducing the average waiting time for operations. This resulted, in addition to many genuine improvements, in some patients 'disappearing' from lists, and in others being made to wait longer before being referred to consultants, since the clock only started ticking once a patient had been referred. Other examples of potentially problematic data include:

- the use of gross domestic product (GDP) to represent people's quality of life. GDP does not account for factors such as social and environmental costs (e.g. accidents, pollution), longer-term environmental damage and depreciation of natural capital (e.g. reduction of fish stocks); inequalities in the distribution of income since the same amount of money is worth more to a poor person than to a rich one; or the value of household labour (Mayo et al, 1997);

- focusing on designated areas such as biodiversity reserves or national parks to represent the totality of a topic. For instance, the condition of areas designated for nature conservation may be very good, but biodiversity may be poor elsewhere or vice versa. That said, at a broad-brush national scale, designated areas might be a helpful indicator; and
- assuming that the existence of a management plan for an area means that the area is well managed.

A subset of this issue is whether the SEA should focus on *outcomes* (the state of the environment; what one is ultimately trying to achieve) or *inputs* (people's responses to pressures on the environment; how to achieve the intended outcomes). Examples of outcomes are good biodiversity status and good access to facilities. Related examples of inputs are protection of wildlife areas and improved provision of cycle trails. Most of the indicators of Table 6.1 are outcome indicators, while all of those of Table 6.2 are input indicators. SEA assessment findings can vary widely depending on whether input or outcome indicators are used, and analysts need to be aware of this.

Authorities generally find it easier to monitor what they do ('input') than final outcomes. They also like to show that they are making an effort to do environmentally beneficial things even if other countervailing factors mean that their effort may not fully achieve the intended outcome.

On the other hand, the only real way to analyse cumulative impacts on the environment is to consider the environmental outcome of multiple inputs. Furthermore, it is the outcomes, not the good intentions, that really matter from an environmental perspective. For instance, in the UK, the transport sector accounts for one quarter of CO_2 emissions. Over the last decade, local authorities have consistently established policies to try to reduce traffic-related air pollution, for instance, by establishing land-use policies on siting new housing near services and jobs, converting units over shops into housing, and promoting home-based working. Many local authorities have also converted their vehicle fleets to low-emission fuels to help reduce emissions. However, despite these very laudable actions, traffic levels in England increased by 14 per cent between 1997 and 2007, falling by only 1 per cent in 2008 as a result of the economic recession, and transport is the only sector in which CO_2 emissions are growing (Department for Transport, 2008).

Figure 6.3 gives an indication of why the link between strategic action inputs (in this case, money to fund more buses) and final environmental outcomes (improvements in air quality) is so tenuous.

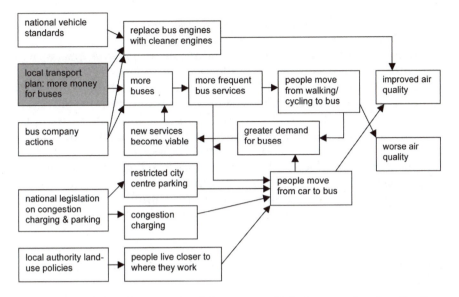

Figure 6.3 *Simple example of the tenuous links between local authority inputs and final environmental outcomes*

In this case, the actions of bus companies, national legislation, other local authority policies, individuals' behaviour and various feedback loops all affect whether an increase in bus numbers leads to better or worse air quality. Individuals' actions are particularly difficult to influence and manage centrally, with sticks typically being less politically acceptable but possibly more effective than carrots.

Ideally, the data for SEA should *already be available*. For the sake of consistency and efficiency, existing themes/objectives and indicators – those used for other strategic actions and other assessment systems – should be employed where possible, as long as they meet the other criteria. Existing monitoring systems and data should also be used to provide information for SEA where possible.

Where the correct data are not be available, it might be possible to make assumptions based on other data. For instance, people's longevity might be a reasonable substitute for the number of years of healthy life that they have; or average distance to open space may substitute for people's perceptions about adequacy of access to open space. However, this opens up the possibility of slowly sliding into a situation where inappropriate indicators are used. In other cases, it may be necessary to collect data specifically for the SEA, for instance, through field surveys or interviews. Particularly for strategic actions that are rewritten on a cyclical basis, it may be worthwhile establishing a monitoring system to collect missing data to inform the next round of SEA.

SEA themes/objectives and indicators should be *needed* and should not duplicate or overlap with others. Obviously they should, at minimum, reflect legal requirements. Data should also be *drawn together into an integrated whole*.

Finally, baseline data collection should be an *iterative process*, with the results of the baseline data collection helping to refine the SEA themes/objectives and indicators. In particular, any environmental problems identified during the baseline analysis may require more data to confirm whether they really are problems, establish the cause of the problems, and suggest measures to deal with the problems and causes. The first list of SEA themes/objectives/indicators should be treated as a draft and as part of a feedback cycle: as more baseline data are collected and problems identified, they should help to focus the objectives on issues of greatest concern, and, in turn, this should help to focus and restrict the collection of further baseline information.

Describing the future baseline without the strategic action

A strategic action's impacts are the difference between the future situation with and without the strategic action. As such, an SEA should predict the likely future as well as the current environment/ sustainability baseline – typically over the length of time that the strategic action is expected to remain operational. This will form the 'business as usual' option for the strategic action and provide the basis for assessing the strategic action's cumulative impacts.

Although some aspects of the current baseline environment may continue into the future, it is unlikely that all of them will. The climate will change, and with it the likelihood of droughts and floods. People may continue to live longer, or else obesity and heart disease may start to reverse the trend. The widespread use of catalytic converters in vehicles is improving air quality, and concerns about food shortages may lead to greater use of genetically modified crops, with yet unknown effects. Unfortunately, few data sources predict future trends, with population, road traffic and greenhouse gas statistics being some of the few exceptions. As such, this will typically need to be done based on an understanding of underlying trends, causes of these trends, and likely future technologies, strategic actions and projects.

Underlying trends include shifts in land use, changes in car use, improvement or deterioration of diffuse air quality, loss of biodiversity, depletion of fish stocks, changes in water levels in aquifers, and climate change. These can often be identified by reviewing past baseline monitoring data and extrapolating these into the future. They may also be identified through records of official plans and environmental assessments; insurance, tax and other records; old maps and photos; and discussions with long-term residents of the area.

Causes of negative environmental trends typically include increased population and household numbers, and greater per capita resource consumption linked to greater wealth. Causes of positive environmental trends include improvements in technology (e.g. renewable energy, electric vehicles); environmental/sustainability legislation, such as the European Water Framework Directive; fiscal mechanisms, such as congestion charging; economic factors such as the recession and changes in the cost of oil; and possibly behavioural change. The SEA needs to consider whether these causes are likely to continue in the future or not, and adapt the projection of underlying trends accordingly.

The SEA also needs to think about how existing and future *technologies, strategic actions and projects* will affect the baseline. Examples include land use and transport plans at the national, regional/provincial/state and local levels; various sectoral plans (e.g. minerals, waste); the high-speed rail construction programmes that several countries are currently embarking on; individual projects such as new regionally important shopping centres or employment areas; and, in London and Rio de Janeiro's case, the forthcoming Olympics.

The significance of likely future changes to the baseline should also be considered in the SEA. Will legal standards be exceeded in the future even if they are not currently? Will environmental limits be breached? How reversible is the change – for instance, will it lead to species extinction, the build-up of persistent pollutants, or loss of productive land? Box 6.4 is an example of a description of the future baseline without the project, which considers some of these questions.

Identifying environmental/sustainability problems

Identifying existing environmental/sustainability problems allows plan-makers to ensure that their emerging strategic action does not make the problems worse, and ideally helps to rectify them. They can also provide a basis for identifying alternatives to the strategic action: what are different ways of dealing with existing problems?

There is no one way of identifying environmental or sustainability problems. The best way is undoubtedly to use a process of triangulation, using a range of different approaches and sources to cross-check each other. One approach is to compare the current baseline data against any *standards or targets* identified as part of the policy context. Does existing air pollution exceed legal standards? Are internationally agreed targets for greenhouse gas emission reductions being met? These targets can be informal as well as formal. In the UK, for instance, the National Playing Fields Association's (now Fields in Trust) 'six acre standard' for provision of outdoor playing space – roughly 1.6 hectares of outdoor sports provision and 0.8 hectares of

Box 6.4 Example of future baseline without the strategic action: Excerpt from the SEA for the Scottish Strategic Transport Projects Review

The Strategic Transport Projects Review puts forward a portfolio of transport 'interventions' for 2012–22 that aims to deliver three strategic outcomes of the National Transport Strategy: improved journey times and connections, reduced emissions, and improved quality, accessibility and affordability. The interventions include a programme of rail electrification, road projects to improve journey time and reliability, and support for bus travel, focused on strategic transport corridors (see Figure 6.4). The SEA for the Strategic Transport Projects Review considered the likely future baseline to 2022. Below is an example, for NO_x.

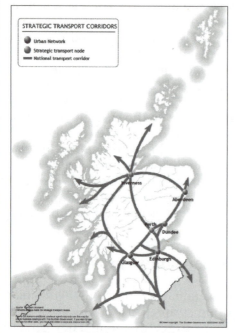

Figure 6.4 *Scottish strategic transport corridors*

'Information used to predict future air quality includes Local Authority applications for new AQMAs [Air Quality Management Areas]. This information has been obtained from the Scottish Government's Air Quality Archive. ENEVAL Scenario modelling has also been used to project NO_2 road related emissions for 2022. The ENEVAL modelling system has been based on data from the Transport Model for Scotland (TMfS) and the TMfS Highland Model.

'National road based nitrogen dioxide (NO_2) emissions are forecast to fall from around 30,000 tonnes in 2005, to around 16,500 tonnes in 2022. However, increases are forecast in the cities of Inverness, Aberdeen, Perth, Dundee, Glasgow, Stirling, the M8 corridor, and Edinburgh. Further AQMAs have been requested for Edinburgh and Glasgow, and NO_2 levels in current Edinburgh AQMAs could exceed EU 2010 targets should the measures contained in the Action Plan fail to be implemented.

'Future changes to rail based NO_x emissions are not possible to forecast on a national level, although data relating to some areas is available. In Edinburgh, rail based NO_x emissions are predicted to remain static, although this could be increased as a result of the Stirling–Alloa–Kincardine Rail Link and increased Glasgow–Edinburgh capacity. The following developments considered within the "Do-Minimum" scenario also have the potential to increase NO_x emission levels; the Glasgow Airport Rail Link, Gourock Transport Interchange, Waverley Route Reopening, and Haymarket Rail Interchange. Within the prediction model, currently electrified rail lines are not considered to produce NO_x emissions.'

Source: Transport Scotland (2008)

Box 6.5 Example of comparative data: Index of Multiple Deprivation for the Eastern Cape province of South Africa

A key objective of the South African government since 1994 has been the improvement of the quality of life for all South Africans and the reduction of poverty and inequality. To assist in targeting deprivation, the National Department of Social Development commissioned a research team at the University of Oxford to develop a small area measure of multiple deprivation. Each 'datazone' covers between 1000 and 3000 people. Based on the 2001 Census, an index was compiled for each datazone which brings together information about income and material deprivation, employment, health, education and living. The figure below shows the results for the Eastern Cape province, with darker areas being more deprived and lighter ones less so. Clearly the north-eastern part of the province is considerably more deprived than the south-western part, and the urban areas are generally less deprived than the rural ones.

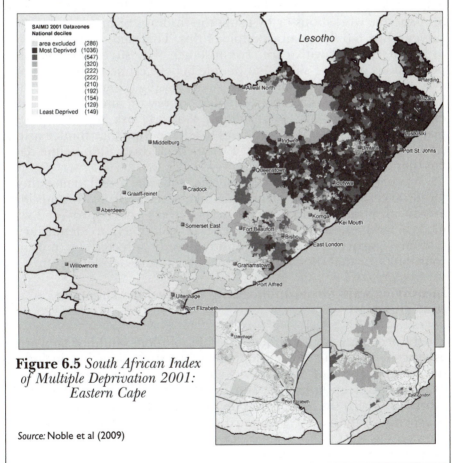

Figure 6.5 *South African Index of Multiple Deprivation 2001: Eastern Cape*

Source: Noble et al (2009)

115

children's playing space for every 1000 population – is widely applied (NPFA, 2001).

Another approach is to compare one authority against *other similar authorities or the national average*: the 'comparator' column of Table 6.2. Where the authority is performing considerably worse than others, this could be a problem. For instance, an 'index of multiple deprivation' has been developed for South Africa, which has allowed areas of relative deprivation to be identified. Box 6.5 shows an example from this index. A similar index is used in the UK, and many local authorities have as an SEA objective to reduce the number of areas in the local authority that are doing poorly in this index.

Trends in the baseline can help to identify problems. Is air quality getting better or worse? If standards are not currently being exceeded but trends are worsening, will standards be exceeded in the future?

The *perceptions* of residents, their representatives (e.g. tribal elders, local politicians), or environmental/sustainability authorities, can also help to identify existing problems. This could be done either through SEA-specific workshops or by using the findings of previous resident surveys. Box 6.6 shows an example of this. That said, such data needs to be interpreted with care. For instance, UK surveys of people's perceptions of crime show that people believe crime to be increasing even though reported crime levels are decreasing (Home Office, 2008).

Finally, *planners* are an invaluable source of information about existing problems. As a consultant, I always ask my clients (the planners) during inception meetings to tell me what they think existing problems are in their authority. I then check this with baseline data, but they are invariably right.

Where problems are spatially specific, it may be useful to map them, for instance, contaminated land, floodplains, areas prone to landslides, areas with poor public transport access, areas poorly provided with medical facilities, or vacant buildings. This could help to identify areas that are particularly sensitive and already affected by multiple constraints, or that should be promoted for future development.

Identifying ways forward; informing the development of the strategic action

Where problems are identified, possible solutions could be suggested as a way of informing the development of the strategic action, including the identification of sustainable alternatives. Table 6.3 shows an example of clear links between identified problems and possible solutions, which, in turn, could be used to help identify and choose between alternative ways forward for the strategic action. Box 6.7 shows the results of a workshop in which participants were asked to propose priority land designations based on existing problems.

Box 6.6 Example of issues and aspirations raised through workshops: SEA for mining sector reform in Sierra Leone

'Environmental and social problems are not addressed satisfactorily by the Sierra Leone mining industry for all scale of mining activities, even where regulations exist. There are a considerable number of schisms between mining companies and various stakeholders. Effective environmental regulation is critically dependent on government monitoring and enforcement capacity, the availability of injunctive measures to help enforce compliance, the use of such measures where appropriate, and the ability of the mining sector to finance the costs of compliance. All of these factors are currently weak or, in some cases, non-existent...

'Stakeholder prioritization workshops were held in each of the four provinces. All major stakeholder groups in the mining sector were represented, including vulnerable groups such a women and youth. There was great similarity in the stakeholder priorities across provinces... The top priorities from cross-regional and regional perspectives are:

Cross-regional priorities

1   Land and crop compensation and village relocations;
2   Sanitation and water pollution;
3   Deforestation and soil degradation;
4   Child labour; and
5   Post-closure reclamation.

Regional priorities

1   Mine employment (southern);
2   Provision of infrastructure (especially paved roads and electricity) (southern);
3   Community development and participation (southern and western); and
4   Blasting effects (eastern).

'When asked to rate the political will to resolve these issues, the respondents all gave very low scores, with only child labour receiving a score suggesting medium to strong political will. Expected remediation or implementation costs to resolve the priority issues were all ranked high.'

Source: World Bank, 2008

Establishing an SEA framework (for objectives-led SEA)

Where an SEA is objectives-led rather than baseline-led, one of the context-setting stages will be the development of a framework of SEA objectives – statements of desired directions of change – and possibly associated indicators and targets. This will provide the structure against which various components of the emerging strategic action will be

Table 6.3 *Example of possible solutions linked to identified problems: Excerpt from the SEA for the Porthcawl Waterfront Supplementary Planning Guidance (Wales)*

Key issues/problems	Opportunities/implications for Porthcawl Waterfront SPG
Flood risk (potential cumulative effect): A significant part of the Porthcawl Development Area foreshore is at risk from tidal flooding during a flood event (1 in 200 year return period). Flood defences currently provide protection to the eastern portion of the Development Area along the west of Newton Bay. Additionally, the Shoreline Management Plan … identifies that the stretch of coast adjacent to the Porthcawl Development Area is being eroded, and that this causes risk to the breakwater structure during high tides and storms	The main potential source of tidal flooding is as a result of overtopping of the existing defences in the western part of Sandy Bay. The Porthcawl Waterfront [plan] should ensure that no new development occurs within the identified floodplain without adequate mitigation in place and that flood defences are adequate to withstand future predicted flood events taking account the implications of climate change
Contaminated land: The Porthcawl Development Area has a history of potentially contaminating land uses that may have introduced soil contamination to the area	The extent of contamination will need to be established by intrusive investigation, and its significance identified and quantitatively risk assessed. Contaminated land will have to be remediated prior to development

Source: Bridgend County Borough Council (2007)

tested, typically in the form of a matrix. The SEA framework as a whole – the totality of the SEA objectives – aims to describe an environmental or sustainability state that acts as a goal that society is striving towards. The assessment process consists in asking, for each plan option or component, 'on the basis of my professional judgement, what is the likely impact of this plan component on this environmental/sustainability objective?'

SEA objectives will normally be different from the objectives of the strategic action and from external objectives. Box 6.8 explains the difference between these different types of objectives. For instance, a transport plan may not have as an objective to protect biodiversity, but its impacts on biodiversity should be tested and minimized, so protection of biodiversity is a typical SEA objective. External objectives are non-SEA objectives that also affect the strategic action, for instance, reduction of congestion or delivery of an agreed national transport network.

Box 6.7 Example of issues and aspirations raised through workshops: Great Sand Hills area, Saskatchewan

The Great Sand Hills (GSH) area in Saskatchewan (Canada) has been subject to conflicts of interest between ranchers, the gas industry and environmental conservation. The GSH Regional Environmental Study aims to provide recommendations to guide future activities in the area. Part of the study involved workshops, in which representatives of different groups (ranchers, First Nations groups, etc.) were asked to identify existing problems, future goals, and zoning or priority land designations. Below are excerpts from the findings of two workshop groups.

Government: Participants in the government sub-groups identified the following points regarding land use. First, the GSH Review area should allow all land uses under a land-use plan, best management practices, and strict regulations. Second, family ranching was identified as the main land use in the GSH, and it should be maintained in family units... Third, where there are active dunes, no traffic should be allowed for oil and gas activity... Fourth, First Nations access is not an issue as long as they are willing to follow conservation rules...

First Nations: It was noted that gas development destroys medicinal plants and disturbs ancestral sites, and it was suggested that no new gas activity be permitted. The File Hills Qu'Appelle sub-group suggested that ranching was not a major concern... Tourism was not seen as an issue for the File Hills Qu'Appelle sub-group or even as a concern. Both the File Hills Qu'Appelle and Blood Tribe sub-groups noted the importance of maintaining intact habitat... A map was derived with input from File Hills Qu'Appelle elders on preferred land uses, which accurately reflected their views on the preservation of First Nations culture...

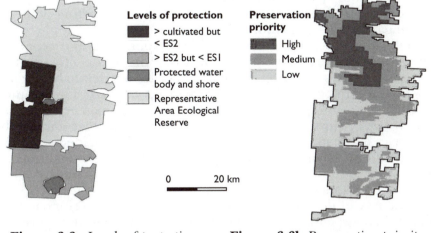

Figure 6.6a *Levels of protection proposed by government participants*

Figure 6.6b *Preservation priority proposed by First Nations participants*

Source: Great Sand Hills Advisory Committee (2007)

Box 6.8 Relation of SEA objectives to other objectives

Strategic action objectives are the objectives of the strategic action in question. They are generally separate from SEA objectives, although the development of SEA objectives may provide inspiration for making the strategic action objectives more environmentally friendly or sustainable. Unless a strategic action is purely conservationist, its objectives will also include economic and social considerations.

External objectives are those other existing objectives to which planners must pay heed independently from the SEA process, for instance, national or international commitments. They may be environmental, but they can also include economic or social objectives.

SEA objectives provide a methodological 'yardstick' against which the environmental and sustainability effects of the strategic action can be tested. SEA objectives will often overlap with strategic-action objectives, although they may go beyond what is achievable solely through the strategic action; they will also often be 'inherited' from environmental-protection objectives, although they may also include additional (often more locally focused) objectives.

Source: Based on ODPM et al (2005)

Table 6.4 shows the UK SA objectives put forward in government guidance. They cover social and economic as well as environmental issues. The table also includes more detailed questions that would be used during the assessment stage to help determine whether the strategic action does or does not promote sustainability. In practice, this framework would be adapted (and normally shortened) to suit the conditions of the plan area and the type of plan being assessed. I have included the full list because it can act as a useful starting point for devising other SEA frameworks.

Table 6.4 is organized into social, environmental and economic categories that are quite different from the more cross-cutting sustainability themes of Box 5.5. This allows an overview to be taken of whether a strategic action has unbalanced impacts: for instance, whether it consistently ignores social issues but is good economically (see Box 5.4). However, it leaves open the possibility that some of the objectives may conflict with each other: Will both sustained economic growth and sustainable sources of water supply always be possible? Is promotion of inward investment always compatible with a sense of community identity?

One way of dealing with this issue may be to use a compatibility matrix (see Appendix C) to test and describe whether SEA objectives are mutually supportive. Typically, economic and environmental objectives are more likely to be in potential conflict than economic v. social or social v. environmental objectives. Where objectives potentially conflict, one or both can be modified to make them compatible, one or

Table 6.4 *Possible SEA objectives and assessment questions*

SA objective	Detailed decision-making criteria
Social objectives	
To reduce poverty and social exclusion and health inequalities	• Will it reduce poverty and social exclusion and health inequalities in those areas most affected? • Will it improve affordability to essential services to the home?
To improve health of the population overall	• Will it reduce death rates? • Will it improve access to high-quality health facilities? • Will it encourage healthy lifestyles? • Will it reduce health inequalities?
To improve the education and skills of the population as a whole	• Will it improve qualifications and skills of young people?
To provide everybody with the opportunity to live in a decent home	• Will it reduce homelessness? • Will it increase the range and affordability of housing for all social groups? • Will it reduce the number of unfit homes?
To reduce anti-social activity	• Will it reduce actual levels of crime? • Will it reduce the fear of crime? • Will it reduce actual noise levels? • Will it reduce noise concerns?
To encourage a sense of community identity and welfare	• Will it encourage engagement in community activities? • Will it increase the ability of people to influence decisions? • Will it improve ethnic relations?
To offer everybody the opportunity for rewarding and satisfying employment	• Will it reduce unemployment overall? • Will it reduce long-term unemployment? • Will it provide job opportunities for those most in need of employment? • Will it help to reduce long working hours? • Will it help to improve earnings?
To improve the quality of where people live	• Will it improve people's satisfaction with their neighbourhoods as places to live?
To improve accessibility to essential services and facilities	• Will it improve accessibility to key local services? • Will it improve accessibility to shopping facilities? • Will it improve the level of investment in key community services?
To improve accessibility for those most in need	• Will it make access more affordable? • Will it make access easier for those without access to a car?
Environmental objectives	
To reduce the effects of transport on the environment	• Will it reduce traffic volumes? • Will it reduce road traffic accidents? • Will it reduce the need for overseas travel? • Will it reduce the effect of heavy goods traffic on people and the environment?

Table 6.4 *continued*

SA objective	Detailed decision-making criteria
	• Will it increase the proportion of journeys using modes other than the car?
To improve water quality	• Will it improve the quality of inland water?
	• Will it improve the quality of coastal waters?
To improve air quality	• Will it improve air quality?
To maintain and enhance biodiversity, flora and fauna	• Will it conserve and enhance natural/semi-natural habitats?
	• Will it conserve and enhance species diversity, and in particular avoid harm to protected species?
	• Will it maintain and enhance sites designated for their nature conservation interest?
	• Will it maintain and enhance woodland cover and management?
To maintain and enhance the quality of landscapes and townscapes	• Will it reduce the amount of derelict, degraded and underused land?
	• Will it improve the landscape and ecological quality and character of the countryside?
	• Will it decrease litter in towns and the countryside?
To conserve, and where appropriate, enhance the historic environment	• Will it protect and enhance sites, features and areas of historical, archaeological and cultural value in both urban and rural areas?
To reduce contributions to climate change	• Will it reduce emissions of greenhouse gases by reducing energy consumption?
	• Will it lead to an increased proportion of energy needs being met from renewable sources?
	• Will it reduce emissions of ozone-depleting substances?
To avoid, reduce and manage flood risk	• Will it minimize the risk of flooding from rivers and watercourses to people and property?
	• Will it minimize the risk of flooding to people and properties on the coast?
	• Will it reduce the risk of subsidence?
	• Will it reduce the risk of damage to property from storm events?
To provide for sustainable sources of water supply	• Will it reduce water consumption?
To minimize the production of waste	• Will it lead to reduced consumption of materials and resources?
	• Will it reduce household waste?
	• Will it increase waste recovery and recycling?
	• Will it reduce hazardous waste?
	• Will it reduce waste in the construction industry?
To conserve soil resources and quality	• Will it minimize the loss of soils to development?
	• Will it maintain and enhance soil quality?

Table 6.4 *continued*

SA objective	Detailed decision-making criteria
Economic objectives	
To encourage sustained economic growth	• Will it improve business development and enhance competitiveness? • Will it improve the resilience of business and the economy? • Will it promote growth in key sectors? • Will it promote growth in key clusters?
To reduce disparities in economic performance	• Will it improve economic performance in advantaged and disadvantaged areas? • Will it encourage rural diversification?
To encourage and accommodate both indigenous and inward investment	• Will it encourage indigenous business? • Will it encourage inward investment? • Will it make land and property available for business development?
To encourage efficient patterns of movement in support of economic growth	• Will it reduce commuting? • Will it improve accessibility to work by public transport, walking and cycling? • Will it reduce the effect of traffic congestion on the economy? • Will it reduce journey times between key employment areas and key transport interchanges? • Will it facilitate efficiency in freight distribution?
To enhance the image of the area as a business location	• Will it attract new investment and additional skilled workers to the area?
To improve the social and environmental performance of the economy	• Will it encourage ethical trading? • Will it encourage good employee relations and management practices?

Source: ODPM et al (2005)

both can be deleted, or one can be made 'dominant' so that it 'wins' where there is conflict. Another option is to keep both conflicting objectives in the framework but explain why this is being done, so that the potential conflict is made explicit and transparent.

Another issue in the development of SEA frameworks is the number of SEA objectives and indicators that they should contain. Clearly, sustainability assessments will require more 'tests' than environmental assessments, since they cover a wider range of issues. However, research into the UK system of SA concluded that SEA frameworks often include too many objectives and indicators, making the resulting assessments unwieldy and unfocused (PAS, 2006; LUC and RTPI, 2008; CLG, 2009b).

To conclude, in his report on the effectiveness and efficiency of the UK system of SA (CLG, 2009b), Steve Smith recommends that the UK should shift towards a more baseline-led approach, in part due to difficulties in carrying out an effective objectives-led assessment framework. His analysis provides a good checklist of things to watch out for by anyone who is setting up an SEA framework:

> *The development of [SEA] objectives generates a host of issues including: getting to grips with, and explaining to stakeholders, the difference between plan and [SEA] objectives; the vexing question as to whether or not a given set of objectives should be consistent with one another in terms of aspiration; the number of objectives that should be generated and the extent to which they assist in distinguishing between competing alternatives; concerns over the 'balance' between economic, social and environmental objectives (the environment is easier to compartmentalise and break down into discrete objectives); the striking similarity between different authorities' objectives (prompting calls for a national, standardised set of objectives); and whether or not, taken together, the aspirations expressed through a set of objectives constitute 'sustainable development'. None of these issues is easily resolved. However, most important is the sense that an objectives-led approach comes at the expense of an assessment against the baseline situation.* (CLG, 2009b)

When to stop collecting information: 'Scoping'

It is perfectly possible to keep collecting baseline data and analysing related strategic actions indefinitely, until the poor researcher becomes a cobweb-ridden skeleton or the strategic action has gone through multiple cycles of implementation and revision. What is 'enough' baseline data? What are 'enough' related strategic actions? At what point do the costs of collecting the information outweigh the information's benefits?

Scoping involves deciding on the topics to be covered by the SEA ('scoped in'), the level of detail into which it will go, the methodology that will be used, and possibly the alternatives that will be considered and how stakeholders will be involved. It can help to identify key issues that require particularly detailed analysis, as well as issues that do not need to be addressed in the SEA – those that can be 'scoped out'. Those environmental components that are very *un*likely to be significantly affected by a strategic action – for instance, the impact of an urban transport plan on soil quality, or of a minerals plan on social equity – will not normally need to be assessed. Box 6.9 gives an example of SEA scoping for a unique strategic action.

Box 6.9 Example of SEA scoping: Excerpts from the SEA for the US Constellation Program of space exploration

The Constellation Program represents the efforts of the US National Aeronautics and Space Administration (NASA) to extend the human presence throughout the solar system. It is focused on providing the capability to transport humans and cargo to the moon, in support of lunar exploration missions, and to the International Space Station. Future efforts would support missions to Mars and beyond. The first chapter of the programmatic environmental impact statement for the Constellation Program explained what topics were and were not considered in the rest of the report:

'On September 26, 2006, NASA published a Notice of Intent (NOI) in the Federal Register ... to prepare a Draft Programmatic Environmental Impact Statement and conduct scoping for the Constellation Program. Scoping meetings to solicit public input on environmental concerns and alternatives to be considered in the PEIS were held on October 18, 2006 in Cocoa, Florida; on October 20, 2006 in Washington, DC; and on October 24, 2006 in Salt Lake City, Utah... The following issues were identified through the public scoping process and are [scoped into] this Final PEIS:

- The economic impact of the Constellation Program, locally and nationally, with an emphasis on the impacts of the Program on jobs near NASA Centers
- Risks to the public associated with launch and Earth atmospheric entry
- Environmental impacts of the use of solid rocket fuels on the ozone layer and impacts associated with the deposition of combustion products near the launch area
- Impacts on local animal species (e.g., sea turtles and manatees) associated with construction and launch activities in the KSC area
- Noise impacts associated with launch events
- Relationship between the Constellation Program and the Space Shuttle Program, including how the socioeconomic impacts of the Space Shuttle retirement and the Constellation Program overlap...

Issues raised that are outside the scope of this Final PEIS [and that are thus scoped out] include the following:

- Possible military applications associated with the Constellation Program
- Legal issues associated with the use of the Moon and its raw materials
- Environmental impacts in outer space, including impacts on the Moon
- Use of nuclear systems in support of the Constellation Program...'

Source: NASA (2008)

Scoping out issues may require some courage, particularly in a litigious context. Certainly, many early SEAs do not seem to have gone through a robust scoping process, resulting in amorphous assessments that were not clearly targeted at significant decisions and so were less influential than they could be. This may reflect a concern about legal challenge rather than environmental precaution, and an unwillingness on the part of environmental/sustainability authorities to 'allow' topics in their remit to be scoped out. Many SEAs also include a huge amount of baseline data and a very lengthy analysis of the policy context, with the assessment stage looking comparatively rushed and incomplete: in such cases, it might be better to spend less energy collecting data and more energy in assessing the strategic action's effects (Snell and Cowell, 2006; Fry, 2007; CLG, 2009b).

Article 5.2 of the SEA Directive gives some guidance on scoping, noting that the level of detail should relate to the:

> *current knowledge and methods of assessment, the contents and level of detail in the plan or programme, its stage in the decision-making process and the extent to which certain matters are more appropriately assessed at different levels in that process in order to avoid duplication of the assessment.* (Art. 5.2)

However, this gives little practical assistance to the potential skeleton.

A possible way forward might be to use what Nicholson (2005) calls the 'so what' test:

> *When presented with a particular piece of baseline information think carefully about what the implications are for the plan that is being appraised; maybe there are none immediately apparent, in which case why include it?* (Nicholson, 2005)

It may also be useful to focus on why the information is needed. One needs baseline data in SEA to allow environmental problems to be identified and addressed; provide a baseline against which future monitoring can be carried out; and provide a basis for impact prediction. Any data that do not do this are superfluous, and enough data are needed to allow this to be done. Where, for instance, locational constraints could affect whether any project is acceptable, then data on these constraints would be needed; where location is clearly not a constraint, then such data are not necessary.

One needs to analyse links with other strategic actions so as to know what constraints are posed on, and by, the strategic action. The importance of another strategic action for the SEA could thus be tested by using criteria such as whether it is a statutory requirement, it has geographical links to the strategic action in question and there is stakeholder concern over the issue covered in that strategic action, and how up-to-date is the strategic action. The reasons for deciding to *not* consider specific issues in the baseline, or specific strategic actions, should be documented.

The scoping 'stage' could also be viewed as being a longer-term process, in which issues are eliminated from further consideration as and when they can be shown to not be significant. Sometimes it is not possible to do this until some data has been collected and some judgements made (CLG, 2009b).

Conclusions

Much of the early, context-setting stages of SEA are not specific to one strategic action. Data collected for one plan's SEA can be re-used for another plan's SEA, as long as the level of detail is appropriate and the information remains up to date. Existing environmental/sustainability problems will not change from plan to plan. Many UK local authorities that have to prepare several plans have chosen to prepare one comprehensive scoping report that applies to all of those plans.

Quality review questions for the context-setting stage that could be used by either a formal reviewer or as a self-test are:

- Is the context-setting information being provided early enough in the plan-making process to fully inform the development of the strategic action?
- Is there a clear description of the strategic action's objectives and structure, and what the strategic action can and cannot do?
- Has the policy context – the links between the strategic action and related higher- and lower-tier strategic actions – been considered? Where strategic actions conflict, have the reasons been clearly documented and have recommendations been made on how to reconcile the strategic actions so as to promote sustainability?
- Is the current baseline situation described? Is it of an appropriate scale, including 'zoom down' to areas likely to be significantly affected by the strategic action? Is it up to date? Is the information appropriate for the strategic action in question (do the indicators say what they mean)? Where appropriate, does the baseline describe the social and economic as well as the environmental situation? Were the methods used to investigate the affected baseline appropriate to the size and complexity of the assessment task?
- Is the likely future baseline situation without the strategic action ('business as usual') described?
- Are existing environmental/sustainability problems explained? Are the causes of these problems discussed? Are they related to possible ways forward for the strategic action, if appropriate?
- For objective-led SEAs, has a framework of SEA objectives (and possibly indicators and targets) been developed? Does it cover an

appropriate range of issues? Has any conflict between the SEA objectives been identified, described and possibly resolved? Have reasons for eliminating issues from further consideration been documented?

- Have any data gaps been clearly documented? Are measures in place to deal with these in the future if appropriate?
- Has a formal scoping process been carried out? Does the SEA address key issues and 'scope out' insignificant ones?
- Have environmental/sustainability authorities, the public and other relevant stakeholders been involved where appropriate?

Chapter 7 considers strategic action alternatives, and how the SEA can help to ensure that environmental/sustainability issues identified in the context-setting stage of SEA are considered in such alternatives.

Chapter 7

Identifying Alternatives

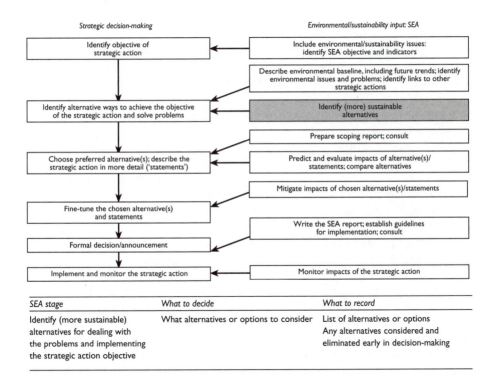

Strategic decision-making	Environmental/sustainability input: SEA
Identify objective of strategic action	Include environmental/sustainability issues: identify SEA objective and indicators
	Describe environmental baseline, including future trends; identify environmental issues and problems; identify links to other strategic actions
Identify alternative ways to achieve the objective of the strategic action and solve problems	Identify (more) sustainable alternatives
	Prepare scoping report; consult
Choose preferred alternative(s); describe the strategic action in more detail ('statements')	Predict and evaluate impacts of alternative(s)/statements; compare alternatives
	Mitigate impacts of chosen alternative(s)/statements
Fine-tune the chosen alternative(s) and statements	
	Write the SEA report; establish guidelines for implementation; consult
Formal decision/announcement	
Implement and monitor the strategic action	Monitor impacts of the strategic action

SEA stage	What to decide	What to record
Identify (more sustainable) alternatives for dealing with the problems and implementing the strategic action objective	What alternatives or options to consider	List of alternatives or options Any alternatives considered and eliminated early in decision-making

The way that alternatives are typically considered in decision-making goes something like this: 'We have congestion in central Standstill, so we will need a bypass from South Standstill to North Standstill. Should we choose route A, B or C?'; or 'Having carried out traffic studies, we district planners recommend a Park and Ride system at Robust Road as a way of solving the congestion problem, but politician Meddlemuch lives near there, so we'd better put it at Sensitive Street instead'.

There are several things to observe here. First, without SEA, alternatives are typically proposed in response to problems rather than as ways of achieving a future vision: they are reactive rather than proactive. Second, the alternatives considered are often detailed, project-level alternatives rather than strategic ones ('Can we avoid congestion in the first place?'). Third, the choice of alternatives is often determined politically.

The development, assessment and comparison of alternatives is a key stage in SEA and is – as can be deduced from the above – inextricably linked to the decision-making process itself. However, it is very hard to do well, and very easy to do badly. For instance:

- Canada: *'The consideration and assessment of a reasonable range of alternatives or scenarios ... was clearly evidenced in only three of the ten cases'* (Noble, 2009).
- England: *'Many local authorities have struggled to generate reasonable alternatives and this has, in turn, reduced the scope for [SEA] to play an effective role in plan-making'* (CLG, 2009b).
- Portugal: *'In most cases [of 12] no alternatives were considered'* (Partidário et al, 2009a).
- Colombia: *'One of the biggest weaknesses was the alternatives analysis. Just one SEA [of 8 reviewed] did the analysis'* (Puyana, 2009).

The role of SEA is to help identify more long-term, sustainable alternatives; identify and assess the environmental/sustainability impacts of different options to help inform and support the choice of alternatives and hopefully make that choice more sustainable; and document how the preferred alternative(s) was chosen as a way of leading to more transparent, inclusive decision-making. In other words, SEA aims to make the decision-making process more proactive, more strategic, more sustainable and less political. SEA can also provide reassurance that, within the constraints facing decision-makers, they have not missed some other markedly better alternative.

This chapter discusses:

- types of alternatives;
- how to identify alternatives;
- how to eliminate alternatives from further assessment; and
- how to document the alternatives generation and selection process.

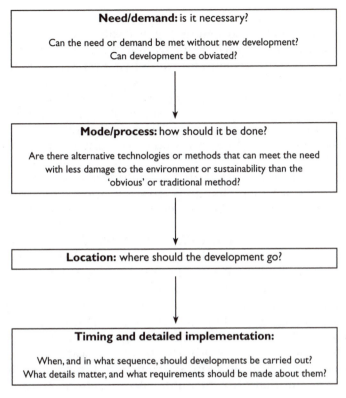

Source: ODPM et al (2005)

Figure 7.1 *'Hierarchy' of alternatives*

Chapter 8 then discusses how alternatives can be compared, and how to document the process of appraising alternatives and choosing a preferred alternative.

Types of alternatives

Most strategic actions involve planning for some form of future action (typically development) in response to a perceived problem or need (either current or projected). Figure 7.1 proposes a basic hierarchy of alternatives for such strategic actions. This hierarchy was initially inspired by the waste hierarchy (reduce, re-use, recycle/recover, dispose), and also by a basic rule used when people install wind turbines or photovoltaics: minimize electricity demand first, and only then install renewables to provide for the reduced demand because demand reduction is cheaper and more environment-friendly than production. The same basic hierarchical thinking holds true for a wide range of other sectors and issues. It goes as follows.

First check whether anything new is really needed: *is it possible to obviate demand?* For instance, before a new reservoir is proposed, is it possible to reduce the demand for water to a level where no new water source is needed? Before a new power station is proposed, can electricity use be reduced? Can we avoid the need for more roads, airports, science parks, golf courses, superstores, incinerators, houses, offshore wind turbines, dams, factories, call centres, landfill sites, mobile phone masts, pylons, wastewater treatment plants, and so on altogether?

Taken to extremes, this approach could lead to a rather grey and bleak dystopia in which change is frowned upon, opportunities for progress are limited, and people wear their clothes until they are in shreds because they don't really have to have new clothes. On the other hand, a look at the second column in Table 7.1 suggests that, in moderation, it could lead to a lively, community-oriented future where people cycle and walk more, cooperate to a greater extent in the provision of childcare and the growing of food, rediscover the pleasure of local holidays, and support local stores serving locally grown foods rather than driving to the newest regional superstore, which is in mad competition with the other new regional superstores.

In the context of worldwide trends towards globalization, consumerism and individualism, restraints on individuals' choices will not happen automatically through citizen action. It can only be achieved through a concerted, planned effort. Box 7.1 discusses this further. SEA is an obvious stage in the decision-making process in which to consider this issue.

Once alternatives for reducing demands have been explored and future needs agreed on, *different ways of providing for these needs*[1] can be identified. Water can be provided by groundwater abstraction, rainwater collection, canal systems, importing and melting icebergs, desalination and many other means as well as different sizes of new reservoirs. People can be moved around by rail (high speed, conventional, light rail, etc.), bike, airplane, foot, bus, boat and (in NASA's case – see Box 6.9) rocket.

Once the type and rough scale of development has been agreed, one can decide *where development should be located and how big it should be.* It is at this point that one thinks about different routes for a bypass, or locations for a Park and Ride site, reservoir, or power station. The issues of location and scale are inter-related: the possible locations will influence the size and type of development that is possible, and the size and type of the proposed development will constrain where it can be sited. For instance, there will be more possible sites for household-level wood chip burners than for an industrial-scale biofuel combined-heat-and-power plant.

Table 7.1 *Examples of alternatives/options*

Topic	Obviation	Mode/type	Location	Implementation/timing
Transport/ accessibility	Reduce the need to travel by: • locating amenities/services nearer their users, or housing the users nearer the amenities they need • helping people meet more needs at home (e.g. homeworking, information technology) Develop community-scale infrastructure and services to reduce the need to transport goods, e.g. small-scale incinerators, reservoirs, wind turbines	Encourage walking and cycling Support good public transport, matched to journey desires (e.g. provide sites for modal interchange, protect rail corridors)	Locate amenities/services together so people can accomplish several errands in one trip – e.g. multifunctional town centres Locate bike stands and bus stops more conveniently than parking	Have walking/cycling infrastructure and public transport services in place before development comes into use If extra traffic capacity is unavoidable, design at minimum necessary capacity, avoid discouraging other modes (e.g. design in traffic calming, safe routes for pedestrians and cyclists), minimize noise, land take and visual intrusion
Economic development	Meet needs or provide occupation *without* more business development, e.g. community/cooperative schemes for childcare, home maintenance, food-growing, play schemes (needing to *spend less* is as good for wealth as *earning more*)	Locally owned and managed; producing goods/services to meet local needs Repairers to avoid the need to buy new things	Near customers and/or raw materials (e.g. market gardens around settlements)	Develop businesses in tandem with housing to reduce the need to commute long distance Develop at a pace and form that takes up 'slack' in staff and buildings as it occurs –

Table 7.1 *continued*

Topic	Obviation	Mode/type	Location	Implementation/timing
Rural economic development, farm conversion and diversification	Save *having to* convert/ diversify by adapting agriculture to new opportunities, e.g. organic, locally distinctive, locally processed and marketed, high value added	Promote activities that require extensive land and not quick or frequent access to urban amenities: e.g. wildlife, study/retreat	Given!	neither displacing old but still viable businesses nor leaving a gap of unemployment/decay Develop in a manner that supports other agricultural/rural uses and the local community
Shopping/ retail development	Provide services in a different way, e.g. wear clothes for longer, make things more durable, create allotments that allow people to grow their own food, introduce local non-monetary exchange schemes Meet demands through: • changes to existing businesses, e.g. village shops also providing banking/postal services; • better use of existing	Buildings adaptable for multiple uses. Promote farm shops and other shops that provide local goods locally	Retail and service centres that allow multiple errands in single trips, near public transport, near users	Ensure that provision is in place and operative before housing is occupied, to avoid anti-sustainable transport habits becoming established

	property, e.g. subdivision, shop within a shop, use store rooms; and • new technologies, e.g. e-commerce (possibly using existing retailers/delivery rounds).			
Tourism	Improve standard of where people live; encourage them to enjoy what they have on their doorsteps reducing the need to travel Provide local recreation/leisure facilities, green areas, etc.	Activities aimed at local/short-distance/non-mechanized visitors Convenient reliable access by foot, cycle, public transport (e.g. coordinated services, integrated ticketing of transport and attractions)	Near users/public transport	Engage local people in decision and implementation
Housing generally	Match supply to needs: • encourage adaptation of buildings to maximize the potential for comfortable occupation (e.g. loft and garage conversions, sub-division of large houses); and • provide high-standard sheltered accommodation for older people as an alternative to staying in unnecessarily large houses. Make best use of existing building stock:	Make best use of land: • encourage infill, development of small sites, rebuilding at higher densities; • promote dense and land-efficient built forms, e.g. terraces, low rise flats, communal open spaces; • maximize density; and • use existing infrastructure in new construction.	Minimize new infrastructure demands (e.g by avoiding locations remote from amenities) Focus new housing on brownfield sites and away from floodplains	Match timing of housing development to needs and to public service provision Encourage self-build or community-build housing as a way of reducing costs and promoting participation

Table 7.1 *continued*

Topic	Obviation	Mode/type	Location	Implementation/timing
	• encourage living above shops; and • promote the conversion of redundant non-domestic buildings, loft conversions, flexible subletting of surplus space Give tax relief for housing developers and buyers in less desirable areas			
Affordable housing	Avoid economic overheating or wealthy in-migration that could price young and local people out of housing	Social landlords, shared ownership/cooperative schemes, shared facilities/communal living	Site and configure housing to maximize opportunities for people to stay near family, community ties and work	Match to demographic profile of customers
	Reduce loss of affordable housing, e.g. disincentives to second homes	Flexible/modular housing where residents can buy a 'starter pack' and add onto this as circumstances permit		
Waste	Reduce generation of waste through waste management plan, limitations on packaging, tax on landfill	Use waste as a resource: recycling, composting, match producers of specialist waste (e.g. pulverised fuel ash) with organizations that can use those wastes, waste-to-energy schemes	Locate waste management sites near source of waste and/or users of waste as resource	Provide recycling facilities at housing and employment sites
			Use waste as infill (e.g. of disused mineral working sites) where appropriate	Use materials efficiently in construction. Use recycled materials

				in construction
Energy	Reduce demand for energy in housing by promoting low-energy lighting and appliances, very efficient boilers, high insulation standards, conservatories and lobbies, large south-facing and small north-facing windows, etc. Reduce the need to travel	Ensure that waste can be used as a resource, e.g. by requiring products to be recyclable, providing facilities for storing recyclable products (e.g. architectural salvage yards, sites for storage of recycled aggregates) Promote renewable energy, energy from waste, combined heat and power Promote use of alternative energy vehicles	Community- and individual-owned renewable energy installations to minimize transmission loss	Use best available energy-efficient technologies in building construction and operation Site housing to optimize solar gain Use materials with low embodied energy (e.g. recycled materials, cob and straw rather than aluminium and concrete)
Water	Reduce demand for water through: • water metering; • increased cost of water, greater increases with increasing consumption; and • in industry, more efficient (or different) processes.	Reduce leakage in water pipes, infill rainwater collection systems, recycle effluent, use canals to move water from wetter to drier areas, etc.	Consider several smaller facilities rather than one larger one	Install water-saving devices e.g. low-flow showers, low-flush toilets Landscaping using plants that do not require much watering

Source: Adapted from ODPM (2002)

Box 7.1 Public v. private decisions, and the myth that 'choice' is always good

'Over the last quarter century, the "long wave" pendulum of political values has swung to an extreme of individualism, market-based solutions, and hostility to and distrust of anything that smacks of central planning and state intervention. This has happened before. But the discrediting and ignominious collapse of the planned economies of Eastern Europe has left the discourse of individualism, choice and liberty so pervasive, and the image of collectivism, social choice and mutuality so tarnished, that we are in danger of forgetting that there is actually a debate to be had or a pendulum that can swing.

'This matters because ... individualism is not increasing wellbeing at all reliably for the wealthy; is disadvantaging the poor; and is making environmental problems insoluble. [We need] to renew the possibility of taking collective solutions seriously. Private choices are always conditioned by the quality of the public goods and wider networks within which any consumer must operate. The use of "choice" as shorthand for personal sovereignty and empowerment as private consumer conceals this. When this happens, what is presented as "choice", and may even be experienced as choice locally, is in fact coercion. In a complex society the choices other people make can be coercive just as much as the choices governments make – but without even the possibility of intelligent direction towards desirable goals...

'Individual choice in markets or quasi-markets does not necessarily lead to the best, good or even tolerable outcomes. Individual choices have cumulatively led to an overall situation that no sane person would have chosen in transport. Parental choice is a major obstacle to providing acceptable standards for all in school education. In food and agriculture, a superabundance of trivial choice masks the absence of more important ones. The shift from state provision to market choice in financial services (especially pensions) has proved oppressive and bewildering, led to exploitation of many vulnerable people and deprived even the most prudent of security.

'Increasing some choices precludes others. It is not good enough just to say that a policy "increases choice": policy makers must consider whether the choices being increased are useful and important ones, and consider the choices thereby being precluded or prevented. Choice should be treated as a means to enable people to get what they want, not an end in itself. Often, the choices that really matter must be taken collectively not by individuals. Government should act to make the right choice *sets* available... Standards should replace choice as the primary basis for appraising public services. Choice should not be allowed to undermine standards...

'All these points lead towards the conclusion that in many areas we need more active government intervention [such as consideration of these issues through SEA]: to move the "choice sets" available to people towards less consumer choice, more social choice, less consumption but more quality of life benefits. This has logic; it makes policy problems soluble; it seems people are increasingly ready for it; it is – and can be presented as – a positive development of progressive ideas. It is also the only plausible and politically remotely practicable approach to address [today's] environmental problems.'

Source: Levett et al (2002)

Finally, at the most detailed level are alternatives about *how the development should be phased, designed and managed*: Should all the wind turbines/houses/business units be put up at once? Should the rail line be operational before anybody moves into the new town?

Clearly the levels of the hierarchy inter-relate, as shown in Box 7.2. Development may actively be needed in some areas, for instance, to regenerate a derelict urban area, so that demand reduction would not be appropriate in these cases. Some modes or types of development are more appropriate in some locations than in others: wind turbines where there is wind, chicken manure power stations where there are chickens. In some areas, certain types of developments are inappropriate, so that location constrains the mode and type of development. For instance, visually intrusive development would normally not be allowed in areas of particular landscape sensitivity, and no reservoirs would be built where the hydrogeology is inappropriate. In some cases, this means that strategic-level decisions about major projects require detailed, local-level information to be collected before a decision can be made.

Generally, the more strategic alternatives (demand reduction, mode/type) are more applicable at the policy and national levels, and the more detailed alternatives (location, implementation) at the programme/project and local/site levels. Swedish planning guidance, for instance, suggests that issues of 'why' and 'if' are strategic, while 'where' and 'how' are more project-specific, and that the former should set the context for the latter (Figure 7.2). For the most part, more alternatives are available at a strategic policy level than at a more detailed programme level; and at a national or regional than at a sub-local level, where decisions made at a 'higher' level will have foreclosed many options.

Alternatives, options, scenarios

So far the discussion has been about 'alternatives' generally. But there are three broad types of alternatives.

Some *alternatives* are discrete, self-contained packages: decision-makers need to choose one option from this limited set ('we could do X or Y or Z'). For instance, politicians may need to decide whether or not to promote nuclear power, or planners may need to select one approach to siting new housing. Box 7.3 is an example of discrete alternatives related to flood risk management.

Box 7.2 Example of tiers of alternatives: SEA for Lao People's Democratic Republic hydropower development

The SEA for hydropower development in the Lao People's Democratic Republic considers the impacts of 23 hydropower projects that are planned until 2020. About two-thirds of the resulting power is expected to be exported to neighbouring countries. The SEA considers several 'tiers' of alternatives:

1. Demand-side management. It notes that power demand in Lao PDR is growing at about 11 per cent per year, but that most of the population is still without access to electricity, and that capacity expansion will remain the country's main focus in the short- and medium-term.

2. Alternative energy resources. The SEA summarizes possible alternatives to hydropower generation: oil and gas, lignite, coal, uranium/nuclear, geothermal, biomass, solar and wind. It concludes that there is no known potential for uranium and geothermal; solar and wind might be important at a local scale but would not provide the amount of energy needed overall; and lignite and coal development plans have so far been halted on grounds of cost and environmental concerns.

3. Alternative hydropower development plans. The SEA explains that several previous hydropower development plans and project rankings have been prepared for the country. In each case, a long-list (30–50) of potential projects was reduced to a short-list based on technical and cost parameters; and, in turn, the short-list projects underwent more detailed assessment and were ranked based on various technical, economic and environmental criteria. It notes that the main weakness of such an approach is that projects are ranked individually, whereas many of the planned projects are located in river basins with many project alternatives, leading to impact interactions between the different projects. This kind of project-based optimization might thus result in a different priority compared to when the projects are judged together (as was done in the SEA). Another alternative is that the development takes place more or less on an ad hoc basis, making an analysis and mitigation of cumulative impacts almost impossible.

4. Export scenarios. The SEA notes that much of the proposed hydropower development is based on the assumption that the resulting energy will be bought by Thailand and Vietnam; and that Cambodia, Myanmar and the People's Republic of China will not effectively compete with Lao to provide power for these markets. It concludes with a 'radical and unrealistic alternative' of the export market for hydropower from Lao disappearing totally, stating that in such a case only 20 per cent of the power generation proposed in Lao's development plan would be needed.

Source: Lao PDR and World Bank (2004)

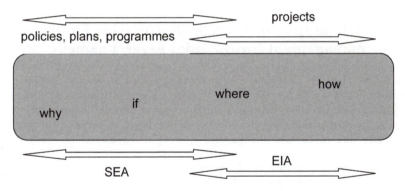

Source: Adapted from Swedish National Board of Housing Building and Planning, and Swedish Environmental Protection Agency (2000)

Figure 7.2 *Different focuses of different levels of decision-making*

Alternatives could also be mix-and-match combinations of individual components of the strategic action ('we could do A and/or B and/or C'). I call these *options*. For instance, Box 7.4 shows various options for regulating genetically engineered organisms in the US. For each bullet-point option, a decision will be made about whether to include that component (option) in the final strategic action or not.

The SEA test for alternatives is 'Which of these is the greenest/most sustainable?' and possibly 'Should we consider any other alternatives?'. The SEA test for options is, for each one, 'Is this option good enough to put in the strategic action?' and possibly 'Should we consider any other options?'.

Finally, alternatives or options could be devised to deal with various *scenarios* – situations that are outside of the control of the strategic action. For instance, one might want to consider alternative provision of employment land under scenarios of high v. low future economic growth; alternative waste management strategies under scenarios of high v. low waste generation (Verheem, 1996); or options for local-level land-use planning where a national-level decision has not yet been made but could significantly affect choices made for that plan. Höjer et al (2008) distinguish between the following:

- Predictive scenarios: both forecasts of what would happen under the most likely situation and 'what-if' scenarios regarding specified external events (e.g. results of an election). In both scenarios, the expectation is that underlying trends are broadly stable.
- Explorative scenarios, which consider the results of possible longer-term, more profound changes. These can be further divided into external scenarios of factors outside the decision-

Box 7.3 Example of discrete alternatives: Flood risk management for the tidal River Thames

Thames Estuary 2100 (TE2100) is a long-term flood risk management plan for the tidal River Thames, which flows through London. Flood protection is currently provided by walls, embankments, gates and the Thames Barrier. However, over the next 100 years, the frequency and severity of flooding is expected to increase, particularly due to climate change, and existing defences will no longer be adequate.

Over a three-year period, the Environment Agency identified and assessed a range of alternative approaches to flood risk management. Alternatives excluded in a first tranche analysis included:

- narrowing of the river mouth (throttle) because this would not be effective in reducing flood risk;
- a tide-excluding barrage because of the adverse impacts that impounding the estuary would cause, including water quality, morphology and drainage;
- a barrier (normally allows water through but can be shut during a flood) with locks downriver of Canvey Island because of cost, environmental impacts and constraints to navigation in the Thames estuary;
- a barrage (always closed) downriver of Canvey Island because of cost and adverse impacts on the estuary environment and navigation; and
- channel-dredging because of its adverse environmental impact.

Four generic options split into ten more specific options formed a short-list that was consulted on in spring 2009:

Option 1. Improve the existing defences
1.1 Raise defences when needed

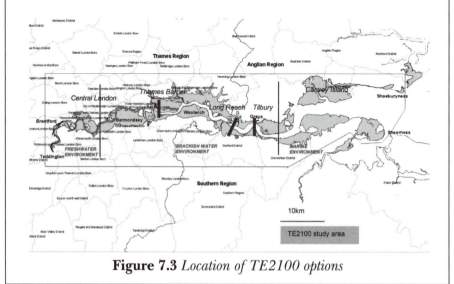

Figure 7.3 *Location of TE2100 options*

1.2 Allow for future adaptation of defences
1.3 Raise defences when they are replaced
1.4 Optimize defence repair and replacement
Option 2. Tidal flood storage
Up to four potential sites could store tidal waters and reduce the level of storm surges
Option 3. New Barrier
3.1 Tilbury location
3.2 Long Reach location
The barrier would be designed to resist the highest surge tides predicted under government climate change guidance.
Option 4. Barrier with locks
4.1 Tilbury location
4.2 Long Reach location
4.3 Convert Thames Barrier to a barrier with locks when the operational limit of closures per year is reached

The Environment Agency recommended two 'front runner' options. In both cases, the existing system would be maintained and improved until about 2070 (option 1.4). Then, option 1.4 could be continued, or a new barrier at Long Reach (option 3.2) could be built.

maker's remit (e.g. economic growth v. recession) and strategic scenarios that describe the possible consequences of policy options or other strategic decisions.

- Normative scenarios that consider how specified targets can be reached, either through incremental adjustments or more fundamental structural changes.

'Business as usual', 'do nothing', 'do minimum', 'best for the environment'

The 'business-as-usual', 'do-nothing' and 'do-minimum' alternatives are often referred to interchangeably. However, they are slightly different, and typically only one of them (often the 'business as usual' alternative) is realistic for a given strategic action.

The *'business-as-usual'* alternative refers to a continuation of the status quo. Why not just keep going with the existing strategic action (or lack thereof)? This provides a very useful sanity check: will the proposed strategic action really improve matters? This alternative also represents the future baseline without the plan discussed at Chapter 6. Carrying out an SEA of the *existing* strategic action (if there is one) early in the development of the *new* strategic action can help to identify the benefits and disbenefits of this alternative, and determine whether a new approach is needed.

Box 7.4 Example of options: Revision of US regulations on genetically engineered organisms

The US Department of Agriculture Animal and Plant Health Inspection Service (APHIS) regulates the introduction of genetically engineered organisms into the environment. In 2004, APHIS began considering whether revisions to its regulations were necessary to address current and future technological trends, ensure a high level of environmental protection, create regulatory processes that are transparent to stakeholders, and ensure conformity with international agreements. Options for these revisions that were considered in a PEIS of 2007 included:

- Whether to widen APHIS's remit beyond genetically engineered organisms that may pose a plant pest risk, to also regulate organisms that may pose a noxious weed risk or that may be used as biological control agents.
- Whether to establish a third approach to regulating genetically engineered organisms beyond (a) restriction and (b) unrestricted commercial use. The third approach could allow commercialization but under restricted conditions or monitoring.
- Whether and how to regulate for the low-level presence in crops, food, feed or seed of genetically engineered materials that have not completed the required regulatory processes.
- Whether to provide expedited review or exemption from review for certain low-risk imported genetically engineered commodities (e.g. food) that have received all necessary regulatory approvals in their country of origin.
- Whether to change APHIS's requirements for containers for the shipment of genetically engineered organisms.

Source: US Department of Agriculture (2007)

The '*do-nothing*' alternative assumes no new strategic action and no continuation of any existing strategic action. Where a new strategic action is being proposed, the 'business-as-usual' and 'do-nothing' alternatives are the same. Where a strategic action already exists and is being refreshed or replaced, then a separate 'do-nothing' alternative is also theoretically (but normally not realistically) feasible. Such an alternative asks 'What if the existing strategic action was neither continued nor replaced?'

The '*do-minimum*' option represents one of minimal ongoing maintenance of existing resources or assets. In Box 7.3, for instance, it would imply simply maintaining existing flood defences at their current level.

Similarly, considering the 'best-for-the-environment' alternative can help to show how far the proposed option is from the ideal state, and can help to identify ways of making it more environmentally sustainable.

Should one consider alternatives to strategic actions that are environmentally benign anyway, such as those for renewable energy or nature conservation? Arguably, even an environmentally positive plan could be made more positive. For example, many renewable energy projects have unavoidable environmental downsides. These may be far less damaging than fossil or nuclear energy alternatives, but obviating the need for energy production in the first place might avoid even these lesser forms of damage. Such analysis would also provide evidence and reassurance that the (benign) strategic action is as benign as possible.

Finally, many SEAs – particularly for developing countries – don't formally consider alternatives at all but do propose mitigation measures for a draft plan. Such mitigation measures could be considered as alternatives, albeit limited ones that are considered only late in the day.

Developing alternatives/options

Given the close links with the plan-making process, the timing of alternatives development is crucial. Nowhere is the concept of 'decision window' more crucial than for alternatives.

In an ideal world, decision-makers would develop a good range of sustainable alternatives/options for their strategic action; and the SEA would simply assess the impact of these alternatives, suggest avoidance/mitigation measures for any adverse impacts, and possibly identify an alternative that is best for the environment/sustainability. In opening the decision-making process to public scrutiny, SEA could also lead to ideas for other alternatives by the public or environmental authorities. The SEA report would document this process of alternatives identification, assessment and decision-making.

In practice, many planners seem to find the process of formally identifying alternatives difficult if not impossible. Many strategic actions are not written from scratch, but rather are adaptations of existing strategic actions. Others arise in response to a problem, with politicians often already having identified and made public the action that they want to implement. Plan-makers' remits are often severely restricted, either by law or by convention. They may be expected to prepare the strategic action in a very short time. In such cases, SEA provides a useful mechanism to help ensure that alternatives are considered, and often also to help develop alternatives.

This section discusses how alternatives can be generated and organized, and their numbers limited, for assessment purposes.

Generating alternatives

As discussed earlier, many possible alternatives to strategic actions will be constrained by higher-level policies, and planners often find it easier to identify alternatives that they do not have rather than those that they do. However, the development of any strategic action will involve choices, even if these are only about how to interpret higher-level policies into a local context. The role of SEA is to help identify those dimensions of the strategic action where alternatives do exist, and to 'tell the story' of how alternatives have been developed. The concept of the 'storyline' is discussed at the end of this chapter.

A range of sources can trigger the generation of alternatives, including analysis of the strategic action objective, policy context and environmental objectives, existing and predicted environmental/ sustainability problems, scenario testing, consideration of the alternatives hierarchy, suggestions raised by key stakeholders and the public, plan-makers' ideas, and previously completed assessments of plans (Desmond, 2007; Höjer et al, 2008; CLG, 2009b).

Alternatives can represent different ways of achieving an objective(s) of the strategy action, for instance, providing enough homes to cater for household growth or providing enough electricity to meet future demand. European Commission (2003) guidance on the European SEA Directive, for instance, notes that 'The first consideration in deciding on possible reasonable alternatives should be to take into account the objectives and the geographical scope of the plan or programme'. Box 7.4 is a clear example of this.

An often surprisingly difficult aspect of this is identifying just what the plan objectives are. Box 7.5 gives an example of a situation where the initially stated plan objectives did not represent the real plan objectives. In this case, the SEA helped to clarify that building a high-speed train line (the original focus of decision-making) was only one way of achieving the true objective of boosting the economy of a peripheral region, and that this could be done more cheaply and with fewer environmental impacts through other means.

Webster and Muller (2006, cited in Partidário (2007)) describe 'strategic thrusts' as sets of cross-cutting interlocking actions delivered through a variety of modes, that are designed to achieve a specified target in the most cost-effective manner possible. An example of this could be increased provision of affordable housing through both direct government investment and support of public–private partnerships. Webster and Muller (2006) suggest that strategic actions should have no more than five such 'strategic thrusts', each of which would be delivered through several more detailed actions. The 'strategic thrust' concept could help to bring together strategic action objectives into a more structured approach. The alternatives assessed in the SEA could represent different ways of delivering each target.

Box 7.5 Alternative ways of achieving an objective: The Netherlands' Zuiderzeelijn (high-speed rail line)

The Zuiderzeelijn was a proposed high-speed rail line between Schiphol Airport or Amsterdam and Groningen, which aimed to boost the lagging economy of the northern Netherlands by improving connections to the country's economic centre. The Zuiderzeelijn concept emerged in the mid-1990s from negotiations between the northern regional authorities and the national government. Much preparatory work was carried out by the Ministry of Transport over about a decade. However, delays and cost overruns – the initial assumed cost of €2.73 billion had risen to more than €4 billion by 2006 – raised doubts about the scheme. In 2005, a parliamentary enquiry committee required a reassessment of the scheme, including an SEA.

Comments were invited on the desired scope of the SEA report, and dozens of meetings were attended by hundreds of people. Several alternative technologies and routes for the rail line were developed, assessed and compared in an SEA report. However, the SEA also noted that the original problem definition – that the distance between the north and the economic centre was the reason for the north's economic problems – was inadequate.

In April 2006, the Cabinet decided that a high-speed rail line would not be economically efficient and that it would have unacceptable environmental impacts. Instead, it agreed a 'transition alternative' that aimed to meet the original objective of boosting the economy of the north. This involved allocating about €2 billion to the northern Netherlands for a range of smaller-scale improvements to the road and rail infrastructure.

> *Strikingly, millions of euros had been spent on developing and assessing alternatives for a project that had not been selected. Although apparently wasteful, such efforts were necessary to decide whether the project would solve any problems, or whether it would instead create many new problems. Stakeholder respondents indicated that, in general, they felt that the money had been well spent. In their eyes, the SEA had contributed significantly to the learning process, as had the societal cost–benefit analysis... The SEA functioned as a generator of alternatives which opened new avenues for stakeholders to think about other agendas.* (van Buuren and Nooteboom, 2009)

Source: Based on van Buuren and Nooteboom (2009)

Alternatives can also aim to achieve a future vision. For instance, community visions can be developed in workshops, and alternatives can be suggested for how the visions can be achieved. The test of the alternative is 'Does it meet the vision/objective?'

Alternatives can be developed in response to an existing or expected future problem, such as climate change, economic recession or an issue raised at public meetings. The test of the alternative in such a case is 'Does it help to solve the problem?' They can also be used to illustrate issues and tensions, which should be addressed as the preferred options are refined, for instance, different ways in which a limited pot of developer contributions can be allocated, or the implications of different approaches to providing infrastructure alongside other development. This can help to develop a preferred alternative that brings together the best elements from several different alternatives.

Environmental/sustainability authorities, other expert bodies or the public can propose alternatives and are often a useful 'sanity check' for possible alternatives. However, they are often consulted on alternatives only late in the decision-making process, when many behind-the-scenes negotiations and discussions have already taken place, and a preferred alternative has already been chosen. This gives them little or no opportunity to meaningfully question and inform the development and choice of alternatives, and puts them in the position of critiquing rather than informing the SEA. Table 7.2 shows a rare example of options proposed by the public that were fully assessed in an SEA and incorporated into the strategic action.

As a counter-example, several English local authorities won a legal challenge against the East of England regional spatial strategy in May 2009, on the basis that the SEA for the strategy did not assess alternatives to the late inclusion of housing sites in the London Green Belt (Government Office for the East of England, 2009). Soon after this ruling, similar challenges were made to two other regional spatial strategies: at the time of writing, no ruling had yet been reached on these further challenges (Planning Resource, 2009a/b).

Morrison-Saunders and Therivel (2006) list decision questions that may help to generate alternatives, from more strategic and potentially sustainable at the top to less so at the bottom:

- What should the future of area X be?
- What is the best way of providing for demand for X?
- What is the best way to address issue/problem X?
- What is the most appropriate activity for site X, and under what circumstances should the activity be allowed to go ahead?
- How can existing activity X be made more sustainable?
- Would proposal X be sustainable?
- Which is the best alternative for undertaking proposal X from given options?
- What is the best site to locate proposal X?
- Is proposal X acceptable at site Y?

Tiers of alternatives, limiting the number of alternatives

The development of most strategic actions will not involve a simple and elegant process of choosing between a limited set of clearly defined

Table 7.2 *Examples of plan options put forward by the public in response to an Issues and Options leaflet: Leicester core strategy*

Topic	Options originally set out in the local planning authority's Issues and Options leaflet	Converse options added to the original options	Additional options identified through consultation responses received about the Issues and Options leaflet
Providing new homes	Continue with planned housing development at Hamilton and Ashton Green	Discontinue the planned housing development at Hamilton and Ashton Green	Maximize the use of vacant land (brownfield sites) and buildings
	Continue to encourage a mix of uses on inner city regeneration sites but make sure that the housing is built early on	Encourage single use (e.g. housing or offices) on inner city regeneration sites	Reduce the vacancy rate of existing Council housing stock
		Restrict infill to maintain current character of the city	
Gypsies and travellers	Identify residential areas for small family sites for gypsy and travellers	Do not use developer contributions for gypsy and traveller sites	Make provision for gypsy and traveller sites outside residential areas
	Use developer contributions for affordable housing to provide sites for gypsy and travellers		
Open space network	Protect and improve all existing open spaces	Do not allow any development in green wedges as shown on current proposals map	Protect and enhance sport and recreation opportunities in the city
	Allow some development on selected open spaces which are unused, poorly located, or of poor quality		
	Review the current green wedge boundary to release some small areas of land that no longer have a strategic green wedge function		

Key: Dark grey shading – options rejected after the initial appraisal
Light grey shading – options discounted after a full appraisal
No shading – options taken forward as preferred options (possibly in amended form)
Source: Adapted from Leicester City Council (2008)

1. Country towns: continuation of existing strategy

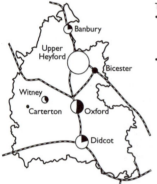

This could achieve:

• growth of jobs and services with population in Banbury, Bicester, Didcot and Witney
• scope for better long distance and public transport links and public transport within the country towns
• a boost to town centres in the country towns, especially Didcot
• continued protection for the green belt and countryside elsewhere in the county

But could also mean:

• potential loss of good quality farmland or landscape around Banbury, Bicester, Didcot and Witney
• growth of commuting to Oxford

New dwellings ◖ Commitments post 2001

⠂ ⠂ Area of search for new dwellings

▬▬ Railway

2. New settlement at RAF Upper Heyford

This could achieve:

• a high quality, self-contained settlement, with potential to plan for public transport, cycling and walking
• scope to travel by rail on the Marylebone and Oxford lines

But could also mean:

• a low quality settlement, heavily dependent on private car use
• poor access to jobs and services
• increased traffic on rural roads
• new road links, including to the M40 (motorway)

Source: Oxfordshire County Council (1995)

Figure 7.4 *Examples of discrete alternatives: Oxfordshire County Council spatial strategy*

alternatives. Most strategic actions have multiple objectives or aim to solve multiple problems, so that there will be several clusters of alternatives to choose from. Development of a strategic action may involve choices of alternatives/options at several different levels, for instance, strategic alternatives on general policy themes, broad spatial alternatives and detailed site alternatives. For many strategic actions there may also be an infinite number of possible alternatives or options: should the local land-use plan aim to deliver 10,000 homes or 10,001 or 9,999, etc.? The SEA process may thus need to help decision-makers to sift through a very complex situation, and document it as a small number of discrete options (Broad, 2006). Several concepts may help to simplify and document this sifting process.

First, the main alternatives will typically be *within* the strategic action rather than to the strategic action. As such, there are likely to be clusters of alternatives rather than a single set.

3. Rail corridors

This could achieve:
• good access to jobs and services in central Oxfordshire by public transport
• scope for developing better long distance public transport links and viable public transport corridors

But could also mean:
• potential loss of good quality farmland and threats to small settlements, high quality landscape, and green belt
• highway problems on minor roads likely
• major investment in public transport links in Oxford in order to achieve benefits

4. Dispersal to smaller towns

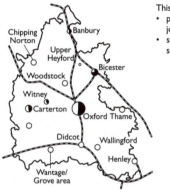

This could achieve:
• potential local balance between jobs and houses
• support and possible expansion of some local shops and services

But could also mean:
• potential loss of good quality farmland and high quality landscape
• possible coalescence of some towns and villages
• heavy reliance on private car use, and would be impossible to serve by public transport effectively
• increased traffic on rural roads

Figure 7.4 *continued*

Many plan-making processes will involve 'tiers' of alternatives, where choices made at an earlier stage of decision-making will limit the subsequent range of available alternatives. For instance, if deciding where to locate 10,000 new homes, the tiers might be:

1 Should the new homes be provided as a free-standing new town, an extension (or two) to an existing town or broken up into smaller developments, as at Figure 7.4? The impacts of these alternatives can be assessed and compared using SEA, and a preferred alternative chosen.
2 Assuming that town extensions are the preferred option, which town or towns should be extended? Again, these can be assessed and compared using SEA.
3 Assuming that Town X is the preferred alternative, should the housing be located to the north, south, east or west?

Box 7.2 is another example of such tiering.

Where a very large number of alternatives is possible (for instance, housing numbers), it may be helpful to artificially choose some points on the continuum for initial assessment purposes, and then close down on a preferred alternative/option through a combination of consultation and further assessment. Similarly, alternatives or options can be chosen which portray different themes or approaches. For instance, alternatives could emphasize renewable energy v. fossil fuels, or siting of new power stations in areas of electricity demand v. in areas of least impact. These may later be adapted, with different aspects of different alternatives brought together, in a final, preferred alternative.

Where many possible areas for development are available and a more limited number needs to be chosen, a hierarchy of criteria could be used. The Planning Advisory Service (PAS) (2009) has suggested the following hierarchy of criteria for English development sites:

- Exclusionary criteria – e.g. flood risk areas, national level landscape designations, areas outside the pattern of development set out in local authority development plans – which may make a site 'unreasonable' as a location for development.
- Discretionary criteria – e.g. relating to public rights of way, agricultural land, local nature conservation designations, etc. These criteria might not necessarily lead to the exclusion of a site but would influence the decision as to whether or not to shortlist a site.
- Deliverability criteria – e.g. land ownership, access, planning history, size – which may have a bearing on whether or not the site is deliverable as a location for development.

The level of detail of the SEA analysis can vary between alternatives. It may be possible to rapidly eliminate some alternatives from further consideration because they are not reasonable (see the next section), are clearly inferior to other alternatives, or in some other way are unlikely to be incorporated in the final strategic action. In such cases, it is not necessary to subject these alternatives to detailed assessment: only a brief explanation of the reasons for eliminating these alternatives is necessary. Other alternatives may merit a more detailed and comprehensive assessment and comparison.

Eliminating alternatives/options from (further) assessment

This section discusses which options do not warrant assessment at all, and how other alternatives can be eliminated from more detailed assessment. It is based heavily on Desmond (2007), PAS (2009) and

Collingwood Environmental Planning et al (2006). Box 7.6 provides a glowing example of alternatives that should never have seen the light of day. Before continuing reading this section, you may want to ask yourself what is wrong with them. I will return to Box 7.6, with my answers, at the end of this section.

A key concept in the consideration and elimination of alternatives is that of 'reasonableness'. For instance the SEA Directive requires the environmental report to assess the environmental impacts of implementing 'the plan or programme and reasonable alternatives' (CEC, 2001). The regulations that implement the US National Environmental Policy Act (40 CFR 1502.14) explain that the lead agency or agencies must 'objectively evaluate all reasonable alternatives', namely those that substantially meet the agency's purpose and need.

So what are unreasonable alternatives? First, alternatives that are *outside of the planning authority's remit* are unreasonable. This includes alternatives that are outside of the planning authority's:

- geographical scope, for instance, locating development in an adjacent local authority or on the moon (except if you are NASA);
- objectives, for instance, proposing higher housing densities as part of a transport plan;
- legal competence, for instance, a local authority proposing congestion charging if this is the remit of the national level transport department. Behavioural change, demand reduction and fiscal measures are (frustratingly) often outside the control of planning authorities; and
- illegal alternatives – for instance, not preparing a plan when the planning authority is legally required to prepare one.

Second, alternatives that are *not feasible* are unreasonable. These include alternatives for which:

- the necessary resources to deliver the alternative are not available;
- sufficient time within the plan period to implement the option is not available;
- the relevant technology will not be available or standards cannot be achieved within the lifetime of the strategic action;
- some extreme alternatives, for instance, providing twice as many homes as are expected to be needed in the plan period; and
- the alternative is unlikely to be fully implemented.

However, this reason for eliminating alternatives needs to be used carefully: there may be good reasons to choose a strategy that forces the development of a new technology or brings about economies of scale for something that is not currently feasible.

Box 7.6 Example of how not to develop alternatives

The following example – which is unfortunately not at all atypical – is based on a real-life case, which I have mercifully rendered anonymous. As a result of new legislation, all local planning authorities in a particular country must now write new land-use plans, which will take over the functions of the former spatial plans. The table below shows the comparison of alternatives for one local planning authority's land-use plan.

Alternative	Positive impact	Negative/uncertain impacts
1. New land-use plan	• Informed by stakeholders and SEA • Achieves environmental objectives of the national spatial plan • Planned and transparent approach • Accommodates national-level flood risk advice • Includes sustainable settlement hierarchy • Environmental protection • Urban and rural regeneration	• Uncertain ecological impact on site X
2. No plan		• Ad hoc land-use decision • No SEA input • No link to environmental objectives of the national spatial plan • Flood risk issues unresolved • Lack of settlement hierarchy • Inadequate environmental protection • No urban and rural regeneration
3. Continue with existing spatial plan	• Has already set out a policy framework for the local authority	• No SEA input • No link to environmental objectives of national spatial plan • Flood risk issues unresolved • Lack of settlement hierarchy • Less environmental protection • Little urban and rural regeneration • Progressively reduced consistency with best practice

The alternatives considered in the SEA should reflect those actually considered by the decision-makers. Alternatives that are *not relevant to the decision-making process* (i.e. they are not genuine, they are 'forced' or 'made up') are unreasonable. These include:

- alternatives that are included simply to make another alternative 'look better', for instance 'do not protect historically important buildings' as an alternative to 'protect historically important buildings';
- most alternatives that deal with the strategic action as a whole, for instance, whether the strategic action should be socially, economically or environmentally led;
- alternatives for minor, inconsequential aspects of the strategic action.

A recent study (CLG, 2009b) concluded that, in England at least, these kinds of 'forced' alternatives are unfortunately very common: '[There are lots] of examples where alternatives are made up just to satisfy regulations, but are not realistic or to do with the Plan.'

Inconvenient alternatives

Inconvenient alternatives are not necessarily unreasonable. They include those that are not politically expedient, not desirable from the planning authority's standpoint, unpopular or not part of the dominant discourse (CEQ, 2007; Runhaar, 2009). The generation and assessment of alternatives for SEA is not a popularity contest, and decision-makers may need to consider alternatives – for instance, about genetically modified organisms, gypsies and travellers, nuclear power or waste incineration – that are unpalatable to most of their constituents. In many cases, the most environmentally friendly alternative is very inconvenient indeed, possibly entailing difficult questions about population size, material wealth or people's behaviour.

It may be also be appropriate to consider alternatives that conflict with higher-level strategic actions, on the basis that the higher-level strategic actions are unsustainable. Desmond (2008) describes 'path dependency' within a tiered decision-making hierarchy as 'the way in which policy decisions create a context for subsequent decisions ... reinforcing the likelihood of similar decisions in the future'. She notes that in some cases – for instance, where the 'path dependency' stresses the waste hierarchy (reduce, re-use, recycle, etc.) – this helps to support sustainable development, but in other cases 'path dependency' may reinforce an unsustainable approach, which should be identified and possibly challenged through SEA. Similarly, in England, 'Inconvenient alternatives are often suppressed... Planners are too quick to assume that an alternative is not reasonable because it is counter to government policy' (CLG, 2009b).

Finally, alternatives that have been rejected previously may become reasonable in time, because they may have been rejected for reasons that are no longer valid. For instance, technologies that were previously too expensive may have become more affordable; or a changing situation may require a new approach. This is the case with nuclear power in the UK: no new nuclear power stations have been built since the electricity system was privatized in 1989, nominally on grounds of cost, but nuclear power is now considered reasonable again as a way of providing energy with few greenhouse gas emissions (DBERR, 2008b).

How not to develop alternatives

This section began with an example of how not to develop alternatives, with three alternatives proposed for a new land-use plan: 1. the new plan; 2. no plan; and 3. continue with the existing plan. This is why those alternatives are problematic:

- The last two alternatives are not legal, since a new plan must be prepared by law.
- The last two have obviously been included to make the 'preferred option' look better.
- The first alternative is clearly so much better than the others that the detailed comparison presented in the table is unnecessary: a single sentence of explanation would have sufficed.
- There is no analysis of the contents of the plan – different ways of meeting the plan objectives, dealing with existing problems, etc.
- The alternatives do not reflect those actually considered by the planners, who are unlikely to have been sitting around the office arguing about whether to write a new plan or not (at least I hope they haven't).

In sum, the alternatives look as though they were made up simply to fulfil the requirements of SEA.

'Telling the story' of alternatives

Documenting the alternatives generation and selection process essentially involves telling the story of how decision-makers, starting with an infinity of possible alternatives for their plan, zeroed in on the final preferred alternative. This is a continuation of the 'story' of the context-setting stage of the SEA. A rough structure for the 'story' is:

Basis for generating alternatives

The geographical and temporal scope of our plan is... Our plan's objectives are... (from the plan description stage). Our plan must... and it should... (from the policy context). Our plan tries to solve the following problems... (from the statement of existing problems). The main strategic thrusts of our plan are...

First sieve of reasonableness

Our plan cannot... and so the following alternatives are not within our remit... The following alternatives have already been precluded by higher-level policy... (though consider querying this if it is unsustainable). We have no alternatives for the following issues because...

Second sieve

We initially considered the following alternatives for topic X (or 'to achieve objective Y' or 'to deal with problem Z')... We discussed these draft alternatives with the environmental/sustainability authorities and the public, who proposed the following additional alternatives... Table A shows the main advantages and disadvantages of the alternatives. The following alternatives are clearly less advantageous than the others because... We have combined/amended/fine-tuned the remaining alternatives as follows to make them more sustainable/reduce their negative impacts/etc....

Subsequent sieves

A full environmental/sustainability assessment was carried out for the remaining alternatives for topic X (again this might be in one or two sieves, for example, first to eliminate policy statements or proposed sites that would affect national-level environmental designations and then to consider the remaining ones in more detail). We again discussed these with the environmental/sustainability authorities and the public, who proposed... We assessed these proposals using the same approach as above. Alternative M is the preferred alternative because...

Conclusions

Quality review questions for the alternatives stage that could be used by either a formal reviewer or as a self-test are:

• Have alternatives been considered that deal with the issues and problems identified as a result of the baseline assessment and/or aim to achieve sustainability?

- Do the alternatives include the 'business as usual', 'do nothing' and/or 'do minimum' alternative, and the 'most environmentally beneficial' alternative if appropriate?
- Are the alternatives in the planning authority's remit (geographical scope, objectives, legal competence)?
- Are the alternatives feasible (available resources, technology, otherwise capable of being implemented)?
- Are the alternatives relevant to the decision-making process (not 'made up', unnecessary or at the wrong level)?
- Are inconvenient but otherwise reasonable alternatives not eliminated – explicitly or implicitly – from consideration?
- Have reasons been given for why alternatives have been eliminated from further consideration?
- Has a preferred alternative(s) been identified?

The next chapter considers how the impacts of the emerging strategic action alternatives and statements can be identified, evaluated and mitigated.

Note

1   A distinction can be made between demands and needs. Demands are what people want; needs are what they need. Demands are almost always greater than needs. The literature on consumption (e.g. Ekins, 1986; Firat and Dholakia, 1998) is full of long discussions about when a demand becomes a need and vice versa, particularly given how, in many countries, consumption has become a vital method of self-expression. I don't intend to go into that here. My only point is that one should try to reduce demand before catering for the remaining demand, which I call 'need'.

Chapter 8

Predicting Impacts

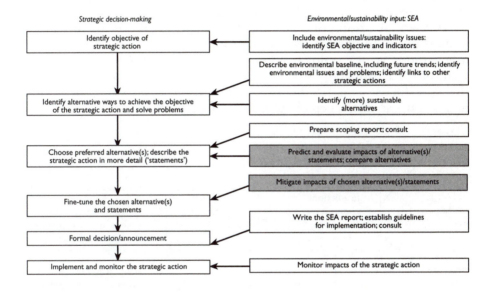

SEA stage	What to decide	What to record
Predict and evaluate impact of alternatives/statements; compare alternatives; mitigate impacts of chosen alternative(s)/statements	What are the effects of the alternatives/options and statements on the environmental/sustainability objectives and indicators; what are the preferred alternatives; what mitigation measures to include	Summary of effects of alternatives/options and statements on the environment and sustainability; list of preferred alternatives; explanation of why these are preferred; mitigation measures proposed

Prediction, evaluation and avoidance/mitigation of the impacts of a strategic action are the core of the SEA process. They are often the most time- and resource-intensive stages of the process. They frequently need to be carried out at several stages of decision-making, for instance evaluation of several alternatives for a broad plan strategy, evaluation and mitigation of more detailed ways of implementing the preferred strategy, and evaluation of the refined/mitigated plan.

Prediction involves determining the scale, duration, likelihood, etc. of the impact[1]. Evaluation involves determining whether the predicted impact is significant or not: this requires an element of judgement. *Avoidance, mitigation and enhancement* involve trying to first avoid any significant negative impacts of the strategic action, and then minimize the remaining negative impacts and enhance the positive impacts. The three stages are closely interlinked (see Figure 8.1).

In the first edition of this book, one chapter sufficed for the inter-related topics of prediction, evaluation and mitigation. However, so much more is now known about these topics, and so many more examples are available, that I have split the original chapter in two – this one focuses on prediction and Chapter 9 on evaluation and mitigation – so as to keep chapter sizes manageable.

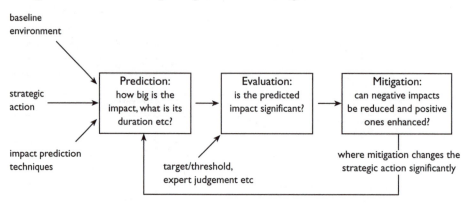

Figure 8.1 *Links between prediction, evaluation and mitigation*

Prediction principles

The aim of impact prediction is to identify various dimensions of a strategic action's likely future impacts. Typical stages in prediction are:

1   Determine, for each environmental/sustainability topic or objective, the scope of the assessment: the geographic area and timescale over which the predictions are being made.
2   Predict what the strategic action/alternatives will 'look' like when implemented, for instance:

– what activities would probably occur?
– where might those activities occur, if appropriate?
– how might they be affected by other parts of the strategic action or other strategic actions?

3 Predict the likely impacts of the strategic action: the difference between the baseline (including future changes within the impact prediction timescale) with and without the strategic action. Impacts may be direct, indirect and induced, and cumulative (including synergistic). The impact prediction stage will involve making a range of assumptions, which should be identified and documented. The impacts of the strategic action can be described in terms of (where relevant):

– whether they are positive or negative;
– their magnitude (large or small impact);
– their spatial distribution;
– their duration (long or short term);
– whether they are reversible or irreversible; and
– their likelihood of occurring.

This chapter begins with a discussion of the main principles of impact prediction. It then discusses each of the above stages in turn. Final sections cover three specific aspects of impact prediction: indirect impacts, cumulative impacts and equality impacts. Specific techniques for impact prediction and evaluation are addressed at Appendix C.

Impact prediction has the potential to be horribly onerous and resource-intensive. Yet its only purpose is to identify key environmental issues to be taken into account in decision-making. As such, a first prediction principle is that *impact prediction should be 'fit for purpose': it should only be detailed enough to allow effective identification of key environmental impacts of the strategic action*. For most impacts of most strategic actions, simple qualitative prediction methods will be perfectly adequate. There is no need to carry out detailed, quantitative predictions simply because they look more robust: they often are not. This is discussed in more detail later in the chapter.

A related principle is that of proportionality of assessment. The *level of detail of the assessment should be proportional to the level of detail of the strategic action*: the more detailed the strategic action, the more detailed the assessment should be. In particular, if a strategic action is spatially specific, then the assessment should also be spatially specific, and based on spatially specific baseline data. The *level of detail of the baseline data should also be proportional to that of the assessment and mitigation*:

The level of abstraction for [SEA] should be balanced with the strategic level of information analysis, especially if details will be further elaborated in a tiered system of SEA/EIA... [T]he causes of the tendency towards unnecessary detail [in SEA] are that the environmental experts are not used to dealing with such a degree of uncertainty and that the public is too impatient to wait for more detailed impact predictions in later stages of decision-making (DHV, 1994).

The assessment *should clearly identify the main negative impacts of the implementation of the strategic action, to help determine the need for avoidance and mitigation measures.* This may involve testing a worst-case scenario as well as the most likely implementation scenario.

Many environmental problems faced today result from the accumulation of multiple small, often indirect, effects rather than a few large, obvious ones. Examples include loss of tranquillity, changes in the landscape, significant loss of some types of habitats and species, global warming and increasing social inequalities in many areas. These effects are very hard to deal with on a project by project basis through EIA: EIA comes too late and is too detailed and focused on the short term. As such, despite the difficulties of doing so, *SEA should make a special effort to consider cumulative, indirect, long-term and equalities impacts.*

The following sections discuss how these principles can be put into practice.

Scope of assessment

The temporal and geographic scope of impact predictions can affect the results of the prediction and so needs careful thought. An over-wide or over-long scope can make a strategic action's impacts seem trivial. A more common problem, however, is an over-narrow scope.

Some impacts of a strategic action will not emerge for years, and may continue for centuries. Housing built today will probably still be around in 2100, as will any (lack of) energy efficiency measures in those homes. Open spaces will only improve the health of local residents in a slow and incremental manner. Changes from greenfield to developed sites tend to be irreversible. The US National Environmental Policy Act wisely called for SEA reports to discuss:

> *the relationship between local short-term uses of man's environment and the maintenance and enhancement of long-term productivity, and any irreversible and irretrievable commitments of resources which would be involved in the proposed action should it be implemented.* (42 USC 4332)

For many impacts – for instance, noise, air pollution and employment benefits – the timescale of SEA predictions will be equivalent to the lifetime of the strategic action. However, an SEA should also clearly identify and document any long-term and irreversible impacts.

Similarly, most impacts of a strategic action are likely to occur within the area covered by that action. However, there may be transboundary impacts to adjacent or even distant countries or districts. In England, an early 'core strategy' (local authority spatial plan) was rejected by an inspector as being unsound, in part because its SA did not consider what impacts a proposed retail centre near the local authority boundary would have on adjacent authorities (Mattocks, 2006). In contrast, the SEA for Ireland's second National Hazardous Waste Management Plan – which aimed to treat more hazardous waste in Ireland and export less of it – concluded that, although the plan would increase local impacts, this was more sustainable overall than shipping the waste abroad and causing impacts there (Environmental Protection Agency, 2008b).

Where an SEA framework was established at the context-setting stage, this should help to ensure that all relevant impacts of the strategic action are identified. However, if at the prediction stage further impacts are identified (or impacts initially thought to possibly occur are found not to), the SEA framework should be adapted accordingly.

What will the strategic action 'look' like when implemented?

For SEA, it is typically not necessary to determine in detail what a strategic action will look like on the ground. However, a strategic action's impacts will often depend on how it is implemented: (a) what types of activities or projects it is likely to generate, and (b) which policy statements are more v. less likely to 'win' in case of conflict. The SEA will need to consider what the actual implementation of a strategic action is likely to be, rather than the plan-makers' intent. Where strategic actions are vague and require assumptions to assess, these assumptions should be clearly stated, and measures should be put in place to try to ensure that any positive assumptions come about in practice. A side benefit of SEA is that it helps to improve the clarity of the strategic action, making it more likely that it will be well implemented.

In terms of the *activities or projects likely to be generated by a strategic action*, take an example from the draft Tooton Rush transport strategy: Wanda and Mohammed are assessing Statement X which Chen has written.

> W: *Let's get on with the assessment. Statement X says that 'The council will discourage the use of unsuitable minor roads.' What will this look like on the ground?*

M: Well, obviously it means that there will be traffic management, like traffic humps and those things that cars need to weave around, on small roads in towns where there are lots of children.

W: I think that it means that lorries will be channelled onto bigger roads, because it's an unsuitable use of minor roads.

M: You're talking about a rural context and I'm thinking about the urban context. We need to figure out what is an 'unsuitable' minor road: unsuitable for what?

W: We need to ask Chen what he means.

M: But we also need to ask what he means by 'discourage'. Does he mean financial disincentives like congestion charging, or bans for certain types of vehicles at certain times like your lorry restrictions, or small-scale building works like traffic humps? The impact of each of those will be different.

In this case, before an adequate assessment can even start, Wanda, Mohammed and Chen need to agree on what is meant by 'discourage', 'unsuitable' and 'minor'. They would not need to know exactly *which* roads are unsuitable and minor, or exactly *how* traffic would be 'discouraged', but would need enough detail to allow reasonable predictions to be made. Chen may have a very clear idea in his head about what he wants his statement to say, but the statement is not clear enough for the SEA team, much less for anyone who needs to implement the statement. Alternatively, Chen may have included the statement because Politician Meddlemuch wants it and it sounds unproblematic, without really thinking about its precise wording. An example of a clearer statement that could result from this discussion is 'In urban areas, the council will discourage through traffic on minor roads (those not marked in red on Map X) by using traffic calming such as speed humps.'

Strategic actions often act as political tools: they try to reconcile opposing views or say unpalatable things by making magnificently vague, 'motherhood-and-apple-pie' type statements. At times, in fact, they seem to say the exact opposite of what they mean. Table 8.1 gives some real-life examples and possible reasons why the mis-wording might have emerged.

Strategic actions typically include several policy statements, some with negative environmental/sustainability impacts, some with positive effects, and some which aim to avoid or minimize the negative impacts. For instance, one policy statement might be about ensuring that sufficient land is available to meet future housing demand, one might propose a new country park, and another might aim to protect

Table 8.1 *Examples of what statements in strategic actions do and do not mean*

Statement	'The conversion of historic agricultural buildings to an alternative use, particularly a use which would make a positive contribution to the local economy, will be permitted unless the proposal: would be significantly detrimental to the form, details, character or setting of the building. Conversion to workshops, meeting halls, indoor sports, storage or camping barns is likely to be more acceptable than conversion to residential uses.'	'The county council will work closely with the district councils to develop comprehensive policies for car parking.'	'The sustainable development of the region's airports will be supported.'
What one might expect the statement at face value to look like when implemented	Sensitive conversion of historic agricultural buildings to workshops, meeting halls, etc.	Policies for short-term and long-term parking, Park and Ride, etc.	Unclear: air travel is inherently unsustainable.
What the statement actually means	All of the recent conversions of historic agricultural buildings have been to housing. We want to slow this down a bit, say to 90% housing and 10% other uses.	Please, district councils, develop parking policies. for us	Development of the region's airports will be supported.
Why the statement might have been written that way	Government guidance states that plans should make positive not negative statements ('you can build under these conditions...', not 'you cannot build...') so we cannot ban conversions to residential use. We are unlikely to see many proposals for conversion to non-residential uses but we'll give it a good try anyway with this strongly worded statement.	County councils have no power to develop parking policies but we need such policies to help achieve our transport targets. District councils control parking. Let's hope that they get the hint.	The national strategy for air travel promotes growth of the region's airports. The government also expects the region to promote sustainable development. The two are inherently contradictory. We are not allowed to choose one or the other, so we will carry on this conflict in our strategic action.

biodiversity and greenfield land. Strategic actions may also include policy statements with potentially conflicting clauses, for instance, 'the sustainable development of the region's airports will be supported' (see Table 8.1).

Assumptions will need to be made about *which policy statements or clauses are likely to 'win' in case of conflict*. This will determine what assumptions need to be made for SEA purposes. Which is the 'winner' will depend on factors such as:

- the likely magnitude of the impact v. magnitude of mitigation;
- the strength of the policy wording ('must' vs. 'seek to');
- whether the issue is within the clear remit of the plan-making authority;
- whether funding mechanisms act preferentially towards one or the other, e.g. housing is privately funded while rail access to the housing requires public funding which is more uncertain;
- whether the issue is monitored and/or highlighted in the news; and
- lifestyle and other trends, e.g. people wishing to fly abroad for holidays.

Box 8.1 is an example of how such assumptions could be made and documented in an SEA report.

By encouraging the strategy authors to be clear about what they have in mind, SEA can help them to consider specific steps that would encourage the 'right' implementation. For instance, new housing could improve conditions for wildlife if it replaces a field of monoculture (say wheat or corn) with wildlife-friendly gardens; or it could replace an area that is rich in wildlife with lots of paving and minimal plantings, and so have a negative effect. The role of the SEA is to highlight this, and to suggest ways of avoiding, mitigating or enhancing these impacts at the implementation stage, for example: 'all existing hedges, woodlands, ponds and ditches will be maintained and enhanced where possible, wildlife corridors will be provided where possible, and communal areas will be planted with indigenous plants'.

Approaches to impact prediction

Once the scope of the assessment and how the strategic action would look when implemented are known, the strategic action's impacts can be predicted. SEA normally deals with large areas and numbers of potential projects/actions, so there will be uncertainty about the strategic action's likely effects. Given these factors, and that SEA aims to help decision-making rather than achieve perfection, the SEA predictions can 'look' quite different from those in EIA. Here are some examples, all for the same impact:

Box 8.1 Example of assumptions about winning v. losing: Excerpt from the SA/SEA for the South East Regional Spatial Strategy (England)

'[Based on monitoring the implementation of the existing Regional Spatial Strategy, the] figure below summarises aspects of the South East region that have shown a clear improvement or deterioration over the last few years. Clearly the economic policies are proving to be effective, as are many *input* social and environmental policies (e.g. dwelling density, per capita water use), and those that reduce *per capita* environmental impacts. Aspects that are deteriorating over time seem to be on social *outcomes* (e.g. homeless households, accessible services) and *total* environmental impacts (e.g. waste generated, ecological footprint). Generally *development* policies (e.g. for housing and renewable energy) seem to be working better than *protective* policies (e.g. for air quality or biodiversity).

	Clear improvement over time	*Clear deterioration over time*
primarily economic	[Gross Value Added] and labour productivity proportion of the population in employment training/qualifications	homeless households children in low income households
primarily social	housing completions, employment land completions higher dwelling density, development on previously developed land rate of traffic growth number of rail journeys health burglaries and vehicle crime	accessibility to services, particularly for people without access to a car traffic and congestion levels robberies risk of flooding
primarily environmental	% waste recycled and incinerated condition of Sites of Special Scientific Interest water quality: biological and chemical per capita water use generation of renewable energy per capita energy use	total waste generated protection of designated nature conservation sites from development population of farmland and woodland birds ecological footprint air quality

'The clearest improvements seem to be single-dimension issues where local authorities have clearly defined remits (e.g. housing completions); clearest deteriorations seem to be multi-dimensional issues where nobody has a clear remit (e.g. accessibility, ecological footprints). These points suggest that some of the policies of the [strategy] are more likely to be implemented than others. For example, the housing policies could be expected to be rolled out with more certainty than those on, say, green infrastructure, reducing the need to travel, or air quality.

'As such, we have generally assumed that the economic and development-oriented policies will be implemented; but have been more cautious in our assumptions about the remaining policies. We have assumed that policies that would carry on an existing trend will be implemented; but have been more cautious about policies that would go counter to existing trends.'

Source: Scott Wilson and Levett-Therivel (2009)

Levels of pollutant Z in Tooton Rush...

a) will get worse over the next 15 years

b) ⬇, *or red (out of red, amber, green), or* ☹

c) would be worse under Scenario A than under Scenario B

d) will exceed national Z standards within the next 15 years

e) will increase from 165 to 203 parts per million between 2010 and 2025

f) will increase by 23 per cent between 2010 and 2025

g) would increase by 23 per cent by 2025 under Scenario A, and by 16 per cent under Scenario B

h) will exceed national Z standards by 6% by 2025

Clearly the latter, more quantitative and detailed predictions look similar to those in project EIA, but the former, 'directional' (getting better, getting worse) ones are much more likely to be seen in SEA.

Table 8.2 summarizes the advantages and disadvantages of different approaches to impact prediction.

Similarly, a range of tools is used in impact prediction, including geographical information systems (GISs), modelling, network analyses and 'expert judgement'. Some prediction techniques from project EIA can be extended to SEA: for instance, topics such as waste and traffic management are already routinely modelled. Specific techniques are discussed further at Appendix C.

Table 8.3 shows part of a typical SEA impact prediction matrix using qualitative 'expert judgement'. It describes the environmental impacts of watercourse management proposed as part of a river basin management plan. It also describes likely impacts on other (mostly economic) activities. In the middle column, it summarizes these impacts as positive or negative, large or small. Information about long- v. short-term and other types of impacts is given in the comments column, but not in a systematic manner. Some limitations of this approach will be discussed later.

Figure 8.2 shows another approach to impact prediction, using maps and a pretty diagram of 'sustainability scores'. In real life, the scores are coloured green for positive impacts and red for negative impacts. This type of 'traffic light' colouring – also amber for neutral impacts or impacts that are both positive and negative – is very common in SEA.

Table 8.2 *Advantages and disadvantages of approaches to impact prediction*

Option*	Advantages	Disadvantages
Qualitative (a–d)	• fast, low resource/staff requirements • decision-makers can 'own' results • arguably no more uncertain than the sum of the uncertainties that result from all of the assumptions used to make quantitative predictions	• vague, subjective, non-rigorous results • not easily replicable or comparable with other predictions • more obviously open to bias • can't be tested against outcomes • not a good basis for cumulative impact assessment
Quantitative (e–h)	• detailed, rigorous, 'scientific', 'objective' • can be used as a basis for cumulative impact assessment • more likely to stand up to audit or inquiry	• resource intensive • assessment process inevitably moves from decision-makers to scientists/technocrats • risks spurious precision/certainty: pseudo-scientific • often requires large number of assumptions (especially at policy level), each with inherent uncertainties, so that the end result may be no more certain than qualitative predictions
Target-based (d and f)	• clear links to monitoring and cumulative impact assessment • in keeping with planning approaches that include targets	• targets/thresholds may not exist for some issues, and may not reflect SEA objectives • targets may not be achievable solely through the strategic action

Note: * letters refer to examples listed on page 168.

Assumptions: What will be the strategic action's impacts?

In many cases, the impacts of a strategic action will be straightforward, dependent on the planned action/projects and the receiving environment. For instance, new housing on a greenfield site will clearly affect the landscape, land use and biodiversity. However, in many cases a strategic action's impacts will not be so clear-cut. For instance, UK roads were for many years assumed to help redistribute existing traffic, reducing congestion and improving air quality. However a seminal report by a high-level government committee (SACTRA, 1994) showed that new roads also generate new traffic, demonstrating that it will never be possible to build one's way out of traffic congestion. Similarly, the assumption that vehicle operation is the primary cause of greenhouse gas emissions may be true for cars, buses and aircraft, but

Table 8.3 *Part of a simple impact prediction matrix: River basin management plan for the Loire-Bretagne basin (France)*

Impact	+/-	Comments
Environmental impact		
Biodiversity	++	Works to maintain watercourses will be carried out in such away as to keep ecosystems in good condition. The works will help migrating fish, aim to limit the proliferation of invasive species, and support awareness and understanding of conservation issues.
Pollution	+	Permission will be denied for proposed projects whose impacts on the [pollution-related] conservation objectives of water bodies cannot be significantly reduced or compensated for. Aquifer protection and reduction in hydromorphological changes will improve the resource.
Flooding	+	The actions needed should not alter the flow of floodwaters.
Landscape	+/-	Could have positive or negative impacts. On the one hand, watercourse management measures will be carried out in order to enhance the natural heritage and landscape. On the other hand, restriction of extraction in the floodplain could lead to an increase in the amount that needs to be extracted elsewhere, leading to an indirect negative impact on the landscape.
Impact on activities		
Agriculture	0	
Fishing	+	Improved conditions for migrating fish species and constraints on the introduction of undesirable species will improve fishing.
Aggregate extraction	-	Reducing the amount of mineral extraction by 4% per year will have a negative impact.

Key:

	environmental impact	*impact on activities*
++	dedicated to the environmental issue	
+	not dedicated to the environmental issue but has positive impacts on it	benefits the activity
0	can have both positive and negative impacts	constraints the activity but could sometimes be beneficial
-	negative impacts	acts to the detriment of the activity

Source: Adapted from Comité de bassin Loire-Bretagne (2007)

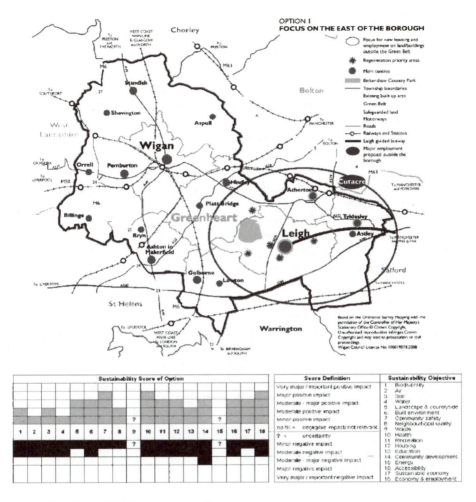

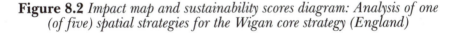

Source: Wigan Council (2008)

Figure 8.2 *Impact map and sustainability scores diagram: Analysis of one (of five) spatial strategies for the Wigan core strategy (England)*

does not necessarily hold true for rail, whose main emissions seem to be from carbon embedded in the construction of the track and stations, and from the operation of train stations and their car parks (Booz Allen Hamilton, 2007; Chester and Horvath, 2009).

In spring 2009, I asked my MSc students to each choose one assumption typically made in 'expert judgement' SEA, and to find out whether these assumptions are supported by actual data. Table 8.4 shows the results from this exercise. The available evidence is patchy and the students were not experts, but the results show a clear consensus, namely that SEA assumptions often simplify a complex

Table 8.4 *Assumption in SEA: Borne out by evidence?*

Assumption	Borne out by the evidence?	Researcher*
Affordable homes go to those who need them	Partly: based on a limited evidence base, they seem to go to those who need them and ask for them	A. Adu-Boatent S. Boyd
Buses get people out of cars	Partly: depends on bus frequency, ease of connections, etc.	P. Gillott
Carbon offsetting works in the long run	Unclear due to lack of robust monitoring of carbon offset projects	S. Cantwell C. Whetstone
Energy efficient technologies decrease energy consumption	Partly: reductions per appliance are often offset by increased use of appliances	N. Majdalani
Green areas are good for health	Yes: strong evidence to show that they are	J. Bowyer H. Mordue
Hedgerows increase biodiversity	Yes for most species, unclear for insects	J. Puyana
Park and Ride sites decrease car use	No: car use in city centre decreases, but it increases elsewhere	M. Tomlinson
Recycled material has real market value	Partly: the market value depends heavily on the quality of the amount of contamination and other factors	C. Whetstone**
Sticks are more effective than carrots in reducing car use	Partly: based on a limited evidence base, it seems that both sticks and carrots are needed to change travel behaviour	S. Lai

* Name of student(s) who carried out research
** Based on his MSc dissertation

issue. This suggests that (a) impact predictions should clearly state and justify any underlying assumptions, and (b) monitoring data should be collected to check assumptions and help inform future impact predictions. The latter is discussed further at Chapter 10.

Dealing with uncertainty

Although the uncertainty inherent in some SEA assumptions can be reduced by clarifying them with plan-makers and by referring to evidence from previous monitoring studies, the remaining uncertainty remains a key feature of SEA. The likely future state of the environment, future technologies, and the effects of other strategic actions, will add to this uncertainty.

SEA should certainly not aim, as a general principle, to replicate the level of certainty of project EIA. In many cases, a 'good enough' result for decision-making can be achieved despite uncertainties, so

Table 8.5 *Examples of techniques for reducing uncertainty*

Technique	Brief example
Worst case scenarios/ assumptions	'Every attempt was made to overcome uncertainty with conservatism… • Model selection. Either very conservative screening-level models were used or more refined models were used in a screening mode… • Assumed the maximum concentrations and depositions could occur at the same time… • Utilized maximum applications rates… • Overestimated the quantity of material that would likely volatilize… • Assumed three applications per treatment option…'
Clarifying assumptions	'Policy H1 on location of housing assumes that housing will be built at 30–50 dwellings per hectare, and that their design will be consistent with Policy D1'
Preparing contingency plans	'In the case of a discharge, the oil terminal has access to six oil spill response contractors and the following on-site equipment: four boats of 4–5 metres; 500 metres of containment boom; two floating suction skimmers; and three oil/water separators. The terminal also has a Spill Prevention, Control, and Countermeasure Plan'
Monitoring	'Little is currently known about the general state of wildlife in the region. Bird populations have been monitored and are used here as an indicator for wildlife generally. As part of the implementation of programme X, we will monitor populations of otters, water voles and bats in the area, to ensure that they are not adversely affected by the programme'

that uncertainties do not need to be dealt with specifically. For instance, future social conditions may clearly be better than current conditions; one alternative may be clearly better than another one; the economic benefits of a strategic action may clearly outweigh its environmental costs. However, even qualitative assessments should be supported by evidence where possible, and details of how that evidence has been assessed; 'qualitative' should not mean 'guessed'.

Techniques for *reducing uncertainty* include scenarios (such as worst case scenarios), sensitivity analysis, clarifying assumptions, identifying risks and preparing contingency plans, and monitoring. Scenarios and sensitivity analyses are discussed in Appendix C. Table 8.5 gives brief examples of the others.

After reducing uncertainty where it makes sense to do so, SEA should document the rest and cope with it. Any data limitations should be recorded, assumptions clearly stated and uncertainties documented. The most common techniques for *recording uncertainty* are to state that it exists or to model it, for instance, as ranges. Box 8.2 gives a

---

Box 8.2 Example of modelling uncertainty using ranges: Air pollution caused by cultural and sporting events resulting from a hypothetical economic strategy

A regional economic strategy includes a statement which 'supports greater cultural and sporting activity to enhance the perceptions of the region'. If we tried to quantify the effect of this statement on air quality, we would need to make assumptions about:

- the number and type of activities that might take place (say 5–10 major sporting events/year plus 5–10 major cultural events/year);
- the number and length of journeys associated with each event (say 200–1000 journeys per event, each 5–20km long);
- the type of journey (say 80–100 per cent by car, 0–20 per cent by bus);
- the amount of car sharing and ridership on buses (say 1–2 people per car, 5–10 per bus);
- the emissions of air pollution x per type of vehicle per kilometre (say 5–10 microgrammes of pollutant x per kilometre for cars, 20–30 for buses).

Multiplying together all of these ranges gives a prediction of 24,000–4,000,000mg of x per year. The end result of multiplying together the different types of uncertainty leads to a range whose high end is more than 100 times greater than the low end.

---

hypothetical example of the latter approach. In this case, uncertainty about the number of events per year is shown as an assumption that between five and ten events per year would take place.

Box 8.2 shows that, with only five assumptions but quite wide ranges for each assumption, the result – the statement's impact on air quality – is so uncertain as to be little better than a statement that 'air pollution would get worse', and the latter is certainly cheaper and easier to derive than the former. This example reinforces the concept that, in SEA, quantified predictions should only be made where the uncertainties inherent in such predictions do not swamp out the predictions themselves, and the additional work is justified by leading to a better strategic action.

Level of detail needed

SEA predictions are a balancing act between getting into enough detail so that one is relatively certain that the predictions are correct, and keeping a firm focus on key impacts i.e. on the wood rather than the trees. The former is done through quantification, consideration of cumulative impacts, consideration of uncertainty and so on – everything that has been discussed until now. The latter is done through scoping of the environmental components and the components of the strategic action.

Discussions with the environmental authorities and possibly the public as part of the scoping process (Chapter 6) should have broadly identified the requisite level of detail needed, and particularly what environmental components the SEA should focus on. However, there are plenty of examples of unbalanced level of detail. In many countries little baseline data exists, and SEAs may propose detailed mitigation measures without a full understanding of how these would affect the environment. In such cases, where the topic is important enough and the significance of the impact depends on the baseline, it may be necessary to collect further baseline data.

On the other hand, in the UK at least, SEAs often present more baseline data than is justified by the subsequent level of detail of the impact prediction and proposed avoidance / mitigation measures. For instance, a recent very handsome-looking SEA presented more than 1500 pages of baseline data but considered only three alternatives (proceed, don't proceed, proceed under certain conditions) in a comparison of only four pages, and only one of its 23 recommendations went beyond generalized statements that could have been made in the complete absence of baseline data. An example of this discrepancy (a small part of the baseline description, followed by the associated recommendation in full) is given below:

> *Pelagic fisheries in the southern North Sea mainly target herring, sprat and horse mackerel. Purse seiners and pelagic trawls are usually used in the herring fishery, with the greatest landings in the 3rd quarter. In spring, landings of herring are concentrated off the Lincolnshire and East Anglia coastline (ICES-FishMap 2008) and important feeding grounds for herring are found off Flamborough Head and in the Humber Estuary.*

> *There should be a presumption against [offshore wind farm] developments which occupy recognized important fishing grounds in coastal or offshore areas (where this would prevent or significantly impede previous activities).* (DECC, 2009)

Where the strategic action proposes little change, the SEA should focus on those aspects that *would* change. As the strategic action's final shape begins to emerge, a screening process can also be carried out on the different sections or policy statements of the strategic action. This would determine what statements are:

- likely to have significant effects: the SEA should particularly focus on these;

Box 8.3 Questions for screening of components/statements of the strategic action

1a   Is the section/statement likely to have significant negative environmental, social or economic impacts?
1b   Is it politically contentious?

If the answer to *either* question is yes (or 'don't know'), then the section/statement needs to be assessed in depth.

2a   Is the section/statement *un*likely to have significant negative environmental, social or economic impacts?
2b   Is the section/statement as good as possible, i.e. is it not possible to enhance it?

If the answer to *both* questions is a clear yes, then the section/statement requires only enough analysis to confirm that its effects are minor (or to move it to one of the other categories).

The remaining sections/statements require an intermediate level of assessment.

3a   Are the effects of the section/statement very similar to those of any other section/statements?

If yes, then consider clustering the sections/statements together for the assessment stage.

Source: ODPM (2002)

- unlikely to have significant effects: the focus should not be on these; or
- in between: these should have an intermediate level of assessment.

The questions in Box 8.3 may help in this process. In case of doubt, the precautionary principle should be applied: the statement should be put in the 'worse' category.

For instance, the statement 'Ensure that new developments reduce the need to travel by car' is economically efficient, socially and environmentally beneficial, and presumably politically acceptable. It would not require detailed assessment. In contrast, statement 'Lobby for and implement the region's most important and strategic transport projects: X, Y and Z' is likely to have significant environmental impacts, might be socially divisive, and, in a real life case, has been very politically contentious. Clearly more effort should be spent assessing and trying to mitigate the impacts of the latter than the former one.

Many strategic actions propose both high-level policies and quite specific projects (for instance, major infrastructure projects 'of regional importance' or 'in the national interest'). These pose a problem in SEA because of the varying levels of analyses needed: strategic and broad-brush for most of the strategic action, but detailed – almost to the EIA level – for specific projects.

The multiple levels of detail will interact:

> *[Strategic decision-making is often] based on the assumption [of] a logical cascade or hierarchy: first you decide you need a project, then where to put it, then the details of how to do it. But in fact the 'higher' or 'earlier' decisions depend on the 'lower' or 'later' ones. The choice where to put a project (and what type of project, and its size) should be influenced by assessment of the different impacts it would have in different places. Even more important, the choice whether to have an infrastructure project [at all] should be influenced by whether there is any location where its impacts would be acceptable...*
>
> *This would seem perfectly reasonable where the national (or broader) benefits of a project were large, and the local disbenefits small, [but major infrastructure projects] are projects where both kinds of interest are substantial and important. Moreover ... many of the most important downsides will often be local in their effects and/or specific to the location where the project takes place... In view of this, deciding whether the project should go ahead after considering only the broader issues would be like conducting a trial where the verdict is decided after hearing only the prosecution case, leaving the defence able only to argue for a more lenient sentence after a 'guilty' verdict had already been passed.* (National Trust, 2002)

This suggests that a fair amount of data and analysis – more equivalent to an EIA than an SEA – may be needed before a strategic action can propose specific projects. Arguably, if a strategic action wants to include reference to projects, it should be tested to the level of detail of a project. Multiple levels of detail of assessment may thus be needed, for example, a general prediction and then a 'zoom down' to individual proposed development sites. Box 8.4 shows an example of this.

Indirect and cumulative impacts

Until now, the focus of this chapter has been on straightforward types of impact: positive v. negative, large v. small, short term v. long term. This section discusses the more complex types of impacts: indirect/induced impacts, and cumulative/synergistic impacts. These are summarized at Figure 8.3.

Box 8.4 Example of two levels of detail of assessment: Plan-wide and 'zoom down' on areas likely to be significantly affected (excerpts from the sustainability appraisal for the South East Regional Spatial Strategy, England)

'Overall, despite [its] protective policies, the Final South East Plan is still likely to have a significant negative impact on biodiversity. The [Habitats Regulations Assessment] shows that increases in the region's population would indirectly lead to increasing recreational pressure, increasing air pollution, and changes to water levels and water quality which would affect nature conservation sites sensitive to these impacts. The [South East Plan] still includes most of the housing allocations and development sites that were identified in the previous SA as being likely to have a significant effect on biodiversity:

- Development of 2500+ homes at the DERA site at Chertsey ... will be directly adjacent the Thames Basin Heaths SPA [Special Protection Area];
- Development of 5000+ homes at Bordon/Whitehill ... will be directly adjacent to the Woolmer Forest SAC [Special Area of Conservation/ Wealden Heaths Phase II SPA; and development of 10,100 homes in Dover district could affect several European sites...
- Several of the employment sites proposed by Policy SCT3 are adjacent or very near to areas designated for their national or international importance for biodiversity, notably Shoreham Airport (the whole eastern end of the airport boundary is adjacent to the Adur Estuary [Site of Special Scientific Interest])...'

Source: Scott Wilson and Levett-Therivel (2009)

Indirect and cumulative impacts have traditionally been poorly considered in project EIA (Piper, 2002; Glasson et al, 2005), in part because project developers find them difficult to identify, and because they are reluctant to be constrained by the actions of other developers. A key purpose behind SEA is to better analyse cumulative impacts. For instance, the SEA Directive requires an assessment of 'secondary, cumulative, synergistic' as well as other types of impacts, and the Chinese PEIA regulations require SEA to analyse 'likely cumulative effects on relevant regional, river basin and marine areas'. Appropriate assessment under the European Habitats Directive requires consideration of 'in combination' impacts' (see Appendix D).

Unfortunately, to date these types of impacts have not been well considered in SEA either (Therivel and Ross, 2007; Wärnbäck and Hilding-Rydevik, 2009). Although some useful guidance on cumulative impact assessment has been published (e.g. CEQ, 1997; Hyder, 1999; Canadian Environmental Assessment Agency, 1999; State of California,

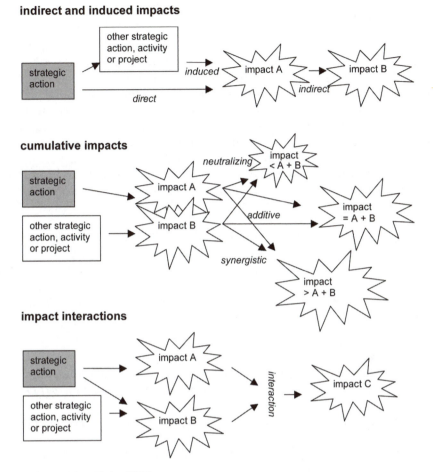

indirect and induced impacts

cumulative impacts

impact interactions

Source: Adapted from Hyder (1999)

Figure 8.3 *Indirect and cumulative impacts, and impact interactions*

2005), this has focused primarily on projects rather than strategic actions; and no guidance has focused specifically on indirect impacts. The techniques needed to identify indirect and cumulative impacts are additional to, and typically more onerous than, those used to identify direct impacts. However, even a rough picture of cumulative impacts is much more useful than no picture at all, and often only a rough picture is needed in order to identify appropriate management measures. As a rule of thumb, I would pick and choose from the following techniques, depending on whether indirect or cumulative impacts (a) are likely to be significant, and (b) require more analysis to allow good decisions to be made.

Indirect impacts

Indirect impacts are impacts that are not a direct result of the strategic actions, but occur away from the original impact and/or as a result of a complex pathway. Examples include development that changes a water table and thus affects the ecology of a nearby wetland, or construction of a new road that attracts other development which, in turn, has air pollution and severance impacts. The road development is an example of *induced impacts*, where one strategic action leads to other actions or developments, which generate further impacts of their own.

The social impact assessment for a proposed Australian liquefied natural gas precinct gives a nice example of how indirect impacts can be documented:

> *A significant downside [of fly-in/fly-out (FIFO) of workers to the precinct] is the 'fly-over' effect, relating to regions missing out on the economic benefits of mining. The 'fly over' effect can be exacerbated by city-based contracting of services and supplies that lead to local industry being overlooked for lucrative contracts. Other criticisms of FIFO include:*
>
> * *lack of community commitment and sense of place;*
> * *limited local investment;*
> * *marginalisation of other industries, for example tourism and the retail sector, due to short-term accommodation being used for FIFO workers;*
> * *anti-social behaviour demonstrated by some transient workers in their work towns; and*
> * *the disruptive influence on personal and family relationships.*
> (Government of Western Australia, 2009)

Indirect impacts can be identified by using a causal flow diagram, such as that in Figure 6.3. Indirect impacts are sometimes described as *secondary impacts*, *tertiary impacts* and so on. In this case, 'more buses purchased' is a secondary impact, 'more frequent services' a tertiary impact, and people changing transport modes a fourth-order impact. However, this concept clearly gets rapidly complicated where there are feedback loops. The main point is that some indirect impacts occur further down the line – possibly also further away or further in the future – than others.

An advantage of causal flow diagrams is that they can help to identify supporting actions needed to help ensure a positive environmental outcome or prevent a negative one. In Figure 6.3, for instance, provision of more buses will (in this example at least) only lead to improved air quality if people move from car to bus use, which will only be achieved if other measures, such as parking restrictions

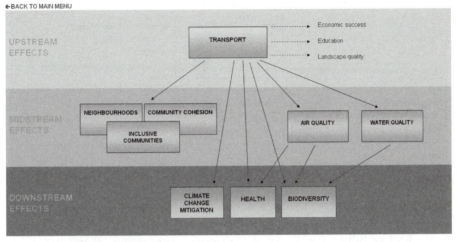

Source: Leeds City Council (2008)

Figure 8.4 *Example of the use of 'upstream', 'midstream' and 'downstream' effects to help streamline the assessment process*

and congestion charging, are also introduced. Causal flow diagrams can help to identify measures that are most likely to lead to the intended effect. In this case, improved air quality is most easily achieved through improved bus engines, although this may not achieve other objectives, such as the social benefits of improved bus services.

Causal flow diagrams can also help to streamline and focus the assessment process. For instance, staff in the Leeds City Development Directorate, working with colleagues across the authority, identified possible effects of their strategic actions. Following the Natural Step framework, they drew the causal flows between them, and identified 'upstream', 'midstream' and 'downstream' effects as shown at Figure 8.4. They now begin their impact assessments by identifying whether the strategic action has any upstream impact. Only if there is an upstream impact are the related mid-stream and downstream effects then assessed.

Cumulative impacts

Cumulative impacts are impacts that result from incremental changes caused by the strategic action together with other past, present or reasonably foreseeable actions (Hyder, 1999). An example of cumulative impacts is several developments, each with insignificant impacts, but which together have a cumulative effect, say a drip-feed increase in traffic leading to significant congestion. This is the concept

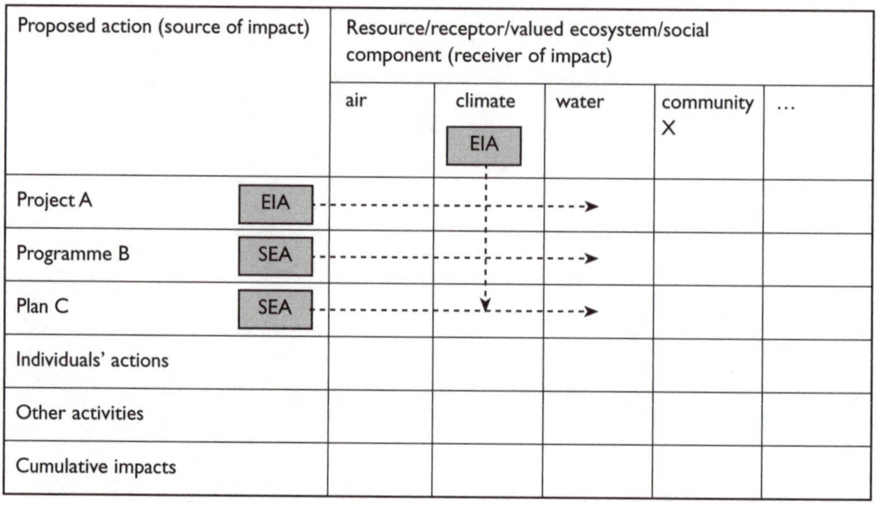

Proposed action (source of impact)	Resource/receptor/valued ecosystem/social component (receiver of impact)				
	air	climate EIA	water	community X	...
Project A EIA					
Programme B SEA					
Plan C SEA					
Individuals' actions					
Other activities					
Cumulative impacts					

Figure 8.5 *Cumulative impact assessment focuses on the receiver*

of 'death by 1000 cuts' or the delightfully pungent German 'Kleinvieh macht auch Mist' (small animals also shit). Cumulative impacts can also refer to the combined impacts of the strategic action (e.g. noise, dust and visual) on a particular receiver.

The defining characteristic of cumulative impact assessment is its focus on the receiver rather than on the source of the impact. This is illustrated by Figure 8.5. Other dimensions of SEA 'look across' at the impacts of the strategic action on various resources, but cumulative impact assessment 'looks down' at all of the changes that could affect the receiver.

Cumulative impacts can be:

- additive, namely the simple sum of all the impacts (e.g. job opportunities in an area of high unemployment);
- neutralizing, where impacts counteract each other, reducing the overall impact (e.g. the impact on birds of one gravel extraction development is neutralized by a new wildlife habitat created through reclamation of another, nearby gravel extraction site); or
- synergistic, where impacts interact to produce an impact greater than the sum of the individual impacts (e.g. closure of the only two footpaths that lead from a housing development to a much wider range of walking trails).

Synergistic impacts often happen as habitats, resources or human communities get close to capacity. For instance, wildlife habitats can become progressively fragmented with limited negative impact until they are so broken up that they hardly support a given population of wildlife or act as a wildlife corridor any more; and then a final

Note: The dots represent windturbines; the lines show flight trajectories
Source: Desholm and Kahlert (2005)

Figure 8.6 *Example of synergistic impact: Westerly oriented flight trajectories of migrating waterbirds around an offshore windfarm*

fragmentation tips them over the edge – the synergistic impact – the population dies, and they cannot be repopulated from other nearby wildlife sites.

Figure 8.6 gives a good example of synergistic impacts: the flight trajectories of migrating waterbirds around a large offshore windfarm. Whereas birds might be able to easily bypass a few turbines, and again another few turbines further away, when all of the turbines are clustered together the birds tend to make significant detours in an attempt to bypass the entire windfarm, with consequent effects on the birds' migratory patterns, energy outlay and so on.

Cumulative impact prediction involves identifying the total effects on a resource arising from (a) different components of the plan (intra-plan or incremental impacts) plus (b) other strategic actions, projects and human activities (called inter-plan impacts here). *Intra-plan impacts* can be identified using a table such as Table 8.6, which also discusses past impacts and proposed mitigation measures. Where the strategic

Table 8.6 *Example of table showing type and location of intra-plan cumulative impacts: SEA for the regional plan for Halle (Germany)*

Cumulation area	Past impacts (current situation)	Proposals of the regional plan	Main expected cumulative impacts	Mitigation measures
Merseburg-Leuna-Bad Dürrenberg Area approx. 26,287ha	The area is characterized by a high proportion of existing settlements and transport infrastructure	Mineral extraction 5 priority areas (564ha) 1 reserved area (65ha) Water abstraction	Cumulative loss of land due to mineral extraction (ca. 870ha) Associated further	Regional plan: Minimization and compensation measures include reforestation,
	(9.6% of the total land area), as well as chemical industry projects (ca. 55ha in Leuna/Spergau). These have a strong influence on the landscape, and jointly form an existing impact on this area.	4 priority areas (1000ha) Agriculture 2 priority areas (1919ha) 4 reserved areas (1478ha) Reforestation 15 reserved areas (408ha).	impacts on the water environment, climate change and the landscape Development of the road network will particularly lead to the further fragmentation of open space. Cumulative impacts on people will be minimized by building bypasses around towns.	establishment of a network of ecological areas, and areas of open space. Beyond the regional plan: Local level development plans will include avoidance and mitigation measures (prevention of impacts). Reinstatement of mineral extraction works will provide opportunities for nature conservation and landscape enhancement.

Source: Based on Planungsgemeinschaft Halle (2009)

Box 8.5 Example of tables and overlay mapping to identify intra-plan cumulative impacts: High Speed 2

High Speed 2 (HS2) is a proposed high-speed rail line between London and the West Midlands, with possible extensions further north and to Scotland. Many possible combinations of route segments exist for this multi-phase programme. To help identify a preferred route, the consultants carrying out the 'appraisal of sustainability' for HS2 Ltd (based on the principles of SEA) brought together the HS2 Ltd team, route engineers and sustainability topic specialists in several workshops in late summer 2009 (A). The workshops identified the impacts of each route segment, and the cumulative impacts of whole routes composed of combinations of route segments (B). They also identified locations where multiple impacts from each route segment (e.g. noise plus landscape plus biodiversity) could have significant cumulative impacts on receivers (C).

A. Appraisal workshops: Engineers and topic specialists identify cumulative impacts

B. Vicky Ward collates the impacts of each route segment in a table

C. Nick Giesler draws locations subject to cumulative impacts on a map

Source: HS2 Ltd., Booz & Company and Temple Group; photos by Riki Therivel and Mark Southwood

---

action is spatially specific, an overlay map showing where different types of significant impacts may occur can also help to identify cumulative impacts. Box 8.5 shows an example of where this was carried out in a workshop format. Even where a strategic action cannot be mapped, it may still be worthwhile asking whether a specific community or areas will be disproportionately cumulatively affected by the strategic action.

Inter-plan impacts are caused by the accumulation of other projects, strategic actions or activities and those of the proposed strategic action. There is no clear agreement about just what other strategic actions, projects and/or activities should be covered in cumulative impact assessment. Guidance by the State of California (2005) is wide-ranging, referring to 'past, present, and future activities or actions of federal, non-federal, public and private entities. Cumulative impacts may also include the effects of natural processes and events.' On the other hand, one UK guidance document on 'in combination' impact assessment under the Habitats Directive recommends a much more limited approach: 'Only other key plans and projects which the [planning authority] consider most relevant should be collected for the 'in combination' test. An exhaustive list could render the assessment exercise unworkable.' (CLG, 2006) In keeping with the spirit of cumulative impact assessment, which focuses on all impacts on receivers, I believe that past actions and general trends should be considered as well as specific plans and projects.

The identification of existing problems in the context-setting stage (Chapter 6) should already have identified cumulative impacts caused by *past and present activities*. Some of these will result from specific activities or projects, for instance, existing fishing activities in a marine area whose impacts would be exacerbated by a proposed programme of offshore windfarms. In other cases, they will have built up over time: for instance global warming, the worldwide decline in global fish stocks, and childhood obesity in some countries have built up slowly over time due to factors such as increasing wealth, greater numbers of households, and changes in people's behaviour. At this stage it might be helpful to formally list existing activities affecting the area in question, and their likely impacts. Table 8.7 provides an example.

The analysis of the 'business as usual' scenario as part of the context-setting stage should help to identify *future trends*, including likely future projects and strategic actions. For near-term future activities, for which good information is available and that are important for the cumulative effect of concern, good impact prediction should be possible. Only a broad-brush picture may be possible for more distant future activities.

Once the possible other strategic actions, projects and activities have been identified, their cumulative impacts with the proposed strategic action should be identified and described. Below is an example of the inter-plan landscape impacts associated with offshore energy developments on the east coast of England. Note that the impacts of underlying trends are described, as well as more specific projects and plans:

Pressures come in the form of further industrial and urban development around Hull and the Thames, and there is limited pressure from caravan, theme park, golf course and water sport development. There is a continuing spread of holiday resorts and homes (e.g. around Cleethorpes, between Mablethorpe and Skegness). Beach nourishment and coastal defence and other engineering is altering the physical form at a number of locations along the coast which may continue in the future and the coastal squeeze of mudflat areas is likely to be exacerbated by any sea-level rise. In some other places, cliff erosion (e.g. Holderness, North Norfolk, Suffolk Coast) will continue to change the form of the coast. Some coastal areas have developed onshore wind energy sites (e.g.

Table 8.7 *Example of other activities with cumulative impacts: SEA for defence activities in the Great Barrier Reef Heritage Conservation Area (Australia)*

Activity	Impact	Spatial and temporal impact
Fishing – trawling, netting, wet lining, etc.	Direct killing of target and by-catch species Direct physical disturbance of substratum and benthos Source of solid waste, including lost nets which 'ghost fish'	Widespread, often seasonal Widespread, often seasonal Chronic
Shipping and boating	Source of underwater noise that could affect cetaceans and other marine organisms Sewage entering the marine environment from vessels	Widespread and persistent Widespread
Civil aviation	Potential disturbance to cetaceans and avian fauna	Widespread but localized; especially intense in some areas (i.e. coastal airports)
Coastal and island development	Source of waste and pollutants (including persistent floating materials, toxicants and nutrients) entering the marine environment Long-term loss/alteration of habitat and coastal processes	Localized and chronic Persistent, long-term, irreversible

Source: Department of Defence (2006)

Out Newton, Humberside and Conisholme Fen). These, and any subsequent developments, could generate cumulative impacts if there is sufficient intervisibility of onshore and offshore structures. (DECC, 2009)

Equality impacts

Equality implies that no group of people should be affected unfairly, particularly by cumulative impacts. Examples of inequality include unequal access to transport or hospital services, fuel poverty (where poor people pay a disproportionate part of their income on keeping warm) and water conflict. Many forms of development have a particularly strong effect on groups that are already disadvantaged. A good example of this is the impact of cars in London:

> *In general, the benefits of car use accrue to those who own and use cars (the better off) but the adverse effects are borne primarily by others. For example, air pollution is worse in more deprived areas and alongside major roads. Injuries show the steepest effect of inequalities. Child pedestrians deaths are five times higher in social class V than I. Children from deprived areas are less likely to be car passengers, more likely to walk, cross more roads that have higher volumes and speeds of traffic, and are less likely to be accompanied by an adult or to have been taught road safety.* (London Health Observatory, 2005)

Whereas SEA considers the impacts of a strategic action on the population as a whole, equality impact assessment (EqIA) focuses on the needs of, and impacts on, sub-groups of the population. EqIA and its variants – for instance, 'rural proofing' or 'gender assessment', are concerned with ensuring that a strategic action responds to the specific needs of particular groups of people, and does not have a disproportionately negative impact – particularly in combination with past impacts and the likely future impacts of other strategic actions and projects – on any sector of the population.

Much regulation and guidance exists on EqIA. This includes the US Executive Order 12898 of 1994, which promotes environmental justice for minority and low-income populations; Section 75 of the Northern Ireland Act 1998, which requires public authorities to support equality of opportunity between persons of different religious belief, political opinion, racial group, age, marital status or sexual orientation, men and women, persons with and without a disability, and persons with and without dependants; the Scottish Government's (2005) *Equality and Diversity Impact Assessment Toolkit*; Australian requirements for regional impact assessment (Hill and Lowe, 2007); the UK Commission for Rural Communities' (2009) rural proofing guidance; and teh Improvement and Development Agency's (IDeA) (2009) guidance on equalities impact assessment, which focuses on 'equalities target groups', namely people of different age, sexuality, faith or belief, race, ethnicity, disability and gender.

All forms of EqIA involve roughly the same steps:

1 Identify relevant sub-groups of the population, ensuring that these are consistent with relevant legislation and guidance.
2 Identify particular problems (health, safety, etc.) currently affecting those sub-groups.
3 Identify and document the needs of the sub-groups. This requires active input from representatives of the sub-groups, possibly in a workshop format.
4 Assess whether the emerging strategic action addresses these needs, and whether it would make conditions for the sub-groups better or worse.

5 Where appropriate, recommend ways in which the strategic action could be changed to better respond to the needs of the sub-groups or ensure that they are not disproportionately affected.
6 Record whether the recommendations have been implemented.

Box 8.6 presents some findings about existing problems (step 2 opposite) from a US Agency for International Development (USAID) (2007) gender assessment for Colombia carried out to inform its 'Plan Colombia' foreign aid programme 2006–2008. As an example of step 4 above, Section 75 of the Northern Ireland Act was applied to the Department of Finance and Personnel's (2002) evolving policy on the location of civil service jobs. The department's EqIA, which was carried out in discussion with a wide range of local authorities, trade unions, commissions on fair employment and human rights and others, noted that the current location of civil service jobs is broadly neutral across the categories of Section 75. However, it identified a range of possible and perceived equality issues that could affect any change in location of jobs, including:

- lobbying for jobs tied to local economic benefits;
- the need to relocate some jobs to more 'religion-neutral' and accessible working environments;
- the need – in the past at least – to relocate jobs from the Greater Belfast area to parts of Northern Ireland that have a higher representation of one section of the community compared to the

---

Box 8.6 Example of identification of existing equalities problems: Excerpts from a gender impact assessment for Colombia

'In Colombia, the forced displacement of over three million people has resulted in major demographic and territorial changes with social, economic and cultural consequences. USAID supports the Colombian government in its programs for displaced people through income generation, housing, and social services...

'The situation of displaced women and children is especially difficult. The most visible and alarming problems are the high rates of domestic and sexual violence in temporary shelters and receiving neighbourhoods. Girls and young women, as well as women who have become heads of households because of the conflict, are especially vulnerable to sexual crimes and exploitation.

'The armed conflict also may create flexibility in gender roles. In urban centers, the skills of rural women are more easily translated to informal employment than those of rural women. Women's increased access to income may foster more independence and control in their households...'

Source: USAID (2007)

other, primarily as a way of encouraging members of the Roman Catholic section of the community to apply for civil service jobs;
• the possibility of using new technologies and home-working to benefit women and people with a disability; and
• the possibility of revitalizing towns, particularly Omagh and Strabane, if jobs were moved outside Belfast.

This allowed the policy to be fine-tuned to manage these possible equality impacts.

Conclusions

This chapter has discussed the first part of the SEA stage of impact prediction, evaluation and mitigation, and Chapter 9 will look at the remaining parts. In real life, this stage is carried out as a seamless whole, with one step segueing directly into the next. Quality review questions on impact prediction that could be used by either a formal reviewer or as a self-test are:

• Is the area and time over which the predictions are made appropriate?
• Are transboundary impacts considered where appropriate?
• Are assumptions about what the strategic action will 'look' like when implemented clearly stated or (if implicit) do they make sense?
• Do the predictions cover all the main likely environmental and sustainability impacts, both short term and long term? If an 'objectives-led' approach is used, is the previously agreed SEA framework being used to structure the impact prediction process?
• Are assumptions about the likely impacts of the strategic action's implementation clearly stated or (if implicit) do they make sense?
• Is the level of detail of prediction appropriate – is it proportional to that of the strategic action, proportional to that of the baseline data, and 'fit for purpose' (not over-detailed)?
• Is uncertainty of predictions identified and documented?
• Do the impacts considered include indirect, cumulative/synergistic and long-term impacts? Do they include impacts on different groups of people, particularly those whom are already negatively affected by environmental impacts and risks?

Note

1   Some people distinguish between effects (changes to the environment) and impacts (the consequences of such changes), but this book treats them both together.

Chapter 9

Evaluating and Mitigating Impacts

The SEA stages of impact evaluation and mitigation are the pinnacle of the process: all the previous stages have been leading up to this. Impact evaluation determines whether an impact is significant or not; and mitigation involves minimizing adverse impacts and enhancing positive ones. There may be several rounds of impact evaluation, mitigation, impact re-prediction and re-evaluation following the mitigation and so on. The information from these stages is then used by decision-makers to help choose and then fine-tune a preferred alternative.

This chapter discusses:

A impact evaluation: using various bases for evaluation, and possibilities for bias in evaluation;
B avoidance, mitigation, compensation and enhancement measures, how they can be identified, and some factors that constrain their effectiveness; and
C approaches to comparing alternatives and making trade-offs.

Evaluating the significance of impacts

The aim of impact evaluation is to translate predicted impacts into statements of importance or significance. This gives the decision-maker information about the significance of individual impacts, and who will be the winners and losers. Impact evaluation brings together information about the characteristics and effects of the strategic action, and the value and sensitivity of the receiving environment.

Annex II of the SEA Directive and Annex III of the SEA Protocol provide an indication of factors that might affect the significance of *characteristics of the strategic action*. Box 9.1 shows this for the SEA Directive. This information can be gleaned from the context-setting stage (see Chapter 6). The more influential the strategic action is for other strategic actions, subsequent projects and environmental

---

Box 9.1 Criteria for determining the likely significance of impacts: Characteristics of the strategic action

- the degree to which the strategic action sets a framework for projects and other activities, either with regard to the location, nature, size and operating conditions or by allocating resources;
- the degree to which the strategic action influences other strategic actions including those in a hierarchy;
- the relevance of the strategic action for the integration of environmental considerations in particular with a view to promoting sustainable development;
- environmental problems relevant to the strategic action;
- the relevance of the strategic action for the implementation of international legislation on the environment (e.g. strategic actions linked to waste-management or water protection).

Source: Adapted from CEC (2001)

---

protection objectives, the more significant will be its impacts.

Effects of the strategic action were discussed at Chapter 8. Characteristics of these effects include their magnitude and spatial extent (geographical area and size of the population likely to be affected, including transboundary impacts); their probability, duration, frequency and reversibility; and any indirect, cumulative or synergistic effects. Clearly the larger, longer and more permanent the effects are, the more significant they will be.

Much information about the *value and sensitivity of the environment* will come from the analysis of the baseline environment and relevant other strategic actions (Chapter 6). Value and sensitivity can be determined in several ways through:

- Designations (e.g. national parks): these indicate areas that are valued because they are rare or particularly important for one or more environmental aspects, such as landscape or biodiversity. The level of their designation – international, national, local – gives an indication of their importance.
- Other measures of value or vulnerability, for instance, areas that are heavily used by people, or are habitats for locally rare species, or buildings/people particularly sensitive to disturbance (e.g. hospitals, groups of people already subject to cumulative impacts).
- Standards and regulations (e.g. air quality standards, standards for insulation in housing): these set thresholds for environmental components, such as air or water.

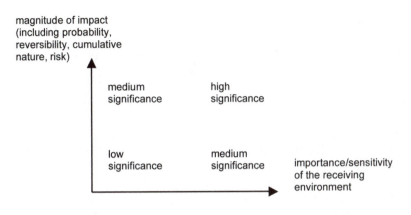

Source: Glasson et al (2005)

Figure 9.1 *Identifying impact significance*

- The public or stakeholders, who can be asked what environmental/ sustainability aspects they consider to be the most important. This would ensure that those people likely to be most affected by a strategic action have a chance to influence it, and to propose mitigation measures. However, their views would need to be complemented by those of experts to ensure a well-rounded analysis, otherwise local interests could outweigh national ones, and cute, furry but common animals (like bunnies) could be given more priority than less lovely but more endangered species (like liverworts).

The more valuable and vulnerable the receiving environment is, and the closer any thresholds are to be exceeded, the more significant is the impact. Figure 9.1 shows how impact magnitude and the value/sensitivity of the baseline environment interact.

Bias in impact evaluation

Most strategic actions have an inbuilt bias towards development. They tend to be written in order to meet social and economic objectives, leaving SEAs to raise the alarm where this would lead to undue environmental harm. In a 2008 survey of UK local authority planners with 152 respondents, 40 per cent felt that their local development plan was biased in favour of the economy, 15 per cent in favour of social issues, 7 per cent in favour of the environment, with only 38 per cent feeling that it was unbiased (Yamane, 2008). Furthermore, planning permission acts like a one-way valve: developers only need to get planning permission once, whereas protection of sensitive sites from development requires successfully arguing against *every* application to develop those sites.

SEA has a clear pro-environment remit. However, even SA is not unbiased, despite nominally considering social and economic as well as environmental issues. In the survey discussed above, half of the respondents felt that the SAs of their plans were well-balanced, but 44 per cent felt that they were balanced in favour of the environment. Some of this may be due to the environmental bias of the statutory consultees, and the need to incorporate the requirements of the SEA Directive (Yamane, 2008). Jackson and Illsley (2007) also argue that the environmental impacts of spatial plans are generally easier to demonstrate than their socio-economic effects, because of limitations in current socio-economic assessment techniques. This suggests that further research is needed on the links between development and socio-economic outcomes (CLG, 2009b).

On the other hand, quantitative predictions, such as those from cost–benefit analyses (see Annex C), will always look more robust than qualitative ones. This means that, unless SEAs are carried out in a demonstrably robust (if not necessarily quantified) manner, it will be easier to 'prove' the benefits of projects (whose benefits are normally quantifiable) than those of the strategies that would avoid the need for the projects in the first place. Projects are often justified on the grounds of, for instance, improved travel times or provision of jobs: these benefits are immediate and quantifiable, even though, in the long term, they may cause problems. For instance, new roads may generate new traffic, and call centres may be moved around to take advantage of cheap labour, leaving large numbers of unemployed people behind. It is much harder to 'prove' the benefits of siting new houses so as to reduce the need to travel, or of policies that reduce reliance on multinational companies by, for example, promoting cooperatives or non-monetary exchange schemes.

Furthermore, given that the impact evaluation stage involves using an element of judgement to 'translate' information about the impacts from the prediction stage into statements about impact significance, that it is meant to inform plan-makers' decisions, and that the SEA report will accompany the proposed strategic action and be made public, there will inevitably be pressure for the SEA report to show the proposed strategic action in a good light. This may result in the impact evaluation stage being influenced more or less subtly so as to support the proposed strategic action. Certainly some SEA reports look more like sales brochures than objective analyses.

This goes back to the points made in Chapter 3 about the mismatch between the rationalist process of SEA and the fluid, politicized nature of decision-making. From the sharp end of SEA practice, Jim Singleton (pers. comm., 2009) suggests that government bodies may be just as prone to bias as commercial organizations:

Strategic assessments should be undertaken in such a way as to avoid their being unduly influenced, or worse still hijacked, by 'elite capture'. This universal problem is surfacing as one that society is increasingly aware of as a core flaw in contemporary governance. We expect private/commercial corporations and businesses to be self-interested – we do not expect government or arms of government to be self-interested (at the negative expense of societal or community interests).

SEA is not a one-way process of providing unbiased information, but rather a multi-loop process, which also includes receiving information from decision-makers, adapting it to suit their needs, and using SEA reports as public relations documents. In my experience, this 'return information' can include decision-makers not wishing the SEA report to discuss some alternatives, suggesting that the intent rather than likely impact of their strategic action should be assessed, proposing different bases of impact evaluation/comparison, directly challenging impact evaluation scores (usually the negative ones), suggesting alternative wording for SEA reports, and arguing that the whole SEA process is anti-development.

Several aspects of impact evaluation can help to avoid this 'undue influence'. These include an informed choice of the basis for impact evaluation; involvement of a range of stakeholders in the evaluation stage; and transparency and honesty in reporting. These are discussed below. Close links between impact evaluation and mitigation are also important because a strategic action's with-mitigation impacts might be very different than those without, or the choice of preferred alternative might be different once mitigation measures are included in the mix.

Basis of evaluation: Current situation, future situation without strategic action, environmental standards

The type and magnitude of a strategic action's impacts can look very different depending on the assumed assessment timeframe and what they are being assessed against: whether the current situation, the future situation without the strategic action, or environmental standards or limits. Figure 9.2 illustrates some of this complexity. At time X, the 'with strategic action' situation would be better than the situation today, worse than the situation without the strategic action, and exceeding the environmental standard. At time Y, the same would hold true but the environmental standard would not be exceeded.

This is the situation facing several English regional strategies in mid-2009. Current air pollution levels in many parts of England are over legal standards. However, air quality is expected to improve rapidly over the next ten years or so due to tightening European vehicle standards, and then level off or get worse again (Grice et al,

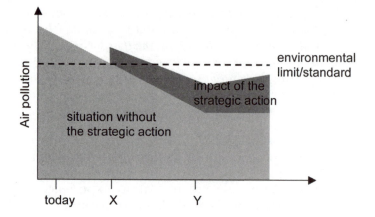

Figure 9.2 *Basis of evaluation: Current situation, future situation, environmental standards*

2006). This (temporary at least) improvement in air quality would allow more polluting developments to be built while still meeting environmental standards or being an improvement over the current situation. Planners are using this as an argument to put forward new development, for instance:

A third runway at Heathrow: argument based on achieving legal standards:

EU annual air quality limit values are currently being exceeded around Heathrow (and elsewhere in the UK)... The position is improving, mainly due to tighter emissions standards on road vehicles... Even on conservative assumptions, the progressive reduction in emissions under current and planned EU vehicle standards should ensure that the UK would be compliant around Heathrow by 2020. For example, [based on modelling] no NO_2 exceedences were identified at residential properties in 2020 even in a third runway were operating fully... (Department for Transport, 2009a)

East of England Regional Transport Strategy: argument based on an improvement over the current conditions:

The limit value for annual mean NO_x concentrations is likely to be exceeded at [four sites of international significance for nature conservation]. However, at all sites, predicted annual mean NO_x concentrations are considerably lower in 2021 with the [strategy] when compared with existing concentrations. (Government Office for the East of England, 2008)

Interestingly, nobody seems to be ensuring that, cumulatively, all of the new strategic actions and projects – each of which is being proposed on the assumption that the improved vehicle standards will provide breathing room (sorry about the bad pun) for new development to be built while still achieving environmental standards – will not again exceed environmental standards.

In contrast, the Chinese PEIA regulations state that the SEAs of special plans will not be approved (and thus the plans will not be adopted) if total emissions of key pollutants in the plans' areas exceed the national or regional limits, and if the plans would increase these emissions (Article 30).

In a complex situation such as that shown in Figure 9.2, it may be necessary to compare a strategic action's impacts against several criteria, for instance, current situation, future situation without the strategic action, *and* environmental standards.

Basis of evaluation: Environmental limits

Environmental limits – the state at which the environment cannot accept more impacts without declining over time – could be a useful basis for the SEA evaluation stage. They would act as a test of environmental sustainability, representing the second part of the Brundtland Commission definition of sustainable development: 'meets the needs of the present without compromising the ability of future generations to meet their own needs' (WCED, 1987). In the UK, 'living within environmental limits' is the first of five principles of sustainable development (Defra, 2005), and recent guidance on Regional Strategies notes that:

> *Responsible regional authorities will... need to consider the environmental limits that should apply in preparing their strategy and how its policies impact on such limits, taking careful account of the findings of their sustainability appraisal.* (CLG and DBIS, 2009)

The Chinese regulations on programmatic EIA require SEA reports to include 'an analysis of carrying capacity', a concept analogous with environmental limits.

However, although the idea of environmental limits is theoretically simple, in practice identifying such limits and determining what they mean for a particular strategic action is fiendishly difficult. In theory, for a renewable resource, an environmental limit is the point beyond which removal of the resource exceeds renewal of the resources for instance, when abstraction of water from an aquifer exceeds the rate at which it is recharged. For non-renewable resources, it is where the resource starts to noticeably decline or where use of the resource affects other environmental limits, for instance, 'peak oil' and climate change impacts.

In practice, it is virtually impossible to pinpoint a state where environmental degradation would result if just exceeded, but no degradation would result if just not exceeded. Not enough is known about the environment. The environment has feedback mechanisms (e.g. climate change resulting in die-back of trees in the rainforest, releasing more carbon dioxide). Various components of the environment interact to increase or decrease each other's limits, for instance, climate change leading to ocean acidification, in turn affecting the sustainability of coral reefs (IPII, 2009). The definition of limits is inherently subjective: even where there may be a clear environmental tipping point, whether this is perceived as a 'limit' also depends on whether we can measure it, and on judgements about what is (un)acceptable or (in)sufficient (Haines-Young and Potschin, 2007).

It is also virtually impossible, even where environmental limits are identified, to determine whether a given strategic action, in combination with other actions, will exceed these limits. A strategic action's effect on environmental limits will depend on mitigation measures, people's behaviour, other strategic actions and projects, timing, and so on. Box 9.2 shows an example of this. Infrastructure and technology can significantly increase the human activities that can be carried out within environmental limits: for instance, new and improved wastewater treatment works can allow more people to live in an area without increased impact on water quality. A strategic action may increase environmental limits: new green areas, for instance, can act as carbon sinks, improve water recharge into aquifers, and provide a site for food production – all possible dimensions of environmental limits. There will inevitably be pressure to show that a strategic action will not exceed limits, with developers arguing that their project can still (just) be accommodated without exceeding environmental limits and/or challenging the assumptions underlying any stated environmental limits.

Finally, even if a strategic action will clearly exceed environmental limits, it is difficult to agree what to do about it. Take the torturous international negotiations concerning climate change. Voluntary, unilateral targets are difficult to set because any target could be perceived to be arbitrary and thus subject to challenge by developers. Strong management measures could be perceived as restricting development, particularly in economically vulnerable areas (Therivel and Ross, 2007). Transfer of resources, for instance, the transportation of water from water-rich to water-poor areas, can have equality implications and typically uses more energy than self-sufficiency of resources. Not proceeding with a strategic action or project may have disproportionately severe social or economic consequences.

Box 9.2 Example of the effect of demographics, behaviour and infrastructure on environmental limits: Water resources in south-east England

Although England has a reputation for being grey and damp, the south-east of the country is under serious water stress. Population density is high, water is scarcer than anywhere else in England and Wales, and there is less water available per person in this region than in many Mediterranean countries. Despite this, average per person water consumption in the region is relatively high, at between 160 and 170 litres per day.

To inform the preparation of a Regional Spatial Strategy for the South East of England, a water supply-demand model was developed and used to test the implications of two new housing growth scenarios to 2026: 28,900 and 40,000 households per year. Six water-efficiency scenarios were considered, and modelled as applying only to new homes or also to 20 per cent and 40 per cent of existing homes: 8, 21 or 47 per cent savings, and per capita consumption capped at 80, 100 or 120 litres per person per day. Different scenarios of water-resource development (e.g. new reservoirs) were also modelled: no resource development beyond that expected by 2009/10, development as proposed in water companies' water resources plans, and an 'integrated' resources scenario developed by the Environment Agency.

The results of the modelling exercises for 2026 varied widely, from a surplus of water resources throughout almost the whole region under some scenarios to a 'water deficit' in most parts of the region under others. A 'deficit' does not mean that the areas run out of water, but indicates that the headroom that water companies use as a contingency is reduced.

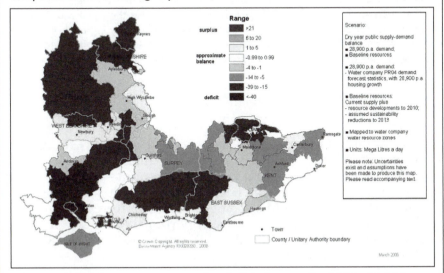

Figure 9.3a *Water resources surplus-deficit forecast for 2026: 28,900 new homes per year, no new water efficiency savings, no new water resources*

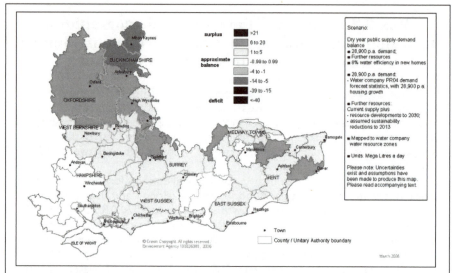

Figure 9.3b *Water resources surplus-deficit forecast for 2026: 28,900 new homes per year, 8 per cent water efficiency in new homes, water resource development as proposed by water companies*

Figure 9.3a shows predicted water resources surplus and deficit in 2026 under a scenario of 28,900 homes per year, with no efficiency measures and no new water resources. The original figure has shading in both red (deficit) and blue (surplus), but inconveniently they both look grey in this book. You'll have to trust me when I say that all of the dark areas in Figure 9.3a are in water deficit, and only a few areas are in slight surplus. Figure 9.3b, instead, shows the predicted situation under a scenario of 28,900 homes, 8 per cent water efficiency in new homes, and water resource developments as proposed by the water companies. Under this scenario, only the Buckinghamshire area in the north-east of the region would be in water deficit by 2026.

Source: Water Resources for the South East (2006)

All this said, it is quite clear that we are already exceeding many environmental limits, for instance, those relating to greenhouse gas levels and fish populations. Our ecological footprint – human pressure on the Earth's ecosystems – has been calculated as already being about 1.3 times that of the world's ecological capacity to regenerate, with wealthy countries having a disproportionately large footprint (Wackernagel and Rees, 1996; Global Footprint Network, 2008).

Possible ways forward include:

- The precautionary principle: act on the assumption that limits are already being exceeded unless it can be shown that they are not. This is the approach required under HDA (see Appendix D), where proponents must show that their proposed plan or project will not affect the 'integrity' of sites of international nature conservation interest, or else face a much more complex, expensive and uncertain authorization process. The use of the precautionary principle here is justified because of the rare and threatened nature of the sites, and the same justification may well not apply to other environmental assets.

- Test for, and enhance, self-sufficiency as a broad indicator of limits: Where do the required resources come from for a given plan area? Where do wastes go to? What proportion of the area's food is grown within the area? On a social level, do young people stay in the area? Economically, how much of the wealth generated locally stays in the area? This approach probably makes more sense at a country or regional, than a local level, since the smaller the area, the less likely it is to be self-sufficient. Cities in particular tend to be heavily dependent on their hinterlands.

- Quality of life assessment and ecosystem services approach: These approaches ask, for a given area or resource, what benefits people gain from it, whether there are already enough of these benefits not, how (if at all) the benefits could be substituted, and, if so, what management of the area or resource is needed. This allows an analysis to be made of resources that are not easily quantifiable, for instance, tranquillity, ecosystems or community interactions. Figure 9.4 shows the main concepts behind the ecosystem services approach, and Appendix C discusses the quality of life assessment approach in more detail.

- Ecological footprints to represent the overall sustainability of an area and proposed activities (Stoeglehner and Narodoslawsky, 2008). For instance, in addition to an existing unsustainable ecological footprint, the development of 1750 new homes through a five-year housing strategy for Aberdeen was found to directly increase the city's ecological footprint by between 105 and 300 hectares; and to indirectly increase it by another 180 to 2200 hectares due to the induced use of material assets, plus a further 300 hectares due to water use and wastewater discharge (Aberdeen City Council, 2007).

The relation of the current status and future trend of an environmental component relative to its target or to environmental limits can help to determine how that issue should be managed, and help to suggest mitigation measures. Tables 9.1 and 9.2 present a more formal structure for deciding how to manage environmental assets. Note that this is starting to suggest approaches for the mitigation of future impacts.

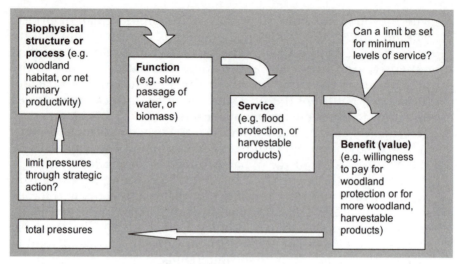

Source: Based on Haines-Young and Potschin (2007)

Figure 9.4 *Ecosystem services approach*

Table 9.1 *Managing non-replaceable environmental assets or benefits*

Importance of asset	Trend relative to target or limit		
	Doing badly: near or exceeding limits	On target	Doing well
High	Proactively promote improvements as a high priority in all relevant decision-making processes. Highest possible protection.	Seek improvements. High protection. Loss only justified by overriding need.	Can be affected if strong need and high compensation.
Medium	Proactively promote improvements. High protection.	Take opportunities for improvement.	Not a priority
Low	Seek improvements. Loss must be justified by need.	Not a priority	Not a priority

Source: Adapted from Countryside Agency et al (2002)

Table 9.2 *Managing replaceable environmental assets or benefits*

Importance of asset	Trend relative to target or limit		
	Doing badly: near or exceeding limits	On target	Doing well
High	Proactively promote enhancement as a high priority in all relevant decision-making processes. Loss must be substituted at greater than 1:1.	Seek improvements. High protection. Loss must be substituted at 1:1 (and preferably higher).	Loss must be justified by need.
Medium	Proactively promote enhancement. Loss should be substituted at greater than 1:1.	Take opportunities for enhancement. Loss should be substituted at 1:1 (and preferably higher).	Loss should be justified by need.
Low	Seek improvements. Loss should be substituted where practicable.	Not a priority	Not a priority

Source: Adapted from Countryside Agency et al (2002)

Basis of evaluation: SEA objectives

In objectives-based SEA, the evaluation stage tests how well the strategic action fulfils each SEA objective in the SEA framework: Does the strategic action help to reduce air pollution, provide more jobs or deliver community facilities? In practice, objectives-based evaluation can again lead to very different conclusions depending on the SEA objectives chosen and the underlying assumptions made during the evaluation.

One difficulty with strategic-level assessment is that most strategic actions are only responsible for some of the effects on a given environmental/sustainability component, and have at best an indirect remit for remediating these effects. As such, rather than testing whether their strategic action, say, improves air quality (an outcome objective), many plan-making authorities opt to test what is within their remit (an 'input' objective), for instance, whether the strategic action supports public transport. Essentially this tests whether a strategic action 'minimizes' its own impacts rather than 'reduces' total environmental impacts.

This may be fine in many cases, but can lead to problems where the input and expected outcome are not closely related. A real-life but anonymous example of this problem is the SEA evaluation:

By making facilities more accessible, the need to travel will be reduced, therefore reducing emissions caused by traffic. Investment in public transport and pedestrian and cyclist infrastructure aims to ease congestion, thus having a positive impact on levels of air pollution.

The inputs (accessible facilities and investment in non-car modes) are several steps away from the desired outcome (improved air quality), with no real certainty that the former will lead to the latter. However, in the above case, the assessor has assumed that the desired outcome will be achieved, without querying whether other factors need to be in place too (see Figure 6.3).

Objectives-based SEAs also involve assumptions about the effectiveness of mitigation measures: Will the mitigation measures be able to fully neutralize the core strategy's negative impacts? Will the mitigation measures be at least as likely to be implemented as the policies causing the negative impacts? In practice, many objectives-led SEAs seem to not only assume that mitigation measures would be fully implemented, but to use mitigation measures to 'upgrade' the SA/SEA evaluation to a rating beyond neutral. One example was shown at Table 8.3:

Pollution   +   *Permission will be denied for proposed projects whose impacts on the [pollution-related] conservation objectives of water bodies cannot be significantly reduced or compensated for. Aquifer protection and reduction in hydromorphological changes will improve the resource.*

Another real but anonymous example is:

[The plan will have a positive environmental effect:] Given that the policy phases the release of land for development, particularly for housing, this will protect greenfield sites and thus during the plan period is likely to cut the effects on biodiversity, flora and fauna, landscape, soil resources and quality, reducing contributions to climate change.

In this case, phasing of development (a mitigation measure) is interpreted as *reducing* environmental impacts, rather than simply minimizing them. These points suggest that positive environmental impacts identified in many objectives-based SEAs may be based more on whether an attempt has been made to mitigate the impacts of what appears to be seen as inevitable economic growth than on whether the overall impact of the strategic action is sustainable: SEAs may assume that 'less bad than before' or 'less bad than other options' means 'good' (Therivel et al, 2009).

Evaluating cumulative impacts

The cumulative impacts of a strategic action – both intra-plan and inter-plan – should be evaluated against the capacity of the receiver to accommodate these impacts. This capacity is equivalent to the concept of environmental limits, and carries with it the same conceptual problems.

Some SEAs incorrectly use their cumulative impact assessment section to highlight just how little impact their strategic action would have, relative to the sum total of all the effects on that receptor. An example of this is:

> *Compared to other human activities [in the Great Barrier Reef World Heritage Area], Defence activities are generally conducted at low spatial and temporal scales. Accordingly, many observed or speculated impacts which may be connected by some observers with Defence actions are usually operating on a much smaller scale than those arising from some analogous civilian activity. Similarly, the scale and intensity of many of the conceivable negative outcomes from Defence activities are insignificant compared to those occurring as a result of natural events such as storms, sediment and nutrient deposition from river systems, or the unexplained natural phenomena of whale strandings.*
> (Department of Defence, 2006)

Transparency

So far, this chapter has shown several questionable examples of impact evaluation: where bases of evaluation were chosen so as to give the 'right' answer; inputs rather than outcomes, and intent rather than likely impacts, were evaluated; mitigation measures were used to unduly 'upgrade' evaluation findings; and the concept of 'cumulative impact' was misinterpreted. However, all of these examples share the clear good point of being transparent. It is possible, in all cases, to understand the logic behind the evaluation, even if the logic itself might be queried.

Take a different (again real-life but anonymous) example, shown at Table 9.3. Here, the logic might be fine, but we have no way of knowing that. The basis of assessment is not clear from the key or the column headings. The assumptions underlying the assessment are not stated, and no explanation is given to support the evaluations. The conclusions give no indication of what, if any, mitigation measures should be considered as a result of the evaluation. If I were a decision-maker, I would have no idea of how to 'take this information into account' when finalizing my plan.

Table 9.3 *Example of a non-transparent impact evaluation matrix*

strategic action component	function of aquatic and terrestrial habitats	conservation of natural habitats and biodiversity	quality of characteristic landscapes	SEA topic — ability to absorb development into the landscape	management of risks linked to erosion, flooding, landslides	adaptation to major natural risks (earthquakes, cyclones, etc.)	health impacts	...
VA1	+	+	+/-		+	+/n	n/-	
VA2	-	-			n/-			
VA3					+	+/-		
VA4						+	+	
VB1					+			
VB2							+	

Conclusion: Programme V will have many positive impacts on risks linked to erosion and flooding, since nine of its measures are dedicated to this topic. However care should be taken with respect to its adaptation to extreme phenomena (notably cyclones), and its impacts on health, landscape and aquatic environments.

Key:

	no impact
+	positive impact
+/n	positive impact under certain conditions
+/-	impact could be positive or negative depending on how the measure is implemented
n/-	negative impact under certain conditions
-	negative impact

This suggests several rules of thumb for transparent impact evaluation:

- Involve a range of relevant stakeholders, including the plan authors.
- Explain underlying assumptions, e.g. about baseline problems, underlying trends, how the strategic action would be implemented, etc. (from the impact prediction stage).
- Use a consistent basis of evaluation and explain what it is: whether the impacts of the proposed strategic action are being tested against the current situation, future situation without strategic action, environmental standards, environmental/sustainability objectives and/or environmental limits.
- For cumulative impact assessment, consider the total impacts of the proposed strategic action and other actions, not the proportion of total impacts due to the proposed strategic action.
- Where there is disagreement about the significance of a strategic action's effects, document all the different points of view.
- Link the evaluation findings clearly to the decision-making process: to the choice of a preferred alternative, fine-tuning of the strategic action, and recommended mitigation measures.

Avoiding, mitigating, compensating for and ameliorating impacts

The impact prediction and evaluation stage will have identified the strategic action's significant positive and negative impacts. The impact mitigation stage aims to minimize any negative impacts, optimize any positive ones, enhance sustainability in other ways if possible, and ensure that these mitigation measures do not themselves have negative impacts. The end result should be a list of agreed measures to change the strategic action, change other strategic actions where relevant, and/or set a context for future projects.

A major advantage of SEA over project EIA is that it allows consideration of a wider range of mitigation measures, particularly measures to prevent impacts at an earlier, more appropriate, stage of decision-making. It allows sensitive areas to be avoided and environmentally beneficial developments to be promoted, rather than individual development proposals being considered on an ad hoc, reactive basis. It also allows for a wider range of environmental/sustainability measures to be considered, for instance, the creation of new wildlife corridors or community facilities.

SEA mitigation measures do not look like those in EIA (which normally focus on location and design). Typical SEA mitigation measures could include:

- changes to the wording of the strategic action (or components/ statements in it);
- the removal of components/statements that are not environmentally sound or sustainable;
- the addition of new components/statements, including 'protective' statements;
- requirements to substitute or offset for certain types of impacts, for instance, through projects that replace any benefits lost through other projects (e.g. a new park near an area of open space that is being developed);
- requirements and terms of reference for EIA of certain types of projects, or sub-components of EIA, such as landscape or traffic assessments (this can increase certainty for developers and speed up scoping of EIA);
- an explanation of why EIA or lower-level SEA might not be needed, or why some environmental or sustainability concerns do not need to be addressed in EIA or lower-level SEA; and
- mitigation measures that should be taken on board in subsequent plans, programmes and projects.

The last three are examples of SEA 'tiering', where decisions made at a higher level can help to streamline decisions at lower levels. This is also where links between SEA and EIA emerge.

Mitigation measures can roughly be divided into those that avoid/prevent impacts altogether, those that reduce/minimize the magnitude and/or severity of impacts, those that 'repair' impacts after they have occurred, those that compensate/offset for impacts (try to balance out negative impacts with other positive ones, but not necessarily in a like-for-like manner), and those that enhance already positive impacts. The detailed classifications are less important than the fact that the different types of measures treat the impact differently. A *'mitigation hierarchy'* exists: generally, avoidance of impacts is preferable to reduction, which in turn is preferable to reparation and compensation. This hierarchy is implicit in the SEA Directive's requirement to discuss 'the measures envisaged to prevent, reduce and as fully as possible offset any significant adverse effects on the environment of implementing the plan or programme' (CEC, 2001).

Box 9.3 shows examples of mitigation measures from real-life SEA reports. They clearly aim to respond to specific impacts identified at the SEA prediction and evaluation stage, and demonstrate a range of levels of 'strategic-ness', stages on the mitigation hierarchy, and overall themes, from improved governance and participation to monitoring. They have not necessarily all been adopted in the final strategic actions.

Box 9.3 Examples of mitigation measures

Governance, participation and capacity-building

- Establish a process by which representatives of local communities and potentially affected stakeholders, including women and youths, are involved in the granting of development licences.
- Develop or strengthen innovative training programmes and marketing opportunities for developers; tie access to these to improved environmental and social performance.
- Steering groups for project implementation should include both men and women, as well as representatives of a diversity of groups within the community. In doing so, special efforts may be required to recruit women and others who have not traditionally had a role in community affairs.
- Change the mandate of the Commission to one of maintaining the ecological integrity and long-term sustainability of the region and its communities.
- Implement and enforce existing environmental policy.

Subsidies, taxation and hypothecation

- Include in the new law a framework for compensation and involuntary resettlement centred on the long-term livelihoods of the affected families, considering standards of international practice.
- Establish an environmental fund from tourist user fees.
- Change the tax policy to promote recovery of the green areas affected by unregulated construction.
- Establish a clear mechanism for benefit sharing of revenues from development.

Zoning and land use

- Exclude new development from environmentally sensitive areas.
- Locate new development on previously developed land.
- In communities with a high density of construction and unfavourable environmental conditions, rezone industrial and agricultural lands as urban green areas of common use.
- Exclude programme support for motorized water sports on water reservoirs.
- For X sites identified as core biodiversity areas, provide a level of protection equal to that of current ecological reserves.

Technical

- Require minimum impact standards for tourism developments.
- Require new housing to be built to Code of Sustainable Construction level X.
- Limit the number of floors of new buildings to X.
- Implement a minimum flow regime for rivers to avoid negative impacts to their ecology.
- Gas leaseholders should be required to use directional/slant drilled wells.
- New development should be accompanied by adequate supporting infrastructure. Infrastructure should also be provided where there are existing deficits.

Implementation, including timing and phasing

- Prioritize improvements to existing developments and infrastructure over development of new ones.
- Prioritize projects that support the coherence and vitality of urban areas.
- Require EIA for all X projects, and prioritize projects that have the least environmental impact.
- Establish guidelines on resettlement planning and implementation.
- Promote a smaller-scale, slower pace of development than proposed in the plan.
- Carry out seismic surveys in marine areas consecutively rather than concurrently, to reduce cumulative impacts.
- Until a firm base of information on marine ecology is available to inform adaptive management, project siting should adopt a precautionary approach: unless evidence indicates otherwise, areas of key importance to waterbird and marine mammal populations should be avoided.

Efficiency and enhancement

- Prioritize projects that make most efficient use of resources (water, energy, etc.).
- Promote forms of tourism that put more into local economies (have lower leakage), have less damaging concentrations of environmental pressure and attract visitors with stronger motivations to come to the country, for example ecotourism, community-based tourism, special interest and non-'packaged' travellers.
- In offshore areas with high renewable energy generation, coordinate decisions on renewable energy leasing and licensing for oil and gas.
- Support marketing of locally produced goods as part of tourism development.

Monitoring and feedback

- Monitor fish catches to ensure compliance with global total allowable catch and ensure that unreported catches are eliminated.
- Continue experimentation with prescribed fire as a means of restoring and maintaining range health.
- Collect more environmental baseline data before finalizing the strategic decision.
- (For local plans that must deliver a specific level of housing), where the local authority can demonstrate to an inspector that neither alternative approaches to plan implementation nor mitigation measures can avoid impacts on the integrity of sites of international nature conservation importance, then lower housing numbers will be agreed.

Source: DECC (2009), DEWHA (2008), Government of Kenya and World Bank (2007), Great Sand Hills Advisory Council (2007), Quasar Consultores (2007), Scott Wilson and Levett-Therivel (2009), UNDP/RECCEE (2005), World Bank (2008)

Identifying mitigation measures

Identifying mitigation measures involves a *mentality* and *timing* rather than a particular set of tools. Decision-makers must be willing to change their strategic action in response to the SEA, and the SEA must be carried out early enough to allow mitigation measures to be incorporated into the strategic action. Article 9 of the SEA Directive requires decision makers to explain how environmental considerations have been taken into account in decision-making: identification and documentation of mitigation measures is a key component of this.

Identifying mitigation measures also means asking the right questions. This is how it could be done, assuming a rapid, qualitative assessment. Get a good SEA team together, one with a wide range of interests and knowledge, ideally including the person who wrote the strategic action, the person(s) who will implement it, and someone with a good understanding of environmental/sustainability issues. Ensure that the recording form – the table in this case – includes somewhere to note down comments and assumptions, and somewhere to make recommendations for changes to the strategic action. Check the checklist in Box 9.4.

Before the assessment starts, the SEA team should repeat several times firmly 'the point of this assessment process is to ensure that the strategic action is as good as possible'. For each alternative, statement or group of statements in the draft strategic action, the SEA team should then carry out the process outlined in Box 9.5.

Box 9.4 Checklist of items to prepare for a prediction, evaluation and mitigation session

✔ Book room(s), ensure that there are enough tables and chairs.
✔ Leave enough time. For a purely qualitative (+/–) analysis of draft statements, leave 30 minutes per statement. The first 2–3 statements will take much longer – say an hour each – as people get used to the process. Also leave 20 minutes in the beginning for introductions, settling in, latecomers, coffee, etc.
✔ Bring plenty of blank assessment forms, maps of the area and scoping reports to refer to for background information.
✔ Bring one copy of the draft strategic action per person. Where different SEA teams are looking at different parts of the strategic action, the teams only need the statements they are assessing.
✔ If the assessment is being carried out by different SEA teams, bring a list of who is on which team (don't assume that anyone will have read your perfectly designed, previously circulated list).
✔ Bring coffee/tea and biscuits. This is not an exercise in martyrdom.

Box 9.5 Questions to ask when predicting, assessing and mitigating impacts

Begin by asking 'What will this statement (or alternative, or group of statements) look like on the ground? Does the statement say what its author means?' If not, it should be rewritten to be clearer. This rewrite is a mitigation measure. Where the decision-maker will definitely change the statement so as to make it clearer, then the new improved statement should be used for the subsequent stages of assessment; otherwise the original statement should be used.

Discuss what impact the statement will have on each environmental component or SEA objective.

- If the statement is likely to have a negative impact, can this be avoided, reduced, repaired or compensated for? If so, rewrite it accordingly, add other statements, etc. These changes are mitigation measures.
- If the statement is likely to have a negative impact that cannot be mitigated, are its benefits so important that they override this negative impact? If so, justify why. If not, consider deleting the statement or giving it a major overhaul. The deletion or overhaul is a mitigation measure.
- Can positive impacts of the statement be enhanced? If so, try rewriting it: this is a mitigation measure.
- If it is unclear what type of impact the statement will have, how can this be determined? What additional information is needed? Obtain that information, or consider setting up a monitoring system to collect it for the next SEA.
- Where the impact depends on how the statement is implemented, use the symbol I (for 'depends on implementation') and try to set measures in place to ensure that the implementation is done correctly. The measures are a mitigation measure.

Document all of these changes: they 'prove' that the SEA process has influenced the plan-making process.

Agreeing and implementing mitigation measures

The final choice of mitigation measures will be influenced by several factors. First, mitigation measures that are within the *planning authority's remit* to implement will be easier to agree and implement than those that are not. Unfortunately, there is often a mismatch between the planning authority's remit to cause environmental problems and to ameliorate them. For instance, a housing authority will have the remit to provide housing, but not necessarily to ensure that the housing is supported by adequate infrastructure to prevent environmental harm. Similarly, it may be easier or cheaper for one authority to provide mitigation measures (e.g. new green spaces) for another authority's impacts than for the other authority to do it themselves, but the first authority may have little incentive to do so.

A particular issue arises with cumulative impacts that have built up over time as a result of past action: how responsible is a particular strategic action for dealing with these past problems? The '*apportionment of blame*' problem arises at all scales: plan-makers argue that it is people's individual actions that have the effects, individuals argue that their actions are constrained by government policies, and both blame China's rapid economic growth for pretty well everything. Decision-makers will argue that their proposed strategic action contributes so little to the existing problem that they should not need to do much in terms of mitigation, but this approach simply perpetuates the problem (Therivel and Ross, 2007). In such cases, mitigation measures may need to be developed and agreed on a multi-authority basis, to ensure consistency and compliance.

Many mitigation measures require substantial *funding*. Public funds may be available, but in other cases developer contributions may be required. Setting a framework for collecting such contributions will probably require some kind of proof that the mitigation measures really are needed, their likely cost and whether they will be delivered on time, as well as a regulatory framework for collecting the contributions. The final choice of mitigation measures will thus depend on a range of issues, and the 'perfect' mitigation package may well be unattainable.

Timescales may also be a constraining factor. Strategic actions can take many years to prepare or revise (although they can also be agreed and implemented extremely quickly), and by the time the strategic action is adopted, circumstances may have radically altered. For example, bus services may have stopped or the arrival of a motorway could have reduced traffic on nearby roads. This also means that it can take a very long time for other, complementary strategic actions to be implemented.

For many plans, impact mitigation is only realistically possible at a project level or through lower-level plans, such as a site allocation or development control plans. Rules of thumb for choosing strategic-level mitigation measures thus include:

- Identify measures that are happening anyway, for instance as a result of other planning authorities' or national government's actions. This ensures that additional proposed measures are commensurate and complementary.
- Focus on measures that are within the remit of the plan-making authority, are feasible, and can be implemented in time. Where appropriate, recommend other measures to other authorities, but be careful about assuming these will be fully implemented.
- Where appropriate, require mitigation measures to be in place before the negative impact begins. For instance ensure that adequate wastewater treatment works are in place before a new

development becomes operational, or that public transport is operational as people move into a new neighbourhood to prevent the establishment of ingrained car-based transport behaviour.

- Similarly, take a proactive approach that doesn't constrain people's behaviour after they have already made decisions and have entrenched views. For instance, it is easier to impose zoning-like conditions letting potential developers know that certain types of future development are not acceptable than to impose management measures retroactively.
- Establish a consistent approach that provides certainty, a level playing field, and an equitable approach so that nobody can claim to be particularly disadvantaged. Thresholds or limits that trigger mitigation measures help to simplify negotiations between multiple organizations. It is much harder to get case-by-case agreements about management measures for multiple individual projects than to have one rule that applies to all projects.
- Choose measures that are practical and not subtly self-defeating (e.g. that do not encourage rebellious counter-behaviour, such as illegal dumping of rubbish, or drivers using side streets to avoid congestion charges on main roads).
- Carry out follow-up monitoring linked to impact management (e.g. requirements to keep fixing things until the established goal has been achieved), to ensure that the measures work as planned (Therivel and Ross, 2007).

Where mitigation measures are recommended through the SEA process and not taken on board in the final strategic action, it may be helpful, for the sake of transparency, to include an explanation of why this is the case in the SEA report. An example of such an explanation is:

> *Given the severe constraints on water resources in the South East, we still believe that there is justification for requiring water efficiency that significantly exceeds current Building Regulations... The extra cost of going from current water standards to Code for Sustainable Homes level 3 would be £125 per dwelling. [The plan-making authority] has decided not to include such a requirement for two main reasons. [First, the policy statement] on sustainable design and construction already points to the pro-active role that both the planning system and local authorities can play on water efficiency [and another policy statement] requires local authorities to 'identify any circumstances under which new development will need to be supported by water efficiency standards exceeding extant Building Regulations standards'... [Second, the strategic action] is in line with national policy and consistent with what the Secretary of State consulted upon. It would be invidious now to*

change that policy without further consultation and collective agreement... (Scott Wilson and Levett-Therivel, 2009)

Informing decisions

By now, the SEA process will have identified the environmental/ sustainability impacts of the proposed alternative or draft strategic action, evaluated their significance, and proposed mitigation measures where appropriate. SEA's role is to inform decisions, not to make them, and so SEA should not now get drawn into 'balancing' or judgements about whether the proposed strategic action's benefits justify any harm it will cause. SEA should clearly identify and report significant positive and negative impacts, and it is then up to the decision-makers to make and justify their decision. That said, the SEA can help to inform these decisions by comparing alternatives, identifying which alternative is most environmentally sound or sustainable, suggesting win–win solutions, and providing information about the impacts of possible trade-offs.

Comparing alternatives

In SEA, alternatives are normally compared using the environmental topics or SEA framework developed earlier (see Chapter 6). The comparison is often summarized in a matrix format, with the alternatives along one axis and the topics or SA objectives along the other. Tables 9.4 and 9.5 are two examples of such comparison from the same SEA on water provision for Dublin: one uses simple +/- symbols to describe impacts on general topics, and the other presents quantitative information where it existed.

The two tables – especially when viewed together – raise interesting issues about how alternatives can be compared and how this comparison is presented. For Table 9.4 these include:

- *Should the total 'marks' for each alternative be added up and compared?* If so, does the fact that climate change and energy overlap mean that the issue is double-counted, and how would this affect the total? Is it appropriate that there are ten environment-related objectives but only one or two on the economy?
- *Are some SEA objectives more important than others, and so should they be given extra weight?* For instance, should economic growth be given more weight than fisheries or energy use?
- *How should missing information be dealt with*, for instance, about cultural heritage?

Table 9.4 *Comparison of alternatives using SEA objectives and +/- symbols: SEA for water provision for Dublin*

SEA objective	A	B	Option C	D	E
Avoid any deterioration in biodiversity, flora and fauna	--	-	+/-	+/-	-
Preserve the integrity of fisheries	-	-	+/-	+/-	-
Ensure no adverse impact on achieving Water Framework Directive objectives	-	-	-	-	0
Avoid adverse changes to current levels, flows and retention times (of water)	--	-	-	-	0
Minimize the contribution to climate change	-	-	-	-	--
Minimize impact on energy use	-	-	-	-	--
Minimize adverse impacts on sites, setting and items of cultural heritage	?	?	?	?	?
Minimize adverse significant impact on landscape quality and visual amenity	-	-	-	-	--
Minimize impact on tourism and amenities	+/-	0	+/-	+	0
Ensure economic growth by provision of a good quality water supply	+	+	+	+	+

Source: Adapted from Dublin City Council (2008)

Table 9.5 *Comparison of alternatives using information that can be quantified: SEA for water provision for Dublin*

SEA objective	A	B	Option C	D	E
Increase in retention time in Lough Derg (+days)	+7	+7	0	~+3	?
Increase in low-flow days in the Shannon Callows	24	?	4	?	?
CO_2 emission (1000 tonnes)	40	45	44	54	198
Energy required per year (million kWh, 2031)	51	58	57	70	256
Area of land potentially rehabilitated (ha)	0	0	2000	2000	0
Area of land impacted by water supply (ha)	1	1	201	101	17
Length of pipeline (km)	104	122	104	127	24
Volume of sludge produced (m^3/day)	340	340	340	340	180

Source: Adapted from Dublin City Council (2008)

- Where there is no difference between the options for some topics (e.g. economy), *would a ranking system provide useful information*, i.e. 'both may be good but A is better than B'?
- *Should some decisions be made before others?* In this case, alternative E would have very different impacts from all the other alternatives: should a choice first be made between E and all the other alternatives, and then (if appropriate) a choice between the other alternatives?

... and for Table 9.5:

- Again, *how should missing information be considered* by decision-makers?
- *How certain are the predictions?* Table 9.5 does not include an indication of the level of (un)certainty of the predictions. If, say, ranges were included to represent uncertainty, would some differences between alternatives disappear (e.g. energy use for the first four alternatives)?
- *How can the quantitative information, which only covers some topics, be considered within the entire SEA and decision-making processes?* For instance, how should the last two topics (pipeline length, sludge produced) be considered given that there are no associated SEA objectives?

The answers to these questions influence the way that the information is presented in the tables, and how the information is 'processed' for decision-makers. The information can be presented as straight – cardinal – statements (either qualitative or quantitative) of impacts, or as a comparison of alternatives against each other, baseline conditions or the 'no action' alternative. Table 9.6 shows some ways of documenting the comparison of alternatives.

In some cases, one alternative will clearly be better than all the others, but in many cases the decision will be more complex. For instance, the choice of one alternative (e.g. location of housing) could also affect the choice of another alternative (e.g. transport infrastructure), or one environmental component may be more important to the local community or decision-makers than another.

Pairwise comparison – comparing each alternative against each other alternative, as in round-robin sports tournaments – may help to omit some options. In Table 9.4, this would eliminate alternative A in favour of B. Some alternatives may trigger 'red flags': their impacts might be so significant that they are immediately eliminated from further consideration, leaving a short-list of remaining alternatives that can be compared in more detail. In situations where some SEA topics/objectives are perceived as being more important than others, multi-criteria analysis (see Appendix C) can be used. Different multi-

Table 9.6 *Examples of comparisons of alternatives: CO_2 emissions of four alternatives*

| | Alternative | | | |
	A	B	C	D
Cardinal/'straight'				
• Category	-	-	-	--
• Quantified (e.g. tonnes per year)	40	45	44	54
Ordinal/comparative				
• Compared to the preferred option	lower than the preferred option	higher than the preferred option	preferred option	much higher than the preferred option
• Compared to the no action alternative	10% lower than the no action alternative	no action alternative	2% higher than the no action alternative	20% higher than the no action alternative
• Ranking	1	3	2	4

criteria analysis runs can be carried out, using different weightings, as a form of sensitivity analysis. This approach can be used to test whether different stakeholders' perceptions of the importance of the various topics affects the final ranking of alternatives.

Again, all of these approaches must clearly be used to inform decisions, not make them. An example of such an analysis, for planned housing levels in Dover, is:

Options 1 and 2 would be unlikely to trigger the level of activity necessary to invigorate and regenerate the District and in particular Dover town. In particular Option 1 risks a continued slow decline in service provision and employment levels and an increasingly aged population (with consequent implications for the local economy and healthcare). Option 3 represents a compromise between the certainty that current trends are not sustainable in the sense that something has to change within the District if investment and regeneration is to take place on a significant scale, and the uncertainty surrounding large-scale growth – i.e. Option 4 – and the risks that this entails...

The choice between Option 3 and Option 4 is not simply about choosing a level of growth for the District. Option 4 would involve construction on greenfield land to the west of Whitfield. This, in turn, would require improved access from the A2 [road], which cannot easily be provided given the road's current configuration... Taking all these factors into account, Option 3 is probably the best option in the short term. However, in our view, it should be viewed as a floor rather than a ceiling and should not be a barrier to otherwise acceptable increases in housing density on allocated sites. (Scott Wilson, 2008b)

The process of documenting and comparing the impact of alternatives may identify a new alternative, perhaps one that includes components of several of the original alternatives or new mitigation measures. Such an alternative would then need to be reassessed and compared with the other alternatives.

The final choice of alternatives will probably be a political decision, encompassing many issues in addition to the environment/ sustainability, for instance higher-level policies, feasibility, cost and security concerns. The reasons for choosing the preferred alternatives and suggested changes to the alternatives should be documented. Where a preferred alternative conflicts with another existing strategic action, this should also be documented and fed back into an early review of the conflicting strategic action. A final question to ask before the preferred alternative is finalized is, as for individual development projects: 'Is this alternative good enough to welcome rather than bad enough to refuse?'

Trade-offs

The development of strategic actions often involves difficult choices, with winners and losers: choices between environment and economic growth, between different groups of people, between current and future generations. SEA aims to ensure that the environment and sustainability issues are fully considered in the decision-making process. Clearly win–win solutions that protect and enhance the environment are ideal. However, after 'full consideration', politicians may still decide to accept some losses in return for greater gains. Table 9.7 discusses various ways in which decisions can be made.

It is not always possible to integrate social, economic and environmental impacts, and different user groups may have very different ideas about what is appropriate integration: one person's cycle lane is another person's obstruction and one person's vibrant neighbourhood may be another person's urban chaos. However, the SEA can identify overall trends in impacts. For instance, does the environment consistently lose out to economic concerns? Are environmental targets always phrased very precisely while social ones are much vaguer? To the extent that SEA can help to steer decisions, there are some obvious rules of thumb to follow:

- avoid irreversible impacts;
- give greater weight to longer-term impacts;
- avoid impacts that would exceed environmental thresholds or limits;

Table 9.7 *Possible types of decision*

Type of decision	How it works	Example
Win–win	Solutions that meet some social, economic and/or environmental objectives, or benefit some groups without harming any others.	Cycle lanes are installed parallel to major roads. They cost little, slightly reduce traffic thus reducing costs to businesses, and improve conditions for people who do not have access to a car.
Net gain/no net loss	Advances in some social, economic or environmental aspects outweigh losses in others; or benefits to some groups outweigh costs to others.	Congestion charging reduces urban traffic by 20%. The revenue is used to improve public transport services. People who continue to drive have to pay but have a faster journey. People who use public transport benefit.
Conflict minimization	Solutions that reduce the potential conflict between different objectives.	The council wants to develop Park and Ride sites so as to reduce congestion in the city centre. Drivers are concerned about the safety of their cars and the price of the Park and Ride service. The council installs security cameras at the Park and Ride sites, and makes the price of parking there considerably cheaper than parking in the city centre.
Strategic coordination	Strategic actions or policy statements support each other.	A plan promotes high-density housing, working from home, and mixed residential–commercial areas. It also encourages public transport.
Addressing all three themes separately	Potentially incompatible objectives are promoted separately within one strategic action.	A plan promotes high-density housing. It also supports good access to open space.

- avoid impacts on particularly sensitive areas;
- avoid impacts that affect ecosystems, resources or communities that have already been cumulatively affected; and
- where impacts cannot be avoided, consider providing compensation.

Gibson (2005) has devised the following sustainability trade-off rules to help avoid inappropriate trade-offs and to demonstrate that a sustainable outcome will be achieved:

- maximum net gains – deliver net progress towards meeting sustainability requirements (i.e. seek mutually reinforcing, cumulative and lasting contributions that favour the most positive, feasible overall result while avoiding significant adverse effects);
- burden of argument on trade-off proponent – the burden of justification (especially where adverse effects in sustainability parameters will result) falls on the proponent of the trade-off;
- avoidance of significant adverse effects – no trade-off that involves a significant adverse effect on any sustainability parameter can be justified unless the alternative is acceptance of an even more significant adverse effect;
- protection of the future – no displacement of a significant adverse effect from the present to the future can be justified unless the alternative is displacement of an even more significant negative effect from the present to the future;
- explicit justification – all trade-offs must be openly identified in an explicit justification in light of the sustainability decision criteria and general trade-off rules; and
- open process – proposed compromises and trade-offs must be addressed and justified through open processes with effective involvement of all stakeholders.

Conclusions

Chapter 8 began with draft alternatives and/or statements. We close this chapter with preferred alternative(s); policy statements that have been analysed and possibly changed to make them clearer and more sustainable; and possibly new or deleted statements, and links to subsequent implementation. As a result of the impact prediction, evaluation and mitigation stages, the strategic action authors should not only obtain ideas for how to improve their strategic action, but should also have a much clearer understanding of their strategic action so that they can better explain, defend and implement it. The other people involved in the SEA should also have a better understanding of the decision-making process and how their work relates to it.

The prediction, evaluation and mitigation stage is often the most fun part of SEA. It is at this stage that grand plans for putting wind turbines on the tops of electricity pylons (you heard it here first...), insulating skyscrapers with straw bales, and installing ski lifts that pull bikes up long hills, are hatched. My favourite assessment session was held in a hotel with erotic Japanese etchings in the ladies' room: the women in the group had a hard time concentrating on the SEA with such an interesting alternative topic of conversation.

Quality review questions on impact prediction that could be used by either a formal reviewer or as a self-test are:

- Has impact evaluation been carried out in relation to a clearly stated and reasonable basis: the current situation, future situation, environmental standards, SEA objectives and/or environmental limits?
- Are any cumulative impacts of the strategic action compared against the capacity of the receiver to accept these impacts?
- Are avoidance, mitigation and compensation measures proposed for all significant adverse impacts of the implementation of the strategic action?
- Has the 'mitigation hierarchy' of first avoidance, then mitigation and finally compensation been followed?
- Are the proposed mitigation measures within the planning authority's remit or control? Do they deal with a fair share of the impacts caused by the strategic action? Will they be funded? Will they be implemented in a timely manner? Are they proactive? Do they provide a level playing field for lower-tier plans and projects?
- If trade-offs have been necessary, do they avoid irreversible impacts; give greater weight to longer-term impacts; steer clear of impacts that would exceed environmental thresholds or limits; preclude impacts on particularly sensitive areas; and avoid impacts that affect ecosystems, resources or communities that have already been cumulatively affected?

Chapter 10 discusses the final steps in SEA: documentation of the process, implementation of the strategic action, and monitoring of the strategic action's impacts.

Chapter 10

Documentation, Implementation and Monitoring

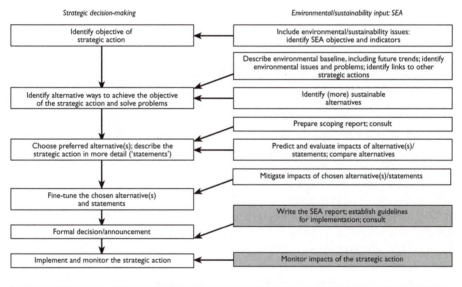

SEA stage	What to decide	What to record
Write the SEA report; establish guidelines for implementation	How to present the data from the previous stages of SEA	Prepare the SEA report
Consult	Whom to consult; how to respond to consultation results	How consultation results were addressed
Monitor environmental/ sustainability impacts of the strategic action	How to deal with any negative impacts of the strategic action	How the strategic action's impacts will be monitored and significant effects dealt with

This chapter considers the last stages of an SEA process: documenting the process in an SEA report, consulting on the SEA report, and setting up a system to monitor the effects of the plan, and documenting the decision-making process in an 'SEA statement'.

The SEA report

Hopefully by now, it should be clear that the SEA report that accompanies the draft strategic action is not the important thing: what *is* important is the process that precedes it. The role of the SEA report is to document the SEA process so that readers can follow how environmental and sustainability considerations have been taken into account in decision-making. A report alone is not an effective way to convince decision-makers to make changes to their strategic action.

The SEA documentation will have several audiences:

- the public, who will want to see why certain alternatives were chosen and how major impacts will be mitigated, but will not be interested in massive assessment tables or complex models;
- the environmental authorities and any organization responsible for quality control of the strategic action, which will want to see the same, will need to ensure that the SEA has been rigorous: they will look at the SEA methodology, and at changes made to the strategic action as a result of the SEA; and
- consultants, academics and other local authorities, which will be interested in the SEA methodology.

None of them will be interested in whether the North Pinksey Lane allotments provide + or ++ benefits to health. All of them will want to know what alternatives were considered to the statement that says that all new energy for Tooton Rush will come from nuclear power stations. So here are some rules for documenting SEA findings:

- DO focus on the big issues.
- DO explain what alternatives and mitigation measures were considered, and why the preferred alternative was chosen. This provides an audit trail of decisions, and shows the role that sustainability issues played in the decisions.
- DO focus on changes made to the strategic action as a result of the SEA. This will show that the SEA has been carried out well, and has influenced the decision-making process.
- DO explain the SEA methodology used: who was involved, how long it took, etc. This again shows that the SEA was carried out well.

- DO present spatial SEA information in maps.
- DO NOT feel obliged to include every single incredibly long and dreary assessment table or policy context description.

Documentation of the SEA process can take various forms. It can be one big report near the end of the decision-making process; or (better) several smaller ones at various stages of the process, which can be brought together into a final report if necessary; or information bulletins; or a website.

The information that must be covered in the SEA report(s) will vary according to legal requirements. For instance, Annex I of the European SEA Directive specifies the minimum SEA report requirements for countries. Chapter 5 noted that SEA reports can be either task-based (structured to follow the stages of the SEA process) or topic-based (structured by environmental/sustainability topic), and showed some typical tables of contents for SEA reports. Table 10.1 shows, for a task-based report structure, where the relevant information is covered in this book.

Several aspects of Table 10.1 are worth specific mention: the non-technical summary, what difference the SEA process has made, and the implementation plan.

Non-technical summary

The non-technical summary (or executive summary) is a particularly important component of the SEA report, since it is the only SEA document that many people will read, and acts as an entry to the rest of the SEA report. Unfortunately, non-technical summaries tend to be written in the last hour of the last day before the report is made public, by exhausted SEA authors, so their preparation probably gets less attention in practice than it deserves. The SEA non-technical summaries that I looked at as part of writing this chapter were between two and 30 pages long. Most were a first section within the main SEA report, but some were free-standing. None, I'm afraid, were particularly inspiring.

Annex I of the European SEA Directive calls for 'a non-technical summary of the information provided under the above headings', which include information about the plan, the policy context, baseline, and so on. This requirement has been carefully phrased: the non-technical summary should not be a description of the SEA *process* but of its *findings*. A legal challenge against two SEAs for local land-use plans in Northern Ireland clarified the importance of including a non-technical summary in the SEA report, and of documenting the findings of the SEA in that summary:

Table 10.1 *Possible structure for a task-based SEA report and where the information is covered in this book*

Structure of report	Information to include	Which chapter in this book discusses this
Summary and outcomes	• Non-technical summary of the SEA report	10
	• What difference the SEA process has made	10
Background and methodology	• Purpose of the SEA	5
	• Who carried out the SEA, when, who was consulted, etc.	5
	• Difficulties in collecting data and limitations of the data	6–9
Context	• Strategic action objectives	2, 5, 6
	• Links to other strategic actions	6
	• Baseline environmental/sustainability data	6
	• Environmental/sustainability visions and problems	6
Plan issues and alternatives	• Significant environmental/sustainability impacts of the strategic action. This may be done for different 'levels' of the strategic action: objectives, alternatives, detailed statements, individual sites, etc.	7–9
	• Why the preferred alternative(s) were chosen, including how environmental/sustainability considerations were taken into account in the choice	9
	• Other alternatives considered, and why these were rejected	7
	• Mitigation measures that have been taken into account	9
	• Where proposed mitigation measures have not been taken into account, the reasons why not	9
Implementation	• Links to project EIA, design guidance, SEA implementation plan, etc.	9, 10
	• Proposed monitoring	10

[The organization challenging the adequacy of the first SEA contends] that there has not been a non technical summary of the information provided under the other paragraphs... Page 1 [of the second SEA report] has the title 'Non Technical Summary' which sets out in seven short paragraphs that it is the SEA for the draft [plan], that it complies with the European Directive, states the objective of the SEA Directive, refers to the objectives of the SEA, explains baseline data collection, refers to the analysis of other relevant plans and programmes and refers to consideration of a range of alternatives for each of the policy groupings. [The legislation implementing the SEA Directive] requires a

summary of the information provided under the preceding nine paragraphs. The non technical summary on page 2 of the report to a large extent does not provide any summary of the information provided under the specified headings... [For both SEAs] there is an inadequate non technical summary for the purposes of paragraph 10 ... I find that the environmental reports ... are not in substantial compliance with schedule 2 of the Regulations and Article 5 and annex 1 of the Directive. (High Court of Justice in Northern Ireland, 2007)

To make sense to the reader, non-technical summaries need to include some preliminary information about why SEA is needed, and how SEAs are carried out and structured. Maps showing the spatial extent of the strategic action and any areas likely to be developed as a result of the strategic action, as well as figures showing any technical information needed to understand the likely impacts of the strategic action, help to break up the text, as well as being (more) easily understandable than a textual description. Readers will be particularly interested in why the strategic action is needed, what alternatives have been considered, the main environmental/sustainability impacts of the strategic action, and proposed mitigation measures. They will also need information about how they can comment on the proposed strategic action and the SEA report.

Difference made by the SEA process

Perhaps the best way of showing that an SEA process has been effective is to show what changes have been made to the strategic action as a result of the SEA. A post-adoption 'SEA statement', such as that required by the European SEA Directive, will provide this information, and is discussed at the end of the chapter. However, I think that as much of this information as possible should already be included in the SEA report, and that this should be done for non-European SEAs too.

To assist in documenting these changes to the strategic action, it is definitely worthwhile writing the SEA report in parallel with the SEA process, rather than in one big effort at the end. SEA authors and decision-makers move, die, go insane: institutional memory is lost. Plans can take years to write, during which the reason for decisions can be forgotten. By the end of an SEA process, the entire SEA team may have changed, and nobody may remember why a particular alternative was chosen or environmental criterion rejected. Make notes as you go along!

SEA implementation plan

The SEA report could include an SEA implementation plan, which helps to ensure that the SEA's recommendations are fully carried out and the strategic action is implemented in the most sustainable manner possible. This plan would bring together the findings of different stages of the SEA process and particularly the proposed mitigation measures. It could include:

- where other strategic actions conflict with the strategic action in question and need to be changed: who needs to be contacted and what might be done;
- what infrastructure is needed to ensure that any proposed development has minimal environmental/sustainability impacts, who will be providing it, and how it will be funded;
- what other actions need to be taken, for instance, encouraging bus companies to provide more buses on route X, or asking the neighbouring authority to revise its parking policies;
- what further guidance needs to be written, for instance, guidance on energy efficiency standards, maximum parking standards or wildlife-friendly design; and
- what needs monitoring.

The plan could identify who is responsible for each action, by when, how one can tell whether it has been put in place and whether it is effective, and what to do if it is not put in place or is not effective.

Consulting on the SEA report(s)

The most important aspects of public participation and the involvement of experts should already have taken place during the SEA process. Consultation on the SEA report(s) – note the deliberate use of that word rather than 'participation', since commenting on reports can be nothing else – will have a limited effect at best in improving the strategic action. Its main aim is to present information about the SEA process.

The final SEA report should be published in parallel with the draft strategic action, and should be made available for public consultation as part of the strategic action consultation process. It should also be made available for comment to the environmental and other authorities, and to other countries whose environment is likely to be significantly affected by the strategic action. SEA reports can be placed on the Internet as well as being made available in hard copy: the former is not only an increasingly common way to disseminate information to the public, but an invaluable tool for others carrying out SEA who can get ideas about report structure, data sources and so on from such reports. For instance, www.levett-therivel.co.uk provides web-links to SEA reports recommended as being of good quality.

Table 10.2 *Example of summary of responses to SEA report consultation*

Plan policy	Consultation comment	Response
General	The process of incorporating the SEA recommendations into successive drafts of the plan has not always been clear or robust	Agreed. Covered in [final SEA report and SEA statement]
DP5	There is a need to include the sustainable transport hierarchy as recommended	Discounted at the submission stage by [the plan-making authority]
RT5	Growth of airports goes against the principles of the plan and the [SEA report]	This issue remains

Source: Based on Scott Wilson (2008a)

Once the public, environmental authorities and other organizations comment on the SEA report, their views must be fully considered by the plan-makers. The SEA Directive requires their views to be 'taken into account' in the final strategic action. The Chinese PEIA Regulations go further: if the public or others disagree with the conclusions of the SEA report, the plan-making authority is required to organize further meetings to discuss them.

In some countries such as China and Korea, the strategic action may not be adopted unless its SEA has been formally examined and approved by a nominated government agency or ministry. For instance, in China, special plans require formal examination by an expert team whose conclusions are used by authorization authorities as a main basis for deciding whether or not the plan should be approved. In the Netherlands, a formal review of SEA reports by the Netherlands Commission for Environmental Assessment (NCEA) is still required, although a similar review of project EIAs has been rescinded (NCEA, 2009).

Changes made to the strategic action as a result of this consultation should be documented. Where consultation responses are not taken into account, an axplanation should be given. Some SEA reports, notably those from the US, include full copies of the consultation comments and of the response sent by the plan-making authority to the consultee. Table 10.2 shows another way of documenting the consultation stage of SEA.

Monitoring and follow-up

Follow-up is an all-purpose word that describes the collection and use of environmental data after the planning decision has been made. It can comprise several activities. Impact *monitoring* involves collecting information about the actual impacts – both predicted and unforeseen – of implementing the strategic action. Impact *auditing/evaluation* involves checking whether impacts of the strategic action comply with targets or standards ('conformance'), whether they are the same as those predicted in the SEA ('performance') and whether proposed mitigation measures have been fully implemented ('implementation'). Impact *management* concerns taking action in response to issues arising from impact monitoring and evaluation. *Communication* relates to informing stakeholders and the public about the results of SEA follow-up (Morrison-Saunders and Arts, 2004).

Monitoring allows environment/sustainability baseline information to be gathered for future strategic actions, and can fill any data/knowledge gaps identified as part of the baseline data collection stage. It can recognise any significant unforeseen impacts of implementing the strategic action and manage them appropriately. Such impacts could include a faster than expected increase in population, unexpected changes in transport patterns, or combinations of expected impacts that have unforseen synergistic or neutralizing effects. Monitoring also helps to identify unforeseen impacts of the strategic action.

Auditing can help to test and confirm/challenge assumptions about the implementation of the SEA, and links between the strategic action and its impacts (e.g. those of Table 8.4). This helps to inform future SEA predictions. In doing so, it 'enhances the rationale and understanding of planning processes, changing the perspective from static to dynamic, from linear to cyclical' (Hanusch and Glasson, 2008). Figure 10.1 illustrates this concept.

Impact management can help to ensure that any unforeseen impacts identified through SEA monitoring are managed appropriately. This could include revisions to the next round of the strategic action as well as more immediate and direct measures. Communication can help to ensure that lessons from this round of SEA are incorporated into subsequent rounds and into other SEA processes, and show that the SEA-monitoring process has been effective.

That said, follow-up of the impacts of strategic actions is hampered by:

- the abstract nature of many strategic actions and corresponding high level of uncertainty in many SEAs, which makes decisions about what to monitor difficult;

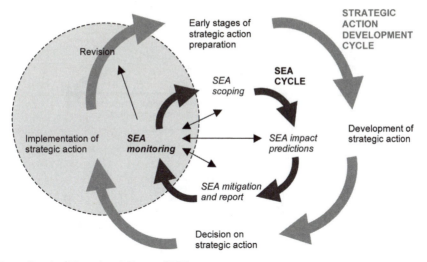

Source: Based on Hanusch and Glasson (2008)

Figure 10.1 *The monitoring cycle*

- the importance of lower-tier decision-making and of parties other than the decision-making authority in implementing the strategic action, and thus the difficulty of identifying what to monitor for the strategic action and who is responsible for this monitoring;
- the difficulty in establishing causal relationships between implementation of a strategic action and environmental changes, making it difficult to link monitored environmental changes to their causes and devise relevant management measures; and
- the dynamic and political nature of strategic level planning (Arts, 1998).

The SEA Directive distinguishes between two stages of evolution of an SEA monitoring system. First, the SEA report is expected to describe 'the measures *envisaged* concerning monitoring in accordance with Article 10' and second, the post-adoption SEA statement should describe 'the measures *decided* concerning monitoring in accordance with Article 10' (my emphases). Article 10, in turn, notes that 'Member States shall monitor the significant environmental effects of the implementation of [strategic actions] in order, inter alia, to identify at an early stage unforeseen adverse effects, and to be able to undertake appropriate remedial action.'

Monitoring is typically carried out using the indicators used for describing the baseline environment and making SEA predictions. The choice of what to monitor is inextricably linked with the questions that the monitoring aims to answer, for instance, whether it aims to provide information on operational aspects of the strategic action or test the

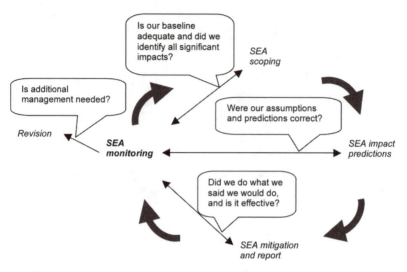

Figure 10.2 *Monitoring questions linked to the monitoring cycle of Figure 10.1*

performance of the strategic action against some criteria (Persson and Nilsson, 2007). Figure 10.2 shows how the following key monitoring questions relate to the monitoring cycle of Figure 10.1:

- Is our *baseline* adequate and did we identify all significant impacts? Monitoring for this would involve maintaining records of long-term environmental/sustainability changes (e.g. river level monitoring), collecting information on the significant impacts of the strategic action, filling in any significant gaps in the baseline data identified in the context-setting stage (e.g. surveys about people's health), and collecting more detailed data for specific areas likely to be significantly affected by the strategic action (e.g. bat population counts in area X). More detailed monitoring could take place where there are known to be existing problems.
- Were our *assumptions and predictions* correct? Monitoring for this would involve collecting data on whether relevant targets or standards were achieved (e.g. average annual air pollution levels) and on assumptions about underlying trends (e.g. population counts, per capita energy use) and about causal relationships between the intentions of the strategic action and its environmental/sustainability impacts (e.g. data on bus use and air quality in area Y).
- Did we *implement* the strategic action as we said we would, and is it effective? Monitoring for this would focus on whether the strategic action was achieving its environmental objectives (e.g. modal shift from car to bus), and on implementation of those aspects of the

Table 10.3 *Example of a monitoring framework: SEA for the Yerevan City master plan (Armenia)*

Indicator	Baseline data	2020 target	Frequency of data acquisition	Responsible authority
Level of water loss in city water systems (percentage)	70%	20%	3 years	Republic of Armenia Ministry of Territorial Administration, Yerevan Water Sewage Company
Level of water pollution			3 years	Republic of Armenia Ministry of Nature Protection
– biochemical oxygen demand	20	6		
– oil products	2–5	-		
– heavy metals	11–13 (copper)	-		
Surface of green areas of common use (m²/person)	543	2382	3 years	Real Estate Cadastre Committee

Source: Adapted from UNDP and RECCEE (2005)

> strategic action that aimed to avoid or minimize environmental/sustainability impacts (e.g. housing density, length of new cycle route built).

The answers to these questions should help to determine whether additional management or revisions to the strategic action are needed.

Once a decision has been made on *what* to monitor and *why*, a monitoring programme or framework can be set up, which specifies *how* to monitor, *when* to monitor, *who* is responsible, what the *management response* should be to any identified problems, and how the monitoring information should be *communicated* (Hanusch and Glasson, 2008). Monitoring of the significant environmental/sustainability impacts of a strategic action is typically undertaken and reported on as part of monitoring the general implementation of the strategic action, though it may require additional indicators. Such monitoring is typically done on an annual basis, but it may be more ad hoc or less frequent. The plan-making authority will often not be the monitoring authority, and may rely on environmental and other authorities to provide them with information.

Of the dozens of SEA reports that I looked at as part of writing this chapter, only about one-third included any monitoring section, and these were all between one and three pages long. Most were, again, uninspiring. Table 10.3 shows an excerpt from one of the better monitoring frameworks. Ideally, it should also include a trigger level for each indicator at which point action would be taken if the actual impacts were too severe; and information about what action would be taken.

Given the relatively short history of SEA, there has been little experience with management responses to SEA monitoring findings. In the short term, the main management response may be to any significant unanticipated environmental/sustainability impacts. This could include application of more effective technical measures, restriction of some activities, or a requirement for further studies before new development is permitted. In the longer term, they should help to improve understanding of the links between strategic actions and their environmental impacts: Persson and Nilsson (2007) suggest that this could be done by measuring indicators at each 'end' of the causal chain from strategic action to ultimate impact, and working towards the 'middle', looking for associations between the various links in the chain. This, in turn, could lead to improvements to impact-prediction models and approaches, and clearer links to avoidance and mitigation requirements for future strategic actions.

Monitoring data are typically communicated to the public in the form of 'annual monitoring reports' on strategic actions, or 'state of the environment' reports on environmental conditions more generally. Persson and Nilsson (2007) note that, due to lack of good monitoring and auditing of SEA findings, decision-makers tend to not be held adequately accountable for the environmental effects of their strategic actions. They suggest that democratic accountability should also figure in SEA follow-up.

The SEA statement

Although a post-adoption 'SEA statement' is only specifically required by Aticle 9.1b of the European SEA Directive, it is such a good idea that I think every country should have a similar obligation. The SEA statement is published alongside, or soon after, the final adopted strategic action, and explains what difference the SEA process has made:

> how environmental considerations have been integrated into the [strategic action] and how the environmental report [and the opinions of the public, environmental/sustainability authorities and other countries] have been taken into account ... and the reasons for choosing the [strategic action] in the light of the other reasonable alternatives dealt with. (CEC, 2001)

Table 10.4 *Documenting how SEA recommendations were taken into account in the strategic action*

SEA recommendation	Politicians' group recommendation	Final agreed change to the strategic action
The Local Transport Plan should take a tougher line on discouraging car use and adopt an approach that involves a greater use of 'sticks', such as congestion charging and increased parking charges. The revenue from road charging could be ring-fenced and channelled into walking, cycling and public transport initiatives (thus creating a virtuous circle)	The group did not accept this recommendation, therefore option A1 effectively represents the preferred alternative	Follows the politicians' group recommendation
Statement X on international transport should be reworded to state: 'The local authority supports the expansion of international traffic through improvements in the rail network and where necessary the strategic road network, which are able to reduce congestion and pollution'	The local authority supports the expansion of international traffic through improvements in the rail network and where necessary the strategic road network, which are able to reduce congestion and pollution	The local authority will press for improvements to the strategic road and rail network to support the expansion of international traffic
The Local Transport Plan should support the principle that revenue from the lorry-charging scheme is used to fund more sustainable modes of transport (e.g. rail freight)	The Local Transport Plan should support the principle that revenue from the lorry-charging scheme is used to fund more sustainable modes of transport (e.g. rail freight)	The Local Transport Plan states that lorry-charging revenue should be used to fund road improvements in the local authority

This rather complex sentence can be summarized as three questions:

1 How does the strategic action incorporate environmental issues?
2 How have the SEA recommendations and various consultation comments been integrated into the strategic action?
3 What alternatives were considered and why was the final strategic action chosen as the preferred alternative?

Starting with question 3, the 'storyline' of alternatives was already discussed at the end of Chapter 7. For question 2, documentation of environmental/sustainability authority and public comments was discussed above. A similar structure can be used to document how the SEA recommendations were taken into account. Table 10.4 shows a transparent and interesting though rather depressing example of this from a real-life, anonymized SEA statement.

For question 1, documentation about how the strategic action has incorporated environmental/sustainability issues and concerns can include information about the timing of the SEA process vis-a-vis the development of the strategic action, how the plan decision-makers were involved in the SEA process, and which sections of the strategic action incorporate environmental safeguards and sustainability enhancements.

All of these points help to show whether the SEA process has achieved the aims noted in the first sentence of this book: to integrate environmental and sustainability considerations into strategic decision-making. Again, as much of this information as possible could already be included in the SEA report, to show that the SEA has been a process of change and improvement, and not just of writing a big report.

Conclusions

If an SEA process has been carried out well, writing the SEA report should be a straightforward process of recording what has been done; most of the consultation will already have been completed before the draft strategic action is published; and devising the implementation and monitoring measures will simply be a way of tying up the loose ends. Otherwise, this is the time to panic.

Here is the last self-check, based on the quality assurance criteria of Box 3.3:

- Has the SEA been conducted as an integral part of the decision-making process, starting when the strategic action objectives were developed and continuing throughout the decision-making process?

- Does the SEA report:
  - identify the decision-maker and who carried out the SEA?
  - describe the methodology used in the SEA, including who was consulted and how?
  - have a clear and concise layout and presentation; is it presented as an integrated whole, and does it use maps and other illustrations where appropriate?
  - use simple, clear language and avoid technical jargon?
  - focus on the big issues?
  - acknowledge external sources of information, including expert judgement and matters of opinion?
  - contain a non-technical summary, which includes an explanation of the overall approach to the SEA; the objectives of the strategic action; the main alternatives considered; and how the strategic action was changed by the SEA?
  - avoid bias and is it presented in an impartial and open manner?
- Is an explanation given in the SEA report (and in a separate post-adoption 'SEA statement' if appropriate) of how environmental/sustainability considerations have been integrated into the strategic action, what changes (if any) were made to the strategic action as a result of the SEA, and the reasons for choosing the strategic action as adopted, in the light of other reasonable alternatives?
- Has a monitoring framework been proposed?
- Is monitoring linked to the provision of future baseline information, closure of any data gaps, testing of assumptions and predictions, and checking whether the strategic action (including recommended mitigation measures) has been well-implemented?
- Have the draft strategic action and SEA report been made available for consultation to the public, relevant environmental/sustainability authorities, and other countries as appropriate? Have they been given an early and effective opportunity within appropriate timeframes to express their opinion on the draft strategic action and SEA report before adoption of the strategic action?
- Have the views of the public and relevant authorities/countries been summarized and addressed?

The next and final chapter discusses how to ensure that SEA is done well.

Part III

Ensuring SEA Effectiveness

Chapter 11

Ensuring that the SEA is Effective and Resourcing It

This last chapter pulls together the material from the rest of the book. It considers what makes SEA effective and how to ensure that an SEA is carried out effectively. It then discusses the resources needed for SEA. Three SEA models are presented – SEA in one, ten and 100 person-days – to give an indication of what is feasible, and what can most usefully be prioritized. Capacity-building for SEA is then covered. The chapter concludes with a brief discussion of future directions in SEA.

Ensuring SEA quality

How does one ensure that an SEA is done 'well'; that it is effective? Having discussed different ways of carrying out each individual stage of the SEA process in Chapters 5–10, this section returns to the concept of SEA quality and how this can be ensured through the SEA process as a whole.

What is an effective SEA process?

The aim of SEA is to help to protect the environment and promote sustainability by helping to integrate environmental or sustainability issues in decision-making. SEA legislation tries to achieve this substantive outcome through procedural means. The two are linked, but are not the same thing: most SEA legislation allows organizations to be challenged in terms of whether they have prepared the right reports at the right times and consulted the right people, but not in terms of whether their decision is environment-friendly and sustainable. In many cases, SEA has become a lawyer's charter, with the focus on jumping through the procedural hurdles rather than on achieving SEA's original aims. The Chinese PEIA regulations are unusual in their inclusion of a substantive basis related to pollution emissions.

On the other hand, it is the substantive, not the procedural, aspects of SEA that are important, and the key test of the effectiveness of SEA is whether it has accomplished its original aims. Unless a strategic action is perfectly sustainable or environmentally benign to begin with, which would be very nice but also very unlikely, one way of testing SEA effectiveness is thus to compare the strategic action before and after SEA, noting any sustainability- or environment-related changes.

To get to such changes, shown as Box B in Figure 11.1, several criteria need to be met. First, the SEA has to identify the strategic action's sustainability or environmental impacts, and suggest possible changes. Such changes could be simple amendments, clearer wording or improvements to the internal consistency of the strategic action, or they could involve a totally new approach to the strategic action. Second, the changes must make the strategic action more sustainable or environmentally benign (see Box 11.1). Since SEA highlights

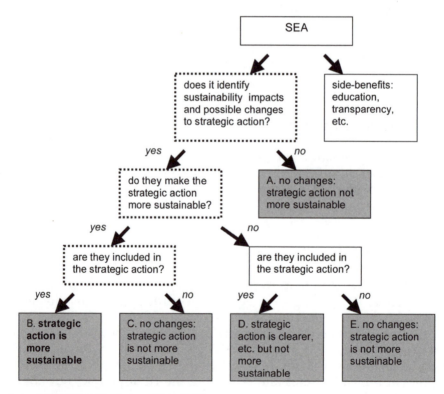

Source: Adapted from Therivel and Minas (2002)

Figure 11.1 *Getting to improved strategic actions through SEA*

Box 11.1 Does the SEA process promote sustainable development? The Bellagio Principles

Assessment of progress towards sustainable development should:

1 Guiding vision and goals
   - be guided by a clear vision of sustainable development and goals that define that vision
2 Holistic perspective
   - include review of the whole system as well as its parts
   - consider the well-being of social, ecological and economic sub-systems, their state as well as the direction and rate of change of that state, of their component parts, and the interaction between parts
   - consider both positive and negative consequences of human activity, in a way that reflects the costs and benefits for human and ecological systems, in money and non-money terms
3 Essential elements
   - consider equity and disparity within the current population and between present and future generations, dealing with such concerns as resource use, over-consumption and poverty, human rights, and access to services, as appropriate
   - consider the ecological conditions on which life depends
   - consider economic development and other, non-market activities that contribute to human/social well-being
4 Adequate scope
   - adopt a time horizon long enough to capture both human and ecosystem time scales thus responding to needs of future generations as well as those current to short-term decision-making
   - define the space of study large enough to include not only local but also long-distance impacts on people and ecosystems
   - build on historic and current conditions to anticipate future conditions – where we want to go, where we could go
5 Practical focus
   - be based on an explicit set of categories or an organizing framework that links vision and goals to indicators and criteria
   - be based on a limited number of key issues for analysis
   - be based on a limited number of indicators or indicator combinations to provide a clearer signal of progress
   - be based on standardizing measurement wherever possible to permit comparison
   - be based on comparing indicator values to targets, reference values, ranges, thresholds, or direction of trends, as appropriate
6 Openness
   - make the methods and data that are used accessible to all
   - make explicit all judgements, assumptions and uncertainties in data and interpretations

7 Effective communication
- be designed to address the needs of the audience and the set of users
- draw from indicators and other tools that are stimulating and serve to engage decision-makers
- aim, from the outset, for simplicity in structure and use of clear and plain language

8 Broad participation
- obtain broad representation of key grass-roots, professional, technical and social groups, including youth, women, and indigenous people – to ensure recognition of diverse and changing values
- ensure the participation of decision-makers to secure a firm link to adopted policies and resulting action

9 Ongoing assessment
- develop a capacity for repeated measurement to determine trends
- be iterative, adaptive, and responsive to change and uncertainty because systems are complex and change frequently
- adjust goals, frameworks and indicators as new insights are gained
- promote development of collective learning and feedback to decision-making

10 Institutional capacity

Continuity of assessing progress towards sustainable development should be assured by:
- clearly assigning responsibility and providing ongoing support in the decision-making process
- providing institutional capacity for data collection, maintenance and documentation
- supporting development of local assessment capacity

Source: Based on Hardi and Zdan (1997)

environmental or sustainability impacts, subsequent changes to the strategic action could be expected to incorporate these concerns. However, an SEA could also identify changes that improve the strategic action (for instance, clearer wording or structure) but do not necessarily improve its sustainability or environmental aspects. Third, the changes have to be incorporated into the strategic action. Suggested changes may not be included where, for instance, the SEA is carried out too late, other factors outweigh sustainability considerations, or the changes are not politically acceptable (Therivel and Minas, 2002).

However, even where the strategic action remains unchanged after the SEA, the SEA may still be effective because it has indirect benefits, such as a better understanding of the strategic action or the environment, more transparent and publicly accountable decision-making processes, or ideas for how to improve the strategic action in the next round of decision-making (see Chapter 3).

Ensuring effective SEA: Personnel, timing, resources

Chapter 2 suggested several principles for achieving an SEA process that improves the strategic action and optimizes 'indirect outcomes':

- start the SEA early in the development of the strategic action;
- involve the decision-maker, stakeholders and the public;
- focus on key environmental/sustainability constraints, thresholds and limits;
- consider alternatives;
- apply the precautionary principle;
- aim to minimize negative impacts, optimize positive ones, and compensate for the loss of valuable features and benefits; and
- be transparent and promote public participation in decision-making.

These principles are supported by six questionnaire surveys of UK local authority planners spanning 13 years (Therivel, 1995, 1996, 1998; Therivel and Minas, 2002; Therivel and Walsh, 2006; Sherston, 2008; Thomas, 2008; Yamane, 2008). Planners responsible for SA – the UK version of SEA – of their plans were asked the open question 'What advice would you give to others carrying out an appraisal?'. The answers to this question have been remarkably consistent over the years:

- *[SEA] should be started early in the plan preparation process, in order to maximize the contribution it can make to guiding the plan process.*
- *Plan it into the timetable for plan preparation.*
- *[SEA] needs to be simple in order to be transparent. It is a tool not a panacea.*
- *Don't underestimate the amount of work involved.*
- *Always discuss issues and reach conclusions between at least two people to minimize subjectivity.*

The more recent surveys also asked questions on factors that could lead to SAs changing plans and having indirect benefits: Who had carried out the appraisal, how many person-days it took, and whether it was carried out early in the plan making or near the end. From this, several factors were identified that improve the likelihood of a plan being changed in response to SA (and presumably SEA):

Appraisal carried out by groups of experienced planners and/or consultants: Plans were least likely to change when only one person in the local authority carried out the appraisal. When consultants and/or more than one planner were involved, plans were much more likely to change. Although involving more people may reduce the consistency of the SEA impact prediction and evaluation stage, this was outweighed by the benefits of a more well-rounded consideration of impacts. Plans were also more likely to be changed as a result of appraisal in authorities with more experience in undertaking appraisals. This suggests that, as planners become familiar with SEA techniques, they start using SEA as a way of improving, rather than just analysing, the plan.

Appraisal carried out early in decision-making: SEA's requirements to establish the policy context, determine the current and future status of the area, and identify problems, are all core elements of sound plan-making. Integrating the two makes efficient use of resources and ensures that SEA data are considered in plan-making. Clearly it is easier to integrate SEA findings into plan-making when the SEA process runs alongside the plan-making process: changing a strategic action when it is nearly completed will present greater barriers.

Over time, in the UK, more and more SAs have become fully integrated into the plan-making process. However, earlier surveys showed that, for those plans *not* changed as a result of SA, nearly 80 per cent of the appraisals were carried out after the plan was largely completed. In contrast, for those plans that *were* changed as a result of SA, 70 per cent of appraisals were integral to the plan-making process (Figure 11.2). Appraisals undertaken as an integral part of plan-making were also more frequently associated with an improvement in planners' awareness of sustainability issues and the plan, and were much more likely to be perceived as an effective use of resources (Figure 11.3).

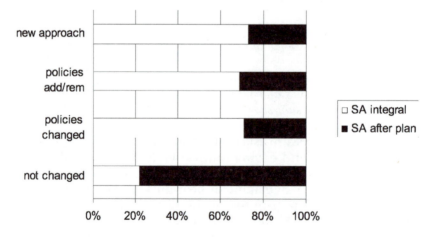

Source: Therivel and Minas (2002)

Figure 11.2 *Changes to the plan with sustainability appraisal carried out as an integral part of plan-making v. after the plan was completed*

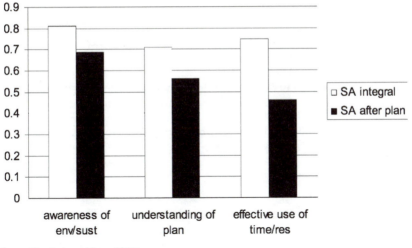

Source: Therivel and Minas (2002)

Figure 11.3 *Timing of appraisal v. indirect benefits and resource efficiency*

More resources, but with commitment to use the appraisal results positively: On average, roughly twice as much time was spent on appraisals that resulted in changes to the plan compared with those that did not: about 60 person-days compared to about 30. Appraisals that were an integral part of the plan-making process also took on average longer than post-hoc appraisals. This suggests that a minimum amount of effort is needed before an appraisal is of a standard that can reveal the need for change. It could also suggest that, in a supportive institutional context where enough resources are put into the appraisal, there is also a willingness to take on board proposed changes from the appraisal process. On the other hand, of those appraisals that took ten days or less, almost 40 per cent led to changes to the plan, suggesting that even rapid SEAs can be effective (Therivel and Minas, 2002).

All three principles together – group appraisal, an early start to appraisal and enough resources – were found to be a particularly potent mixture. Of the appraisals that involved more than one person *and* were integral to plan-making *and* took more than 15 person-days, 95 per cent resulted in some change to the plan (Therivel and Minas, 2002).

A more recent study carried out for the European Commission (2009b) suggests that a typical SEA takes very roughly 50 person-days and costs about €20,000 (see Table 11.1). Longer ones can take multiple person-years, though one must query whether such SEAs could not be done faster with the same effect. For environmental authorities, being consulted on an SEA might take a few days per SEA. SEA effectively shifts some of the burden of environmental data collection and analysis

Table 11.1 *Estimated cost of typical SEA processes*

Member state	Estimated cost (€)
Denmark	2700–9400 per SEA
Estonia	4000–30,000 per SEA
Hungary	20,000–40,000 per SEA for a national-level strategic action, for preparation of the environmental report only
Slovenia	5000–100,000 per SEA
UK	35,000–80,000 per SEA, based on the person-days needed to complete a typical SEA

Source: Based on European Commission (2009b)

from the private (project EIA) to the public sector. However, even where SEA feels like an unnecessary frill in the short run, it may save money in the longer term by preventing costly delays and legal challenges.

Ensuring effective SEA: Improved SEA process

Although the European Commission (2009b) study gives frustratingly little information on how to ensure an effective SEA process, research for the UK Department of Communities and Local Government (CLG, 2009b) concludes with many helpful recommendations on this topic. Many of them echo previous chapters of this book. Those that are internationally relevant and additional to points already covered are summarized below. Essentially, given the definite costs of carrying out SEAs where they are legally required, the recommendations help to ensure that the *benefits* of SEA are maximized.

First, the SEA (and strategic action) evidence basis should be spatial, where appropriate. Understanding geographical differences across the planning area can help to develop alternatives related to the needs, character and roles of different areas, and to prepare strategic actions that are spatially specific in the distribution of development and the management of change.

Second, early consultation on the scope and level of detail of the SEA should include consultation on the alternatives to be considered. Scoping involves judging what evidence will be required to inform the assessment and this, in turn, requires an understanding of the nature of the alternatives to be assessed. Only a limited number of truly realistic alternatives should be considered in SEA: many SEAs, to date, have either considered alternatives for too many small, unnecessary issues or have considered unrealistic alternatives that feel like they have been artificially developed for the purposes of SEA.

Third, practitioners should be braver about scoping issues out of further SEA analysis, to allow the SEAs to focus on key impacts. That said, the scope of the SEA will evolve with the strategic action. As the evidence base for the strategic action is progressively built up, further alternatives may emerge, and issues may be scoped back into the SEA. As new alternatives emerge, it may also be necessary to add further information to the evidence base to ensure that the alternatives' implications are properly understood.

SEA should help to identify, and test the impacts of the strategic action on, environmental limits. These limits can provide a benchmark for assessing the impacts of alternatives and policy statements, and help to ensure environmental sustainability. This would necessitate a more quantitative approach to impact identification and evaluation than has been used in many SEAs to date, and a baseline-led rather than objectives-led approach.

The level of detail of the SEA should reflect the level of detail of the strategic action: if the strategic action identifies particular sites for development or management, then the SEA should evaluate impacts at the site scale. The levels of detail of the baseline data and subsequent assessment should also be proportional.

When assessing a strategic action's impacts, the SEA should query the strategic action's deliverability. Rather than assessing the intentions, aspirations or specific wording of alternatives or policy statements, assessors should question the degree to which these aspirations will be effectively implemented, and focus on the strategic action's likely on-the-ground effects.

The assessment process should generate explicit recommendations to which plan-makers should formally respond. This could help to ensure that proposed mitigation measures are reasonable, and that the SEA findings are fully and actively considered by the plan-makers. It would also improve transparency in understanding how the SEA findings have been 'taken into account'.

Finally, responding to problems raised by the UK's predominantly objectives-based SEA system (see Chapter 5), the report comes out strongly in favour of a baseline-led approach:

The development of [SEA] objectives generates a host of issues including: getting to grips with, and explaining to stakeholders, the difference between plan and [SEA] objectives...; the vexing question as to whether or not a given set of objectives must be consistent with one another in terms of aspiration; the number of objectives that should be generated and the extent to which they assist in distinguishing between competing alternatives; concerns over the 'balance' between economic, social and environmental objectives...; the striking similarity between different authorities' objectives...; and whether or not, taken together, the aspirations expressed through a set of objectives constitute 'sustainable development'. None of these issues is easily resolved.

However, most important is the sense that an objectives-led approach comes at the expense of an assessment against the baseline situation...

A shift towards a more baseline-led approach would yield numerous benefits. Firstly, it would render the intractable issues associated with an objectives-led approach significantly less relevant and, secondly, it would promote an approach to appraisal more in keeping with the requirements of the SEA Directive and the outcomes in terms of impact identification and evaluation anticipated by stakeholders... Thirdly, and ultimately perhaps most importantly, it would signal a shift away from a matrix-based methodology. (CLG, 2009b)

Ensuring a good SEA report: Quality assurance review

A post-hoc check of an SEA report can indirectly help to test whether the SEA process that underlies it has been carried out well. There is already a tradition of testing the quality of project EIAs (e.g. Lee and Colley, 1990; European Commission, 2001a; Glasson et al, 2005), and a similar approach can be used for SEA reports.

Box 3.3 presented a quality assurance checklist for SEA. Such a checklist can be used by government officials, inspectors/auditors, organizations carrying out SEA, or members of the public. In carrying out an SEA review, reviewers would normally carry out the steps in Box 11.2.

Box 11.2 Typical steps in a SEA report review

- Familiarize yourself with the content of the SEA report.
- Identify whether the quality assurance questions (e.g. the SEA process criteria of Box 3.3) are relevant to the strategic action under review, and which are legally required (if applicable).
- Determine, for each quality assurance question, whether the SEA report has performed this to a high standard, adequately or inadequately.
- Identify:
  - major omissions: shortcomings of the SEA report so serious that they require immediate correction in the form of a supplement to the report or a new SEA, typically those associated with a breach of legal requirements;
  - significant omissions: shortcomings that can be rectified fairly easily by means of explanations and conditions; and
  - secondary omissions: shortcomings that are not worth remedying immediately but should be kept in mind for the next SEA.
- Decide what corrective action is needed if the report fails to meet the standards required.
- Document the above information in a review report.

Ensuring an ineffective SEA process

Just to hammer these points home, here is a five-step programme showing how to spend a lot of resources on SEA with minimal benefit:

1   Find out that you need an SEA when the strategic action is almost completed; alternatively 'forget' that you need an SEA until then. Decide that none of your staff can do the SEA because they are too busy putting final touches on the strategic action.
2   Hire the cheapest consultant you can find, who happens to live far away and be unfamiliar with the area: justify this by saying that you need 'independent' assessment of the strategic action. Alternatively, get your most junior planner to do the SEA: explain that this will be 'a good introduction to our strategic action'.
3   Put the consultant/junior planner into a room with the strategic action and some blank tables on a computer. Give them detailed and esoteric rules for filling out the tables, e.g. '+ +' *is totally different from* '+ ? +', *and* '+ + / ?' *has a completely different meaning again. When adding the assessment symbols up, subtract 0.5 for each* '?' *that comes after a* '+' *but multiply the total of* '+'*s by 0.667 where the* '?' *comes before.* Forget about them for three weeks while you put further finishing touches on the strategic action. Rebuff attempts to involve you or any other member of your team in the SEA process.
4   When the bleary-eyed consultant/planner has filled in all the tables, pay the consultant lots of money. Expect the planner to either quit at the first opportunity (with consequent costs in terms of hiring someone new), or else demand, in an annoying manner, changes to the strategic action that simply cannot be accommodated before it is due at the printer (wasting their own time and that of the other planners).
5   Print out the SEA tables, wrap them in a handsome cover that says 'SEA report', and place this on a prominent shelf. When the strategic action is put out to consultation and people ask where the SEA report is, let them look at the report only at limited and variable times, and provide only the corner of a cramped desk for them to do so.

Then the inspector, or judge, or audit commission asks for the SEA, prompted by public comments about the poor quality and lack of accessibility of the SEA report. The inspector decides that the SEA report does not provide the required information, and that the SEA process (as described – or not – in the SEA report) does not inspire confidence. They want to know why you chose the preferred alternative, and why you did not consider several alternatives and mitigation measures suggested by the public and other consultees. The inspector sends the strategic action back to you and asks you to re-do the SEA, getting it right this time. Several months and lots of resources after you started the SEA, you start again ...

How to carry out SEA in one, ten and 100 person-days

An SEA process does not have to be long-winded and expensive to be effective. Most of the effectiveness of SEA comes from decision-makers taking on board the SEA findings. A short SEA process can thus be effective, and in contrast even a huge commitment of time and energy can be wasted if decision-makers are unwilling to take account of the SEA findings.

To illustrate some of these points, three models of SEA are presented below: one-day, ten-day and 100-day SEA. All of them include fundamentals of good SEA practice: involvement of the decision-makers, group assessment, and a focus on improving the strategic action. The first one is primarily of use as a training exercise, so that decision-makers can get a feel for the kind of thinking and process involved in SEA. However, even such a short SEA can lead to improvements in some aspects of the strategic action. The second example is a 'quick and dirty' but effective process that would identify key issues: for a larger SEA, it could act as a scoping stage. The third model would allow the legal requirements of, for example, the SEA Directive to be achieved. All of them are in person-days, not time elapsed. Please beware: the main purpose of this section is to suggest a rough allocation of the time that should be spent on each SEA stage, not to be a definitive work schedule.

SEA in one person-day

What this process will do:

- give initial ideas for possible improvements (if appropriate) to four to six statements or alternatives of the strategic action; and
- give a rough feel for several stages of SEA and an indication of what an entire SEA process is like, as an educational process for the decision-makers involved.

The process can be carried out at any stage of the strategic action decision-making process where alternatives or strategies are developed in enough detail so that they can be assessed. One planner – the SEA coordinator ϒ – spends slightly over an hour getting ready for the assessment. They and the author(s) of the strategic action statements/alternatives ⚲ – I assume that there are two in addition to the coordinator – then spend another three hours each carrying out the assessment. There is no formal documentation of the process.

9:00 ϒ Coffee (get the priorities right)

9:02 ϒ Adapt the SEA objectives of Table 6.4 to the circumstances of the strategic action: take out objectives that are not appropriate to the context, add any other relevant ones, convert to topics if you prefer. Aim for 6–12 objectives or topics.

9:30 ϒ Brainstorm: what are the worst environmental problems in the area? Put stars (*) next to the SEA objectives or topics that symbolize the most serious problems.

9:40 ϒ Identify six policy statements from the strategic action that are most likely to cause significant environmental/sustainability impacts; alternatively, identify up to six alternative approaches to a given issue or constraint. You only have one morning to do all of this, so don't agonize. The aim is to focus on more, rather than less, important parts of the strategic action.

10:10 ϒ Draw up a table like Table 3.2, with the six statements or alternatives in the first column, and the SEA objectives or topics in the first row. Make sure to include a column on comments and proposed changes to the strategic action. Make enough copies of the table so that everyone involved in the SEA has a copy.

10:15 ϒ ⋔ Gather together the strategic action authors. Give them coffee.

10:20 ϒ ⋔ Take the first statement/alternative. Fill in the table using the process outlined in Box 9.5. Focus particularly on any changes to the statement/alternative that would help to minimize negative impacts: the idea is to identify ways in which the strategic action could be improved. Focus particularly on those SEA objectives that you put a * next to.

11:10 ϒ ⋔ Now that you know how to do it, do the same thing for the other statements/alternatives, spending 20–25 minutes on each. If you are assessing alternatives, spend the last ten minutes thinking about which alternative is best in terms of the environment or sustainability (using the SEA findings, focusing particularly on those objectives with * next to them).

13:00 Done!

SEA in ten person-days

What this process will do:

- identify, in a rough and ready manner, key environmental/sustainability constraints to a strategic action;
- suggest some alternative approaches for dealing with these constraints;

- give ideas for possible improvements (if appropriate) to up to 60 statements or alternatives;
- result in an SEA report (though not necessarily a legally compliant one); and
- start ensuring that the SEA report findings are implemented.

The process should be begun early in the development of the strategic action.

Day 1:
- ⅄ ♔, one to two hours: Agree on how the SEA will be carried out. Agree SEA topics or objectives and an initial list of key environmental/sustainability problems, as for the one-day exercise
- ⅄, one hour: Document the findings.

Day 2:
- ⅄, all day: Telephone local authority, environmental authority, etc. officials; and do a web-search to confirm key environmental/ sustainability problems and get data on them if available. Put together a folder of relevant maps: a general map of main settlements and transport corridors; maps showing areas designated for their nature conservation, landscape, historical value; other maps of environmental/sustainability problems if easily available. If appropriate, in light of this work, suggest which SEA topics or objectives are most important. Document the findings. (*Variant: if the strategic action has many alternatives or possible statements, spend part of the day identifying those that are most likely to have significant impacts so that the rest of the assessment process can focus on these*).

Day 3:
- ⅄ ♔, two hours: Discuss what constraints ♔ are facing as they are devising their strategic action, and what they must do and cannot do. Discuss what alternatives ♔ are already considering for their strategic action. Using Figure 7.1 or the questions proposed by Morrison-Saunders and Therivel (2006) at Chapter 7, brainstorm other strategic action alternatives that deal with the environmental/sustainability constraints and/or achieve the strategic action's objectives. Eliminate those that are clearly not feasible or appropriate.
- ⅄, one hour: Document the findings.

At this stage, ♔ would elaborate the alternatives/options into statements as part of their normal decision-making functions. The SEA resumes once this has been done.

Days 4–8:
- ϒ ﷼, two days: In groups of two to three (strategic action author, sustainability expert, plus one other person who knows the area, subject of the policy statement or alternative, or sustainability), using the SEA topics or objectives agreed on Day 1 (focusing particularly on key topics or objectives identified on Day 2), analyse the policy statements or alternatives as in the 10:20 and 11:10 sessions of the one-day SEA (*Variant: assess broad alternatives, and then a limited number of more detailed statements. Another variant: assess fewer statements but in more depth, using some of the techniques in Appendix C.*) Document the SEA findings and proposed changes to the strategic action as the assessment progresses.

Days 9 and 10:
- ϒ, all day: Follow up the SEA findings: discuss the SEA results with key decision-makers, try to ensure that they are actively taken on board, document the SEA methodology, put together the previously written documents into an SEA report, make sure the report appears on the organization's website.

SEA in 100 person-days

What this process will do:

- achieve a full SEA process in accordance with, say, the SEA Directive or Protocol;
- inform decision-makers about sustainability and environmental issues; and
- result in an SEA report capable of withstanding inquiry/audit.

The SEA process of Table 11.2 allows for generous timing if little quantification of impacts is done; tight timing if significant quantification is done. It assumes that most of the SEA will be carried out in-house by a planning team of four to five people, with support from an external SEA coordinator or consultant.

Table 11.2 *The Full Monty: 100 person-day SEA process*

SEA stage	Person-days	Comments and advice
Early in the development of the strategic action		
SEA training for decision makers	3	The SEA coordinator/consultant gives the planning team a half-day training course on SEA, focusing on legal requirements and a good practice SEA case study similar to that being worked on.
Devise SEA objectives	2	Identify and agree SA topics or objectives, ensuring that they cover all legal requirements. Check whether other assessment requirements (e.g. appropriate assessment) apply and integrate them with SEA if appropriate. Carry out an internal compatibility appraisal (see Appendix C) of the SEA objectives.
Quick SEA of the existing strategic action	optional: 5	The planning team quickly assesses the (old) existing strategic action, if one exists, using the agreed SEA topics or objectives, Table 3.2 and Box 9.5 (as in the one-day SEA). This provides a starting point for drafting the new version of the strategic action.
Collect baseline data and identify environmental/ sustainability problems and issues	15	Set a specific timeframe for this stage, as it can in theory take forever. Use a cyclical process: collect some data, identify key environmental/sustainability problems and issues, collect more data on these issues, etc. Identify the need for any maps and request these from the GIS team (or collate any that are available). Start discussions with consultees. Document the findings.
Identify and describe links to other relevant strategic actions	4	Use existing lists of strategic actions and their requirements where possible to save time. Document the findings.
Write draft scoping report	5	Documentation of the above stages as they are being carried out helps to ease this process, leaving only the following aspects: methodology, purpose of the SEA, difficulties, limitations, etc. Test the quality of the report so far by using the checklist in Box 3.3.
Consult on, and agree, the scoping report (this could also be done after alternatives are identified)	4–7	This could be done (preferably) in a meeting of key stakeholders, or by correspondence. The extra days may be needed if the public is also consulted (e.g. through a website or newspaper announcement).

SEA stage	Person-days	Comments and advice
As the strategic action evolves ...		
Identify reasonable alternatives or options	4	Members of the planning team identify draft options for their topic areas, starting with the options they do not have, then using Table 7.1 and the 'generating alternatives' section of Chapter 7 as inspiration. Unreasonable options are eliminated using the 'tests of unreasonableness' from Chapter 7: not within the planning authority's remit, not feasible, not relevant to the decision-making process.
Discuss and fine-tune the draft alternatives	4	Planning team members discuss their draft options with each other or with the SEA coordinator/consultant, and adapt the options in response to these discussions.
Test the alternatives/options against the SEA objectives; mitigate impacts; test whether the preferred alternatives/options are compatible with each other	10	This is done in small groups, to definitely include members of the planning team but possibly also other officers from the authority, outside experts, politicians and/or members of the public. Table 3.2 and Box 9.5 provide a template for assessing the alternatives. Check the cumulative impacts of the preferred alternatives/options (e.g. Table 8.6), and revisit the options if cumulative impacts are significant
Document the alternatives' identification and assessment stage	3	The 'storyline' concept from the end of Chapter 7 may be helpful.
... preferred alternatives/options are chosen and evolved into detailed policy statements		
Screen the policy statements	1	Use the questions in Box 8.3 to ensure that those statements with the most significant impacts are given the most attention and vice-versa.
Test the policy statements against the SEA topics or objectives; mitigate impacts	20	This could involve small group 'expert judgement' sessions again, but could also involve research and possibly quantification for issues that need more detail (Appendix C). Remember to keep documenting limitations and any problems or uncertainty encountered.

SEA stage	Person-days	Comments and advice
Implement the SEA findings, propose a monitoring programme	4	The decision-makers put procedures in place to ensure that the SEA findings are implemented and monitored.
Write the SEA report	8	Use Table 10.1 as a template. Allow plenty of time for formatting and editing. Test the quality of the report using the checklist in Box 3.3.
Consult on the SEA report; take consultation comments on board; document how this was done	6-8	Use Table 10.2 as a template.
Celebrate the completion of the SEA	0.5	

Capacity building, setting a supportive context

This section discusses possible ways of promoting a positive 'SEA culture' that helps to avoid the uncertainty and confrontational aspects of SEA through training, efficiencies of scale and central support.

Promoting a culture of 'doing SEA'

Where SEA is not (yet) legally required, as a way to improve experience and confidence with SEA, decision-makers could voluntarily carry out SEA as part of their plan-making processes. This could have multiple advantages:

- It produces more sustainable strategic actions as soon as possible.
- It gives decision-makers hands-on experience and confidence.
- It allows problems in implementing SEA to be identified and ironed out before SEA becomes mandatory, and thus reduces the risk of problems and challenges when it does.
- It helps to improve people's skills and establishes a new type of 'green business' sector.
- It increases the chances that when local or small-scale strategic actions come up for statutorily required SEA, the higher level strategic actions that constrain and guide them will already have undergone SEA and are therefore less likely to limit sustainable options.

Early examples of SEAs can act as invaluable models for others who are (considering) carrying out SEAs themselves. For instance, they can provide examples of relevant related strategic actions, suggest sources of baseline data, give an indication of the amount of work required, and encourage organizations to collaborate in carrying out common SEA requirements, such as provision of baseline data and identification of problems. 'SEA pioneers' should ideally make their SEA reports publicly available, possibly at a central website.

Central government has a key role to play in both promoting an 'SEA culture' and improving SEA efficiency and effectiveness. A central SEA support centre, such as the Netherlands Commission for Environmental Assessment or the Scottish SEA Gateway, can publish SEA guidance and case studies, commission relevant studies and ensure SEA quality. It can act as a cross-departmental coordinating body to ensure that different departments with different remits (agriculture, energy, etc.) understand SEA requirements and good practice, are aware of each other's emerging strategic actions, and carry out SEAs in a consistent manner. A central SEA website could provide information on legal requirements and guidance documents on SEA, good practice examples of SEA, reasonable assumptions to make about the links between policy input and outcomes on the ground, how SEAs should link to other types of assessment such as health impact assessment or HDA, and information on further references, training courses and so on.

Cost efficiencies

Legal SEA requirements influence the minimum amount of work needed (more than a day, I'm afraid), but even then an efficiently run SEA can be carried out in a fraction of the time taken by an inefficient SEA. Factors that affect how long SEA takes and how much it costs include: when the SEA is started in the decision-making cycle; the amount and quality of baseline data (including maps/GIS) that already exists; whether stakeholders are willing to share data and/or collaborate in collecting data; whether there is consensus on key environmental/ sustainability problems and issues; whether lists of other relevant strategic actions and their requirements already exist; and what consultation processes already exist. Again, a central support agency that facilitates these aspects of SEA can greatly reduce costs for individual authorities that need to carry out SEA.

Some aspects of SEA only need to be done once, well, for each authority and then periodically updated:

- an analysis of existing strategic actions that could affect the development of strategic actions in that authority;

- the description of the baseline environment, including maps, and a description of likely future trends;
- identification of key existing environmental problems and sustainability issues;
- identification of relevant environmental limits; and
- monitoring.

This information – with slight variants to reflect different countries' legislative requirements – is necessary for each SEA within a given authority or region, though it will vary by level (national v. regional v. local) and between authorities at the same level. It would make sense to collect it once (if need be, with joint funding from the departments that would gain most from economies of scale) and make it available to everyone within the authority, say through a regularly updated website with downloadable documents. Then, any given SEA team would only need to cut and paste those data or those other strategic actions' requirements that apply to their strategic action, and not have to reinvent the wheel each time.

In authorities where many SEAs are carried out, it might be worthwhile appointing an officer who is responsible for SEA data provision, support and training.

Training

Planners, engineers, consultants, environmentalists and politicians will all need training on how to carry out effective SEAs. SEA courses will be needed, possibly tailor-made for different types of audiences:

- Planners and bureaucrats need information on basic SEA requirements, how these will affect their organization, and what strategic actions require SEA. In my experience, support on generation of reasonable alternatives is often also very helpful.
- Senior government officials, politicians and elected representatives need a basic understanding of legal SEA requirements, and how to take the results of an SEA into account in decision-making.
- Environmental/sustainability authorities and non-governmental organizations, who will generally be responsible for SEA quality assurance, will require some training, as well as internal guidance and review of criteria/checklists to enable them to efficiently provide consistent and comprehensive feedback.
- Consultants and academics involved in plan-making, policy appraisal and law will need training on SEA legal requirements and ideas on SEA good practice techniques. Given the large amount of group work, consensus-building and community involvement required in many SEAs, training on negotiation skills is also likely to be useful.

- Consultants and academics involved in EIA, engineering, economic and other 'technical' subjects, will need training on the more 'strategic' aspects of SEA, for instance, how to generate alternatives, deal with uncertainty and keep SEA from being the compilation of lots of EIAs. Training on negotiation skills is also likely to be beneficial. I personally find these professionals hardest to train in SEA techniques because they are so good at detailed work that they find it difficult to deal with the subjective aspects and inevitable uncertainties associated with SEA.
- The public is unlikely to be interested in formal SEA training. A website explaining the SEA process and sources of further information might, however, be helpful.

The future of SEA

Over the last 40 years, we have gone from a single formative sentence in the US National Environmental Policy Act –

include in every recommendation or report on proposals for legislation and other major Federal actions significantly affecting the quality of the human environment, a detailed statement by the responsible official on the environmental impacts of the proposed action

– via years of evolving EIA procedures, to legal requirements to carry out SEAs in several dozen countries. Just in the six years since the publication of the first edition of this book, the number of SEAs prepared each year has mushroomed, overall SEA quality has improved dramatically, much greater use has been made of technologies such as the Internet and GIS to inform SEA practice, and much better understanding has been gained on how SEAs are, and can be, used in decision making.

Where does SEA go from here? Based on experience with project EIA, the number of SEAs carried out will continue to rise rapidly, as will their quality. SEA will expand to cover other strategic actions and other countries: for instance, national government decision makers will feel pressure to carry out SEAs of their policies when local and regional level decision makers start arguing that the un-SEAed national policies do not provide them with a robust, coherent and sustainable framework for their decisions. Those countries with SEA systems will start requiring other countries to have SEA systems in place before they provide funding or collaborate with them.

Most notably, decision makers will start 'thinking SEA' as they develop their strategic actions. Instead of perceiving SEA as a separate process that is 'done on' their strategic actions, they will start integrating environmental and sustainability thinking into their strategic actions ... to the point where ultimately, hopefully, SEA will make itself (and this book) redundant.

Appendices

Appendix A

European Union Directive 2001/42/EC

**DIRECTIVE 2001/42/EC OF THE EUROPEAN PARLIAMENT
AND OF THE COUNCIL**

of 27 June 2001

**on the assessment of the effects of certain plans and
programmes on the environment**

THE EUROPEAN PARLIAMENT AND THE COUNCIL OF THE
EUROPEAN UNION,

Having regard to the Treaty establishing the European Community,
and in particular Article 175(1) thereof,

Having regard to the proposal from the Commission ([1]),

Having regard to the opinion of the Economic and Social Committee
([2]),

Having regard to the opinion of the Committee of the Regions ([3]),

Acting in accordance with the procedure laid down in Article 251 of
the Treaty ([4]), in the light of the joint text approved by the Conciliation
Committee on 21 March 2001,

Whereas:

(1) Article 174 of the Treaty provides that Community policy on the
environment is to contribute to, inter alia, the preservation, protection
and improvement of the quality of the environment, the protection of

human health and the prudent and rational utilisation of natural resources and that it is to be based on the precautionary principle. Article 6 of the Treaty provides that environmental protection requirements are to be integrated into the definition of Community policies and activities, in particular with a view to promoting sustainable development.

(2) The Fifth Environment Action Programme: Towards sustainability – A European Community programme of policy and action in relation to the environment and sustainable development ([5]), supplemented by Council Decision No 2179/98/EC ([6]) on its review, affirms the importance of assessing the likely environmental effects of plans and programmes.

(3) The Convention on Biological Diversity requires Parties to integrate as far as possible and as appropriate the conservation and sustainable use of biological diversity into relevant sectoral or cross-sectoral plans and programmes.

(4) Environmental assessment is an important tool for integrating environmental considerations into the preparation and adoption of certain plans and programmes which are likely to have significant effects on the environment in the Member States, because it ensures that such effects of implementing plans and programmes are taken into account during their preparation and before their adoption.

(5) The adoption of environmental assessment procedures at the planning and programming level should benefit undertakings by providing a more consistent framework in which to operate by the inclusion of the relevant environmental information into decision-making. The inclusion of a wider set of factors in decision-making should contribute to more sustainable and effective solutions.

(6) The different environmental assessment systems operating within Member States should contain a set of common procedural requirements necessary to contribute to a high level of protection of the environment.

(7) The United Nations Economic Commission for Europe Convention on Environmental Impact Assessment in a Transboundary Context of 25 February 1991, which applies to both Member States and other States, encourages the parties to the Convention to apply its principles to plans and programmes as well; at the second meeting of the Parties to the Convention in Sofia on 26 and 27 February 2001, it was decided to prepare a legally binding protocol on strategic environmental assessment which would supplement the existing provisions on environmental impact assessment in a transboundary context, with a

view to its possible adoption on the occasion of the 5th Ministerial Conference 'Environment for Europe' at an extraordinary meeting of the Parties to the Conventions, scheduled for May 2003 in Kiev, Ukraine. The systems operating within the Community for environmental assessment of plans and programmes should ensure that there are adequate transboundary consultations where the implementation of a plan or programme being prepared in one Member State is likely to have significant effects on the environment of another Member State. The information on plans and programmes having significant effects on the environment of other States should be forwarded on a reciprocal and equivalent basis within an appropriate legal framework between Member States and these other States.

(8) Action is therefore required at Community level to lay down a minimum environmental assessment framework, which would set out the broad principles of the environmental assessment system and leave the details to the Member States, having regard to the principle of subsidiarity. Action by the Community should not go beyond what is necessary to achieve the objectives set out in the Treaty.

(9) The Directive is of a procedural nature, and its requirements should either be integrated into existing procedures in Member States or incorporated in specifically established procedures. With a view to avoiding duplication of the assessment, Member States should take account, where appropriate, of the fact that assessments will be carried out at different levels of a hierarchy of plans and programmes.

(10) All plans and programmes that are prepared for a number of sectors and set a framework for future development consent of projects listed in Annexes I and II to Council Directive 85/337/EEC of 27 June 1985 on the assessment of the effects of certain public and private projects on the environment ([7]), and all plans and programmes which have been determined to require assessment pursuant to Council Directive 92/43/EEC of 21 May 1992 on the conservation of natural habitats and of wild flora and fauna ([8]), are likely to have significant effects on the environment, and should as a rule be made subject to systematic environmental assessment. When they determine the use of small areas at local level or are minor modifications to the above plans or programmes, they should be assessed only where Member States determine that they are likely to have significant effects on the environment.

(11) Other plans and programmes which set the framework for future development consent of projects may not have significant effects on the environment in all cases and should be assessed only where Member States determine that they are likely to have such effects.

(12) When Member States make such determinations, they should take into account the relevant criteria set out in this Directive.

(13) Some plans or programmes are not subject to this Directive because of their particular characteristics.

(14) Where an assessment is required by this Directive, an environmental report should be prepared containing relevant information as set out in this Directive, identifying, describing and evaluating the likely significant environmental effects of implementing the plan or programme, and reasonable alternatives taking into account the objectives and the geographical scope of the plan or programme; Member States should communicate to the Commission any measures they take concerning the quality of environmental reports.

(15) In order to contribute to more transparent decision-making and with the aim of ensuring that the information supplied for the assessment is comprehensive and reliable, it is necessary to provide that authorities with relevant environmental responsibilities and the public are to be consulted during the assessment of plans and programmes, and that appropriate time frames are set, allowing sufficient time for consultations, including the expression of opinion.

(16) Where the implementation of a plan or programme prepared in one Member State is likely to have a significant effect on the environment of other Member States, provision should be made for the Member States concerned to enter into consultations and for the relevant authorities and the public to be informed and enabled to express their opinion.

(17) The environmental report and the opinions expressed by the relevant authorities and the public, as well as the results of any transboundary consultation, should be taken into account during the preparation of the plan or programme and before its adoption or submission to the legislative procedure.

(18) Member States should ensure that, when a plan or programme is adopted, the relevant authorities and the public are informed and relevant information is made available to them.

(19) Where the obligation to carry out assessments of the effects on the environment arises simultaneously from this Directive and other Community legislation, such as Council Directive 79/409/EEC of 2 April 1979 on the conservation of wild birds (⁹), Directive 92/43/EEC, or Directive 2000/60/EC of the European Parliament and the Council of 23 October 2000 establishing a framework for Community action in the field of water policy (¹⁰), in order to avoid duplication of the

assessment, Member States may provide for coordinated or joint procedures fulfilling the requirements of the relevant Community legislation.

(20) A first report on the application and effectiveness of this Directive should be carried out by the Commission five years after its entry into force, and at seven-year intervals thereafter. With a view to further integrating environmental protection requirements, and taking into account the experience acquired, the first report should, if appropriate, be accompanied by proposals for amendment of this Directive, in particular as regards the possibility of extending its scope to other areas/sectors and other types of plans and programmes.

(1)   OJ C 129, 25.4.1997, p.14 and OJ C 83, 25.3.1999, p.13.
(2)   OJ C 287, 22.9.1997, p. 101.
(3)   OJ C 64, 27.2.1998, p.63 and OJ C 374, 23.12.1999, p.9.
(4)   Opinion of the European Parliament of 20 October 1998 (OJ C 341, 9.11.1998, p.18), confirmed on 16 September 1999 (OJ C 54, 25.2.2000, p.76), Council Common Position of 30 March 2000 (OJ C 137, 16.5.2000, p.11) and Decision of the European Parliament of 6 September 2000 (OJ C 135, 7.5.2001, p.155). Decision of the European Parliament of 31 May 2001 and Decision of the Council of 5 June 2001.
(5)   OJ C 138, 17.5.1993, p.5.
(6)   OJ L 275, 10.10.1998, p.1.
(7)   OJ L 175, 5.7.1985, p.40. Directive as amended by Directive 97/11/EC (OJ L 73, 14.3.1997, p.5).
(8)   OJ L 206, 22.7.1992, p.7. Directive as last amended by Directive 97/62/EC (OJ L 305, 8.11.1997, p.42).
(9)   OJ L 103, 25.4.1979, p.1. Directive as last amended by Directive 97/49/EC (OJ L 223, 13.8.1997, p.9).
(10) OJ L 327, 22.12.2000, p.1.

HAVE ADOPTED THIS DIRECTIVE:

Article 1. Objectives
The objective of this Directive is to provide for a high level of protection of the environment and to contribute to the integration of environmental considerations into the preparation and adoption of plans and programmes with a view to promoting sustainable development, by ensuring that, in accordance with this Directive, an environmental assessment is carried out of certain plans and programmes that are likely to have significant effects on the environment.

Article 2. Definitions
For the purposes of this Directive:

(a) 'plans and programmes' shall mean plans and programmes, including those co-financed by the European Community, as well as any modifications to them:
- which are subject to preparation and/or adoption by an authority at national, regional or local level or which are prepared by an authority for adoption, through a legislative procedure by Parliament or Government, and
- which are required by legislative, regulatory or administrative provisions.

(b) 'environmental assessment' shall mean the preparation of an environmental report, the carrying out of consultations, the taking into account of the environmental report and the results of the consultations in decision-making and the provision of information on the decision in accordance with Articles 4 to 9;

(c) 'environmental report' shall mean the part of the plan or programme documentation containing the information required in Article 5 and Annex I;

(d) 'The public' shall mean one or more natural or legal persons and, in accordance with national legislation or practice, their associations, organisations or groups.

Article 3. Scope
1. An environmental assessment, in accordance with Articles 4 to 9, shall be carried out for plans and programmes referred to in paragraphs 2 to 4 that are likely to have significant environmental effects.

2. Subject to paragraph 3, an environmental assessment shall be carried out for all plans and programmes,
(a) which are prepared for agriculture, forestry, fisheries, energy, industry, transport, waste management, water management, telecommunications, tourism, town and country planning or land use and which set the framework for future development consent of projects listed in Annexes I and II to Directive 85/337/EC, or
(b) which, in view of the likely effects on sites, have been determined to require an assessment pursuant to Article 6 or 7 of Directive 92/43/EEC.

3. Plans and programmes referred to in paragraph 2 which determine the use of small areas at local level and minor modifications to plans and programmes referred to in paragraph 2 shall require an environmental assessment only where the Member States determine that they are likely to have significant environmental effects.

4. Member States shall determine whether plans and programmes, other than those referred to in paragraph 2, which set the framework for future development consent of projects, are likely to have significant environmental effects.

5. Member States shall determine whether plans or programmes referred to in paragraphs 3 and 4 are likely to have significant environmental effects either through case-by-case examination or by specifying types of plans and programmes or by combining both approaches. For this purpose Member States shall in all cases take into account relevant criteria set out in Annex II, in order to ensure that plans and programmes with likely significant effects on the environment are covered by this Directive.

6. In the case-by-case examination and in specifying types of plans and programmes in accordance with paragraph 5, the authorities referred to in Article 6(3) shall be consulted.

7. Member States shall ensure that their conclusions pursuant to paragraph 5, including the reasons for not requiring an environmental assessment pursuant to Articles 4 to 9, are made available to the public.

8. The following plans and programmes are not subject to this Directive:
- plans and programmes the sole purpose of which is to serve national defence or civil emergency,
- financial or budget plans and programmes.

9. This Directive does not apply to plans and programmes co-financed under the current respective programming periods(^{1}) for Council Regulations (EC) No 1260/1999(^{2}) and (EC) No 1257/1999(^{3}).

Article 4. General obligations
1. The environmental assessment referred to in Article 3 shall be carried out during the preparation of a plan or programme and before its adoption or submission to the legislative procedure.

2. The requirements of this Directive shall either be integrated into existing procedures in Member States for the adoption of plans and programmes or incorporated in procedures established to comply with this Directive.

3. Where plans and programmes form part of a hierarchy, Member States shall, with a view to avoiding duplication of the assessment, take into account the fact that the assessment will be carried out, in accordance with this Directive, at different levels of the hierarchy. For the purpose of, inter alia, avoiding duplication of assessment, Member States shall apply Article 5(2) and (3).

Article 5. Environmental report

1. Where an environmental assessment is required under Article 3(1), an environmental report shall be prepared in which the likely significant effects on the environment of implementing the plan or programme, and reasonable alternatives taking into account the objectives and the geographical scope of the plan or programme, are identified, described and evaluated. The information to be given for this purpose is referred to in Annex I.

2. The environmental report prepared pursuant to paragraph 1 shall include the information that may reasonably be required taking into account current knowledge and methods of assessment, the contents and level of detail in the plan or programme, its stage in the decision-making process and the extent to which certain matters are more appropriately assessed at different levels in that process in order to avoid duplication of the assessment.

3. Relevant information available on environmental effects of the plans and programmes and obtained at other levels of decision-making or through other Community legislation may be used for providing the information referred to in Annex I.

4. The authorities referred to in Article 6(3) shall be consulted when deciding on the scope and level of detail of the information, which must be included in the environmental report.

Article 6. Consultations

1. The draft plan or programme and the environmental report prepared in accordance with Article 5 shall be made available to the authorities referred to in paragraph 3 of this Article and the public.

2. The authorities referred to in paragraph 3 and the public referred to in paragraph 4 shall be given an early and effective opportunity within appropriate time frames to express their opinion on the draft plan or programme and the accompanying environmental report before the adoption of the plan or programme or its submission to the legislative procedure.

3. Member States shall designate the authorities to be consulted which, by reason of their specific environmental responsibilities, are likely to be concerned by the environmental effects of implementing plans and programmes.

4. Member States shall identify the public for the purposes of paragraph 2, including the public affected or likely to be affected by, or having an interest in, the decision-making subject to this Directive, including relevant non-governmental organisations, such as those

promoting environmental protection and other organisations concerned.

5. The detailed arrangements for the information and consultation of the authorities and the public shall be determined by the Member States.

Article 7. Transboundary consultations
1. Where a Member State considers that the implementation of a plan or programme being prepared in relation to its territory is likely to have significant effects on the environment in another Member State, or where a Member State likely to be significantly affected so requests, the Member State in whose territory the plan or programme is being prepared shall, before its adoption or submission to the legislative procedure, forward a copy of the draft plan or programme and the relevant environmental report to the other Member State.

2. Where a Member State is sent a copy of a draft plan or programme and an environmental report under paragraph 1, it shall indicate to the other Member State whether it wishes to enter into consultations before the adoption of the plan or programme or its submission to the legislative procedure and, if it so indicates, the Member States concerned shall enter into consultations concerning the likely transboundary environmental effects of implementing the plan or programme and the measures envisaged to reduce or eliminate such effects.

Where such consultations take place, the Member States concerned shall agree on detailed arrangements to ensure that the authorities referred to in Article 6(3) and the public referred to in Article 6(4) in the Member State likely to be significantly affected are informed and given an opportunity to forward their opinion within a reasonable time-frame.

3. Where Member States are required under this Article to enter into consultations, they shall agree, at the beginning of such consultations, on a reasonable timeframe for the duration of the consultations.

Article 8. Decision-making
The environmental report prepared pursuant to Article 5, the opinions expressed pursuant to Article 6, and the results of any transboundary consultations entered into pursuant to Article 7 shall be taken into account during the preparation of the plan or programme and before its adoption or submission to the legislative procedure.

Article 9. Information on the decision

1. Member States shall ensure that, when a plan or programme is adopted, the authorities referred to in Article 6(3), the public and any Member State consulted under Article 7 are informed and the following items are made available to those so informed:

(a) the plan or programme as adopted;

(b) a statement summarising how environmental considerations have been integrated into the plan or programme and how the environmental report prepared pursuant to Article 5, the opinions expressed pursuant to Article 6, and the results of consultations entered into pursuant to Article 7 have been taken into account in accordance with Article 8 and the reasons for choosing the plan or programme as adopted, in the light of the other reasonable alternatives dealt with; and

(c) the measures decided concerning monitoring in accordance with Article 10.

2. The detailed arrangements concerning the information referred to in paragraph 1 shall be determined by the Member States.

Article 10. Monitoring

1. Member States shall monitor the significant environmental effects of the implementation of plans and programmes in order, inter alia, to identify at an early stage unforeseen adverse effects, and to be able to undertake appropriate remedial action.

2. In order to comply with paragraph 1, existing monitoring arrangements may be used if appropriate, with a view to avoiding duplication of monitoring.

Article 11. Relationship with other Community legislation

1. An environmental assessment carried out under this Directive shall be without prejudice to any requirements under Directive 85/337/EEC and to any other Community law requirements.

2. For plans and programmes for which the obligation to carry out assessments of the effects on the environment arises simultaneously from this Directive and other Community legislation, Member States may provide for coordinated or joint procedures fulfilling the requirements of the relevant Community legislation in order, inter alia, to avoid duplication of assessment.

3. For plans and programmes co-financed by the European Community, the environmental assessment in accordance with this Directive shall be carried out in conformity with the specific provisions in relevant Community legislation.

Article 12. Information, reporting and review

1. Member States and the Commission shall exchange information on the experience gained in applying this Directive.

2. Member States shall ensure that environmental reports are of a sufficient quality to meet the requirements of this Directive and shall communicate to the Commission any measures they take concerning the quality of these reports.

3. Before 21 July 2006 the Commission shall send a first report on the application and effectiveness of this Directive to the European Parliament and to the Council.

With a view further to integrating environmental protection requirements, in accordance with Article 6 of the Treaty, and taking into account the experience acquired in the application of this Directive in the Member States, such a report will be accompanied by proposals for amendment of this Directive, if appropriate. In particular, the Commission will consider the possibility of extending the scope of this Directive to other areas/sectors and other types of plans and programmes.

A new evaluation report shall follow at seven-year intervals.

4. The Commission shall report on the relationship between this Directive and Regulations (EC) No 1260/1999 and (EC) No 1257/1999 well ahead of the expiry of the programming periods provided for in those Regulations, with a view to ensuring a coherent approach with regard to this Directive and subsequent Community Regulations.

Article 13. Implementation of the Directive

1. Member States shall bring into force the laws, regulations and administrative provisions necessary to comply with this Directive before 21 July 2004. They shall forthwith inform the Commission thereof.

2. When Member States adopt the measures, they shall contain a reference to this Directive or shall be accompanied by such reference on the occasion of their official publication. The methods of making such reference shall be laid down by Member States.

3. The obligation referred to in Article 4(1) shall apply to the plans and programmes of which the first formal preparatory act is subsequent to the date referred to in paragraph 1. Plans and programmes of which the first formal preparatory act is before that date and which are adopted or submitted to the legislative procedure more than 24 months thereafter, shall be made subject to the obligation referred to in Article 4(1) unless Member States decide on a case-by-case basis that this is not feasible and inform the public of their decision.

4. Before 21 July 2004, Member States shall communicate to the Commission, in addition to the measures referred to in paragraph 1, separate information on the types of plans and programmes which, in accordance with Article 3, would be subject to an environmental assessment pursuant to this Directive. The Commission shall make this information available to the Member States. The information will be updated on a regular basis.

Article 14. Entry into force
This Directive shall enter into force on the day of its publication in the *Official Journal of the European Communities*.

Article 15. Addressees
This Directive is addressed to the Member States.

Done at Luxembourg, 27 June 2001.

For the European Parliament, The President, N. FONTAINE

For the Council, The President, B. ROSENGREN

(1) The 2000-2006 programming period for Council Regulation (EC) No 1260/1999 and the 2000-2006 and 2000-2007 programming periods for Council Regulation (EC) No 1257/1999.
(2) Council Regulation (EC) No 1260/1999 of 21 June 1999 laying down general provisions on the Structural Funds (OJ L 161, 26.6.1999, p.1).
(3) Council Regulation (EC) No 1257/1999 of 17 May 1999 on support for rural development from the European Agricultural Guidance and Guarantee Fund (EAGGF) and amending and repealing certain regulations (OJ L 160, 26.6.1999), p.80.

Annex I. Information referred to in Article 5(1)
The information to be provided under Article 5(1), subject to Article 5(2) and (3), is the following:

(a) an outline of the contents, main objectives of the plan or programme and relationship with other relevant plans and programmes;

(b) the relevant aspects of the current state of the environment and the likely evolution thereof without implementation of the plan or programme;

(c) the environmental characteristics of areas likely to be significantly affected;

(d) any existing environmental problems which are relevant to the plan or programme including, in particular, those relating to any areas of a particular environmental importance, such as areas designated pursuant to Directives 79/409/EEC and 92/43/EEC;

(e) the environmental protection objectives, established at international, Community or Member State level, which are relevant to the plan or programme and the way those objectives and any environmental considerations have been taken into account during its preparation;

(f) the likely significant effects([1]) on the environment, including on issues such as biodiversity, population, human health, fauna, flora, soil, water, air, climatic factors, material assets, cultural heritage including architectural and archaeological heritage, landscape and the interrelationship between the above factors;

(g) the measures envisaged to prevent, reduce and as fully as possible offset any significant adverse affects on the environment of implementing the plan or programme;

(h) an outline of the reasons for selecting the alternatives dealt with, and a description of how the assessment was undertaken including any difficulties (such as technical deficiencies or a lack of know-how) encountered in compiling the required information;

(i) a description of the measures envisaged concerning monitoring in accordance with Article 10;

(j) a non-technical summary of the information provided under the above headings.

Annex II. Criteria for determining the likely significance of effects referred to in Article 3(5)

1. The characteristics of plans and programmes, having regard, in particular, to:
- the degree to which the plan or programme sets a framework for projects and other activities, either with regard to the location, nature, size and operating conditions or by allocating resources,
- the degree to which the plan or programme influences other plans and programmes, including those in a hierarchy,
- the relevance of the plan or programme for the integration of environmental considerations in particular with a view to promoting sustainable development,
- environmental problems relevant to the plan or programme,
- the relevance of the plan or programme for the implementation of Community legislation on the environment (e.g. plans and programmes linked to waste-management or water protection).

2. Characteristics of the effects and of the area likely to be affected, having regard, in particular, to:
- the probability, duration, frequency and reversibility of the effects;
- the cumulative nature of the effects;
- the transboundary nature of the effects;
- the risks to human health or the environment (e.g. due to accidents);
- the magnitude and spatial extent of the effects (geographical area and size of the population likely to be affected);
- the value and vulnerability of the area likely to be affected due to:
  - special natural characteristics or cultural heritage;
  - exceeded environmental quality standards or limit values;
  - intensive land use; and
- the effects on areas or landscapes that have a recognised national, Community or international protection status.

Appendix B

Chinese Plan Environmental Impact Assessment Regulations 2009

Translated by Kai-Yi Zhou

Chapter 1 General provisions

Article 1

The objective of these regulations is to strengthen plan environmental impact assessment (PEIA), improve scientific rationality of planning, avoid environmental pollution and ecological degradation from the beginning, and promote economic, social and environmental development in a harmonious way.

Article 2

1. PEIA should apply to plans developed by relevant ministries and commissions of the State Council, governments and their departments of administrative level above municipal with districts[1] regarding land use, regional development, watershed and marine development, construction and utilization ('comprehensive plans'), and industry, agriculture, animal husbandry, forestry, energy, water resources, transport, urban construction, tourism and natural resources ('special plans').

2. Subject to Para. 1, Art. 2, the detailed scope of sectors to which PEIA applies will be drafted by the competent authority of environmental protection (CAEP) of the State Council jointly with relevant ministries and commissions of the State Council, and implemented after the State Council has ratified it.

Article 3
PEIA application must comply with the principles of objectivity, openness and impartiality.

Article 4
1. The State will develop a system to make PEIA information publicly available.

2. Governments and their departments whose administration level is municipal with districts and above shall make PEIA information publicly available.

Article 5
The costs of PEIA application should be part of the budget for the development of a proposed plan. PEIA-related expenditure must be strictly supervised and audited.

Article 6
Any organization or person has the right to report activities that breach these regulations, or any plan implementation that has significantly adverse environmental impacts to the planning examination approval authority (PEAA), planning authorities or the CAEP. After any relevant departments have received a report, they should investigate and manage the case according to regulations.

Chapter 2 Assessment

Article 7
Planners should apply PEIA during the course of plan-making.

Article 8
The PEIA should analyse, predict and evaluate the following:

1. Likely cumulative effects on relevant regional, river basin and marine areas due to the implementation of the plan;

2. Likely long-term effects on the environment and communities due to the implementation of the plan;

3. The relationship between economic, social and environmental benefits; and current and long-term benefits due to the implementation of the plan.

Article 9
1. When applying PEIA, there should be compliance with relevant environmental protection standards and PEIA technical guidelines and specifications.

2. The technical guidelines of PEIA are formulated by the CAEP of the State Council jointly with relevant ministries and commissions of the State Council. The technical specifications of PEIA[2] are formulated by ministries and commissions of the State Council according to the guidelines. A copy of the technical specifications should be sent to the CAEP of the State Council to serve as a record.

Article 10
1. When drafting a comprehensive plan, an environmental impact chapter or note should be compiled on the likely environmental effects of implementing the plan.

2. When drafting a special plan, an environmental impact report (EIR) should be compiled before the plan is submitted for approval. When drafting a conceptual (or directive) plan for a special plan, an environmental impact chapter or note should be compiled subject to Para. 1, Art. 10.

3. A conceptual (or directive) plan in Para. 2 is a type of special plan mainly addressing development strategies.

Article 11
1. An environmental impact chapter or note shall contain the following:

    1. Analyses, prediction and assessment of the likely environmental effects of plan implementation, including an analysis of carrying capacity, analysis and prediction of adverse environmental impacts, and analysis of the environmental compatibility of the plan with other relevant plans;
    2. Counter measures and solutions that can avoid or reduce adverse environmental impacts, mainly including policies, management measures and technical measures.

2. In addition to the above contents, the EIR should contain the conclusions of the PEIA process, including the environmental rationality[3] and feasibility of the draft plan, the rationality and feasibility of counter measures and solutions for avoiding and reducing adverse environmental impacts, and suggestions for how to adjust the draft plan.

Article 12
The planner or organization in charge of PEIA applications should compile the environmental impact chapter or note, or the EIR. The planner is responsible for the quality of the document.

Article 13
1. For special plans that may have adverse environmental impacts and directly involve the interests of the public,[4] before the plan is submitted for approval, the planner should publicly solicit comments and suggestions on the EIR from institutions concerned, experts and the public through questionnaires, forums, meetings and/or hearings. These requirements do not apply to plans that have been legally classified.[5]

2. If institutions concerned, experts and the public have major divergence on the conclusions of the EIR, the planner should make further contacts by hearings, meetings, etc.

3. The EIR submitted for approval should document comments or suggestions made by the public, state whether they have been adopted or not, and explain the reasons for doing so.

Article 14
To make significant changes or revisions to a plan's implementation area or period of application, or the scale, structure and layout of a plan that has been formally approved, the planner should reapply PEIA or apply PEIA to the changes according to these regulations.

Chapter 3 Examination

Article 15
When a planner submits a draft comprehensive plan or a conceptual plan of a special plan for examination and approval, the environmental impact chapter or note should also be submitted as a part of the plan to the PEAA. Where a draft plan is submitted without an environmental chapter or note, the PEAA should require the planner to supply this. If the planner does not supply this, the PEAA shall not examine and approve the plan.

Article 16
When a planner submits a draft special plan, the plan's EIR should also be submitted to the PEAA. If an EIR is not submitted, the PEAA should require the planner to supply it. If the planner does not supply it, the PEAA shall not examine and approve the plan.

Article 17
1. For special plans that only local governments at or above the level of municipal with districts have the authority to examine and approve, before the examination and approval procedure may begin, the CAEP of the sector that the given special plan belongs to should convene an EIR examination team comprised of experts and representatives from relevant departments to examine the given plan's EIR. The team should provide written conclusions.

2. For special plans that only provincial governments and above have the authority to examine and approve, the EIR examination and approval process and procedure is formulated by the CAEP of the State Council working with ministries and commissions of the State Council.

Article 18
1. The members of an EIR examination team should be selected randomly from a number of experts in relevant topic areas within the national statutory expert database.

2. Those experts that participated in the compilation of the EIR are not eligible to be members of the team.

3. More than half of the members of the EIR examination team should be experts. If the number of experts is fewer than half, the examination conclusions made by the team are not valid.

Article 19
1. The members of an EIR examination team shall prepare written EIR examination conclusions, basing them on their objective, fair and independent judgements. During the course of the EIR examination, the PEAA, the planner and the organization that convenes the team shall not intervene.

2. The EIR examination conclusions shall include the following:

    1. The authenticity of the original materials and data used;
    2. The rationality of the assessment methods used;
    3. The reliability of the environmental impact analysis, prediction and evaluation;
    4. The reasonableness and effectiveness of the adopted counter measures and solutions for avoiding or reducing adverse environmental impacts;
    5. The rationality of explanations of the reasons for whether comments and suggestions made by the public have been adopted;
    6. The scientific rationality of the conclusion of the PEIA process.

3. The EIR examination conclusions should be agreed and signed by three-quarters of the members of the examination team. If members of a team have different opinions, those opinions should be truthfully documented and reported.

Article 20
If the following conditions occur, the EIR examination team shall suggest that an EIR must be revised and the revisions should be reassessed:

1. inauthenticity of the original materials and data;
2. irrationality of the assessment methods used;
3. the analysis, prediction and evaluation of adverse environmental impacts is not correct and not thorough, therefore further examinations are required;
4. the adopted counter measures and solutions for avoiding or reducing adverse environmental impacts have serious flaws;
5. the conclusions of the PEIA process are unclear, unreasonable and wrong;
6. the EIR does not include an explanation of the reasons for whether comments and suggestions made by the public have been adopted, or the explanation for why comments and suggestions made by the public were not adopted are clearly unreasonable;
7. the contents of the EIR have other serious flaws and omissions.

Article 21
The EIR examination team shall not approve an EIR where:

1. according to current levels of knowledge and technological conditions, it is very difficult to come to a scientific judgement on the scale and extent of adverse environmental impacts caused by the implementation of a plan;
2. the implementation of the plan may cause significantly adverse environmental impacts and there are no feasible prevention or mitigation measures and solutions.

Article 22
1. When the PEAA examines and approves a draft special plan, its final decision should be made mainly based on the conclusions of the EIR and the conclusions of the EIR examination.

2. If the PEAA does not adopt the conclusions of an EIR and the comments and suggestions made by the EIR examination team, the PEAA shall provide written explanations for each individual conclusion, comment or suggestion of why it was not adopted, and

those written explanations should be archived for future examination. Institutions concerned, experts and the public have the right to apply to review those explanations. These requirements do not apply to plans that have been legally classified.[6]

Article 23
If a plan that has undergone PEIA includes specific construction projects, when project EIAs are carried out for construction projects under the plan, the conclusions of the PEIA should be seriously taken into account and the contents of the project EIAs could be simplified based on the outcomes of the PEIA.

Chapter 4 Follow-up assessment

Article 24
Soon after a comprehensive plan or a special plan that is likely to have significant adverse impacts on the environment[7] has been implemented, the planner should organize a follow-up assessment for the PEIA. The planner should report on the outcomes of the follow-up assessment to the PEAA, and inform departments concerned, including the environmental protection authority.

Article 25
The follow-up assessment of a PEIA should include the following contents:

1. comparative analysis and evaluation between those environmental impacts that occur due to the implementation of a plan and those environmental impacts documented in the EIR;
2. analysis and evaluation of the effectiveness of those counter measures and solutions adopted in the plan aimed at preventing or reducing adverse environmental impacts;
3. the public's comments on environmental impacts associated with the implementation of the plan; and
4. conclusions of the follow-up assessment.

Article 26
During the course of PEIA follow-up assessment, the planner should organize questionnaires, on-site interviews, hearings and/or other methods to solicit opinions from relevant departments, experts and the public.

Article 27
The planner should identify remedial measures without delay if

significant adverse environmental impacts have been identified during the course of plan implementation; report the event to the PEAA, and inform the relevant departments, including the environmental protection authority.

Article 28
Where the CAEP identifies significant adverse environmental impacts occurring during the course of plan implementation, the CAEP should recheck the findings without delay. Once confirmed, the CAEP should put in place improvement measures or suggest revisions to the adopted plan to the PEAA.

Article 29
After the PEAA receives a report from the planner or suggestions from the CAEP, the PEAA should organize a formal discussion, and the adopted plan should be reformulated or new mitigation measures should be adopted.

Article 30
If the total emissions of a key pollutant exceed the national limit or regional limit within the implementation area of a given plan, the examination and approval of EIR of new plans that increase the concentration of the key pollutant within the area should be suspended.

Chapter 5 Legal liabilities

Article 31
If, during the course of a PEIA application, a planner commits fraud or is negligent of their duties, and this causes the PEIA process to be seriously inconsistent with the facts, punishments should apply to the person in charge and other personnel with direct responsibilities of conforming with legal regulations.

Article 32
Where the PEAA is responsible for the following, punishments should apply to the person in charge and other personnel with direct responsibilities of conforming with legal regulations:

1. Approval is granted to a comprehensive plan or a conceptual plan of a special plan for which an environmental impact chapter or note should have been compiled according to law but was not;
2. Approval is granted to a draft special plan for which an EIR should have been compiled according to law but was not; or to a draft special plan whose EIR has not been examined by the EIR

examination team.

Article 33

1. Where the authority that brings together an EIR examination team practises fraud or misuses its power during the course of an EIR examination, and this causes the PEIA process to be seriously inconsistent with facts, punishments should apply to the person in charge and other personnel with direct responsibilities of conforming with legal regulations.

2. Where a PEIA process is seriously inconsistent with facts due to fraud or neglect of duty by any experts of the EIR examination team, the CAEP in charge of developing the national statutory expert database shall remove the experts from the database and make an announcement to this effect. If representatives from the departments concerned practise similar activities, punishments should apply according to law.

Article 34

Where an EIR is seriously inconsistent with facts due to fraud or neglect of duty by any PEIA consultants, the CAEP of the State Council should circulate a notice to this effect. The fine is more than one time and below three times the consultation fee. If the PEIA consultants' activities constitute a crime, responsibility for the crime should be investigated according to law.

Chapter 6 Supplementary provisions

Article 35

Provincial level governments will require their lower level governments to apply PEIA to their plans according to the local situation. Detailed application measures shall be formulated by provincial governments according to the provisions of the EIA law and these regulations.

Explanatory notes by Kai-Yi Zhou and Riki Therivel (not part of the regulations)

1. The levels of Chinese administration are: national, provincial, municipal with districts, municipal without districts, and village.
2. The technical guidelines are for the whole country. The technical specifications vary by sector.
3. The term 'rational' comes up several times in this legislation. Its meaning should be defined by the government in future official explanations.

4. The legislation does not specify who decides whether a plan will have significant impacts and involves the public interest.
5, 6. The legislation does not specify what plans are legally classified, or how they become legally classified.
7. The legislation does not specify who decides whether a plan will have significant adverse impacts on the environment.

Appendix C

SEA Prediction and Evaluation Techniques

The aim of this appendix is not to make the reader an expert on different types of SEA prediction and evaluation techniques: that would require at least one book of this size per technique. Rather, it aims to give an introduction to a range of techniques, an understanding of the circumstances under which their use might be appropriate in SEA, and sources of further information.

The appendix begins by discussing factors to keep in mind when choosing SEA prediction and evaluation techniques. It then presents brief information on a range of commonly used SEA techniques, starting with the least technical and most commonly used qualitative techniques, then techniques for mapping and simple spatial analysis, techniques for ensuring that all impacts are identified and for quantifying them, and finally evaluation techniques and compatibility assessment. Table C.1 summarizes how these techniques could be used in SEA.

Some of the techniques partly overlap, for instance, overlay maps can be done using GIS; vulnerability assessment involves multi-criteria analysis (MCA) and GIS. I have included some techniques despite my personal doubts about them – which will emerge quickly enough in the 'advantages and disadvantages' sections – because they are widely advocated as ways of improving the robustness of SEA, and thus its ability to withstand critique (e.g. in lawsuits and inquiries).

Choosing prediction and evaluation techniques

There is no one set of SEA techniques that is best under all circumstances. Doing SEA is like planning a dinner party, with different tools and approaches providing possible menus, lighting and table decoration: one chooses the menu and lighting that one thinks will

Table C.1 *Possible applications of SEA prediction and evaluation techniques*

Type of technique	Technique	Describe baseline	Identify impacts	SEA stage Predict impacts	Evaluate impacts	Ensure coherence
Qualitative, participatory	Expert judgement	✔	✔	✔	✔	✔
	Public participation (see Chapter 5)	✔	✔		✔	
	Impact matrices (see Chapters 8 and 9)		✔	✔	✔	
	Quality of life assessment/ecosystems services approach	✔			✔	
Mapping and simple spatial analysis	Overlay or constraints maps	✔		✔		
	Geographical information systems	✔		✔	✔	
	Land unit partitioning analysis			✔		
Impact prediction	Network analysis		✔	✔		
	Modelling			✔		
	Scenario/sensitivity analysis			✔		
Impact evaluation	Cost–benefit analysis				✔	
	Multi-criteria analysis				✔	
	Life cycle analysis				✔	
	Vulnerability analysis			✔	✔	
	Carrying capacity, ecological footprints				✔	
	Risk assessment					
Sound planning	Compatibility appraisal					✔

Table C.2 *Streamlined v. comprehensive SEA techniques*

	Streamlined	Comprehensive
Examples of techniques	Expert judgement Public participation Impact matrices Overlay or constraints maps	Modelling Sensitivity analysis Life cycle assessment GIS
Carried out by	Decision-maker	Consultants
Relation to decision making	Integral	Independent
Based on	Policy appraisal	Project EIA
Cost/resources needed	Low	High
Scientific validity/rigour	Low	High
Accessibility/ownership	High	Low
Effectiveness in improving the strategic action	?	?

make the guests happiest. This section considers how one might choose which SEA techniques to use to ensure that the environment/sustainability are best integrated in decision-making.

A rough distinction can be made between SEA techniques that are 'streamlined' and those that are 'comprehensive'. Table C.2 summarizes the differences between these techniques.

In project EIA, the more detailed and scientifically robust the impact prediction and evaluation technique is, the better it is. The 'comprehensive' techniques would thus be preferred. The same does not necessarily hold true in SEA for several reasons.

First, SEA processes must keep pace with decision-making processes, which are often very rapid. This means that techniques that take much time, require lots of data, need comprehensive datasets, and rely on the skills of busy specialists, are often inappropriate. Some SEA approaches focus on identifying 'decision windows': moments in the decision-making process that are critical to the environmental outcome of the decision (ANSEA Team, 2002). Others, for instance, the 'rapid appraisal' approaches of Brown (1997, 1998) and Lucht and Jaubert (2001), aim to respond quickly once a 'decision window' opens up.

Second, strategic actions are inherently fluid, nebulous and often not spatially specific. Applying sledgehammer prediction techniques to the equivalent of cloud formations is inappropriate; the concept of proportionality of assessment was discussed at Chapter 8. Techniques such as GIS or cost–benefit analysis (CBA) may also provide only limited information in situations where only partial data are available.

Third, for the SEA to inform and influence decision-making, techniques are needed that convey environmental information effectively. Simple educational and psychological approaches, and techniques that foster good governance are thus often more appropriate than technical ones. Jansson (1999) argues that 'quantitative assessment works fairly well when comparing similar alternatives, but if there are differences in principle, or a possibility of shifts in paradigm, measurement becomes nearly useless'. Stirling (1999) also notes that:

> *serious theoretical and methodological difficulties, including those related to the selection and framing of 'problems' and 'options', the treatment of deep uncertainties and the impossibility of aggregating in analysis the divergent social interests and value judgements which govern the prioritisation of the different dimensions of 'sustainability'... render futile any attempt to develop an 'analytical fix' for the problems of appraisal. In this light, systematic public participation is ... not just an issue of political efficacy and legitimacy, but also ... a fundamental matter of analytical rigour.*

In other words, there are good reasons why 'expert judgement' (including by an informed public) is the most commonly used SEA technique. It is quick, cheap, needs little equipment, can cope with qualitative as well as quantitative data, and can take on board political sensitivities.

However, Kidd and Fischer (2007) postulate that the use of participatory approaches to the exclusion of more technical methods could lead to assessments that are skewed in favour of economic over environmental concerns. They cite Peterson's (1981) theory on redistributive policies, which suggests that local communities generally subordinate environmental values to economic ones, and Giddens' (1998) view that, as people become more sensitive to individualistic concerns, they tend to overlook long-term connections between the community and the environment. More robust and replicable techniques are likely to be particularly needed where the decision is contentious, where public scrutiny is expected to be intense, or where environmental impacts are complex: cumulative, reversible, dependent on implementation, and so on.

Factors that determine which SEA techniques are appropriate thus include:

- What decision needs to be taken: the scale (international, national, regional, local) and strategic-ness (policy, plan, programme) of the strategic action. Qualitative approaches are often more applicable for policy-level and large-scale strategic actions, while quantitative techniques may be more relevant at the programme level and small scale.

- The type of decision: some techniques are particularly good at identifying mitigation measures, or helping to choose between sites, or making broad policy decisions (see Table C.1).
- Who the SEA audience is/who would use the outputs: the more 'scientific' techniques may be appropriate for a specialist audience but not for public participation and vice-versa.
- The context in which the SEA is being carried out. If the decision is, for instance, a political and contentious choice between a few distinct alternatives, then more 'scientific', data-based techniques that avoid the possibility of bias will be appropriate. Where, instead, innovative solutions to a problem are being sought by a like-minded group of people, then quite different techniques will be best.
- The time available. More data-hungry and specialist-intensive techniques are fine where there is reasonable time in which to carry out the SEA. But quick-and-dirty techniques may be the only ones that can keep up with a rapid decision-making process.
- The resources, staff and equipment available. Some techniques require computer facilities, new data or specialist expert input that may simply not be available in the time available for the SEA. On the other hand, this is not a permanent excuse ('sorry, we don't have the resources so we'll never be able to do it'). The first round of SEA can help to identify what future SEAs might require, and resources and staff can then be put in place in time for subsequent rounds of SEA.
- What kind of data the technique requires as input. Some techniques require little or nothing in the way of data, while others require a great deal of data and cannot work until they are all comprehensively in place.
- Tradition and mindset. In some countries or situations, some techniques are simply more acceptable than others. In particular, streamlined techniques that are perceived as perfectly appropriate by some could be seen as woefully flabby by others, whereas comprehensive techniques may seem terrifying and a waste of resources by those who are comfortable in the hurly-burly of streamlined techniques.

Table C.3 shows key situations in which various SEA techniques could be used, and Figure C.1 shows the resource and data requirements of these techniques.

It may be appropriate to use a sequence of SEA prediction and evaluation techniques, starting with cheap, rapid SEA techniques to identify key issues and then, as more information is gleaned, using more comprehensive techniques as needed. For instance, an initial analysis by expert judgement may identify the need for further analysis

Table C.3 Situations in which SEA techniques could be used

Technique	Technique works for…								Technique copes with…			
	Policy level*	Programme level*	Non-spatially specific plan	Spatially specific plan	Large area	Small area	Land use plan	Sectoral plan	Incomplete data	Uncertain data	Qualitative data	Few data resources
Expert judgement	✓	✓	✓	✓	✓	✓	✓	✓	✓	✓	✓	✓
Impact matrices	✓	✓	✓	✓	✓	✓	✓	✓	✓	✓	✓	✓
Quality of life assessment	✓	✓	✓	✓	✓	✓	✓	✓	✓	?	✓	?
Maps/GIS	?	✓	✓	✓	✓	✓	✓	✓	?	?	?	?
Land unit partitioning anal.	?	?		✓	?	✓	?	✓	✓	✓	✓	
Network analysis	✓	✓	✓	✓	?	✓	?	✓	✓	✓	✓	✓
Modelling	?	?	✓	✓	?	✓	?	✓	?	?	?	
Scenario/sensitivity anal.	?	?	✓	✓	?	✓	?	✓		?		
Cost–benefit assessment	?	?	✓	✓	?	✓	?	✓		✓		
Multi-criteria analysis	?	✓	✓	✓	?	?	?	?	✓	✓	✓	?
Life cycle analysis	?	?	?	?	?	✓		✓		?	✓	
Vulnerability analysis	?	?	✓	✓	✓	✓	✓	✓		?	✓	
Carrying capacity, ecological footprints	?	?	?	?	?	✓	?	?	?	?	?	
Risk assessment	?	✓	✓	✓	?	✓	✓	✓	✓	✓	?	
Compatibility appraisal	✓	✓	✓	✓	✓	✓	✓	✓	✓	✓	✓	✓

Note: * The tool's effectiveness at the plan level will be between that for policy and programme level
Key: ✓ fully; ? partly; or in some situations (blank) does not
Source: Adapted from Therivel and Wood (2005)

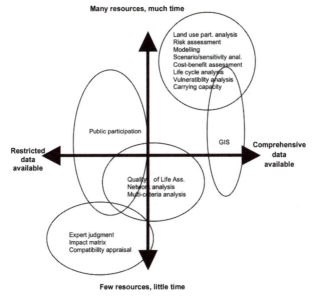

Source: Adapted from Therivel and Wood (2005)

Figure C.1 *Resource and data requirements of SEA techniques*

using, say, network analysis and constraints maps, which in turn may suggest the need for detailed modelling of a key issue.

Whatever technique is used, though, please do not add up the assessment results (e.g. 27 'plusses' and 15 'minuses' equal 12 net 'plusses'): different criteria will have different importance in different contexts, and any summing up will only graft a spurious veneer of 'scientificness' onto something that is essentially a subjective process aimed at improving the strategic action.

Expert judgement

What the technique aims to do

Expert judgement can be used for a wide range of applications: collecting data, developing alternatives from the most strategic policy level to the very detailed site level, analysing and ranking them, predicting impacts and suggesting mitigation measures.

What it involves

One or preferably several experts whose specialisms cover the range of impacts of the strategic action, brainstorm/discuss/consider the relevant issue. This has been formalized in some situations, for instance, through the Delphi Technique which uses consecutive cycles of questionnaires of expert participants until agreement on a subject is reached.

What the outputs look like

'Expert' data, ideas, decisions.

Advantages

- quick and cheap;
- requires no specialist equipment;
- can take account of unquantifiable, partial, political, etc. information;
- can lead to innovative win–win solutions;
- fosters information sharing and education between the expert participants; and
- the level of uncertainty of the results is not necessarily higher than that of much more complex techniques.

Disadvantages

- potential for bias depending on the experts involved; and
- non-replicable, not scientific.

Quality of life assessment (QoLA)

(This approach also forms the basis for the ecosystem services approach.)

What the technique aims to do

QoLA aims to identify what matters and why in an area, so that the quality of life consequences (both good and bad) of strategic actions can be better taken into account. The core idea of QoLA is that the environment, the economy and society provide a range of benefits for people, and that it is these benefits that need to be protected and/or enhanced. For example, a small woodland on the edge of a town does not matter because it provides X hectares of woodland, but rather because it provides recreation, a habitat for rare species, carbon 'fixing', jobs for foresters, and so on. Analysing these benefits gives an indication of how the area should be managed in the future.

Table C.4 *Part of quality of life assessment for major new development proposal west of the A1(M) at Stevenage*

Feature (B)	Benefit (C)	Reason it matters/ to whom it matters	Answers to evaluation questions (D)			Management implications (E)
			Scale at which it matters	Importance	Trend relative to target	Substitutability
Rights of way network (including bridle-ways)	Circular routes/ choice of routes	Recreation, links to west of valley. Cross country loops, e.g. 'pony riding route'	Local	High	From public consultation exercise not enough	Substitute with other non-vehicular access Ensure footpaths lead to and connect with area beyond development. Give access from town X without going through the new development. Bridleways to connect to the 'pony riding route'. Allow mobility vehicles for people with disabilities but not motorbikes
	Alignment associated with historic movement and ancient boundary patterns	Historians, specialist interest	Local ?	?	Cannot replace historic features	Retain alignment and existing character; improve signage and information for users

Source: CPM (1999)

What it involves

QoLA involves six steps (A–F). Having identified the purpose of the assessment (A) and described the area to be studied (B), the benefits/disbenefits that the area offers to present and future generations are identified (C). The technique then asks (D): How important is each benefit or disbenefit, to whom, and why? On current trends, will there be enough of each of them? What (if anything) could substitute for the benefits? The answers to these questions lead to a series of management implications (E), which allow a 'shopping list' to be devised of things that any development/management of that area should achieve, how they could be achieved, and their relative importance. The 'shopping list' stipulates the benefits that any development would have to provide before it was considered acceptable and, as a corollary, indicates where development would not be appropriate. Monitoring of the benefits (F) should be carried out to ensure that they are actually provided.

What the outputs look like

The main output of a QoLA exercise is a list of management implications for the area in questions. Stages B–E are normally documented as a table such as Table C.4.

Advantages

- sets a context for development proposals by stipulating benefits that any development should provide to an area;
- offers flexibility for developers in terms of *how* they provide the benefits;
- encourages public participation; enhances public ownership and transparency of decision-making;
- acknowledges the complementary role of experts and local residents;
- focuses on management and enhancement of an area, rather than just minimizing impacts on it;
- values the uniqueness, scarcity and diversity of assets affected, not just quality: goes beyond just protecting a limited number of 'best' areas;
- most effectively protects those sites that provide the most benefits; and
- provides an equitable basis for comparing sites in terms of the benefits they offer and the degree to which those benefits can be substituted.

Disadvantages

- not well-understood or widely used; and
- does not compare alternative types of development, i.e. does not consider potential benefits.

Further information

Quality of Life Assessment: Countryside Agency et al (2002) Ecosystem services: POST (2007), Haines-Young and Potschin (2007), Bröring and Wiegleb (2005)

Overlay or constraints maps

What the technique aims to do

Overlay maps help to identify areas that would be appropriate or inappropriate for development.

What it involves

Maps of areas of constraint – for instance, areas of importance for landscape or wildlife, areas that are already developed, or areas with particular problems – are superimposed using computer mapping (e.g. GIS) or transparencies.

What the outputs look like

A map showing constraints (or lack of constraints) to development. Figure 6.2 is a typical constraints map, which shows nature conservation, landscape and historical designations: areas with no designations pose fewer constraints to development than areas with designations. Figure C.2 shows two maps of 'tranquil areas' in England. The maps superimpose (in white):

- 4km radius from the largest power stations;
- 3km buffers from the most heavily used roads and from major industrial areas;
- 2km buffers from other heavily used roads and from the edge of smaller towns;
- 1km buffers from roads with medium disturbance, some main line railways, 400KV and 275KV power lines;
- noise lozenges from military and civil airfields; and
- areas of very extensive opencast mining.

Early 1960s   Early 1990s

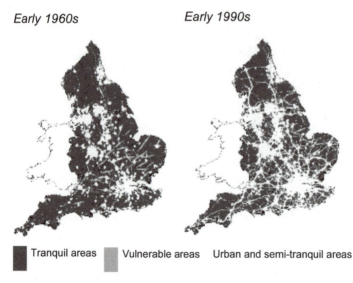

▉ Tranquil areas   ▉ Vulnerable areas   Urban and semi-tranquil areas

Source: CPRE and Countryside Commission (1995)

Figure C.2 *Example of overlay maps: Tranquil areas*

The dark tranquil areas are those in which special efforts should be made to preserve tranquillity. The maps also highlight the impact that development had on tranquil areas between the early 1960s and early 1990s. These maps have since been superseded by maps that use more complex indicators of tranquillity, but the concept remains the same.

Advantages

- gives easily understandable results that can be used in public participation exercises;
- can be carried out by non-experts; and
- applicable at all scales.

Disadvantages

- can only be used with impacts/developments that have a spatial component (that are 'mappable'), and so are unlikely to be useful at policy level;
- can be time-consuming and expensive, especially if done through GIS; and
- can be difficult to keep up to date if *not* done through GIS.

Further information

Hyder (1999)

Geographical information systems

What the technique aims to do

GISs are often only used to map data, but they can also be valuable analytical tools. They can, for instance, calculate areas and distances (straight line and sometimes also along a network), identify viewing areas from a point, construct buffer zones around features, draw contour-lines using interpolated values between points, and superimpose maps of the above to produce combined maps.

What it involves

GISs link attribute data to map data. Map data (spatial reference points) are essentially points or lines on a map. Attribute data are characteristics of map-features, for instance, land use of an area or slope of a road. GISs are thus a combination of a computerized cartography system that stores map data, and a database management system that stores attribute data. Links between map data and attribute data allow maps of the attribute data to be displayed, combined and analysed with relative speed and ease.

GISs require an appropriate computer system, compilation or purchase of map data and related attribute data, and analysis of these data. Specialist skills are required.

What the outputs look like

Figure C.3 shows an example where GIS was used in association with a decision tree (e.g. 'if a site with land use X is close to deciduous woodland then convert it to...') to identify potential sites for expansion of UK Biodiversity Action Plan priority habitats in the Chiltern Natural Area (Lee et al, 2002).

Advantages

- helps to draw together multidisciplinary data and supports other SEA techniques;
- relatively easy manipulation of large amounts of data;
- allows spatially specific impacts to be clearly visualized;
- its zoning features and its ability to consider several layers of information at a time can be used in sensitivity mapping;
- long-term cost-savings in map-making; and
- results can easily be used in public participation exercises, sometimes in an interactive manner.

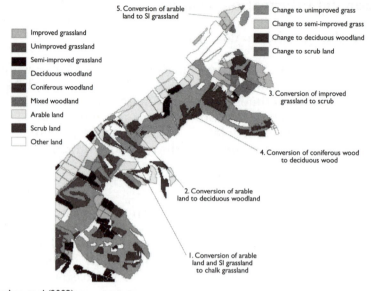

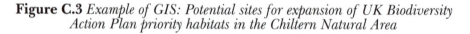

Source: Lee et al (2002)

Figure C.3 *Example of GIS: Potential sites for expansion of UK Biodiversity Action Plan priority habitats in the Chiltern Natural Area*

Disadvantages

- carries out only a limited range of analytical tasks: essentially it provides data description rather than real spatial analysis;
- can be expensive with high start-up costs, although these are dropping with more widespread use of GIS;
- requires technical expertise; and
- limited to impacts that have a direct spatial component.

Further reading

European Environment Agency (1998), Rodriguez-Bachiller (2004), Therivel and Wood (2005), Geneletti et al (2007)

Land-partitioning analysis

(Also called land-fragmentation analysis or landscape-fragmentation analysis)

What the technique aims to do

Linear infrastructure cuts across land and divides it into smaller parcels. This affects nature conservation because it fragments habitats: landscape because it reduces the scale of the landscape; tranquillity because it reduces the size of tranquil areas; the viability of agricultural businesses because it reduces the cost-effectiveness of large field sizes; peoples' ability to move from one area to another, and so on. Land use partitioning aims to identify, assess and record this fragmentation.

What it involves

Land-use partitioning analysis involves looking at the size and possibly the environmental quality of areas of non-fragmentation before and after a programme of linear infrastructure construction. At its simplest, it requires identifying the number and size of non-fragmented areas using GIS and/or remote sensing. It can also involve:

- identifying the size and per cent of urban, transitional and 'interior' (far from fragmenting infrastructure or development) areas;
- overlaying fragmentation data with information on nature conservation, landscape or other types of value (e.g. designations and land uses);
- comparing the number, area and/or quality of land areas before and after proposed development.

Fragmentation can be shown on maps, or in a graph of the number of land units versus their cumulative area. The latter shows how the same cumulative area (e.g. 1000ha) would be formed by more individual land units after the strategic action than before.

What the outputs look like

Figure C.4 shows the results of a land-use partitioning analysis.

Advantages

- deals with a topic that would otherwise be poorly (or not) considered; and
- provides a good visual representation of impacts.

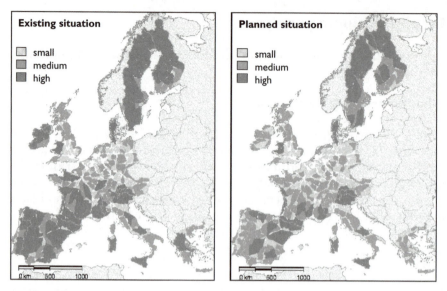

High = More than 50% of the area is designated by international conventions and more than 50% of the area is forest or semi-natural habitat.
Small = Less than 50% of the area is designated by international conventions and less than 50% of the area is forest or semi-natural habitat.
Medium = Intermediate ranking.

Source: European Environment Agency (1998)

Figure C.4 *Example of land-use partitioning analysis:*
European Trans-European Network

Disadvantages

- typically needs GIS and/or remote-sensing technologies;
- requires lots of data;
- is expensive and time-consuming;
- its application is limited to only a few subjects: it supports other techniques rather than being a 'main' SEA technique.

Further information

European Environment Agency (1998), Lacoul and Samarakoon (2005), Walz and Schumacher (2005)

Network analysis

(Also called cause–effect analysis, consequence analysis or causal chain diagrams)

What the technique aims to do

Network analysis explicitly recognizes that environmental systems consist of a complex web of relationships, and that many activities' impacts occur at several stages removed from the activity itself. It aims to identify the key cause–effect links that describe the causal pathway from initial action to ultimate environmental outcome. In doing so, it can also identify assumptions made in impact predictions, unintended consequences of the strategic action, and possible measures to ensure effective implementation. It is particularly useful for identifying cumulative and indirect impacts.

What it involves

Network analysis requires, through expert judgement, drawing the direct and indirect impacts of an action as a network of boxes (activities, outcomes) and arrows (interactions between them). These can include feedback loops and symbols to denote positive and negative impacts.

What the outputs look like

Figures 6.3 and 8.4 show examples of network analyses.

Advantages

- easy to understand, transparent, good for public participation;
- rapid and not cost-intensive;
- identifies the main impacts on environmental receptors, makes mechanisms of cause and effect explicit;
- identifies cumulative and indirect impacts;
- identifies constraints to effective implementation of a strategic action; and
- a useful input to other SEA techniques, e.g. modelling.

Disadvantages

- not quantitative, not replicable;
- can miss important impacts if not done well;
- does not deal with spatial impacts or impacts that vary over time; and
- the diagram can easily become very complex.

Further reading

Perdicoúlis (2005), Perdicoúlis et al (2007)

Modelling

(Also called forecasting)

What the technique aims to do

Modelling techniques aim to predict likely future environmental conditions with and without the strategic action (the strategic action's impacts are the difference between the two).

What it involves

Modelling involves making a series of assumptions about future conditions under various scenarios, and calculating the resulting impacts. Models typically deal with quantifiable impacts, such as air pollution, noise and traffic. For instance, the likely noise and air pollution impacts of a proposed road network can be calculated based on assumptions about expected traffic volumes on the network, the ratio of heavy goods vehicles, average speeds along the network and noise recipients. Most models used in SEA have evolved from EIA techniques. Many are computerized.

What the outputs look like

Numbers (possibly with ranges to denote uncertainty); graphs that show future air, noise, etc. levels under different scenarios; and maps that show spatial modelling outputs. Box 9.2 showed the results of modelling water resource demand and supply in south-east England. Figure C.5 shows an example of hydrological modelling of water levels in Lough Ree in Ireland, based on assumptions about rainfall, abstraction of water from the river, management of river water levels and so on, and using a dry year (1995) as a basis. The findings of this model were used to calculate the number of low-flow days in the lough under alternative scenarios for water provision in Dublin.

Booz Allen Hamilton (2007) used assumptions about the CO_2 emissions of different forms of transport, people's willingness to shift between transport modes, technological improvements in the fuel efficiency of vehicles and the future carbon content of transport fuels, to model the carbon impact of building a new north–south rail line in Great Britain using conventional rail, high-speed rail and magnetic levitation technology. The report controversially suggested that, over the 60-year appraisal period, the CO_2 emissions saved from operating a new rail line between London and Manchester would not cancel out the emissions generated in building the line, but that the opposite would be the case for a (longer) route between London and Glasgow/Edinburgh.

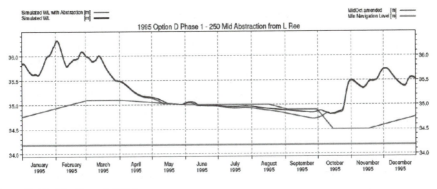

Source: Dublin City Council (2008)

Figure C.5 *Example of modelling: Water levels in Lough Ree (Ireland)*

Another example is an accident modelling exercise carried out for a network of high-speed roads in Poland. This used as inputs information about road length for eight different categories of road, accident rates for these categories and costs of accidents. Future accident rates were expected to be lower than current ones because it was presumed that Poland would reach Western European standards of road network hierarchization, signing and quality of pavements. The study concluded that:

> *Transferring a large part of the [vehicle-kilometres onto] motorways and expressways, i.e. roads with lower accident rates, will decrease [the] number of accidents. According to moderately optimistic prediction for [2025] the number of accidents will be reduced by 17,000, number of injured by 22,000 persons and [number] killed by 360–380 persons, and reduction in costs of about 3.6–3.9 billion [zloty]* (Tracz, 1999)

Advantages

- objective, scientific, rigorous (as rigorous as possible given uncertainties); and
- can deal with cumulative and indirect impacts.

Disadvantages

- It is limited to impacts that can be quantified/modelled.
- It can require large amounts of expensive and/or possibly unreliable data.
- Many models are 'black boxes': technocratic, complex and not transparent. They generally do not encourage participation or ownership by those people affected by the strategic action.

- Many models are based on untested assumptions, and have not been verified/monitored on the ground, particularly over longer timeframes. For instance, UK traffic models assumed for many years that new roads merely dispersed existing traffic over a greater road length: monitoring later showed that new roads also generate new traffic (SACTRA, 1994). The current assumptions on which models are based (e.g. height of 1 in 100 year flood) may also not be appropriate in the future.
- Because most models used in SEA were initially used in EIA, they promote project-level rather than strategic thinking.
- Many models can only compare like with like (e.g. road with road, not road with rail).

Further information

The entire June 1998 issue of *Impact Assessment and Project Appraisal* (vol 16, no 2) is on modelling, though primarily in the context of EIA. Also Hyder (1999).

Scenario/sensitivity analysis

What the technique aims to do

Often the impacts of a strategic action, or the relative benefits and disbenefits of different options, depend on variables outside the strategic action's control. For instance, the benefits provided by flood prevention measures could change depending on future climatic conditions; or future water use could rest in part on whether water meters are installed in people's homes. Scenarios can be used to describe a range of future conditions. The impact of a strategic action can be forecast and compared for different scenarios – sensitivity analysis – to test the strategic action's robustness to different possible futures. Chapter 7 discussed the difference between predictive, explorative and normative scenarios.

What it involves

Forecasts based on current trends and/or scenarios representing trends outside the decision-makers' control are generated and the strategic action's impacts are predicted based on these forecasts/scenarios. Sensitivity analysis measures the effect on predictions of changing one or more key input values about which there is uncertainty.

What the outputs look like

The following are examples of scenarios:

The SEA of the Dutch waste management plan 1992–2002 was based on two explorative scenarios for future waste production. The 'policy scenario' assumed that national objectives regarding waste prevention, reduction and so on would be fully achieved. The 'headwind scenario' assumed that they would not be fully achieved, and that therefore more waste would have to be dealt with (Verheem, 1996).

The SEA for the 100-year flood risk management strategy for the tidal River Thames considered several scenarios of future climate change and associated sea-level rise. These helped to inform the choice and proposed timing of flood alleviation measures, which in turn affected the likely environmental impacts of the strategy (Environment Agency, 2009).

Advantages

- reflects uncertainties;
- helps to generate ideas for reducing uncertainties, leads to more robust strategic actions; and
- supports the precautionary principle.

Disadvantages

- can be time- and resource-intensive.

Further information

Finnveden et al (2003), Höjer et al (2008), Partidário et al (2009b)

Cost–benefit analysis (CBA)

What the technique aims to do

CBA compares the monetary value of a strategic action's benefits with the monetary value of its costs. It aims to help decision-makers by translating environmental and social costs into a single, well-understood and widely used unit of measure: money. In theory, this allows all impacts to be put on the same footing.

What it involves

The two broad approaches to carrying out CBA involve identifying stated preferences – preferences stated by a respondent to a question – and revealed preferences – preferences inferred from an individual's behaviour.
Stated preference techniques include:

- contingent valuation: asks individuals about their willingness to pay and/or accept compensation for changes in environmental resources; and
- contingent ranking: asks individuals to rank several alternatives.

Revealed preference techniques include:

- replacement cost approach: estimates the cost of restoring the environment to its original state if it was damaged;
- avertive expenditures: measures expenditures undertaken by individuals to offset some environmental risk (e.g. noise abatement);
- travel cost method: surveys visitors to a site (e.g. a nature area) to determine how they value the (mainly recreational) characteristics of the site and how much time they spent travelling to the site;
- hedonic price methods (house prices approach): cross-sectional data on house prices are assembled, together with data on factors likely to influence these prices (e.g. noise, views). Links between factors and prices are analysed using multiple regression techniques; and
- dose-response approach: determines the links between pollution (dose) and its impacts (response), and predicts the costs of the impacts (e.g. cost of crop/forest damage from air pollution).

What the outputs look like

Table C.5 shows a partial CBA of a local transport plan. Note that the last row only adds up the monetary values, not the other values such as landscape.

Advantages

- is widely accepted by economists and decision-makers;
- allows all impacts to be considered on the same footing: 'integrates' different types of impact assessment;
- makes transparent the value of things that have not traditionally been considered in economic analyses; and

Table C.5 *Example of part of a cost–benefit assessment*

Journey times and vehicle operating costs	Overall, public transport should enjoy reduced journey times, as general congestion will be reduced. A new bus lane in Wellington Road will benefit buses travelling inbound to the bus station	Trunk road journey time savings: 2.46 minutes	Low growth: present value of benefits (PVB) £7.99m High growth: PVB £8.98m
Cost	The cost to Railtrack (now Network Rail) of maintaining and operating the level crossing barriers and signalling would be negated Not applicable	Present value of costs (PVC) £4.023m	
Local air quality	Slight decrease in air quality with the opening of the bridge. Slight improvement to air quality in town centre	No. properties experiencing: better air quality: 747 worse air quality: 1685	Neutral to slight adverse effects

Low growth PVB £7.99m; PVC £4.02m; net present value £3.97m
High growth PVB £8.98m; PVC £4.02m; net present value £4.96m

Source: Adapted from Somerset County Council (2000)

- may be the only way that environmental values can be taken into account in some decision-making processes.

Disadvantages

- Many CBA techniques are very indirect – for instance, house values in a given neighbourhood may have little to do with air pollution levels – and the techniques used can greatly affect the results.
- It is unclear over what time period costs and benefits should be compared: a strategic action's impact on jobs may last for 20 years, on climate change for hundreds of years.
- The discount rate – the reduced cost of future impacts (the flip side of interest rates) – used can have a large impact on the CBA's results. There is no agreement on what discount rates to use. Anything other than no discount rate – future impacts given the same cost as today's – contradicts the intra-generational principle of sustainable development.
- Economic efficiency is not the only principle that matters in decision-making and efficiency is not value-free: placing an economic value on nature or a human life is seen by many as an alien, reductionist approach.

- It does not consider who wins and who loses. For instance, it does not distinguish whether the noise increases are borne by people with already high noise levels or not.
- It can be perceived as unethical. It relies on individuals' judgements about their personal interests, which is arguably neither an appropriate approach to, nor always a realistic model of, how people make decisions about public goods.
- It is probably limited to projects and programmes.
- It requires much data, and takes much time/resources.

Further information

UK Treasury (1997), Weiss (1998), Pearce et al (2006)

Multi-criteria analysis (MCA)

(Also called multiple attribute analysis or multi-objective trade-off)

What the technique aims to do

MCA reflects the concept that different SEA topics, objectives or indicators may carry different weights in decision-making. It analyses and compares how well different alternatives achieve different objectives, taking into account the 'weight' of each objective, and identifies a preferred alternative.

What it involves

MCA involves choosing relevant assessment criteria/impacts and alternatives; assigning a weight (value of importance) to each criterion; assessing how each alternative affects each criterion; and aggregating the score and weight of each alternative. Table C.6 shows different scoring systems, using noise as the criterion:

Weighting of the criteria aims to reflect the fact that different criteria can have different relative importance. For instance, noise may have been identified in the SEA baseline stage as being much more important than air pollution and landscape: it could be given a weighting of, for instance, three compared to the other weightings of one. Weighting would normally be carried out by a panel of experts or public participation.

The scores and weightings are then multiplied and the results added up for each alternative. The alternative that scores most highly 'wins'. Table C.7 shows a hypothetical example of this, using the 'value' approach to scoring from Table C.6. In Table C.7, alternative B 'wins';

Table C.6 *Scoring systems for multi-criteria analysis*

Scoring method	Alternative A	B	C	D	Basis of the score
Absolute	65	62	71	75	Measured L_{10}dBA levels
Interval	0	-3	+6	+10	Difference in L_{10}dBA levels compared to alternative A
Ordinal	B	A	C	D	Ranking according to ascending L_{10}dBA levels
Binary	0	0	1	1	0 = less than 70 L_{10}dBA; 1 = more than 70 L_{10}dBA
'Value'	0	+1	-2	-3	+1 = good, -3 = very poor

Source: Lee (1987)

despite very good scores for air and landscape, alternative D comes out poorly because of the significance of the noise criterion.

What the outputs look like

A choice of preferred alternative(s) underpinned by a table similar to Table C.7. For instance, Tkach and Simonovic (1998) used MCA to explore four alternative floodplain management strategies for the Red River Valley in Manitoba, Canada.

Advantages

- acknowledges that society is composed of diverse stakeholders with different goals and values, and makes these views transparent;
- reflects the fact that some issues 'matter' more than others;
- is simple and can be used in a variety of settings, including public participation;
- can compare alternatives; and
- can be used with both quantifiable and unquantifiable data.

Table C.7 *Example of ranking of alternatives based on weighted scores*

Criterion	Weight (w)	A score (a)	a x w	B a	a x w	C a	a x w	D a	a x w
Noise	3	0	0	+1	+3	-2	-6	-3	-9
Landscape	1	+2	2	-2	-2	+1	+1	+2	+2
Biodiversity	1	-2	-2	0	0	0	0	+3	+3
Total			0		+1		-5		-4

Disadvantages

- can be used to 'twist' data; can lead to very different results depending on who establishes the weightings and scoring systems; and
- generally does not cope well with irreversible/critical limits; 'show stoppers', which mean that no matter how important other aspects are, they cannot outweigh the adverse implications of one factor.

Further information

Glasson et al (1999), Finnveden et al (2003)

Life cycle analysis (LCA)

What the technique aims to do

LCA analyses the entire impacts of a strategic action throughout its 'life', from initial development ('cradle') to implementation ('grave'). It considers not only the strategic action's direct impacts, but also its impacts up and down the line: for instance, where the aggregates would come from for road construction, or how to dispose of the wastes from an energy generation programme.

What it involves

LCA involves four main steps:

1 Agreement on objectives, the alternatives to be assessed, system boundaries, etc.: for instance, comparison of landfilling v. recycling in the UK over the next 10 years;
2 Compilation of an inventory of relevant inputs (e.g. materials, energy) and outputs (e.g. emissions to air, water and soil) associated with each alternative (landfilling, recycling);
3 Evaluation of the magnitude and significance of potential environmental impacts associated with those inputs and outputs. This may involve grouping the data into impact categories (e.g. global warming, soil pollution); assigning the inventory data to the impact categories; and quantifying the alternatives' impacts on the impact categories; and
4 Interpretation of the results to identify the preferred alternative, ways of improving the strategic action, etc.

What the outputs look like

Information about the impacts of different alternatives and help in choosing a preferred alternative. LCA has been applied to the development of the Dutch national waste management plan 2002 and second national plan on mineral resources (Ministry of the Environment and Mitsubishi Research Institute (Japan), 2003), and to three policy scenarios for a waste incineration tax in Sweden (Björklund et al, 2003).

Chester and Horvath (2009) carried out an ex-post analysis of the whole-life energy use, greenhouse gas emission and air pollution impacts of different forms of transport – a restricted form of LCA – and found that the whole-life impacts of all transport modes were significantly higher than their mere operating impacts. For instance, the whole-life greenhouse gas emissions of rail were found to be 2.5 times greater than those of train operation due to, for example, infrastructure construction and operation, and the whole-life SO_2 emissions of cars were about 20 times greater than operational emissions due to, for example, vehicle manufacturing, road construction and operation and gasoline production. Most examples of LCA have been for products (e.g. disposable v. reusable nappies) or sites.

Advantages

* comprehensive, deals with all impacts from a strategic action, from cradle to grave; and
* can be used to compare alternatives.

Disadvantages

* agreement/standardization has not yet been reached on many aspects of LCA, for instance, what is 'cradle' and 'grave', or whether to consider second generation impacts, such as the energy needed to produce building materials;
* requires judgements that balance apples and oranges, e.g. impacts on water v. on air;
* because of this, LCAs to date have not been particularly replicable: LCAs have reached different and sometimes contradictory conclusions about similar products because they used different assumptions;
* probably limited to programme SEA; and
* requires large amounts of detailed data.

Further information

Tukker (2000), International Organization for Standardization (2006a, b)

Vulnerability analysis

What the technique aims to do

Vulnerability analysis allows different development scenarios to be evaluated in terms of how they affect the vulnerability of the receiving environment.

What it involves

Vulnerability analysis combines GIS and MCA to assess the impacts of a planned activity on the vulnerability of an area. Vulnerability in this context is the combination of an environmental component's sensitivity and its value. A typical vulnerability analysis follows the following steps:

1 Identification of the environmental components for which the vulnerability assessment will be carried out. For instance, a motorway network could affect flora and fauna through habitat destruction, fauna through disturbance, the landscape and habitats through fragmentation, and people through noise.
2 Preparation of maps that show, for each environmental component, (a) the sensitivity of that component (e.g. national level designation is more sensitive than local level or no designation), and (b) the value of that component, standardized as classes (for instance, 0 not valuable – 100 very valuable).
3 Identification of the potential risk of impact to each environmental component, for instance, its distance from future areas of development.
4 Integration of the vulnerability of, and risk of impact to, each environmental component in a map for that component, and bringing these maps together into an overall map showing vulnerability to environmental impacts.

What the outputs look like

An environmental vulnerability analysis of possible sites for refugee camps in Liberia (UNEP, 2006) considered the environmental components of land cover, ecological service value and protection status. Risks to each component were calculated on the basis of how accessible the components were to camp locations (based on 'cost–distance', which takes into account not only distance as the crow flies but the type of landscape that would need to be traversed). From this, different levels of vulnerability around each possible refugee camp site were identified, and development could be prioritised towards sites that are in less vulnerable areas.

Advantages

- allows a quantitative expression of spatial impacts, which is useful in comparing alternatives; and
- because vulnerability analysis uses the local (geographical) characteristics of the environment, it is also useful for site-specific EIA.

Disadvantages

- can be costly and time-intensive;
- only works with impacts that can be mapped;
- the concept of vulnerability involves value judgements, but these are 'hidden' in the final analysis; and
- not much used to date.

Further information

van Straaten (1996), UNEP (2006), Cork County Council (2007)

Carrying capacity, ecological footprints

What the technique aims to do

Identify limits to growth, that is where human activities go beyond the capacity of the environment to support them.

What it involves

The concepts of carrying capacity and ecological footprinting take as a basis that:

total human impact on an area = the area's population × per capita impact.

Carrying capacity analysis aims to determine the human population that can be 'carried' by a particular area based on given per capita consumption levels. Carrying capacity analysis has a long history, for instance, in tourism planning ('how many tourists should be allowed on this island each year so that its quality as a tourism destination does not decline?') or to determine whether a given area can accommodate more dwellings. However, it has been mired in controversies over what exactly 'capacity' is, how land can be managed to increase capacity, whether a few more people can't be moved in after all, and so on.

Ecological footprinting looks at the equation from the other side. It identifies how much productive land and water area is required to support a given area's population indefinitely at current consumption levels (if the required land/water area is larger than that which exists, then the area is over capacity); or the maximum rate of resource consumption and waste discharge that can be sustained indefinitely by a given population in a given area.

What the outputs look like

- Carrying capacity: the maximum number of people/households/etc. that can be sustained by an area; *or*
- Ecological footprint: the average amount of productive land and sea required per person (or for a given population) to maintain a particular consumption level. For instance, the Global Footprint Network (2009) has calculated that the average American's footprint in 2008 was 9.4ha, compared to the average Indian's 0.9ha; *or*
- 'Earthshares': the average amount of productive land and sea available globally per capita. For instance, Chambers et al (2000) calculate that worldwide 'earthshares' were 2.1ha in 2000 but, because of increases in human population, will only be 1.4ha in 2050.

All of these can also be presented as timelines, for instance, of changes to a country's ecological footprint over the last 40 years.

Advantages

- directly linked to concepts of sustainability;
- can be carried out at any scale;
- results can be easily understood; and
- educational: can help to trigger behavioural change.

Disadvantages

- complicated process which can only really be carried out by experts; and
- makes huge assumptions, not easily replicable.

Further information

www.footprintnetwork.org, Wackernagel and Rees (1996), Chambers et al (2000)

Risk assessment

What the technique aims to do

Risk assessment estimates the risk that products and activities cause to human health, safety and ecosystems.

What it involves

It requires identifying possible hazards (e.g. oil spills, new wind farms), identifying and analysing their consequential impacts (e.g. on human health, bird populations), and estimating their frequency. It may also translate these risks into costs, for instance, by multiplying likely risks (frequency × consequential impacts) by the nominal value of a human life, bird population or job.

What the outputs look like

Statements about:

- the probability of a specified (hazardous) event, e.g. 1 in 10,000 chance of an oil spill in area X in a given year;
- the number of consequential impacts across a defined population, e.g. 10 premature deaths in community A due to the health effects of accidental hydrocarbon exposure, 600 additional bird strikes per year in a bird population of size B due to a new windfarm complex;
- the incidence of impacts per unit of exposure, e.g. X per cent increase in premature deaths per unit of hydrocarbon; and/or
- 'no effect' level of exposure, e.g. no bird strikes are likely if the windfarm is limited to X turbines (Pearce et al, 2006).

For instance, a post-conflict SEA of depleted uranium in Kosovo (UNEP, 2001) included a (horror-inducing in its 'neutrality') assessment of the risks to 7–12-year-old children of picking up solid pieces of depleted uranium (DU):

The only significant exposure may be by external beta radiation... The surface radiation dose rate is about 2 mSv [per hour]. If the piece of DU is put in the pocket the beta radiation is somewhat reduced, 50% is assumed. The exposed skin area will be quite small each time and from day to day it may shift a little making the skin dose smaller. By keeping the piece of DU in the pocket for several weeks it might be possible that the skin dose will exceed values corresponding to the limit for the public (50 mSv/year) and workers (500 mSv/year). It is out of the question that there will be any deterministic effects (skin burns)... The gamma dose rate at different distances from a penetrator, about 300 g DU, has been measured at the approximate dose rates are ...

external dose rate (μSv/h)	distance from the penetrator (m)
2.7	*0.05*
0.85	*0.1*
0.25	*0.2*

Advantages

- can be used to compare alternatives on the basis of the risk that they cause; and
- can incorporate the precautionary principle.

Disadvantages

- only considers one aspect of the 'environment', namely risk/safety;
- often extrapolates the risks at high dose levels of a pollutant to low dose levels, with consequent uncertainties;
- results can vary enormously depending on the assumptions made; and
- where it is used in cost–benefit assessment, values placed on human life or ecosystems can be highly contentious and possibly not politically acceptable.

Further information

Finnveden et al (2003), Schmidt et al (2005), Stewart (2007)

Internal compatibility appraisal

What the technique aims to do

Internal compatibility appraisal aims to ensure that the SEA objectives or the various components of the strategic action are internally coherent.

What it involves

An internal compatibility matrix plots different components/statements of the strategic action (or different SEA objectives) on one axis and the same components/ statements on the other axis. The 'mirror image' cells are eliminated, leaving a triangular matrix that looks like a road mileage chart. Matrix cells are filled in by asking 'Is this component compatible with that component (tick) or not (cross)?'. Where

	1	2	3	4	5	6	7	8	9	10	11	12	13	14
1														
2	✔													
3	–	–												
4	✔	–	✔											
5	✔	✔	✔	✔										
6	–	–	✔	–	–									
7	✗	✗	✔	–	✔	✔								
8	✗	✔	✔	–	✔	✔	✔							
9	✗	✔	✔	–	✔	✔	✔	✔						
10	✗	–	✔	–	–	–	✔	✔	✔					
11	–	✔	✔	✔	✔	–	✔	✔	–	✔				
12	–	✔	–	–	–	–	–	–	–	–	✔			
13	–	–	–	–	–	–	–	–	–	✔	–	✔		
14	–	–	–	–	–	–	✗	✗	✗	✔	–	✔	✔	
	1	2	3	4	5	6	7	8	9	10	11	12	13	14

Key
✔ Compatible
✗ Incompatible
– No link/insignificant
? Uncertain/unknown

Source: Gedling Borough Council (2009)

Figure C.6 *Example of an internal compatibility matrix*

incompatibility is found, one or both components may need to be changed.

What the outputs look like

Figure C.6 shows an example of an internal compatibility matrix. This would typically be supplemented by an explanation of why any non-compatible statements or objectives are being taken forward.

Advantages

- helps to ensure that a strategic action or group of SEA objectives is internally coherent;
- clarifies trade-offs, e.g. between social benefits and environmental costs; and
- is easy to understand.

Disadvantages

- is subjective;
- can be time intensive; and
- outputs can look daunting.

Appendix D

Appropriate Assessment under the Habitats Directive

In Europe, 'appropriate assessment' of plans is required under the Habitats Directive (European Commission, 1992), which assesses plans' impacts on the 'integrity' of sites of international nature conservation importance. Plans that, 'in combination' with other plans and projects, affect this integrity may only be adopted under limited and stringent conditions. Appropriate assessment thus acts as a precautionary decision-*making* tool, and an interesting contrast to the balancing decision-*informing* tool of SEA, which has a broader focus but whose findings must only be 'taken into account'.

This appendix introduces the legal requirements for, and describes the stages of, appropriate assessment. It presents two short case studies of strategic level appropriate assessment, which exemplify a range of good practice approaches. It concludes with a brief discussion of how appropriate assessment links with SEA.

Legal requirements

The Directive on Conservation of Natural Habitats and of Flora and Fauna 92/43/EEC – the so-called Habitats Directive – is the key European legislation for protecting biodiversity. The Directive aims to 'contribute towards ensuring bio-diversity through the conservation of natural habitats and of wild fauna and flora' (Article 2). One of the main mechanisms by which it attempts to achieve this is by identifying a pan-European ecological network – Natura 2000 – of Special Protection Areas for birds and Special Areas of Conservation for habitats and species, and by protecting these sites against development through 'appropriate assessment'. The Natura 2000 network comprises over 26,000 protected areas covering about 850,000km^2, and representing more than 20 per cent of total European Union territory (European Commission, 2009c).

Article 6(3) of the Habitats Directive requires an appropriate assessment to be prepared for any plan or project, alone or in combination with other plans or projects, that is likely to have a significant effect on the 'integrity' of a Natura 2000 site. If the appropriate assessment shows that a plan or project could affect the integrity of the site – essentially the reason why that site has been designated as a Natura 2000 site – then Article 6(4) states that the plan or project may not be adopted unless three stringent requirements – 1. no alternatives, 2. 'imperative reasons of overriding public interest', and 3. provision of compensatory measures – are met:

6(3) Any plan or project not directly connected with or necessary to the management of the site but likely to have a significant effect thereon, either individually or in combination with other plans or projects, shall be subject to appropriate assessment of its implications for the site in view of the site's conservation objectives. In the light of the conclusions of the assessment of the implications for the site and subject to the provisions of paragraph 4, the competent national authorities shall agree to the plan or project only after having ascertained that it will not adversely affect the integrity of the site concerned and, if appropriate, after having obtained the opinion of the general public.

6(4) If, in spite of a negative assessment of the implications for the site and in the absence of alternative solutions, a plan or project must nevertheless be carried out for imperative reasons of overriding public interest, including those of social or economic nature, the Member State shall take all compensatory measures necessary to ensure that the overall coherence of Natura 2000 is protected. It shall inform the Commission of the compensatory measures adopted. Where the site concerned hosts a priority natural habitat type and/or a priority species the only considerations which may be raised are those relating to human health or public safety, to beneficial consequences of primary importance for the environment or, further to an opinion from the Commission, to other imperative reasons of overriding public interest (EC, 1992).

Although the Habitats Directive was adopted in 1992, many European member states have only transposed its requirements for appropriate assessment of plans into national legislation since 2000 (IWAPHD, 2009), and in some cases only after being taken to the European Court of Justice (e.g. ECJ, 2005). Some member states (e.g. the Netherlands, UK) have developed specific guidance on appropriate assessment of plans, while many others use European Commission (2001b) guidance oriented to both plans and projects.

Stages of appropriate assessment

The European Commission (2001b) guidance explains how appropriate assessment can be carried out in up to four steps, with the findings of each step determining whether the next step is needed:

1. *Screening* – the process which identifies the likely impacts upon a Natura 2000 site of a project or plan, either alone or in combination with other projects or plans, and considers whether these impacts are likely to be significant in view of the sites' conservation objectives.
2. *Appropriate assessment* – consideration of the impact on the integrity of the Natura 2000 site of the project or plan, either alone or in combination with other projects or plans, with respect to the site's ecological structure and function in respect of the habitats and/or populations of species for which the site is designated. Additionally, where there are adverse impacts, an assessment of the potential mitigation of those impacts.
3. *Assessment of alternative solutions* – the process examines alternative ways of achieving the objectives of the project or plan that avoid adverse impacts on the integrity of the Natura 2000 site.
4. *Assessment where no alternative solutions exist and where adverse impacts remain* – in the light of an assessment of imperative reasons of overriding public interest (IROPI), where it is deemed that the project or plan should proceed, an assessment of whether effective compensatory measures can be delivered.

Additional European Commission guidance interprets the Article 6.4 concepts of no alternatives, IROPI and compensatory measures:

- The sequential order of first Article 6(3) and then Article 6(4) must be followed: the provisions of Article 6(4) apply only when the plan will adversely affect the integrity of one or more Natura 2000 sites; or doubts remain as to the absence of adverse effects on the integrity of the site(s) linked to the plan concerned.
- Alternative solutions include the 'zero option', alternative locations or routes, different scales or designs of development, and alternative processes.
- Imperative reasons of overriding public interest may include human health, public safety, environmental benefits or other forms of public interest. Public interest is assumed to be 'overriding' only if it is a long-term interest. For IROPI, the balance between these interests and the conservation objectives of the affected Natura 2000 site must be shown to favour the former.
- Compensatory measures constitute measures specific to the plan, additional to the normal implementation of the 'nature' directives.

They aim to offset the negative impact of a project and provide compensation corresponding precisely to the negative effects on the species or habitat concerned. Compensatory measures constitute the 'last resort', and should be used only when the Directive's other safeguards are ineffectual.

• To ensure the overall coherence of Natura 2000, the compensatory measures proposed for a project should address, in comparable proportions, the habitats and species negatively affected; and provide functions comparable to those which justified the selection of the original site, particularly in terms of geographical distribution.

• The result of implementing compensation should normally be operational by the time that damage to site integrity takes place (European Commission, 2007).

It is difficult to imagine how most plans could achieve all of these points, suggesting that plan-makers should make every effort to avoid and mitigate their plans' impacts on Natura 2000 sites rather than try to get plans adopted through Article 6(4) processes.

Plan-makers have understandably struggled to put these tough requirements into practice. Points of ongoing (as of autumn 2009) contention include what Natura 2000 sites need to be considered in a given appropriate assessment; what 'in combination' impacts need to be considered and whether these include past trends; where the screening stage stops and the appropriate assessment stage begins; whether mitigation measures or only avoidance measures can be considered at the screening stage; and under what circumstances a strategic action can be screened out from further appropriate assessment.

Approaches to appropriate assessment of plans

Boxes D.1 and D.2 show two examples of strategic level appropriate assessment. One relates to disturbance of ground-nesting birds by residents of new homes, the other to changes in species composition in sensitive habitats due to nitrogen deposition from traffic and agricultural activities. Both exemplify good practice approaches to several issues that arise in strategic-level appropriate assessment.

First, both try to deal with a strategic,-level issue in a correspondingly strategic manner. A problem that besets many appropriate assessments (and SEAs) is that a strategic action's impacts may depend on the location of its consequent development, but the strategic action itself may not specify where that development will take place. In these cases, it is clear that development near the Natura 2000

Box D.1 Example of strategic level appropriate assessment: Recreational disturbance at the Thames Basin Heaths Special Protection Area

The Thames Basin Heaths Special Protection Area (SPA) is a network of heathland sites covering about 8400ha in an area of south-east England subject to significant development pressure – see Figure D.1. The SPA is designated for three species of ground-nesting birds, which are all sensitive to recreational disturbance, particularly from dog walkers: woodlark, nightjar and Dartford warbler. New housing near the SPA could generate more visits to the SPA by the new residents and their pets, increasing the current significant levels of disturbance.

Source: Riki Therivel

Figure D.1 *Thames Basin Heaths SPA: Chobham Common*

In the wake of the European Court of Justice ruling that required appropriate assessment of plans in the UK, English Nature (now Natural England), the government agency responsible for nature conservation, objected to most new housing proposed near the Thames Basin Heaths SPA and to draft plans proposing more housing. It also drafted a 'delivery plan' of proposed mitigation standards for new residential developments near the SPA, to achieve a consistent and comprehensive approach for the 15 local authorities whose housing proposals might affect the SPA (English Nature, 2006). The 'delivery plan' consisted of a combination of development-free buffer zone and provision of Suitable Accessible Natural Green Space ('SANGS'), which aimed to draw dog walkers away from the SPA:

- Zone A: within 400 metres of the SPA, no new housing would be permitted;
- Zone B: between 400m and 2km, 16ha of SANGS would need to be provided per 1000 new population; and
- Zone C: between 2km and 5km, 8ha of SANGS would need to be provided per 1000 new population.

SANGS would be easily accessible, near centres of population, semi-natural with varied topography, allow for dogs to roam off the lead, accommodate walks of about 2.5km, and, where possible, create a feeling of 'peace and quiet'.

The draft delivery plan raised a host of objections from affected local authorities and developers, including:

- whether pet-free development would be acceptable within 400m of the SPA through restrictive covenants or by only permitting nursing homes, student accommodation, etc. (raising the intriguing possibility of birds being protected by a 400m wide buffer of very young and very old people);
- whether a development that is, for instance, 4.8km from the SPA in a direct line but 5.2km away by road should have to provide SANGS;
- whether enough SANGS land was available within each authority, either in public ownership or in private ownership, with a reasonable potential for conversion;
- whether the SANGS 'rules' would allow new development only in rural areas quite far away from amenities, that is in locations that were otherwise unsustainable.

Source: Riki Therivel

Figure D.2 *Example of a SANGS: Chobham Place Wood*

These points were debated at the public enquiry for the South East of England Regional Spatial Strategy. An inspector for the inquiry recommended a variant on the 'delivery plan' (Burley, 2007). Zone A would remain development-free unless such development would not lead to further recreational use of the SPA or otherwise have a significant effect on its integrity. Most development between 400m and 5km from the SPA would require SANGS at 8ha per 1000 population (e.g. schemes of more than ten dwellings); and development of over 50 houses between 5km and 7km from the SPA might require SANGS provision under certain circumstances. The inspector also recommended that all new developments should pay into a fund that would be used to identify and manage SANGS.

The adopted Regional Spatial Strategy for the South East has included most of Inspector Burley's recommendations in Policy NRM6, which is specifically about the SPA (Government Office for the South East, 2009). The principle of SANGS provision is currently being implemented by the local authorities. Authorities are requiring developers to pay a SANGS contribution of roughly £800–3500 ($1300–5700) per new house, depending on the location and size of the dwelling. These contributions are being used to improve existing or provide new green spaces (see Figure D.2 for an example). The buffer zone plus SANGS approach is also being considered by authorities near other similar SPAs.

sites could have a significant impact (more dog walkers, more NH_3 deposition), but development further away might have few or no impacts. In both case studies, the solution has been to establish 'rules' that are generic to all development, but that are more stringent in areas nearer the Natura 2000 site.

In both cases, the 'rules' relate specifically to the factors that support the integrity of the Natura 2000 site (lack of disturbance, low nitrogen input) and they apply to all plans and projects that could affect that site. More general statements of protection (e.g. 'development will only be permitted if it does not affect the integrity of Natura 2000 sites') would certainly be easier to agree at the strategic level, but would leave the difficult business of interpreting and implementing them to lower-tier planning decisions. This could lead to inconsistent approaches to mitigation being used at the lower tiers.

Devolving mitigation measures to lower, more local tiers might also make it easier to 'salami slice' impacts, and thus not ignore impacts that should be mitigated. A local authority could argue that, say, the 1000 new homes that it proposes would not require measures to deal with recreational disturbance. However, if this argument was used by each of the, for instance, 20 local authorities that comprise a region, then no mitigation would be implemented, even though the impacts of the region's 20,000 new homes should be addressed.

Both cases promote the hierarchy of first avoidance and then mitigation. New development is steered away from Natura 2000 sites,

Box D.2 Example of strategic level appropriate assessment: Nitrogen deposition in the Netherlands

This example relates to an issue that is a problem in several European member states but for which no agreed solution has been found to date. I have included it because it shows some of the complexities of dealing with a large-scale problem involving multiple stakeholders, some from other countries.

Nitrogen deposition acts like a fertilizer. It tends to favour fast-growing and taller plant species over slow-growing and shorter species, and can increase the risk of damage from drought, frost, pests, etc. (APIS, 2009). It can thus reduce the integrity of Natura 2000 sites, which depends on plant species or habitats that require low levels of nitrogen deposition.

Nitrogen deposition in much of the Netherlands exceeds the critical loads of several Natura 2000 habitat types. Average annual deposition in the east and south of the country is 15–20kg of nitrogen per hectare per year (N/ha/yr), whereas transition mires, quaking bogs and European dry heaths have critical loads of 7–8kg N/ha/yr, and lowland hay meadows have critical loads of 14kg N/ha/yr. About half of Dutch habitat types (though not half of their surface area) are thus already 'overloaded' by nitrogen deposition.

The pollutants that contribute to nitrogen deposition derive mainly from nitrogen oxides (NO_x) and ammonia (NH_3) emissions. In the Netherlands, the great majority of NH_3 emissions come from agriculture. About two-thirds of NO_x emissions come from the transport sector, and much of the rest is a result of industry and energy production. Dutch agriculture is responsible for half of the country's total nitrogen deposition; almost one-third originates in other countries; and about 9 per cent comes from Dutch traffic. Although NO_x emissions have been decreasing steadily for the last decade due in part to tightening European vehicle standards, NH_3 emissions and depositions have been broadly steady during that time. Some major Natura 2000 sites in the Netherlands, situated on sandy and oligotrophic soils that are most vulnerable to eutrophication, are near or even in the middle of the areas of most intensive animal husbandry. On average, between half and three-quarters of nitrogen depositions at a given Natura 2000 site come from within 15km of that site.

The provincial government is not permitting any extensions of farms that could increase nitrogen emissions because of concerns that, 'in combination', they will exacerbate these problems. This has led to polarization between farmers and environmentalists. To try to resolve this impasse, a possible strategy could be:

- progressively remove farms from the edge of vulnerable Natura 2000 sites;
- reduce background nitrogen deposition through action at the national and international level (e.g. on vehicle emissions, legislation aimed at stricter measures for livestock housing); and
- improve other environmental conditions at the Natura 2000 sites, e.g. better site management, reduced fragmentation, improvements to hydrological conditions.

Source: Bakker (2009)

and then additional measures are proposed to deal with the remaining impacts.

In both cases, the Natura 2000 sites were already subject to significant 'in combination' impacts, and environmental limits for those sites could already be shown to be breached. The English Nature (2006) 'delivery plan' referred to a range of research papers showing links between bird populations and recreational disturbance. Considerable research has been carried out about the levels of various air pollutants that different habitats can cope with (APIS, 2009). It may well be more difficult to show that limits are being breached for other types of Natura 2000 habitats and species, or in SEA (see Chapter 9). Neither of the case studies' mitigation measures attempts to actually get to within environmental limits: this is not required by appropriate assessment although it is an implicit aim of the Directive. Rather they aim to negate the effects of the plan concerned.

Other types of avoidance and mitigation measures that have been put in place in response to strategic level appropriate assessment include:

- new topic-specific policy statements about, e.g., protection zones to avoid disturbance to bats and destruction of their feeding and roosting areas, reduction of water abstraction, protection of water quality, and management of Natura 2000 sites to reduce pressures of urbanization;
- new policy statements on air quality;
- removal of certain locations from consideration as sites for future development;
- strengthening of policy statements on nature conservation; and
- policy statements requiring appropriate assessment for specific types of projects, or for projects in specified areas.

Links between SEA and appropriate assessment

Clearly there are large areas of overlap between SEA and appropriate assessment. They both aim to protect biodiversity, fauna and flora. Their broad methodologies are similar. The requirement for appropriate assessment of a plan also triggers the requirement for SEA: Article 3.2 of the SEA Directive states that:

Subject to paragraph 3 [on small area plans and minor modifications to plans], an environmental assessment shall be carried out for all plans and programmes... (b) which, in view of the likely effect on sites, have been determined to require an assessment pursuant to Article 6 or 7 of Directive 92/43/EEC. (CEC, 2001)

Table D.1 *Appropriate assessment v. SEA*

	Appropriate assessment	Strategic environmental assessment
Aim of process is to...	maintain the integrity of the Natura 2000 network and its features	provide for a high level of protection of the environment
Emphasis of process is on...	preventing development that could harm European sites	providing information on environmental impacts, consultation, documenting decisions
	'protection led'	'baseline led'
Legal 'bite': court cases hinge on...	substantive: whether the plan would have significant impacts on the integrity of European sites	procedural: whether the right reports have been written and the right people consulted
Level of detail, quantification	narrow focus on Natura 2000 sites, detailed	wider focus on environment
Skills needed	Ecological expertise; understanding of potentially affected sites and impacts on them	Data collection, developing alternatives and assumptions, impact prediction and mitigation

On the other hand, appropriate assessment covers a much narrower scope than SEA and has legal teeth that can stop plans, whereas SEA merely informs the plan-making process. Table D.1 summarizes these points.

Some European member states (e.g. Estonia, Poland, Slovenia) have integrated the SEA and appropriate assessment processes, while others (e.g. Ireland, UK) carry them out in parallel (IWAPHD, 2009). A close link between appropriate assessment and SEA processes would help to promote joined-up thinking and reduce duplication of work. It could also help to identify environmental limits and ensure that strategic actions do not breach them. However, it would also have disadvantages:

- Joint SA and SEA, as carried out in parts of the UK, is already perceived as potentially diluting the environmental emphasis of SEA. Joint SEA and appropriate assessment could similarly be perceived as diluting the strong protection element of appropriate assessment.
- Conversely, the focus on Natura 2000 sites of appropriate assessment could unbalance SEA, and lead to neglect of non-Natura 2000 sites. In some situations, measures that protect the integrity of Natura 2000 sites could be otherwise unsustainable, for instance, where measures to maintain water quality in a Natura 2000 river would entail pumping wastewater to another non-

Natura 2000 river, using more energy and affecting the ecology of that river.
• Very different skills are required, particularly for SA and appropriate assessment.

The examples above show just how influential appropriate assessment can be. This is due to its precautionary nature (the planner has the onus of showing that the strategic action will not affect a Natura 2000 site) and the fact that the strategic action may not be adopted unless it has no significant 'in combination' impacts on site integrity or can jump through the onerous triple hurdle of no alternatives, IROPI and compensatory measures. An analysis of the 'schedules of change' for six UK regional spatial strategies (Therivel, 2009) showed that, between them, they mentioned SA 47 times and appropriate assessment (or equivalent) 92 times, testifying to the weight given to appropriate assessment in decision-making. Appropriate assessment is likely to influence European SEA practice significantly in the coming years, and already is an interesting example of a narrow but powerful form of SEA.

References

All web-links were active as of 27 October 2009.

Aberdeen City Council (2007) *Environmental Report for the Aberdeen Local Housing Strategy 2006–2011*, www.aberdeencity.gov.uk/nmsruntime/saveasdialog.asp?lID=15152&sID=3427

ANSEA Team (TAU Consultora Ambiental et al) (2002) *Towards an Analytical Strategic Environmental Assessment*, Madrid, Spain

APIS (Air Pollution Information System (2009) 'Nitrogen deposition', www.apis.ac.uk/overview/pollutants/overview_N_deposition.htm

Argyris, C. and Schön, D. A. (1978) *Organisational Learning: A Theory of Action Perspective*, Addison-Westley, Reading

Arts, J. (1998) *EIA Follow-up – On the Role of Ex Post Evaluation in Environmental Impact Assessment*, Geo Press, Groningen

Aschemann, R., Partidário, M., Verheem, R., Fischer, T. and Dusik, J. (eds) (2011 forthcoming) *Handbook of Strategic Environmental Assessment*, Earthscan, London

Asian Development Bank (2009) *Harnessing Hydropower for Development: A Strategic Environmental Assessment for Sustainable Hydropower Development in Viet Nam*, www.gms-eoc.org/CEP/Comp1/docs/SEA_HarnessHydropower.pdf

Audit Commission (1999) *Listen Up! Effective Community Consultation*, www.audit-commission.gov.uk/SiteCollectionDocuments/AuditCommissionReports/NationalStudies/listenup.pdf

Bakker, J. (2009) 'N deposition in the Netherlands: Implications for Natura 2000', presentation to International Workshop on Assessment of Plans under the Habitats Directive, www.levett-therivel.co.uk/pres9.ppt

Bass, R. (2005) 'United States', Chapter 16 in C. Jones, M. Baker, J. Carter, S. Jay, M. Short and C. Wood (eds) *Strategic Environmental Assessment and Land Use Planning: An International Evaluation*, Earthscan, London

Bass, R., Herson, A. and Bogdan, K. (2001) *The NEPA Book: A Step-by-Step Guide on How to Comply With the National Environmental Policy Act*, Solano Press Books, Pt. Arena, California

Bass, R., Summerville, A., Bogdan, K. and Smith, M. (2009) *Economic Stimulus and NEPA: Streamlining the Environmental Review Process*, ICF International, Fairfax, USA, www.icfi.com/docs/economic-stimulus-nepa.pdf

Bina, O. (2007) 'A critical review of the dominant lines of argumentation on the need for strategic environmental assessment', *Environmental Impact Assessment Review*, vol 27, no 7, pp585–606

Bina, O. (2008) 'A context-specific interpretation of SEA in China', in Au, E., Lam, K.-C., Zhu, T. and M. Partidário (eds), *International Experience on Strategic*

Environmental Assessment, www.grm.cuhk.edu.hk/en/research/docs/Exp_SEA.pdf

Björklund, A., Johansson, J., Nilsson, M., Eldh, P. and Finnveden, G. (2003) *Environmental Assessment of a Waste Incineration Tax: Case Study and Evaluation of a Framework for Strategic Environmental Assessment*, Forskningsgruppen för Miljöstrategiska Studier, Stockholm

BPA (Bonneville Power Administration) (2003) *Bonneville Power Administration Fish & Wildlife Implementation Plan Final EIS*, www.efw.bpa.gov/environmental_services/ Document_Library/Implementation_Plan/

Booz Allen Hamilton (2007) *Estimated Carbon Impact of a New North–South Line*, report to the Department for Transport, www.dft.gov.uk/pgr/rail/researchtech/ research/newline/carbonimpact.pdf

Bridgend County Borough Council (2007) *Porthcawl Waterfront Supplementary Planning Guidance, Sustainability Appraisal/Strategic Environmental Assessment*, www.bridgend.gov.uk/web/groups/public/documents/report/030345

Broad, M. (2006) 'Fine intention adds to workplace grief', *Planning*, vol 13, January

Bröring, U. and Wiegleb, G. (2005) 'Assessing Biodiversity in SEA', Chapter 36 in M. Schmidt, E. João and E. Albrecht (eds) *Implementing Strategic Environmental Assessment*, Springer, Berlin

Brown, A. L. (1997) 'The environmental overview in development project formulation', *Impact Assessment*, vol 15, no 1, pp73–78

Brown, A. L. (1998) 'The Environmental Overview as a Realistic Approach to Strategic Environmental Assessment in Developing Countries', in A. Porter and J. Fittipaldi (eds) *Environmental Methods Review: Retooling Impact Assessment for the New Century*, US Army Environmental Policy Institute, The Press Club, Fargo, USA, pp127–134

Burgos, C., Garcia, J., Alvarado, B., Garcia, J. and Garcia, C. (2008) *Evaluación Ambiental Estratégica (EAE) para la Formulación de Política en Materia de Salud Ambiental para Colombia, con Énfasis en Contaminación Atmosférica en Centros Urbanos. Informe Final. Documento Técnico ASS/1487B Proceso Facilitado por el MAVDT con la Participacion de Multiples Actores Públicos*, Pontificia Universidad Javeriana, CENDEX, Colombia

Burley, P. (2007) 'Report to the Panel on the Thames Basin Heaths Special Protection Area and Natural England's Draft Delivery Plan', Draft South East Plan Examination in Public, www.eipsoutheast.co.uk/news/story.aspx?id=49

CAG Consultants (2000) *Integrating Policies in Development Plans, Phase 1*, report to Countryside Agency, Cheltenham

California Department of Food and Agriculture (2009) *Light Brown Apple Moth Eradication Programme, Programmatic Environmental Impact Report*, State Clearinghouse No. 2008022076, www.cdfa.ca.gov/phpps/pdep/lbam/ envimpactrpt.html

Canadian Environmental Assessment Agency (1999) *Addressing Cumulative Environmental Effects*, www.ceaa-acee.gc.ca/Content/D/A/C/ DACB19EE-468E-422F-8EF6-29A6D84695FC/cea_ops_e.pdf

Cashmore, M., Gilliam, R., Morgan, R., Cobb, D. and Bond, A. (2004) 'The interminable issue of effectiveness: Substantive purposes, outcomes and research challenges in the advancement of environmental impact assessment theory', *Impact Assessment and Project Appraisal*, vol 22, no 4, pp295–310

CEC (Commission of the European Communities)(1985) 'Council Directive on the assessment of the effects of certain private and public projects on the environment (85/337/EEC)', *Official Journal of the European Communities* L175/40, Brussels

CEC (2001) 'Directive 2001/42/EC on the assessment of the effects of certain plans and programmes on the environment', http://ec.europa.eu/environment/eia/sea-legalcontext.htm

CEQ (Council on Environmental Quality) (1997) *Considering Cumulative Effects Under the National Environmental Policy Act*, http://ceq.hss.doe.gov/NEPA/ccenepa/ccenepa.htm

CEQ (2007) *A Citizen's Guide to the NEPA*, http://ceq.hss.doe.gov/nepa/Citizens_Guide_Dec07.pdf

Chambers, N., Simmons, C. and Wackernagel, M. (2000) *Sharing Nature's Interest: Ecological Footprints as an Indicator of Sustainability*, Earthscan, London

Cherp, A., Watt, A. and Vinichenko, V. (2007) 'SEA and strategy formation theories: From three Ps to five Ps', *Environmental Impact Assessment Review*, vol 27, no 7, pp624–644

Chester, M. V. and Horvath, A. (2009) 'Environmental assessment of passenger transportation should include infrastructure and supply chains', *Environmental Research Letters*, vol 4, pp1–8, www.iop.org/EJ/article/1748-9326/4/2/024008/erl9_2_024008.pdf?request-id=2599581f-71ad-4698-8f7a-ad2381b929c1

CLG (Communities and Local Government) (2006) *Planning for the Protection of European Sites: Appropriate assessment*, www.communities.gov.uk/archived/publications/planningandbuilding/planning2

CLG (2007a) *Eco-towns prospectus*, www.communities.gov.uk/publications/housing/ecotownsprospectus

CLG (2007b) *Using Evidence in Spatial Planning: Spatial Plans in Practice – Supporting the Reform of Local Planning*, www.communities.gov.uk/publications/planningandbuilding/spatialplanspracticelessons

CLG (2009a) *Eco-towns*, www.communities.gov.uk/housing/housingsupply/ecotowns/

CLG (2009b) *Towards a more efficient and effective use of strategic environmental assessment and sustainability appraisal in spatial planning*, prepared by Scott Wilson, London

CLG and DBIS (Department for Business, Innovation and Skills) (2009) *Policy statement on regional strategies and guidance on the establishment of leaders' boards: Consultation*, www.communities.gov.uk/archived/publications/planningandbuilding/regionalstrategiesconsultation

Collingwood Environmental Planning, Land Use Consultants, Levett-Therivel sustainability consultants, Scott Wilson, Treweek Environmental Consultants and C4S (2006) *Working with the SEA Directive: Do's and Don'ts Guide to Generating and Developing Alternatives*, www.sea-info.net/files/general/Options_Do's_Dont's_Guide_(Dec_06).pdf

Comité de bassin Loire-Bretagne (2007) *Schéma Directeur d'aménagement et de Gestion des Eaux du Bassin Loire-Bretagne: Rapport d'évaluation Environnementale*, www.eau-loire-bretagne.fr/sdage_et_sage/projet_de_sdage

Commission for Rural Communities (2009) *Rural Proofing Guidance*, www.ruralcommunities.gov.uk/files/rural%20proofing%20toolkit.pdf

Cork County Council (2007) *Draft County Development Plan, Strategic Environmental Assessment Environmental Report*, www.corkcoco.ie/co/pdf/265619842.pdf

Countryside Agency, Environment Agency, English Nature and English Heritage (2002) *Quality of Life Assessment – What matters and why*, http://p1.countryside.gov.uk/Images/LAR_LOF_Position_Statement_tcm2-29989.pdf

Countryside Council for Wales (2007) *Strategic Environmental Assessment Guidance for Practitioners*, prepared by C4S, www.sea-info.net/content/sectors.asp?pid=40

Cowell, R. and Owens, S. (2006) 'Governing space: Planning reform and the politics of sustainability', *Environment and Planning C: Government and Policy*, vol 24, pp403–421

CPM (1999) *The Results of the Environmental Capital Approach for Land West of the A1(M)*, CPM, Coln St Aldwyns

CPRE (Council for the Protection of Rural England) and Countryside Commission (1995) *Tranquillity*, www.cpre.org.uk/campaigns/landscape/tranquillity

CPRE (Campaign to Protect Rural England), WWF-UK and Friends of the Earth England (2007) *Environmental Sustainability and English Regional Strategies*, report by Levett-Therivel sustainability consultants, www.cpre.org.uk/news/view/410

Dalal-Clayton, B. and Sadler, B. (2005) *Strategic Environmental Assessment: A Sourcebook and Reference Guide to International Experience*, Earthscan, London

Dalal-Clayton, B. and Sadler, B. (2010 forthcoming) *Sustainability Appraisal*, Earthscan, London

DBERR (Department for Business, Enterprise and Regulatory Reform) (2008a) *Consultation on Strategic Environmental Assessment Scoping Report for Proposed National Policy Statement for New Nuclear Power*, www.berr.gov.uk/files/file45240.pdf

DBERR (2008b) *Meeting the Energy Challenge: A White Paper on nuclear power*, www.berr.gov.uk/files/file43006.pdf

DCENR (Department of Communications, Energy and Natural Resources) (2008) *Third Strategic Environmental Assessment for Oil and Gas Activity in Ireland's Offshore Atlantic Waters: IOSEA3 Rockall Basin, Environmental Report*, www.dcenr.gov.ie/Natural/Petroleum+Affairs+Division/Irish+Offshore+Strategic+Environmental+Assessment+(IOSEA+3)/

DECC (Department of Energy and Climate Change) (2009) *UK Offshore Energy Strategic Environmental Assessment: Future Leasing for Offshore Wind Farms and Licensing for Offshore Oil & Gas and Gas Storage, Environmental Report*, www.offshore-sea.org.uk/consultations/Offshore_Energy_SEA/index.php.

Defra (2005) *Securing the future: UK government sustainable development strategy*, www.defra.gov.uk/sustainable/government/publications/uk-strategy

Department of Defence, Australia (2006) *Strategic Environmental Assessment of Defence Activities in the Great Barrier Reef World Heritage Site*, www.gbrmpa.gov.au/corp_site/management/eim/docs/strategic_env_assessment_defence.pdf.pdf

Department of Finance and Personnel (Northern Ireland) (2002) *Developing Policy on the Location of Civil Service Jobs: An Equality Impact Assessment*, Belfast

Department of Health (2007) *Draft Guidance on Health in Strategic Environmental Assessment*, www.dh.gov.uk/en/Consultations/Liveconsultations/DH_073261.

Department for Transport (2008) *Transport Statistics Great Britain 2008 edition*, www.dft.gov.uk/pgr/statistics/datatablespublications/tsgb/.

Department for Transport (2009a) *Britain's transport infrastructure: Adding capacity at Heathrow, decision following consultation*, www.dft.gov.uk/pgr/aviation/heathrowconsultations/heathrowdecision/decisiondocument/decisiondoc.pdf

Department for Transport (2009b) Ports: National Policy Statement for England and Wales – Appraisal of Sustainability (AoS) Report, www.dft.gov.uk/consultations/closed/portsnps/aos.pdf

Desholm, M. and Kahlert, J. (2005) 'Avian collision risk at an offshore windfarm', *Biology Letters*, vol 13, pp1–4, www.rsbl.royalsocietypublishing.org/content/1/3/296.full

Desmond, M. (2007) 'Decision criteria for the identification of alternatives in SEA', *Impact Assessment and Project Appraisal*, vol 25, no 4, pp259–269

Desmond, M. (2008) 'Identification and development of waste management alternatives for strategic environmental assessment (SEA)', *Environmental Impact Assessment Review*, vol 29, no 1, pp51–59

DEWHA (Department of the Environment, Water, Heritage and the Arts, Government of Australia) (2008) *Assessment of the Southern Bluefin Tuna Fishery*, www.environment.gov.au/coasts/fisheries/commonwealth/southern-bluefin-tuna/pubs/report08.pdf

DEWHA (2009) *Comparative Analysis of the Feasibility of Alternative Locations for the Development of a Liquefied Natural Gas Precinct*, www.environment.gov.au/epbc/notices/assessments/kimberley.html

DHV Environment and Infrastructure BV (1994) *Existing Strategic Environmental Assessment Methodology*, report prepared for the European Commission DGXI, Brussels

Dublin City Council (2008) *Water Supply Project – Dublin Region (Draft plan), Strategic Environmental Assessment (SEA Phase 1), Environmental Report*, prepared by Veolia Water and RPS, www.dublincity.ie/WaterWasteEnvironment/waterprojects/Pages/WaterSupplyProject-DublinRegion.aspx

Dusik, J. and Xie, J. (2009) *Strategic Environmental Assessment in East and Southeast Asia: A Progress Review and Comparison of Country Systems and Cases*, prepared for the World Bank, http://siteresources.worldbank.org/INTEAPREGT OPENVIRONMENT/Resources/SEAprogressreviewinEAPFINAL.pdf

East Cambridgeshire District Council (2008) *Sustainability Appraisal Scoping Report*, www.eastcambs.gov.uk/docs/publications/devservices/sascopingrep.pdf.

ECJ (European Court of Justice) (2005) Commission of the European Communities vs. United Kingdom of Great Britain and Northern Ireland, Case C-6/04, ECR I-9017, http://eur-lex.europa.eu/JCHtml.do?uri=OJ:C:2007:056:SOM:EN:HTML

Ekins, P. (ed) (1986) *The Living Economy*, Routledge, London

El-Jourbagy, J. and Harty, T. (2005) 'Improved Decision-making Through SEA – Expectations and Results in the United States', Chapter 17 in Schmidt, M., João, E. and Albrecht, E. (eds), *Implementing Strategic Environmental Assessment*, Springer, Berlin

English Nature (2006) Thames Basin Heaths Special Protection Area: Mitigation Standards for Residential Development, www.eipsou/heart.co.uk/documents/documents.aspx?ct=13

English Nature, Environment Agency, The Countryside Agency and English Heritage (2004) *Strategic environmental assessment: Consultation Bodies' Services and Standards for Responsible Authorities*, www.environment-agency.gov.uk/static/documents/Research/sea_sos_eng_1705376.pdf

Environment Agency (2009) *Thames Estuary 2100 Strategic Environmental Assessment, Environmental Report Summary*, www.environment-agency.gov.uk/static/documents/Research/TE2100_Environment_Summary-LR.pdf

Environmental Protection Agency (2008a) *Strategic Environmental Assessment SEA Process Checklist*, Johnstown Castle Estate, County Wexford, Ireland, www.epa.ie/downloads/consultation/Strategic_Environmental_Assessment_Jan086.pdf

Environmental Protection Agency (2008b) *Second National Hazardous Waste Management Plan: Environmental Assessment*, www.epa.ie/downloads/pubs/waste/haz/name,25129,en.html

Environmental Protection Agency and National Development Planning Commission (EPA and NDPC) (2003) *Strategic Environmental Assessment of the Ghana Poverty Reduction Strategy*, Accra, Ghana

EPDGHKSAR (Environmental Protection Department of the Government of the Hong Kong Special Administrative Region) (2009) *Strategic Environmental Assessment (SEA) Knowledge Centre*, www.epd.gov.hk/epd/SEA/eng/index.html

Eskom Distribution (2007) *Eskom Master Plan – Central region, Strategic Environmental Assessment*, prepared by Eco Assessments, Linden, South Africa, www.eskom.co.za/content/APPENDIX%204D%20Workshop%20Discussion%20Document.pdf

European Commission (1992) Council Directive 92/43/EEC of 21 May 1992 on the conservation of natural habitats and of wild fauna and flora, http://eur-lex.europa.eu/LexUriServ/LexUriServ.do?uri=CELEX:31992L0043:EN:HTML

European Commission (2001a) *Guidance on EIA: EIS Review*, Brussels, http://ec.europa.eu/environment/eia/eia-guidelines/g-review-full-text.pdf

European Commission (2001b) *Assessment of plans and projects significantly affecting Natura 2000 sites: Methodological Guidance on the Provisions of Article 6(3) and 6(4) of the Habitats Directive 92/43/EEC*, Brussels, http://ec.europa.eu/environment/nature/natura2000/management/guidance_en.htm

European Commission (2003) *Implementation of Directive 2001/42 on the Effects of Certain Plans and Programmes on the Environment*, Brussels, http://ec.europa.eu/environment/eia/pdf/030923_sea_guidance.pdf

European Commission (2007) Guidance document on Article 6(4) of the 'Habitats Directive' 92/43/EEC, http://ec.europa.eu/environment/nature/natura2000/management/docs/art6/guidance_art6_4_en.pdf

European Commission (2009a) *Strategic Environmental Assessment (SEA) of the Implementation of the National Sugar Adaptation Strategy for Trinidad & Tobago, Draft strategic environmental assessment*, EU Ref. No. 110860/C/SV/Multi, prepared for EuropeAid Co-Operations Office, Brussels www.detto.ec.europa.eu/en/docs/SEA%20Final%200609.pdf

European Commission (2009b) *Study concerning the Report on the Application and Effectiveness of the SEA Directive (2001/42/EC), Final Report*, http://ec.europa.eu/environment/eia/pdf/eia_study_june_09.pdf

European Commission (2009c) 'Nature and biodiversity', http://ec.europa.eu/environment/nature/index_en.htm

European Environment Agency (1998) *Spatial and Ecological Assessment of the TEN: Demonstration of Indicators and GIS Methods*, Environmental Issues Series No 11, Copenhagen, www.eea.europa.eu/publications/GH-15-98-318-EN-C

Feldmann, L., Vanderhaegen, M. and Pirotte, C. (2001) 'The European Union's Strategic Environmental Assessment Directive: Status and links to integration and sustainable development', *Environmental Impact Assessment Review*, vol 21, no 3, pp203–222

Finnveden, G., Nilsson, M., Johansson, J., Persson, A., Moberg, A. and Carlsson, T. (2003) 'Strategic Environmental Assessment methodologies: Applications within the energy sector', *Environmental Impact Assessment Review*, vol 23, no 1, pp91–123

Firat, A. F. and Dholakia, N. (1998) *Consuming People: From Political Economy to Theatres of Consumption*, Routledge, London

Fischer, T. B. (2007) *Theory and Practice of Strategic Environmental Assessment*, Earthscan, London

Fischer, T. B. (2010) 'Reviewing the quality of strategic environmental assessment reports for English of spatial plan core strategies', *Environmental Impact Assessment Review*, vol 30, no 1, pp62–69

Fischer, T. B. and Gazzola, P. (2006) 'SEA effectiveness criteria – Equally valid in all countries? The case of Italy', *Environmental Impact Assessment Review*, vol 26, no 4, pp396–409

Fischer, T. B. and He, X. (2007) *Differences in Perceptions of Effective Strategic Environmental Assessment Application in the UK and China*, www.liv.ac.uk/civdes/staff/survey20062007.ppt

Fischer, T. B., Kidd, S., Jha-Thakur, U., Gazzola, P. and Peel, D. (2009) 'Learning through EC Directive based SEA in spatial planning? Evidence from the Brunswick Region in Germany', *Environmental Impact Assessment Review*, vol 29, no 6, pp 421–428

Fothergill, J. (2008) 'Objective led SEA – Is there another way?', presentation at the IEMA Environmental Assessment Forum 2008, www.iema.net/stream.php/download/conferences/EA%20Forum%202008/20080424W1/1F%20Josh%20fothergill%20-%20%20Objective%20led%20SEA.pdf

Fry, C. (2007) 'Towards the next wave of SEA', *The Environmentalist*, issue 47 (May), p19

Gedling Borough Council (2009) *Core Strategy Sustainability Appraisal Scoping Report*, www.gedling.gov.uk/gedling_sa_scoping_report.pdf

Geneletti, D., Bali, S., Napolitano, P. and Pistocchi, A. (2007) 'Spatial decision support for strategic environmental assessment of land use plans. A case study in southern Italy, *Environmental Impact Assessment Review* vol 27, no 5, pp408–423

George, C. (2001) 'Sustainability appraisal for sustainable development: integrating everything from jobs to climate change', *Impact Assessment and Project Appraisal*, vol 19, no 2, pp 95–106

GTZ (Gesellschaft für Technische Zusammenarbeit) (2009) *Strategic Environmental Assessment*, www.environmental-policy.cn/focus-areas/strategic-environmental-policy/strategic-environmental-assessment.html

Gibson, R. (2005) *Sustainability Assessment: Criteria and Processes*, Earthscan, London

Giddens, A. (1998) *The Third Way*, Policy Press, Cambridge

Glasson, J., Therivel, R. and Chadwick, A. (2005) *Introduction to Environmental Impact Assessment*, 3rd edition, Routledge, London

Global Footprint Network (2008) 'Data sources', www.footprintnetwork.org/en/index.php/GFN/page/data_sources/

Global Footprint Network (2009) 'Footprint for Nations', www.footprintnetwork.org/en/index.php/GFN/page/footprint_for_nations/

Government of Kenya and World Bank (2007) *Institution Centred Strategic Environmental Assessment of the Forest Sector in Kenya*, prepared by FRR/IDL/Matrix Consultants, http://web.worldbank.org/WBSITE/EXTERNAL/TOPICS/ENVIRONMENT/0,,contentMDK:20667165~isCURL:Y~menuPK:549265~pagePK:148956~piPK:216618~theSitePK:244381,00.html

Government of Western Australia, Department of State Development (2009) *Kimberley LNG Social Impact Assessment, Volume 1: Scope and Profile*, Perth

Government Office for the East of England (2008) *East of England Plan Supporting Document*, www.gos.gov.uk/goee/docs/Planning/Regional_Planning/Regional_Spatial_Strategy/final_text_supporting1.pdf

Government Office for the East of England (2009) 'Legal challenge to the East of England Plan', www.gos.gov.uk/goeast/planning/regional_planning/837825/

Government Office for the South East (2009) *The South East Plan*, www.go-se.gov.uk/gose/planning/regionalPlanning/815640/?a=42496

Great Sand Hills Advisory Committee (2007) *Great Sand Hills Regional Environmental Study*, www.environment.gov.sk.ca/2007-104GreatSandHillsEnvironmentalStudy

Grice, S., Bush, T., Stedman, J., Vincent, K., Kent, A., Targa, J. and Hobson, M. (2006) *Baseline Projections of Air Quality in the UK for the 2006 Review of the Air Quality Strategy*, report to Defra, www.airquality.co.uk/archive/reports/cat16/0604041040_baselineprojectionsreport5.pdf

Haines-Young, R. and Potschin, M. (2007) *The Ecosystem Concept and the Identification of Ecosystem Goods and Services in the English Policy Context*, review paper to Defra, project code NR0107, www.ecosystemservices.org.uk/docs/NR0107_pos%20paper%20EA_D1.3.pdf

Hanusch, M. and Glasson, J. (2008) 'Much ado about SEA/SA monitoring: The performance of English Regional Spatial Strategies, and some German comparisons', *Environmental Impact Assessment Review*, vol 28, no 8, pp601–617

Hardi, P. and Zdan, T. (1997) 'Assessing sustainable development: Principles in practice', presented at conference held by International Institute for Sustainable Development, Bellagio, Italy

Heiland, S. (2005) 'Requirements and Methods for Public Participation in SEA', Chapter 29 in M. Schmidt, E. João and E. Albrecht (eds) *Implementing Strategic Environmental Assessment*, Springer, Berlin

High Court of Justice in Northern Ireland, Queen's Bench Division (2007) *(1) An Application by Seaport Investments Limited; (2) An Application by Magherafelt District Council, F P McCann (Developments) Limited, Younger Homes Limited, Herron Bros Limited, G Small Contracts and Creagh Concrete Products Limited*, [2007] NIQB 62, www.courtsni.gov.uk/NR/rdonlyres/BD682D62-7F68-497D-9947-445B786B03C5/0/j_j_WEAC5799Final.htm

Hill, E. and Lowe, J. (2007) 'Regional impact assessment: An Australian example', *Impact Assessment and Project Appraisal*, vol 25, no 3, pp189–197

Höjer, M., Ahlroth, S., Dreborg, K.-H., Ekvall, T., Finnveden, G., Hjelm, O., Hochschorner, E., Nilsson, M. and Palm, V. (2008) 'Scenarios in selected tools for environmental systems analysis', *Journal of Cleaner Production*, vol 16, pp1958–1970

Home Office (2008) *Crime in England and Wales 2007/08*, www.homeoffice.gov.uk/rds/pdfs08/hosb0708.pdf

Hong Kong Environmental Protection Department (2009) *Strategic Environmental Assessment Knowledge Centre*, www.epd.gov.hk/epd/SEA/eng/index.html

Hyder (1999) *Guidelines for the Assessment of Indirect and Cumulative Impacts as well as Impact Interactions*, report prepared for European Commission DG XI, Brussels, http://ec.europa.eu/environment/eia/eia-studies-and-reports/guidel.pdf

IAIA (International Association for Impact Assessment) (2002) *Strategic Environmental Assessment Performance Criteria*, www.iaia.org/publicdocuments/special-publications/sp1.pdf

IDeA (Improvement and Development Agency) (2009) *Equality Impact Assessments (EqIAs)*, www.idea.gov.uk/idk/core/page.do?pageId=8017247

Institute of Environmental Management and Assessment (2002) *Perspectives: Guidelines on Participation in Environmental Decision-making*, www.iema.net/shop/default.php?cPath=27_26

International Organisation for Standardization (2006a) *ISO 14040: 2006 Environmental Management – Life Cycle Assessment – Principles and Framework*, Geneva, www.iso.org/iso/catalogue_detail?csnumber=37456

International Organisation for Standardization (2006b) *ISO 14044: 2006 Environmental Management – Life Cycle Assessment – Requirements and Guidance*,

Geneva, www.iso.org/iso/catalogue_detail?csnumber=38498

International Union for the Conservation of Nature (IUCN) (1991) *Caring for the Earth: A Strategy for Sustainable Living*, Geneva

IPII (Interacademy Panel on International Issues) (2009) *IAP Statement on Ocean Acidification*, www.interacademies.net/Object.File/Master/9/075/ Statement_RS1579_IAP_05.09final2.pdf

IWAPHD (International Workshop on Assessment of Plans under the Habitats Directive) (2009) *Status of Assessment of Plans under the Habitats Directive in Different European Member States*, www.levett-therivel.co.uk/IW.htm

Jackson, T. and Illsley, B. (2007) 'An analysis of the theoretical rationale for using strategic environmental assessment to deliver environmental justice in the light of the Scottish Environmental Assessment Act', *Environmental Impact Assessment Review*, vol 27, no 7, pp607–623

Jansson, A. (1999) 'Transport SEA: A Nordic perspective', presented at the OECD/ECMT conference on SEA of transport, Warsaw, 14–15 October

Jha-Thakur, U., Gazzola, P., Fischer, T. B., Peel, D. and Kidd, S. (2009) 'SEA effectiveness – The significance of learning', *Impact Assessment and Project Appraisal*, vol 27, no 2, pp133–144

João, E. (2007) 'A research agenda for data and scale issues in strategic environmental assessment', *Environmental Impact Assessment Review*, vol 27, no 5, pp479–491

Jones, C., Baker, M., Carter, J., Jay, S., Short, M. and Wood, C. (2005) *Strategic Environmental Assessment and Land Use Planning: An International Evaluation*, Earthscan, London

Kidd, S. and T.B. Fischer (2007) 'Towards sustainability: Is integrated appraisal a step in the right direction?', Environment and Planning C: Government and Policy, vol 25, pp233–249

Killarney Town Council (2008) *Killarney Town Plan 2009–2016 Strategic Environmental Assessment*, Killarney, Ireland

Kläne, C. and Albrecht, E. (2005) 'Purpose and Background of the European SEA Directive', Chapter 2 in M. Schmidt, João, E. and Albrecht, E. (eds) *Implementing Strategic Environmental Assessment*, Springer, Berlin

Lacoul, M. and Samarakoon, L. (2005) 'Study of landscape fragmentation to characterize of urban sprawl', *Proceedings of the Asian Conference on Remote Sensing 2005*, www.a-a-r-s-acrs.org/acrs/proceeding/ACRS2005/Papers/URM2-5.pdf

Lao PDR (People's Democratic Republic) Ministry of Industry and Handicrafts and the World Bank (2004) *Lao PDR Hydropower – Strategic Environmental Assessment*, prepared by Norplan, http://siteresources.worldbank.org/INTLAOPRD/Resources/ SIAnovember2004.pdf

Latham and Watkins (2009) *Client Alert: American Recovery and Reinvestment Act of 2009 – Land Use Implications for Cleantech projects*, www.lw.com/upload/pubContent/ _pdf/pub2515_1.pdf

Lee, J., Griffiths, G., Warnock, S., Bailey, N., Bayliss, J., Vogintzakis, I. and Thompson, S. (2002) *Development of a Biodiversity and Landscape Map for the Chilterns Using a GIS Based Model*, Chilterns Area of Outstanding Natural Beauty, English Nature, Forestry Commission and Oxford Brookes University, Oxford

Lee, N. (1987) *Environmental Impact Assessment: A Training Guide*, 2nd edition, Occasional Paper No 18, Department of Planning and Landscape, University of Manchester, Manchester

Lee, N. and Colley, R. (1990) *Reviewing the Quality of Environmental Statements*, Occasional Paper No 24, EIA Centre, University of Manchester, Manchester

Lee, N. and Wood, C. (1987) 'EIA: A European perspective', *Built Environment*, vol 4, pp101–110

Leeds City Council (2008, unpublished) 'Review of Leeds Local Development Framework sustainable development methodology: Notes of workshop (25 April 2008) with statutory bodies', LCC, Leeds

Leicester City Council (2008) *Core Strategy Sustainability Appraisal*, www.leicester.gov.uk/your-council-services/ep/planning/plansandpolicy/ldf/ ldfcore-strategy/sustainability-appraisal-/

Levett, R. and McNally, R. (2003) *A Strategic Environmental Assessment of Fiji's Tourism Development Plan*, http://assets.panda.org/downloads/sea_adb_final_ report_0503.pdf

Levett, R., with Christie, I., Jacobs, M. and Therivel, R. (2002) *A Better Choice of Choice?*, report to the Sustainable Development Commission, London

Li, W., Li, Z. and Li, T. W. (2006) *Strategic Environmental Assessment: Development, Experiences and Practice*, Chemical Industrial Press, Beijing

Local Government Management Board (1994) *Sustainability Indicators Research Project: Report of Phase 1*, Luton

London Health Observatory (2005), *Health in London – Determinants of Health – Transport*, www.lho.org.uk/LHO_Topics/Health_Topics/Determinants_of_ Health/Transport.aspx

Lozano, M. T. P., Rojas, A. C., Cammaert, C., Romero, C., Mejía, S., Valbuena, S., Franco, C., Rincón, S. A. and Guzmán, S. L. (2008) *Evaluación Ambiental Estratégica de Políticas, Planes y Programas de Biocombustibles en Colombia con Enfasis en Biodiversidad*, Instituto de Investigación de Recursos Biológicos 'Alexander von Humboldt' and others, Bogotá, Colombia

LUC (Land Use Consultants) and RTPI (Royal Town Planning Institute) (2008) *Research Review of Sustainability Appraisal in Spatial Planning*, prepared for the Sustainable Development Research Network, www.rtpi.org.uk/item/2077/ pg_dtl_art_news/pg_hdr_art/pg_ftr_art

Lucht, J. and Jaubert, L. (2001) *Rapid Site Assessment Guide*, Environmental Data Centre, University of Rhode Island, Providence

Marsden, S. (2008) *Strategic Environmental Assessment in International and European Law*, Earthscan, London

Mattocks, J. R. (2006) *Report to Lichfield District Council: Report on the Examination into the Core Strategy Development Plan Document*, www.lichfielddc.gov.uk/downloads/ Report_on_the_Examination_into_the_Core_Strategy.pdf

Mayo, E., MacGillivray, A. and McLaren, D. (1997) *The Index of Sustainable Economic Welfare for the United Kingdom*, www.icsu-scope.org/downloadpubs/scope58/ box3w.html

Ministry of the Environment and Mitsubishi Research Institute (Japan) (2003) 'Effective SEA system and case studies', http://docs1.eia.nl/os/sea/casestudies/ japan_effective_sea_and_cases_6xnl_6xee_4xuk_03.pdf

Mintzberg, H. (1987) 'The Strategy Concept 1: Five Ps for Strategy', *California Management Review*, vol 30, no 1, pp11–25

Morris, P. and Therivel, R. (eds) (2009) *Methods of Environmental Impact Assessment*, 3rd edition, Routledge, London

Morrison-Saunders, A. and Arts, J. (2004) *Assessing Impact: Handbook of EIA and SEA Follow-Up*, Earthscan, London

Morrison-Saunders, A. and Therivel, R. (2006) 'Sustainability integration and assessment', *Journal of Environmental Assessment Policy and Management*, vol 8, no 3, pp281–298

NASA (National Aeronautics and Space Administration) (2008) *Final Constellation Programmatic Environmental Statement*, Houston, TX, www.nasa.gov/mission_pages/constellation/main/peis.html

National Trust (2002) *In the National Interest? Government Proposals for Planning Major Infrastructure Projects*, report by Levett-Therivel, London

Natural Resources Canada (2007) *Public Statement of Environmental Effects: Federal Mountain Pine Beetle Program*, www.nrcan-rncan.gc.ca/com/envamb/public-beetlecoleop-eng.php

NCEA (Netherlands Commission for Environmental Assessment) (2009) *Views and experiences from the Netherlands Commission on Environmental Assessment 2009*, http://docs1.eia.nl/mer/diversen/views_experiences_2009.pdf

NEPA (National Environmental Policy Act) Task Force (2003) *Modernizing NEPA Implementation*, http://ceq.hss.doe.gov/ntf/report/finalreport.pdf

Nicholson, S. (2005) 'Sustainability Appraisal – Adding value', *The Environmentalist*, issue 32 (November), p25

Nilsson, M., Wiklund, H., Finnveden, G., Johnsson, D. K., Lundberg, K., Tyskeng, S. and Wallgren, O. (2009) 'Analytical framework and tool kit for SEA follow-up', *Environmental Impact Assessment Review*, vol 29, no 3, pp186–199

Noble, B. F. (2009) 'Promise and dismay: The state of strategic environmental assessment practices in Canada', *Environmental Impact Assessment Review*, vol 29, no 1, pp66–75

Noble, M., Barnes, H., Wright, G., McLennan, D., Avenell, D., Whitworth, A. and Roberts, B. (2009) *The South African Index of Multiple Deprivation 2001 at Datazone Level*, Pretoria, Department of Social Development, www.casasp.ox.ac.uk/docs/SAIMD%20report%2022%20June%202009.pdf

NPFA (National Playing Fields Association) (2001) *The Six Acre Standard: Minimum Standards for Outdoor Playing Space*, NPFA, London

Nykvist, B. and Nilsson, M. (2009) 'Are impact assessment procedures actually promoting sustainable development?', *Environmental Impact Assessment Review*, vol 29, no 1, pp15–24

ODPM (Office of the Deputy Prime Minister) (2002) *Draft Guidance on the Strategic Environmental Assessment Directive*, London

ODPM, Scottish Executive, Welsh Assembly Government and Department of the Environment, Northern Ireland (2005) *A Practical Guide to the Strategic Environmental Assessment Directive*, www.communities.gov.uk/publications/planningandbuilding/practicalguidesea

OECD (Organisation for Economic Co-operation and Development) (2006) *Applying Strategic Environmental Assessment: Good Practice Guidance for Development Co-operation*, www.seataskteam.net/guidance.php

O'Faircheallaigh, C. (2009) 'Effectiveness in social impact assessment: Aboriginal peoples and resource development in Australia', *Impact Assessment and Project Appraisal*, vol 27, no 2, pp95–110

Orloff, N. and Brooks, G. (1980) *The National Environmental Policy Act: Cases and materials*, Bureau of National Affairs, Washington DC

Owens, S., Rayner, T. and Bina, O. (2004) 'New agendas for appraisal: Reflections on theory, practice and research', *Environment and Planning A*, vol 36, no 11, pp1943–1959

Oxfordshire County Council (1995) *Oxfordshire County Council Structure Plan: Alternative Actions*, public consultation leaflet, Oxford

Partidário, M. R. (2007) 'Scales and associated data – What is enough for SEA needs?', *Environmental Impact Assessment Review*, vol 27, no 5, pp460–478

Partidário, M. P. and Clark, R. (eds) (2000) *Perspectives on Strategic Environmental Assessment*, Lewis Publishers, Boca Raton

Partidário, M. R., Augusto, B., Vincente, G. and Lobos, V. (2009a) 'Learning the practice of strategic-based SEA', presented at 29th annual conference of the International Association for Impact Assessment, Accra, Ghana, www.iaia.org/iaia09ghana/documents/cs/CS8-4_Partidario_etal_Learning_the_practice.pdf

Partidário, M. R., Sheate, W. R., Bina, O., Byron, H. and Augusto, B. (2009b) 'Sustainability assessment for agricultural scenarios in Europe's mountain areas: Lessons from six study areas, *Environmental Management*, vol 43, no 1, pp 144–165

PAS (Planning Advisory Service) (2006) *LDF Learning and Dissemination Project: Making Sustainability Appraisal Manageable and Influential*, www.pas.gov.uk/pas/aio/25127

PAS (2009) *Local Development Frameworks: Guidance on options generation and appraisal*, www.pas.gov.uk/pas/core/page.do?pageId=57128

PDGHKSAR (Planning Department of the Government of the Hong Kong Special Administrative Region) (2007) *Agreement No. CE 25/2001 Hong Kong 2030: Planning Vision and Strategy – Strategic Environmental Assessment*, www.epd.gov.hk/epd/SEA/eng/file/FinalSEAReport.pdf

Pearce, D., Atkinson, G. and Mourato, S. (2006) *Cost–benefit Analysis and the Environment: Recent Developments*, OECD Publishing, Paris

Perdicoúlis, A. (2005) 'A Structural and Functional Strategy Analysis for SEA', Chapter 32 in M. Schmidt, E. João and E. Albrecht (eds) *Implementing Strategic Environmental Assessment*, Springer, Berlin

Perdicoúlis, A., Hanusch, M., Kasperidus, H. D. and Weiland, U. (2007) 'The handling of causality in SEA guidance', *Environmental Impact Assessment Review*, vol 27, no 2, pp176–187

Persson, Å. and Nilsson, M. (2007) 'Towards a framework for SEA follow-up: Theoretical issues and lessons from policy evaluation', *Journal of Environmental Assessment Policy and Management*, vol 9, no 4, pp473–496

Peterson, P. E. (1981) *City Limits*, University of Chicago Press, Chicago

Piper, J. M. (2002) 'CEA and sustainable development: Evidence from UK case studies', *Environmental Impact Assessment Review*, vol 22, no 1, pp17–36

Planning Resource (2009a) 'Fresh challenges to South East Plan', 15 June, www.planningresource.co.uk/news/ByDiscipline/environment/913134/Fresh-challenges-South-East-Plan/

Planning Resource (2009b) 'Legal challenge delays South West Strategy', 17 June, www.planningresource.co.uk/news/ByDiscipline/Development-Control/913845/Legal-challenge-delays-South-West-strategy/

Planungsgemeinschaft Halle (2009) *Umweltbericht zum Regionaler Entwicklungsplan für die Planungsregion Halle (Entwurf)*, www.regionale-planung.de/halle/pdf/Rep_Umw03.pdf

Pope, J., Annandale, D. and Morrison-Saunders, A. (2004) 'Conceptualising Sustainability Assessment', *Environmental Impact Assessment Review*, vol 24, no 6, pp595–616

POST (Parliamentary Office of Science and Technology) (2007) *Postnote 281: Ecosystem Services*, www.parliament.uk/documents/upload/postpn281.pdf

Puyana, J. (2009) 'Analysing the SEA system in Colombia', unpublished MSc dissertation, Oxford Brookes University, Oxford

Quasar Consultores (2007) *Evaluation environnementale strategique: Programme operationnel de cooperation transfrontaliere France-Espagne, 2007–2013*, Quasar Consultores, Madrid

RDC (République Démocratique du Congo) (2009) *Etude Environnementale Stratégique – PNFoCo*, www.rdc-conversiontitresforestiers.org/atelier-2/etude-environnementale-strategique-pnfoco/index.php

Republic of Slovenia, The Government Office for Local Self-Government and Regional Policy (2007) *Environmental Report for Strategic Environmental Assessment of Instrument for Pre-Accession Assistance Cross-border Cooperation Operational Programme Slovenia – Croatia 2007–2013*, www.svlr.gov.si/fileadmin/svlsrp.gov.si/pageuploads/cilj_3/SEA_OP_Slo-Cro_27.7.07__Eng_.pdf

Retief, F. (2007) 'A quality and effectiveness review protocol for strategic environmental assessment (SEA) in developing countries, *Journal of Environmental Assessment Policy and Management*, vol 9, no 4, pp443–471

Retief, F., Jones, C. and Jay, S. (2008) 'The emperor's new clothes – Reflections on strategic environmental assessment (SEA) practice in South Africa', *Environmental Impact Assessment Review*, vol 28, no 7, pp504–514

Rodriguez-Bachiller, A. (2004) *Expert Systems and Geographic Information Systems for Impact Assessment*, Taylor and Francis, London

Royal Commission on Environmental Pollution (2002) *Environmental Planning*, CEP Twenty-third report, London, www.rcep.org.uk/reports/23-planning/documents/2002-23planning.pdf

Runhaar, H. (2009) 'Putting SEA in context: A discourse perspective on how SEA contributes to decision-making', *Environmental Impact Assessment Review*, vol 29, no 2, pp200–209

SACTRA (Standing Advisory Committee on Trunk Road Assessment) (1994) *Trunk Roads and the Generation of Traffic*, Department for Transport, London

Sadler, B. and Verheem, R. (1996) *SEA: Status, Challenges and Future Directions*, Report 53, Ministry of Housing, Spatial Planning and the Environment, The Hague, Netherlands

Schmidt, M., João, E. and Albrecht, E. (eds) (2005) *Implementing Strategic Environmental Assessment*, Springer, Berlin

Scott Wilson (2008a) *Consolidated SA Report for the North West Regional Spatial Strategy*, prepared for the Government Office for the North West, www.gos.gov.uk/497468/docs/248821/457370/consolidatedSAreportNWRSS

Scott Wilson (2008b) *Dover Core Strategy: Sustainability Appraisal Report*, prepared for Dover District Council, www.doverdc.co.uk/pdf/Dover%20Pre-Submission%20SA%20Report%20v2.1.pdf

Scott Wilson and Levett-Therivel (2009) *Regional Spatial Strategy for the South East: Sustainability Appraisal and Habitats Regulations Assessment/Appropriate Assessment of the Secretary of State's Final Revisions*, www.go-se.gov.uk/497648/docs/171301/815607/fSA_and_HRA_Assessment.pdf

Scottish Executive (2006) *Strategic Environmental Assessment Toolkit*, www.scotland.gov.uk/Resource/Doc/148434/0039453.pdf

Scottish Government (2005) *Equality and Diversity Impact Assessment Toolkit*, www.scotland.gov.uk/Publications/2005/02/20687/52421

SEPA (State Environmental Protection Agency) (1993) *Circular on Strengthening EIA Management of Construction Projects Financed by International Financial Organizations*,

http://english.sepa.gov.cn/Policies_Regulations/policies/EIA1/200711/
t20071121_113206.htm

SEPA (2003) *Technical Guidelines for Plan Environmental Assessment* (on trial) (HJ/T130-2003), Beijing

Sherston, T. (2008) 'The effectiveness of strategic environmental assessment as a helpful development plan making tool', unpublished MSc dissertation, Oxford Brookes University, Oxford

Somerset County Council (2000) *Local Transport Plan for Somerset 2001–2006, Annex 6 North West Taunton Package*, Taunton, Somerset

Snell, T. and Cowell, R. (2006) 'Scoping in environmental impact assessment: balancing precaution and efficiency?', *Environmental Impact Assessment Review*, vol 26, no 4, pp359–376

State of California (2005) *Guidance for Preparers of Cumulative Impact Analysis: Approach and Guidance*, www.dot.ca.gov/ser/cumulative_guidance/downloads/Approach_and_Guidance.pdf

Stewart, G. (2007) *Environmental risk management and strategic environmental assessment: Guidance note*, www.grdp.org/static/documents/Research/risk_man_v6_850000.doc

Stirling, A. (1999) 'The appraisal of sustainability: Some problems and possible responses', *Local Environment*, vol 4, no 2, pp111–135

Stoeglehner, G. and Narodoslawsky, M. (2008) 'Implementing ecological footprinting in decision-making processes', *Land Use Policy*, vol 25, pp421–431

Stoeglehner, G., Brown, A. L. and Kørnøv, L. B. (2009) 'SEA and Planning: "Ownership" of strategic environmental assessment by the planners is the key to its effectiveness', *Impact Assessment and Project Appraisal*, vol 27, no 2, pp111–120

Sustainable Development Commission (SDC) (2001) *Sustainability Appraisal of Policies for Farming and Food*, www.sd-commission.org.uk/publications/downloads/011201%20Sustainability%20appraisal%20of%20policies%20for%20farming%20and%20food.pdf

Swedish National Board of Housing, Building and Planning and Swedish Environmental Protection Agency (2000) *Planning with Environmental Objectives! A Guide*, Stockholm

Tao, T., Tan, Z. and He, X. (2007) 'Integrating environment into land-use planning through strategic environmental assessment in China: Towards legal frameworks and operational procedures', *Environmental Impact Assessment Review*, vol 27, no 3, pp243–265

Therivel, R. (1995) 'Environmental appraisal of development plans: Current status', *Planning Practice and Research*, vol 10, no 2, pp223–234

Therivel, R. (1996) 'Environmental appraisal of development plans: Status in late 1995', *Report*, March, pp14–16

Therivel, R. (1998) 'Strategic environmental assessment of development plans in Great Britain', *Environmental Impact Assessment Review*, vol 18, no 1, pp39–57

Therivel, R. (2009) 'Appropriate assessment of plans in England', *Environmental Impact Assessment Review*, vol 29, no 4, pp261–272

Therivel, R. and Brown, L. (1999) 'Methods of Strategic Environmental Assessment', in J. Petts (ed) *Handbook of Environmental Impact Assessment, Vol. 1*, Blackwell Science, Oxford, pp441–464

Therivel, R. and Minas, P. (2002) 'Ensuring effective SEA in a changing context', *Impact Assessment and Project Appraisal*, vol 29, no 2, pp81–91

Therivel, R. and Partidário, M. R. (eds) (1996) *The Practice of Strategic Environmental Assessment*, Earthscan, London

Therivel, R. and Ross, B. (2007) 'Cumulative effects assessment: Does scale matter?', *Environmental Impact Assessment Review*, vol 27, no 5, pp365–385

Therivel, R. and Walsh, F. (2006) 'The Strategic Environmental Assessment Directive in the UK: One year on', *Environmental Impact Assessment Review*, vol 26, no 7, pp663–675

Therivel, R. and Wood, G. (2005) 'Tools for SEA', Chapter 24 in M. Schmidt, E. João and E. Albrecht (eds) *Implementing Strategic Environmental Assessment*, Springer, Berlin

Therivel, R., Wilson, E., Thompson, S., Heaney, D. and Pritchard, D. (1992) *Strategic Environmental Assessment*, Earthscan, London

Therivel, R., Christian, G., Craig, C., Grinham, R., Mackins, D., Smith, J., Sneller, T., Turner, R., Walker, D. and Yamane, M. (2009) 'Sustainability-focused impact assessment: English experiences', *Impact Assessment and Project Appraisal*, vol 27, no 2, pp155–168

Thissen, W. (2000) 'Criteria for Evaluation of Strategic Environmental Assessment', in M. R. Partidário and R. Clark (eds) *Perspectives on Strategic Environmental Assessment*, Lewis Publishers, Boca Raton, pp113–127

Thomas, P. (2008) 'Four years on from the implementation of the SEA Directive', unpublished MSc dissertation, Oxford Brookes University, Oxford

Tkach, R. J. and Simonovic, S. P. (1998) 'A new approach to multi-criteria decision making in water resources', *Journal of Geographic Information and Decision Analysis*, vol 1, no 1, pp25–43

Tracz, M. (1999) 'SEA of planned network of motorways and expressways in Poland', presented at OECD/ECMT Conference on SEA for Transport, Warsaw, 14–15 October, www1.oecd.org/cem/topics/env/SEA99/SEAtracz.pdf

Transport Scotland (2008) *Strategic Transport Projects Review: Environmental Report*, www.transportscotland.gov.uk/files/documents/reports/j10194b/j10194b-00.pdf

Tukker, A. (2000) 'Life cycle assessment as a tool in EIA', *Environmental Impact Assessment Review*, vol 20, no 4, pp435–456

UK Treasury (1997) *The Green Book*, www.hm-treasury.gov.uk/d/green_book_complete.pdf

UNDP (United Nations Development Programme) and RECCEE (Regional Environmental Centre for Central and Eastern Europe) (2005) *Strategic environmental assessment of the Yerevan City Master Plan, Report*, www.unece.org/env/eia/documents/SEA_CBNA/Armenia_SEA_Yerevan_en.pdf

UNECE (United Nations Economic Commission for Europe) (1998) *Convention on Access to Information, Public Participation in Decision-Making and Access to Justice in Environmental Matters*, www.unece.org/env/pp/documents/cep43e.pdf

UNECE (2003) *The Protocol on Strategic Environmental Assessment*, www.unece.org/env/eia

UNEP (United Nations Environment Programme) (2001) *Depleted Uranium in Kosovo: Post-Conflict Environmental Assessment*, Kenya, http://postconflict.unep.ch/publications/uranium.pdf

UNEP (2006) *Environmental Vulnerability Mapping in Liberia*, work in progress, http://postconflict.unep.ch/liberia/displacement/documents/EnvironmentalVulnerabilityMapping100306.pdf

United Nations University (2005) *Strategic Environmental Assessment Open Educational Resource*, http://sea.unu.edu/

USAID (United States Agency for International Development) (2007) Gender assessment: USAID/Colombia, http://pdf.usaid.gov/pdf_docs/PDACJ922.pdf

USDAAPH (United States Department of Agriculture Animal and Plant Health Inspection Service) (2007) *Introduction of Genetically Engineered Organisms*, draft programmatic environmental impact statement, www.aphis.usda.gov/brs/pdf/complete_eis.pdf

USDoE (United States Department of Energy) and USDoI (United States Department of the Interior, Bureau of Land Management) (2008) *Programmatic Environmental Impact Statement, Designation of Energy Corridors on Federal Land in the 11 Western States*, DoE/EIS—386, http://corridoreis.anl.gov/documents/fpeis/index.cfm#vol1

van Buuren, A. and Nooteboom, S. (2009) 'Evaluating strategic environmental assessment in The Netherlands: Content, process and procedure as indissoluble criteria for effectiveness', *Impact Assessment and Project Appraisal*, vol 27, no 2, pp145–154

van Straaten, D. (1996) 'Methodological Considerations to Strategic Environmental Assessment', in R. Verheyen and K. Nagels (eds) *Methodology, Focalization, Evaluation and Scope of Environmental Assessment: Fourth report: Strategic environmental assessment: Theory versus practice*, University of Antwerp, Wilrijk, Belgium, pp135–143

Verheem, R. (1996) 'SEA of the Dutch Ten-year Programme on Waste Management', in R. Therivel and M. R. Partidário (eds) *The Practice of Strategic Environmental Assessment*, Earthscan, London, pp86–94

Wackernagel, M. and Rees, W. (1996) *Our Ecological Footprint: Reducing Human Impact on the Earth*, New Society Publishers, Gabriola Island, British Columbia

Walz, U. and Schumacher, U. (2005) 'Landscape fragmentation in the Free State of Saxony and the surrounding border areas', *Proceedings of the 19th International Conference on Informatics for Environmental Protection*, Masaryk University, Brno, Czech Republic, www2.ioer.de/recherche/pdf/2005_walz_schumacher_enviroinfo.pdf

Wärnbäck, A. and Hilding-Rydevik, T. (2009) 'Cumulative effects in Swedish EIA practice – Difficulties and obstacles', *Environmental Impact Assessment Review*, vol 29, no 2, pp107–115

Water Resources for the South East (2006) *Response to Latest South East Plan Housing Provision and Distribution Received from Seera*, www.southeast-ra.gov.uk/documents/sustainability/water_resources-may06.pdf

WCED (World Commission on Environment and Development, Brundtland Commission) (1987) *Our Common Future*, Oxford University Press, Oxford

Webster, D. and Muller, L. (2006) *City Development Strategy Guidelines: Driving Urban Performance*, City Alliances, Washington DC

Weiss, J. (1998) 'Cost–benefit analysis and assessing privatisation projects in transitional economies', *Impact Assessment and Project Appraisal*, vol 16, no 4, pp289–294

White House (1994) *Executive Order 12898, Federal Actions to Address Environmental Justice in Minority Populations and Low-Income Populations*, www.epa.gov/Region2/ej/exec_order_12898.pdf

Wigan Council (2007) *Core Strategy Issues & Options Interim Sustainability Appraisal*, www.wigan.gov.uk/NR/rdonlyres/11B6009A-7B33-4B6A-ACA1-CF2574D3E475/0/InterimSAReport1456kb.pdf

Wood, C. (1988) 'EIA in Plan Making', in P. Wathern (ed) *Environmental Impact Assessment*, Unwin Hyman, London

Wood, C. and Djeddour, M. (1991) 'Strategic environmental assessment: EA of policies, plans and programmes', *The Impact Assessment Bulletin*, vol 10, no 1, pp3–22

World Bank (1996) *Participation Source Book*, www-wds.worldbank.org/external/default/WDSContentServer/WDSP/IB/1996/02/01/000009265_3961214175537/Rendered/PDF/multi_page.pdf

World Bank (2007) *Strategic Environmental Assessment Study: Tourism Development in the Province of Guizhou, China*, Reference 0045664, http://siteresources.worldbank.org/INTEAPREGTOPENVIRONMENT/Resources/Guizhou_SEA_FINAL.pdf

World Bank (2008) *Sierra Leone Mining Sector Reform*, http://siteresources.worldbank.org/INTRANETENVIRONMENT/Resources/244351-1222272730742/SierraLeoneMiningSectorReformReport.pdf

World Bank (date unknown) *SEA Toolkit*, http://go.worldbank.org/XIVZ1WF880

Yamane, M. (2008) 'Achieving sustainability of local plan through SEA/SA', unpublished MSc dissertation, Oxford Brookes University, Oxford

YEPB (Yunan Environmental Protection Bureau) and Sida (2009) Core training material on strategic environmental assessment, version 2, YEPB

Zhu, D. and Ru, J. (2008) 'Strategic environmental assessment in China: Motivations, politics, and effectiveness', *Journal of Environmental Management*, vol 88, pp615–626

Index